FOR KING AND COUNTRY

In Memoriam.

Christmas Message from Queen Victoria to the
Commander-in-Chief, South Africa, 1899:

"I WISH YOU, AND ALL MY BRAVE SOLDIERS, A HAPPY CHRISTMAS. GOD PROTECT AND BLESS YOU ALL."

FOR KING AND COUNTRY

BEING A RECORD OF

FUNDS AND PHILANTHROPIC WORK

IN CONNECTION WITH

THE SOUTH AFRICAN WAR

1899—1902

BY

COLONEL GILDEA, C.V.O., C.B.

The Naval & Military Press Ltd

Published by

The Naval & Military Press Ltd
Unit 5 Riverside, Brambleside,
Bellbrook Industrial Estate,
Uckfield, East Sussex,
TN22 1QQ England

Tel: +44 (0) 1825 749494
Fax: +44 (0) 1825 765701

www.naval-military-press.com
www.nmarchive.com

In reprinting in facsimile from the original, any imperfections are inevitably reproduced and the quality may fall short of modern type and cartographic standards.

𝔇𝔢𝔡𝔦𝔠𝔞𝔱𝔢𝔡
(*by permission*)
TO
HIS MAJESTY THE KING
AND
HER MAJESTY QUEEN ALEXANDRA

NOTE.

THE profits arising from the sale of this Record, after the cost of publication, will be devoted to the Homes for Officers' Widows and Daughters, now amalgamated with the Officers' Branch of the Soldiers' and Sailors' Families Association, 23, Queen Anne's Gate, Westminster, S.W., from whence copies can be obtained. Price One Guinea, nett. For particulars of these Homes, see Appendix, page 198.

PREFACE.

THE Mansion House was the medium, as was right, through which the general appeal to the Nation for Funds in connection with the War was made. A new departure, however, in this instance was taken in the Appeal being for four objects, as enumerated in Sir John Voce Moore's letter to the Press of the 21st October 1899, and the saving clause of which, as to the allocation of contributions not specially earmarked for one of the four objects, subsequently led to the establishment of what was known as the Lord Mayor's " Discretionary Fund."

The action of Lords Lieutenant of Counties, Lord Mayors, Mayors and Provosts of Boroughs, whose assistance and co-operation was at the same time invited, was not in all cases identical, some appealing for contributions on behalf of the Mansion House Fund and remitting the same direct; some retaining Funds subscribed in their own hands, and making grants according to their discretion to local organisations; some, in many cases, enlarging the scope of the Lord Mayor's Appeal to that for Yeomanry and Volunteer Equipment, special hospitals, ambulances, extra comforts for men, and such like; whilst others formed their own Committees, made independent appeals for some particular object or objects and administered the Funds themselves.

In some instances again, such as in the case of *The Daily Telegraph*, *The Daily Mail*, *The Birmingham Daily Mail*, *The Scotsman*, *The Liverpool Courier Express*, and *The Irish Times*, the proprietors of these newspapers and others, on their own account raised and distributed Funds, whilst more generally, and this was specially so in the Counties, large Funds were raised by the proprietors of the Provincial Press, and handed over to local organisations for administration, many also advertising free of cost local contributions received by administering bodies. Later on in the War *The Morning Post* also took an active part in furthering the interest of the Field Force Fund, and *The Globe* in raising a Fund for the Indian Stretcher Bearers.

The Patriotic Commissioners, the British Red Cross Society, Lloyd's Patriotic Fund, and the Soldiers' and Sailors' Families Association, the four bodies named in the Lord Mayor's Appeal, received also contributions direct, *exclusive* of the Funds sent to the Mansion House earmarked for their several objects, the three first to the amount of £114,063 0s. 1d. the latter to the extent of £1,015,404 4s. 3d.

Appeals innumerable for other objects connected with the War were made by Committees formed for these purposes, and in many cases by private individuals who administered the same. Of the former, probably the most successful were those for the Bisley Convalescent Home, the Children's Penny Fund, the Princess Christian's Cottage Homes, all in connection with the Soldiers' and Sailors' Help Society; and the Officers' Families Fund (more generally known as Lady Lansdowne's Fund) in connection with The Soldiers' and Sailors' Families Association.

In India and the British Dominions beyond the seas large contributions were made, part of which was sent to the Mansion House and part retained for local purposes. Additional and very material help, the extent of which will never be known and never recorded, was afforded by the generosity of the "fellow workmen" of the men themselves, especially of the Reservists, who in many districts made weekly contributions from their wages for their comrades' families from the time the men left till they returned; and by the patriotism of employers of labour, landed proprietors, railway and other companies of every description, who, besides keeping the men's places open, have, some wholly, some partially, enabled the families to keep their homes together during the absence of the breadwinner, and also in many cases made provision for the fatherless children.

To these should also be added the gratuitous attendance of the medical profession throughout the Kingdom; the provision for invalided and wounded men made by the Committees of Hospitals and Convalescent Homes, as well as by a large number of owners of private houses, who not only placed these at the disposal of the Authorities, but provided a staff of nurses and attendants at their own expense.

The same may be said of the supply of extra comforts for the men, sent out direct by relatives, friends, and others, not only to those in whom they were most interested, but to different regiments, corps, and hospitals, far exceeding similar work undertaken by the Special Funds raised for this particular object.

It may be stated that the Lord Mayor's Appeal for the Transvaal Refugees (Part VII.) was made previous to the National Appeal described above.

The contents of the following pages may, it is hoped, prove of some interest, and will be a record of what has been done by those at home, when our soldiers and sailors went forth to fight for King and Country.

JAMES GILDEA.

11, Hogarth Road, S.W.
Coronation Day, 26th June 1902.

NOTE.—The compiler begs to offer his grateful thanks to the Managers of Funds and others for particulars supplied; his apologies for any errors or omissions; and his regrets that information, which would have made the record more complete, has, in some few instances, not been supplied.

CONTENTS.

	PAGE
IN MEMORIAM (QUEEN VICTORIA) [*Photogravure*] ...	*Frontispiece*
HIS MAJESTY THE KING	... xiii
HER MAJESTY QUEEN ALEXANDRA ...	xv
QUEEN VICTORIA'S CHOCOLATE BOX ...	117
QUEEN ALEXANDRA'S PIPE	 119

PREFACE   vii

PART I.

THE MANSION HOUSE FUND ...	1

WIDOWS AND ORPHANS.

THE PATRIOTIC FUND ...	7
THE "DAILY TELEGRAPH" FUND...	8
THE IMPERIAL WAR FUND... ...	10

WIVES AND FAMILIES.

THE SOLDIERS' AND SAILORS' FAMILIES ASSOCIATION ...	11
OFFICERS' FAMILIES FUND (THE LANSDOWNE FUND) ...	14
COUNTY AND BOROUGH FUNDS (TABULAR STATEMENT)	17
REGIMENTAL FUNDS (TABULAR STATEMENT)	72
THE BIRMINGHAM "DAILY MAIL" RESERVISTS' FUND	73
THE WAR EMPLOYMENT BUREAU	74
SUMMARY OF APPROXIMATE AMOUNT SUBSCRIBED	75

PART II.

THE CENTRAL BRITISH RED CROSS COMMITTEE	79
NATIONAL SOCIETY FOR AID TO SICK AND WOUNDED IN WAR ...	80
THE CENTRAL BRITISH RED CROSS COMMITTEE'S WORK IN SOUTH AFRICA	81
ST. JOHN AMBULANCE ASSOCIATION	82
ST. JOHN AMBULANCE BRIGADE ...	82
ARMY NURSING SERVICE RESERVE	83
QUEEN ALEXANDRA'S IMPERIAL MILITARY NURSING SERVICE...	83

HOSPITAL SHIPS.

THE "PRINCESS OF WALES"	84
AMERICAN SHIP "MAINE" ...	86

HOSPITAL TRAINS.

THE "PRINCESS CHRISTIAN"	88
NO. 4	88

CONTENTS.

PRIVATE HOSPITALS.

	PAGE
THE PORTLAND	89
THE LANGMAN	90
THE VAN ALEN	90
THE IRISH	91
THE "PRINCESS CHRISTIAN"	91
THE WELSH	92
THE EDINBURGH AND EAST OF SCOTLAND	92
THE SCOTTISH NATIONAL RED CROSS	93
THE IMPERIAL YEOMANRY	94
SUMMARY OF APPROXIMATE AMOUNT SUBSCRIBED	95

PART III.

DISABLED OFFICERS AND MEN—CONVALESCENT HOMES.

LLOYD'S PATRIOTIC FUND	99
GEORGINA, COUNTESS OF DUDLEY'S FUND	100
THE LAYARD HOME FOR OFFICERS	100
MEDICAL AND SURGICAL AID FOR SICK AND WOUNDED OFFICERS (THE DUKE OF ABERCORN'S FUND)	101
INCORPORATED SOLDIERS' AND SAILORS' HELP SOCIETY	102
REGIMENTAL COTTAGE HOMES	103
THEIR MAJESTIES' CONVALESCENT HOME AT BABINGLEY	104
H.R.H. THE PRINCESS LOUISE'S (DUCHESS OF ARGYLL) TRANSFER HOSPITAL, ROSENEATH	105
KING EDWARD'S HOSPITAL (THE MISSES KEYSER)	106
THE EARL OF SANDWICH'S HOME AT HINCHINGBROOKE	107
WOUNDED OFFICERS' FUND, CANNES	107
SIR ALFRED COOPER'S PRIVATE MILITARY HOSPITAL, SURBITON	108
GLENEARN CONVALESCENT HOME (MISS KER DUNLOP)	109
THE GROSVENOR HOME, DOVER (MISS L. HARDY)	109
GOLDER'S HILL, HAMPSTEAD (BRIGADE OF GUARDS)	109
SYRACUSA CONVALESCENT HOME, TORQUAY	110
WESTERN COUNTIES CONVALESCENT HOME, COMBE DOWN, BATH	110
CONVALESCENT HOMES—PRIVATE HOUSES, &c. (TABULAR STATEMENT)	111
SUMMARY OF APPROXIMATE AMOUNT SUBSCRIBED	114

PART IV.

EXTRA COMFORTS, &c.

QUEEN VICTORIA'S CHOCOLATE BOX (ILLUSTRATED)	117
QUEEN ALEXANDRA'S PIPE (ILLUSTRATED)	119
THE "ABSENT MINDED BEGGAR" FUND	120
WOMEN AND CHILDREN FROM SOUTH AFRICA (SOUTHAMPTON)	121
FIELD FORCE FUND	122
LITERATURE FOR THE TROOPS	123
LADY WHITE'S LADYSMITH FUND	124
KIMBERLEY AND MAFEKING (IN MEMORIAM) SOLDIERS' FUND	125
SUMMARY OF APPROXIMATE AMOUNT SUBSCRIBED	126

PART V.
VARIOUS.

	PAGE
THE COUNTESS CARRINGTON'S FUND (COLONIALS)	129
MAFEKING RELIEF FUND	130
BARALONG RELIEF FUND	131
THE AUSTRALIAN BUSHMEN CONTINGENT FUND	131

EQUIPMENT.

YEOMANRY AND VOLUNTEER EQUIPMENT	132
LORD LOCH'S HORSE	132
THE CITY OF LONDON IMPERIAL VOLUNTEERS (THE C.I.V.)	132
THE MOUNTED SHARPSHOOTERS' CORPS	133
SUMMARY OF APPROXIMATE AMOUNT SUBSCRIBED	134

PART VI.
INDIA.

THE NORTH-WESTERN PROVINCE AND OUDH TRANSVAAL WAR FUND	137
THE INDIAN FOLLOWERS' RELIEF FUND	138
THE INDIAN STRETCHER-BEARERS' FUND	139

BRITISH DOMINIONS BEYOND THE SEAS.

THE CANADIAN PATRIOTIC FUND ASSOCIATION	140
LORD STRATHCONA'S HORSE	140
THE SOUTH AFRICAN WIDOWS' AND ORPHANS' FUND	141
GOOD HOPE SOCIETY FOR AID TO SICK AND WOUNDED	142
NATAL VOLUNTEER WAR FUND	143
SOUTH AUSTRALIA TRANSVAAL PATRIOTIC FUND	144
TASMANIA TRANSVAAL PATRIOTIC FUND	145
SUMMARY OF APPROXIMATE AMOUNT SUBSCRIBED	146

PART VII.
REFUGEES.

THE MANSION HOUSE TRANSVAAL REFUGEES' FUND	149
BRITISH REFUGEES' FUND } (VICTORIA LEAGUE)	151
THE DUTCH WOMEN AND CHILDREN'S FUND	
SOUTH AFRICAN WOMEN AND CHILDREN'S DISTRESS FUND	152
THE BOER WOMEN AND CHILDREN'S CLOTHING FUND	152
THE JOHANNESBURG REFUGEES' FUND	153
SUMMARY OF APPROXIMATE AMOUNT SUBSCRIBED	154

PART VIII.

MISCELLANEOUS.

	PAGE
Soldiers' Christian Association Work in South Africa	157
South Africa General Mission	158
The Church Army Work in South Africa	159
Army Scripture Readers' and Soldiers' Friend Society	160
Royal Army Temperance Association	161
Transvaal Clergy Relief Fund	163
The Girls' Friendly Society (Two Orphans)	163
Soldiers' Graves (Victoria League)	164
Capetown Cathedral Memorial Fund	165
Summary of Approximate Amount Subscribed	166
Summary of Approximate Amounts Subscribed Part I., II., III., IV., V., VI., VII., VIII.	167
Schedule of Funds over Twenty Thousand Pounds	168

APPENDIX.

Letter from Lord Lansdowne and Lord Wolseley	171
Letter from Lord Roberts	172

ALLOCATION OF SUBSIDIARY FUNDS.

The Artists' War Fund	173
The National Bazaar	174
The Naval and Military Exhibition, Crystal Palace	174
The Great County Sale, Earl's Court	175
The Children's Penny Fund	176
Brigade of Collecting Dogs	177
The Cricketers' National War Fund	178
His Majesty the King's (as Prince of Wales) Committee	179
The War Relief Funds Committee	180
War Relief Funds Organisation	188
Joint Select Committee of the House of Lords and Commons	189
The Forces in South Africa	193
Table of Casualties	194
Diary of the War	195
Homes for Officers' Widows and Daughters	198

King of the United Kingdom of Great Britain and Ireland, and of the British Dominions beyond the Seas, Defender of the Faith, Emperor of India.

Christmas Message from Queen Alexandra,
at the time Princess of Wales:

"Sandringham, *December 9th,* 1899.

"My heart bleeds for the poor widows and fatherless, whose loved ones have met a glorious death fighting for their Queen and Country.

"May God help and comfort them in their saddened Christmas, and give them that peace which passeth understanding.

"'Peace, perfect peace, with loved ones far away,
In Jesu's keeping we are safe and they.'

"ALEXANDRA,
"Princess of Wales."

PART I.
WIDOWS AND ORPHANS.
WIVES AND FAMILIES.

CONTENTS.

	PAGE
The Mansion House Fund	1

WIDOWS AND ORPHANS.

The Patriotic Fund	7
The "Daily Telegraph" Fund	8
The Imperial War Fund	10

WIVES AND FAMILIES.

The Soldiers' and Sailors' Families Association	11
Officers' Families Fund (The Lansdowne Fund)	14
County and Borough Funds (Tabular Statement)	15
Regimental Funds (Tabular Statement)	72
The "Birmingham Daily Mail" Reservists' Fund	73
The War Employment Bureau	74
Summary of Approximate Amount Subscribed	75

THE MANSION HOUSE OR LORD MAYOR'S FUND

RAISED DURING THE MAYORALTIES OF

Sir John Voce Moore	1899.
Sir Alfred James Newton, Bart.	1899-1900.
Sir Frank Green, Bart.	1900-1901.
Sir Joseph C. Dimsdale, M.P.	1901-1902.

Private Secretary—WM. JAMESON SOULSBY, Esq., C.B., C.I.E.

APPEAL OF SIR JOHN VOCE MOORE.

Letter to the Press.

Sir,—In response to the accompanying appeal from his Royal Highness the Duke of Cambridge I have consented to open a fund for the benefit of the widows, orphans, and other dependents of the officers and men of Her Majesty's forces who may unfortunately lose their lives in the war operations in South Africa. At the same time I think it right to say that there are cognate objects for public philanthropy in connection with our gallant troops engaged in those operations.—I allude to the soldiers themselves who may get disabled by wounds and the wives and children separated at home here from their husbands and fathers by the exigencies of the war.

I therefore propose, in order to give the public the widest scope for their benevolence, that contributions for widows, orphans, and other dependents of those who may lose their lives shall be handed to the Patriotic Fund Commission for administration; those for sick and wounded while under treatment to the British Red Cross Society; those for soldiers disabled by wounds (for their benefit after they leave the service) to that excellent organisation Lloyd's Patriotic Fund, founded in the City in 1803; and those for wives and children separated to the Soldiers' and Sailors' Families' Association. All contributions should, therefore, be clearly indicated by donors as follows:—(1) Widows and orphans; (2) sick and wounded; (3) disabled soldiers; (4) wives and children. Any not marked will be handed over for the benefit of widows and orphans, as it is upon the Duke of Cambridge's appeal that I ask the public to give liberally. As this is a national emergency, I would earnestly invite the co-operation and assistance of my brother mayors to whom I have already had occasion this year to apply for help in other matters.

Donations may be sent to the Secretary's Office, Mansion House, or to the Bank of England, to the credit of the "Transvaal War Fund." I would especially request donors to send their contributions in such a way that they may not be confused with the simultaneous appeal for the Transvaal Refugees Fund, which, in spite of its great success, is still urgently in need of assistance.

I am, Sir, your obedient servant,

JOHN VOCE MOORE, Lord Mayor.

The Mansion House, London, October 21, 1899.

Royal Commission of the Patriotic Fund,
53, Charing Cross, London, S.W., Oct. 21, 1899.

My dear Lord Mayor,—The engagement of our forces with the enemy in Natal yesterday resulted, so the telegrams state, in killed and wounded among our troops. This means soldiers' widows and orphans to be provided for.

Parliament has placed upon the Patriotic Fund Commission the responsibility of appealing to the public for contributions for the benefit of widows, orphans, and other dependents of officers and men of Her Majesty's naval and military forces.

You, my Lord Mayor, are yourself a Patriotic Fund commissioner.

It is, therefore, my duty, as president of the Patriotic Fund Commission, to ask you to at once kindly open a fund for the benefit of the widows, orphans, and other dependents of those who may lose their lives by wounds or disease in the war operations in South Africa.

Arrangements have already been made, as in the case of our recent war operations on the North-West Frontier of India and similar operations in various parts of Africa, to afford immediate relief to the widows, and the War Office authorities will give us the earliest intimation of every casualty so that the relief may be prompt.

I will only add that the object of the fund to be raised will be to provide the widows with regular allowances during widowhood, according to their circumstances, and regular allowances to the children, boys under 14 years of age and girls under 16 years of age, as has been done by this commission in the case of every widow and orphan of those who fell in the recent campaigns to which I have alluded. Such children as it may be desirable to place in orphanages will be placed in the Royal Victoria Patriotic Asylum for Girls or other available homes.

I have every confidence that the nation will respond liberally to this appeal if your Lordship will be so good as to open a Mansion House fund, and, thanking you in anticipation, allow me to remain,

My dear Lord Mayor, yours very faithfully,

GEORGE, President.

The Right Hon. the Lord Mayor of the City of London.

Donations from The Queen and The Prince of Wales.

Balmoral Castle, Nov. 4, 1899.

My Lord Mayor,—By command of the Queen I beg to enclose a cheque for £1,000 as a donation to the Transvaal War Fund, and I am to add that Her Majesty will be glad that £400 should be allotted for the benefit of the wives and children of those serving in South Africa and £200 to each of the other three objects enumerated in your Lordship's appeal.

I have the honour to be, my Lord Mayor,

Your obedient servant,

FLEETWOOD J. EDWARDS.

The Right Hon. the Lord Mayor.

Marlborough House, Nov. 4, 1899.

Dear Lord Mayor,—I am directed by the Prince of Wales to send your Lordship a cheque for 250 guineas as a donation from His Royal Highness towards the Transvaal War Fund lately opened at the Mansion House. The Prince wishes this donation to be credited to that portion of the fund marked No. 4 on your list—viz., "The Soldiers' and Sailors' Families Association Fund," which has been so strongly brought to the notice of the British public by Lord Lansdowne and Lord Wolseley in their letter to *The Times* of the 1st inst.*

I remain, dear Lord Mayor, yours faithfully,

D. M. PROBYN, General.

The Right Hon. the Lord Mayor.

A Donation of £100 was also received from The Duke and Duchess of York, and £100 from the Grand Duchess of Mecklenburg-Strelitz.

OPENING OF "THE DISCRETIONARY FUND" BY SIR ALFRED NEWTON.

Letter to the Press.

Sir,—At to-day's conference held at the Mansion House the application of this fund was fully discussed. It was strongly urged, amongst other equally laudable suggestions, that a substantial sum should be allocated for the benefit of our colonial troops, and that our disabled soldiers and sailors in particular should be especially cared for.

In my opinion these suggestions will recommend themselves to all contributors to the fund, but it is my duty to point out that all donations received up to now have been subscribed on certain conditions, which it may be held do not meet these or similar cases.

Of the splendid patriotism and benevolence displayed throughout the Empire we are justly proud, and our anxiety should be now directed that the fund under consideration should be so applied as to embrace within its scope the claims of such established and recognised institutions as have for their object the amelioration of the condition of those who have suffered in the cause of Queen and country. To achieve this result it is highly desirable that where no specific instructions are given by donors the Lord Mayor should have power so to apportion the subscriptions received by him as to benefit, amongst others, such institutions, for instance, as the Princess Christian's Bisley Homes for Disabled Soldiers and Sailors.

---

* For copy of Lord Lansdowne and Lord Wolseley's letter, see Appendix, page 171.

I beg, therefore, to take this opportunity of notifying to future subscribers that in those cases where specific instructions do not accompany remittances I hold myself at liberty to apply them in the way I may be best advised for the relief of distress arising from the present war.

I am, Sir, your obedient servant,

ALFRED J. NEWTON, Lord Mayor.

The Mansion House, London, Dec. 8, 1899.

NATIONAL CHURCH COLLECTION.

Letter to the Archbishop of Canterbury from the Home Secretary enclosing the Queen's Commands.

Whitehall, 18th December, 1899.

My Lord Archbishop,—In obedience to the Queen's commands I have the honour to transmit to your Grace the accompanying Royal letters (signed by Her Majesty) authorising your Grace to take proper measures for promoting a church collection within your Province to increase the funds in aid of the sick, wounded, and disabled in the war in South Africa, and for the succour of the wives and children and widows and orphans of the men engaged.

I am to inform your Grace that it is Her Majesty's desire that these letters shall not be taken as a command in regard to any parish where, owing to the recent making of a collection or for other good reasons, it is not convenient to make a collection for the above purposes.

I have the honour to be, my Lord Archbishop, your Grace's obedient servant,

M. W. RIDLEY.

His Grace the Archbishop of Canterbury.

(Enclosure.)

VICTORIA R.

Most Reverend Father in God, Our Right Trusty and Right Entirely Beloved Councillor, We greet you well!

Whereas a large portion of Our Forces is presently engaged in operations of War in South Africa by reason of which many men must We grieve to think lose their lives and even a greater number be wounded:

And whereas it has been represented unto Us

That many of those so engaged have left at home wives and families dependent upon them:

That large sums of money are needed in order not only that special care may be given to the sick and wounded on the field of battle, but also that assistance may be rendered to those who are disabled in after-life and succour offered to the women and children who may either be separated for a time from their husbands and fathers or have to endure the great loss which makes them widows and orphans:

That Funds for the purposes aforesaid have been set on foot to which contributions of no small amount have been made by all classes of Our people: and

That if We were pleased to issue Our Royal Letters authorising a general Collection throughout the Churches of England and Wales the Funds aforesaid would be greatly increased as is most desirable:

We taking the same into Our Royal Consideration and being always ready to give the best encouragement and countenance to any movement which may tend to show the approval and high regard felt by Ourself and by Our whole Empire for loyalty and devotion to duty such as is now being manifested in South Africa, are graciously pleased to condescend to the prayer which has been addressed to Us on behalf of the Church of England, and do hereby direct you that these Our Letters be communicated to the several Suffragan Bishops within your Province, expressly requiring them to take care that publication be made thereof in such manner within their respective Dioceses as the said Bishop shall direct; and that upon this occasion the Minister in each Parish do effectually excite his Parishioners to a liberal contribution which shall be collected in the Church on Sunday, the Seventh day of January next ensuing, or if that day be inconvenient on any other Sunday which the said Bishops shall appoint; and that the said Ministers do cause the sums so collected to be paid immediately to Our Right Trusty and Well-beloved the Lord Mayor of Our City of London to be accounted for by him, and to be bestowed amongst the Funds aforesaid in such manner as you and Our Right Trusty and Right Entirely Beloved Councillor the Lord Archbishop of York shall in your joint discretion appoint for the furtherance of the above-mentioned good designs.

And so We bid you heartily Farewell.

Given at Our Court at Saint James's, the Sixteenth day of December, 1899, in the sixty-third year of Our Reign.

By Her Majesty's Command,

M. W. RIDLEY.

THE DECISION OF THE ARCHBISHOP OF CANTERBURY AND THE ARCHBISHOP OF YORK, AS TO THE ALLOCATION OF THE COLLECTION.

We desire that the Funds collected under the Queen's letter should be equally divided between the Red Cross Society, Lloyd's Patriotic Fund, and The Soldiers' and Sailors' Families Association.

F. CANTUAR.
WILLELM EBOR.

20 January, 1900.

Amount collected . . £70,377 11 8

Letter to the Lord Mayor from the Queen's Private Secretary.

Osborne, January 22nd, 1900.

My Lord Mayor,—I am commanded by the Queen to express to you the gratification with which Her Majesty has learnt from your letter of yesterday, of the large sum which has been so generously given in compliance with the Queen's letter.

I have the honour to be, My Lord Mayor,

Your most obedient servant,

ARTHUR BIGGE.

The Right Hon. The Lord Mayor.

THE PRINCESS OF WALES'S (QUEEN ALEXANDRA) APPEAL.

Letter from the Secretary of State for War.

War Office, January 1st, 1901.

My Lord Mayor,—I shall be happy to mark my sympathy with the appeal* made in this morning's papers by Her Royal Highness The Princess of Wales by contributing £100 to the funds of the Soldiers' and Sailors' Families Association. I trust the Fund may receive the assistance which it deserves.

I am, My Lord Mayor,

Yours very faithfully,

ST. JOHN BRODRICK.

The Right Hon. The Lord Mayor.

THE MANSION HOUSE FUND.

October, 1899 to 31 December, 1901.

RECEIPTS.	£	s.	d.	PAYMENTS.	£	s.	d.
To Contributions for:—				By Amounts allocated to:—			
No. 1 Patriotic Fund	445,761	0	0	No. 1 Patriotic Fund	440,600	0	0
„ 2 Red Cross Society	98,113	0	0	„ 2 Red Cross Society (in addition to Grants from Discretionary Fund)	96,759	0	0
„ 3 Lloyd's Patriotic Fund	112,303	0	0	„ 3 Lloyd's Patriotic Fund (in addition to Grants from Discretionary Fund)	111,009	0	0
„ 4 Soldiers' and Sailors' Families Association	197,920	0	0	„ 4 Soldiers' and Sailors' Families Association (in addition to Grants from Discretionary Fund)	194,827	0	0
„ 4A „ „ (Queen Alexandra's Appeal)	62,873	0	0	„ 4A Queen Alexandra's Appeal	62,261	0	0
„ 5 Lord Mayor's Discretionary Fund	214,835	0	0	„ 5 Lord Mayor's Discretionary Fund	208,156	0	0
	1,131,805	0	0		1,113,612	0	0
Less—				By Balance not allocated to date, 31st December, 1901,			
Advertising, Printing, Stationery, Postages, and Clerical Staff	11,438	0	0	General Fund .. £1,073 0 0			
	1,120,367	0	0	„ Lord Mayor's Discretionary Fund 8,892 0 0			
Add—					9,965	0	0
Profits and Interest on temporary Investments (Lord Mayor's Discretionary Fund), &c.	3,210	0	0				
	1,123,577	0	0		1,123,577	0	0

* For copy of Appeal, *see* page 12.   For allocation of Discretionary Fund, *see* following three statements.

LORD MAYOR NEWTON'S DISCRETIONARY FUND.

RECEIPTS.	£	s.	d.
To Contributions received at the Mansion House	207,027	18	6
" " " Bank of England	97	1	7
" Profits on Monies Invested	2,474	11	6
	209,599	11	7
Less—			
Returned to Williams, Deacon & Co., they having paid a contribution a second time in error	12	3	2
	209,587	8	5

PAYMENTS.	£	s.	d.
By Soldiers' and Sailors' Families' Association	110,000	0	0
" British Red Cross Society, Special Grant	5,000	0	0
" Imperial War Fund	2,600	0	0
" Georgina, Countess of Dudley's Fund, for Convalescent Officers sick and wounded in the war	9,000	0	0
" Royal School for Officers' Daughters, for admission of Children	245	0	0
" Duke of Abercorn's Sick and Wounded Officers' and Surgical Medical Aid Fund	1,250	0	0
" H.R.H. Princess of Wales, for charitable purposes in connection with the War	5,000	0	0
" H.R.H. Princess Louise (Duchess of Argyll) for disabled Soldiers	2,000	0	0
" Lloyd's Patriotic Fund: temporarily disabled Soldiers	1,331	0	6
" Imperial Yeomanry Hospital	4,000	0	0
" Soldiers' and Sailors' Help Society's Homes at Bisley	3,100	0	0
" Portland Hospital (Red Cross Society)	1,000	0	0
" County of Nottingham Reservists' Families Fund (contributed in the County)	5,631	8	5
" Soldiers' Daughters' Home for Maintenance of Children	2,788	0	0
" Soldiers' and Sailors' Help Society	4,500	0	0
" " " " (Irish Branch)	2,000	0	0
" Countess Carrington, for Colonial Troops in London	1,000	0	0
" Mafeking Relief Fund: Lady Georgina Curzon	339	12	9
" The American Hospital Ship *Maine*	3,000	0	0
" Western Counties Convalescent Home	300	0	0
" Miss Agnes Keysers (King Edward's Hospital)	200	0	0
" The Army Guild	143	0	0
" Household Brigade	400	0	0
" Isle of Man	500	0	0
" The Layard Home, Matjesfontein	500	0	0
" Cape Colony Widows' Fund	200	0	0
" Indian Followers' Families' Fund	200	0	0
" Addenbrookes Hospital, Cambridge	110	0	0
" The Louise Margaret Hospital, Aldershot	210	0	0
" Officers' Convalescent Home at Pietermaritzburgh	105	0	0
" City of London Regiment Families' War Fund	500	0	0
" Augmentation of Home Remittances by Wesleyan Soldiers	222	3	6
" St. John Ambulance Society	105	0	0
" Gloucester Regiment Wives' Fund	100	0	0
" Indian Stretcher Bearers' Fund	250	0	0
" Queen Charlotte's Lying-in Hospital, for attendance on Soldiers' Wives	225	0	0
" Nurses' Convalescent Holiday Fund	1,000	0	0
" Army and Navy Pensioners' Society	25	0	0
" The Welsh Hospital (per Sir David Evans)	1,000	0	0
" City of London Regiment, extra clothing	273	14	9
" Grants to Relations of Officers and Men killed and wounded in the War, and to wounded Officers, &c.	2,124	6	0
" Expenses of Staff, including Audit of Georgina, Countess of Dudley's Accounts	129	3	3
" Central War Relief Funds Organization	1,280	18	5
" Transvaal War General Account, proportion of Advertising Expenses	1,460	0	0
" Bank Cheque Books	1	10	10
	175,349	18	5

Balance—
By London County Council Loan, £12,600 Stock	£12,223	11	2			
" Consols, £10,000	9,781	6	0			
" On Deposit, London Joint Stock Bank	9,000	0	0			
				31,004	17	2
" Cash at the Bank of England transferred to the Right Hon. Frank Green, Lord Mayor				3,232	12	10
				209,587	8	5

ALFRED NEWTON, Lord Mayor,
Treasurer.

29 March, 1901.

Examined and found correct,
(Signed) TURQUAND, YOUNGS, BISHOP & CLARKE,
Chartered Accountants.

LORD MAYOR GREEN'S DISCRETIONARY FUND.

RECEIPTS.		£	s.	d.
To Balance of Lord Mayor Newton's Discretionary Fund Investments—				
London County Council Loan (sold as below) .. £12,600	£12,223 11 2			
Consols 10,000	9,781 6 0			
Deposit at London Joint Stock Bank (withdrawn)	9,000 0 0			
	£31,004 17 2			
„ Cash at Bank of England		3,232	12	10
„ Withdrawn from Deposit		9,000	0	0
„ Sale of London County Council Loan—				
Loan £12,600 .. .. Cost £12,223 11 2				
Profit on Sale 168 2 7				
		12,391	13	9
„ Interest on £9,000 Deposit		183	8	3
„ Interest on £10,000 Consols		194	15	11
„ Interest on County Council Loan		125	0	2
„ Contributions Received at Mansion House ..		7,504	1	7
		32,631	12	6

PAYMENTS.	£	s.	d.
By the Mayor of Melbourne, for Widows and Orphans and Wounded Soldiers in the Colony of Victoria ..	10,000	0	0
„ Georgina, Countess of Dudley's Fund, for Convalescent Officers wounded in the War	10,500	0	0
„ City and County of Nottingham Reservists' Fund ..	1,500	0	0
„ Soldiers' Daughters' Home, Maintenance of Children	1,777	0	0
„ Royal School for Officers' Daughters, Admission of Children	1,435	0	0
„ Assistance to Refugees in the War Districts	1,000	0	0
„ Royal British Female Orphan Asylum, Admission of Children	730	0	0
„ Indian Followers' Families' Fund	2,000	0	0
„ Prince Christian Victor's Memorial Homes for disabled Soldiers	500	0	0
„ Duke of Abercorn's Sick and Wounded Officers Surgical and Medical Aid Fund	250	0	0
„ Soldiers' and Sailors' Help Society	455	12	9
„ Household Brigade Convalescent Fund	500	0	0
„ City of London Regiment Families' War Fund ..	250	0	0
„ Field Force Fund, Comforts for the Troops	300	0	0
„ Mayor of Cape Town Committee for Christmas Comforts, Literature, &c., for the Troops	250	0	0
„ The Aldershot Farnborough Camp Ladies' Association	150	0	0
„ Charing Cross Hospital, for Treatment of Convalescent Soldiers	100	0	0
„ Harrismith Hospital	100	0	0
„ Christmas Comforts, 2nd Battalion, The Buffs ..	100	0	0
„ Mr. Johnstone's work in supplying Literature to the Troops	50	0	0
„ Army and Navy Pensioners' Employment Society ..	75	0	0
„ Queen Charlotte's Lying-in Hospital, Soldiers' Wives	77	12	6
„ Army Guilds Home	52	0	0
„ Soldiers' Institute, Mafeking	20	0	0
„ Grants to Relations of Officers and Men killed and wounded in the War	395	0	0
„ Cheque Book and Bank charges		5	2
	32,567	10	5
„ Cash Balance at Bank of England	64	2	1
	32,631	12	6

There is also £10,000 Consols costing £9,781 6 0

Frank Green, Lord Mayor,
Treasurer.
20 December, 1901.

Audited and found correct.
(Signed) Turquand, Youngs, Bishop & Clarke, *Chartered Accountants.*

LORD MAYOR DIMSDALE'S DISCRETIONARY FUND.

Supplemental Statement to complete Accounts to 31 December, 1901, in order to coincide with Statement of Contributions received to same date.

RECEIPTS.	£	s.	d.
To Balance Cash at Bank (in addition to Consols £10,000 costing £9,781 6s. 0d.)	64	2	1
„ Interest on London County Council Loan	14	16	8
„ Return of Grant (E. C. Hankinson)	50	0	0
„ Sale of portion of Consols above	3,499	8	6
„ Additional Contributions to 31 December, 1901 ..	208	12	9
	3,837	0	0

PAYMENTS.	£	s.	d.
By Georgina, Countess of Dudley's Fund, for Convalescent Officers wounded in the War	1,000	0	0
„ Soldiers' Daughters' Home, for Alice May Phillips, born, 4 February, 1895, whose Father, Serjeant Phillips (Sussex Regiment), died of pneumonia at Bloemfontein	183	0	0
„ Royal British Female Orphan Asylum, for case of Eva Howlett	21	0	0
„ Mrs. Spinks, aged 70 (blind), additional, per Miss Ida Weekes	10	0	0
„ Messrs. Hayter & Hayter: Expenses of Transport of Comforts for the Troops	10	3	1
„ Ditto for Packing, Carriage paid on Parcels, &c.	2	13	0
	1,226	16	1
„ Balance Cash at Bank	2,610	3	11
	3,837	0	0

There is also £6,167 Consols.

The Mansion House, E.C.

THE ROYAL COMMISSION OF THE PATRIOTIC FUND.

Transvaal War Fund for Widows, Orphans, and other Dependents of Officers and Men losing their lives in the War in South Africa.

(*Communicated.*)

Letters from His Royal Highness the Duke of Cambridge to the Lord Mayor of London, and the Lord Mayor's letter to the Press.*

October 21, 1899.

My Dear Lord Mayor,—The engagement of our forces with the enemy in Natal yesterday resulted, so the telegrams state, in killed and wounded among our troops. This means soldiers' widows and orphans to be provided for. Parliament has placed upon the Patriotic Fund Commission the responsibility of appealing to the public for contributions for the benefit of widows, orphans, and other dependents of officers and men of her Majesty's Naval and Military Forces.

You, my Lord Mayor, are yourself a Patriotic Fund Commissioner.

It is, therefore, my duty as President of the Patriotic Fund Commission to ask you to at once kindly open a Fund for the benefit of the widows, orphans, and other dependents of those who may lose their lives by wounds or disease in the war operations in South Africa.

Arrangements have already been made, as in the case of our recent war operations on the North-west frontier of India and similar operations in various parts of Africa, to afford immediate relief to the widows, and the War Office authorities will give us the earliest intimation of every casualty, so that the relief may be prompt.

I will only add that the object of the Fund will be to provide the widows with regular allowances during widowhood, according to their circumstances, and regular allowances to the children—boys under fourteen years of age and girls under sixteen years of age—as has been done by the Commission in the case of every widow and orphan of those who fell in the recent campaigns to which I have alluded. Such children as it may be desirable to place in orphanages will be placed in the Royal Victoria Patriotic Asylum for Girls or other available homes.

I have every confidence that the nation will respond liberally to this appeal if your Lordship will be so good as to open a Mansion House Fund, and thanking you in anticipation, allow me to remain, my dear Lord Mayor, yours very faithfully,

GEORGE,
President.

The Right Hon. The Lord Mayor of the City of London.

October 21, 1899.

To the Press.

Sir,—In response to the accompanying appeal from H.R.H. the Duke of Cambridge, I have consented to open a Fund for the benefit of the widows, orphans, and other dependents of officers and men of Her Majesty's Forces, who may unfortunately lose their lives in the war operations in South Africa.

At the same time I think it right to say that there are cognate objects for public philanthropy in connection with our gallant troops engaged in those operations. I allude to the soldiers themselves who may get disabled by wounds, and the wives and children separated at home here from their husbands and fathers by the exigencies of the war.

I therefore propose, in order to give the public the widest scope for their benevolence, that contributions for widows, orphans, and other dependents of those who may lose their lives shall be handed to the Patriotic Fund Commission for administration; those for sick and wounded while under treatment to the British Red Cross Society; those for soldiers disabled by wounds (for their benefit after they leave the service) to that excellent organization, Lloyd's Patriotic Fund, founded in the City in 1803; and those for wives and children separated to the Soldiers' and Sailors' Families' Association. All contributions should, therefore, be clearly indicated by donors as follows: (1) Widows and Orphans; (2) Sick and Wounded; (3) Disabled Soldiers; (4) Wives and Children. Any not marked will be handed over for the benefit of widows and orphans, as it is upon the Duke of Cambridge's appeal that I ask the public to give liberally. As this is a national emergency, I would earnestly invite the co-operation and assistance of my brother Mayors, to whom I have already had occasion this year to apply for help in other matters.

Donations may be sent to the Secretary's Office, Mansion House, or to the Bank of England, to the credit of "The Transvaal War Fund." I would especially request donors to send their contributions in such a way that they may not be confused with the simultaneous appeal for the Transvaal Refugees' Fund, which, in spite of its great success, is still urgently in need of assistance.

I am, Sir, your obedient Servant,
JOHN VOCE MOORE,
Lord Mayor.

STATEMENT OF RECEIPTS AND PAYMENTS.

October, 1899 to 31st December, 1901.

RECEIPTS.	£	s.	d.	PAYMENTS.	£	s.	d.
To Contributions from the Mansion House	440,600	0	0	To Expenditure..	77,412	18	7
" " " other sources	25,753	2	1	„ Balance	388,940	3	6
	466,353	2	1		466,353	2	1

Numbers assisted	Widows	3,519
	Orphans	4,600
	Other Dependents...	1,229

The assistance rendered to Widows and Orphans was firstly—in the shape of a donation, and subsequently in the shape of regular allowances after investigation of each case. The assistance rendered to other dependents was in the shape of donations and in some cases of regular allowances to aged parents.

Until the War is over, and the number of eligible applicants for assistance has been definitely ascertained, all allowances issued must necessarily be provisional.

53, Charing Cross, W.C.

---

* A note is necessary to account for the repetition of the above two letters which already appear in the previous Article, the information supplied by the Secretary of the Patriotic Commissioners being given conditionally only on their being again inserted here, and in reversed order.

THE "DAILY TELEGRAPH" SHILLING FUND.
(Communicated.)

The *Daily Telegraph* Shilling Fund for our Soldiers' and Sailors' Widows and Orphans was opened on October 28th, 1899, as a result of an appeal written by Sir Edwin Arnold, K.C.I.E., C.S.I. It was intended to collect contributions in small sums, as a branch of the Mansion House Fund, but upon the strong representations of the first subscribers, with the consent of the then Lord Mayor, the distribution of the money was undertaken by the *Daily Telegraph*.

A Register, arranged upon the plan of a regimental and alphabetical card catalogue, was immediately opened, and a check provided against error and fraud, no entry being made in the Register without official notification of death. Whilst the Fund was in full operation the Register was maintained, and it contains a complete record of the 11,823 soldiers who were killed, or died of disease, to the end of 1900.

The Fund placed itself in communication with the Military and Naval authorities throughout the Country, Mayors, Magistrates, Guardians of the Poor, Local Societies, and Conductors of Provincial Funds; and it obtained the co-operation of the Secretary of State for War, and the First Lord of the Admiralty, and the active support of Lady Roberts and Lady Audrey Buller.

It received recommendations in favour of the widows and fatherless children of men losing their lives in the South African Campaign from all sources without regard to locality, creed, or denomination, and during the first few months it treated all Widows and Orphans, who had been properly verified, alike.

The first idea was to give each Widow a Post Office Banking Account, into which was paid £20, with £3 for each child, and to add annuities and children's endowments as far as the money available would permit.

This scheme was carried out in its entirety in respect to the first 250 eligible Widows and their children (about 300), and for these women £15 immediate Life Annuities were purchased of the State through the Post Office Savings Bank, and Trust Accounts, in £50 each, were opened for their children.

As local funds, municipal and county, multiplied, and many of these were assisting Widows and Orphans, The Shilling Fund, whilst scarcely limiting its Post Office Bank Book, or other grants throughout the country, and in the Colonies, restricted its permanent benefits to those districts furnishing money specially "ear-marked" for their own Widows.

The £15 Annuities were continued for awhile, chiefly in the Metropolis, the series of fifty-four carnivals providing for that purpose upwards of £46,000; but with the constant multiplication of claims upon the Fund, it was found necessary in the summer of 1900, to reduce the grants to Widows in counties and towns where local assistance was being given, to the initial registration grant of £3, and instead of the £15 Annuities in London, Scotland, and elsewhere, £10 Annuities were purchased.

In several instances supplemental £5 Annuities were subsequently issued, raising the recipients to an equal status. This plan was pursued largely in Scotland, in which country, through the advocacy of the *Scotsman*, the *Daily Telegraph* plan of distribution was continued until the autumn of 1901, some weeks later than July 1st, on which date the parent Shilling Fund in London published its closing list with a total of 5,210,024½ shillings.

The appeal of the *Daily Telegraph*, however, had ceased on January 1st, 1901, and the growth of the Fund to that date, and the claims upon it, were as shown below:—

Date.	Shillings.	Widows.
November 9, 1899	521,100	4
November 22 ,,	1,010,969	9
December 12 ,,	1,514,652	43
January 9, 1900	2,015,725	162
February 22 ,,	2,510,068	357
April 5 ,,	3,035,456	665
June 18 ,,	3,504,197	1,319
July 28 ,,	4,003,610	1,649
November 20 ,,	4,500,212	2,222
December 31 ,,	4,735,476	2,353

In the ensuing six months to July 5th, the Grand Total was raised to £254,800, and since the Balance Sheet was published on July 16th, 1901, audited by Messrs. Saffrey, Sons & Co., Chartered Accountants, belated subscriptions have been received and administered. In Scotland they have amounted to some thousands of pounds, so that the grand aggregate of the *Daily Telegraph* and *Scotsman* Fund, exceeds £261,500.

At the end of 1901 the total number of annuities issued was 727, exclusive of others in course of arrangement.

The number of Post Office Accounts opened to June 30th, 1901, was 2,364, but grants were subsequently made in Scotland through Trustees Savings Banks, and the work of the Shilling Fund was not finally wound up at the end of the year.

The difficulty of bringing the Fund to a termination was due to the fact that large numbers of benevolent people were not content that widows should receive Government Pensions only. These were first payable on the day of the publication of the Shilling Fund closing list, July 1, 1901. The public was at a loss to know where to send money for Widows and Orphans, the recommendations of the Joint Committee of the House of Lords and the House of Commons in favour of the establishment of Military and Naval Pension Boards, with power to administer money placed at their disposal for the purpose of being expended in pensions to Widows and allowances to Orphans, not having been to that time carried into effect.

Whilst its main work was that of providing temporarily, and, as far as possible, permanently, for as many Widows and Orphans, other duties were undertaken by the Fund. During the Christmas of 1899 there was a strong feeling of sympathy with the wives of Reservists whose husbands were at the front, and monies were sent for them at a time when it was being influentially represented that enough had been collected for the needs of Widows and Orphans. In this work again the *Daily Telegraph* was compelled by circumstances to distribute upon its own system, which was based upon an independent register, to which was added mechanical checks which had the desired result of entirely safe-guarding the Fund against fraud. A similar system was applied to the relief of disabled and wounded soldiers to the extent of the money specially subscribed for them, and the full number of these compassionate grants was, on July 1st, 1901, 1,188.

In the following Christmas other agencies were at work, and it was not necessary to repeat Christmas Gifts in money, clothing (for the distribution of which a special depôt had been opened in the winter of 1899–1900) or kind, but to most of the fatherless soldiers' children in the country a doll was presented.

In the Colonies the Fund had its own Committee at Cape Town, with Sir J. Gordon Sprigg as Chairman, and a member of the *Daily Telegraph* Staff as Hon. Secretary, and at Natal it worked through the Government, and in Pietermaritzburg, Mrs. Hamilton, wife of the Postmaster, assisted Widows on its behalf. Every co-operation was forthcoming in Australasia through the Agents General, and in India the India Office afforded valuable help, whilst at Gibraltar, Malta, and other military stations, the Authorities heartily assisted the Fund.

Throughout its operations the Shilling Fund was never defrauded by any applicant, and it was not found necessary to institute a single prosecution in the Police Courts.

It is calculated that the contributors numbered upwards of twelve millions, the average of the items received being considerably below the shilling. Few large sums were acknowledged, and the greater part of the West of Scotland, the suburbs of London (through copper collections at Carnival times), the regular workshop payments, and the children's cards, severally accounted for thousands of pounds wholly amassed in pence.

In addition to contributions in cash all kinds of jewellery, curiosities, and odds and ends were sent to the Fund, and a series of public auctions were held for their disposal. Large sums were received as entrance payments to exhibitions of war relics which were also arranged by the Fund.

All expenses in connection with the collection, acknowledgment, and distribution of the quarter of a million sterling, were borne by the proprietors of the *Daily Telegraph*. From the opening of the Fund to its close, eleven hundred columns of the paper were filled with lists, articles, and correspondence created by the movement.

The principles, working, and full details of the organization were supplied to the War Relief Funds Committee in March, 1900, by Mr. J. Hall Richardson, Manager of the Shilling Fund, and to the Joint Select Committee of the House of Lords and House of Commons in May, 1901, by Sir Edward Lawson, Bart., the Founder.

STATEMENT OF RECEIPTS AND PAYMENTS.
25TH OCTOBER, 1899 TO 5TH JULY, 1901.

RECEIPTS.	£	s.	d.	PAYMENTS.	£	s.	d.
To Contributions	254,800	0	6	By Cash Grants to Widows and Orphans	38,154	0	0
				,, Annuities, Post Office and Savings Bank	190,006	3	3
				,, Trust Account (Children)	14,716	15	0
				,, Grants to Natal	2,100	0	0
				,, Ditto Cape Colony	1,568	9	3
				,, Reservists' Families, disabled Soldiers and Dependents	5,389	16	4
				,, Officers' Families and Yeomanry Widows (Imperial War Fund)	1,294	15	9
				,, Funerals of Soldiers' Wives	69	16	0
				,, Grant to Bournemouth (at request of Subscribers)	100	0	0
				,, Red Cross Society	21	0	0
				,, Lloyd's Patriotic Fund	17	3	0
				,, Chocolate Boxes (paid to Wives for Boxes sold and credited to General List)	101	6	6
				,, Cash remitted to *Scotsman*	1,123	18	0
				,, Balance in hand, 5 July, 1901	136	17	5
	254,800	0	6		254,800	0	6

Audited and found correct, SAFFREY, SONS & Co., *Chartered Accountants*.

NOTE.—The *Daily Telegraph* has received and distributed since 5 July, 1901, further sums. The final distribution of this and the *Scotsman* Fund (*see* under Edinburgh, in tabular statement of Counties) was not completed on this date.

141, *Fleet Street*, E.C., 25 *March*, 1902.

IMPERIAL WAR FUND.
(Communicated.)

THE object of this Fund (founded in 1882) was for the relief of relatives of Soldiers and Sailors consequent on the latter going on active service, as well as to assist Widows, Mothers, or Sisters, owing to the death (by wounds or disease) of husbands, sons, or brothers; as also Soldiers themselves invalided whether from wounds or disease.

The amount of Contributions received for the South African War was as follows:—

	£	s.	d.	
From the Mansion House Fund	2,600	0	0	} £5,688 19s. 9d.
,, ,, *Daily Telegraph*	1,140	0	0	
,, ,, *Daily Mail*	650	0	0	
,, ,, Lord Mayor of Liverpool	500	0	0	
,, Other sources	798	19	9	

Number of Cases relieved:—

Widows, with 648 children	551	} 999.
Wives	11	
Dependent Relatives	313	
Relations of Officers	34	
Insurance of Men	90	

Relief to South African Cases ceased after the sum of £8,568 8s. 4d. had been expended.

Cash Account for the period December 1st, 1899, to November 30th, 1901.

RECEIPTS.	£ s. d.	£ s. d.
To Balance, December 1st, 1899:—		
Cash at bank	76 11 4	
Petty cash	15 0 0	
		91 11 4
,, Subscriptions		5,688 19 9
,, Dividends on investments		146 4 0
,, Hospital Accounts:—		
Net returns, Netley	34 6 9	
,, Woolwich	37 15 0	
		72 1 9
,, Sales of Stock:—		
£2,500 New South Wales, cost £2,571 17s. 6d., realised	2,907 9 0	
£700 Canada, cost about £642 5s., realized	717 9 0	
		9,623 14 10

PAYMENTS.	£ s. d.	£ s. d.
By Relief:—		
General	7,693 8 0	
Officers' branch and Yeomanry	647 10 0	
Extra war premiums	227 10 4	
		8,568 8 4
,, General Expenses:—		
Office administration, typewriting, and clerical assistance	440 4 3	
Printing and stationery	167 16 6	
Advertising	261 3 3	
Postage, &c.	82 4 7½	
Miscellaneous	9 13 4½	
		961 2 0
,, Balance in Hand, November 30th, 1901:—		
Cash in bank	56 4 2	
In Secretary's hands	38 0 4	
		94 4 6
		9,623 14 10

Investments Account, November 30th, 1901.

RECEIPTS.	£ s. d.
To In Hand, December 1st, 1899:—	
£2,500 New South Wales, 4 per cent.	2,571 17 6
£2,200 Canada, 3½ per cent.	2,018 10 0
,, Appreciation	572 0 6
	5,162 8 0

PAYMENTS.	£ s. d.
By Sold:—	
£2,500 New South Wales, 4 per cent.	2,907 9 0
£700 Canada, 3½ per cent.	717 9 0
,, Balance, £1,500 Canada, estimated value, at 102½ per cent.	1,537 10 0
	5,162 8 0

Balance-sheet, November 30th, 1901.

RECEIPTS.	£ s. d.
To Total funds in hand, November 30th, 1901	1,631 14 6
	1,631 14 6

PAYMENTS.	£ s. d.
By Investment:—	
£1,500 Canada, 3½ per cent.	1,537 10 0
,, Cash at bank	56 4 2
,, In Secretary's hands	38 0 4
	1,631 14 6

561/20, Bucklersbury, E.C.

Correct, J. WILSON WITTON, 16, Charing Cross, *November 29th,* 1901.

THE SOLDIERS' AND SAILORS' FAMILIES ASSOCIATION.

Patron :
THE KING.

President ;
QUEEN ALEXANDRA.

The above Association was founded in February 1885, with the object of aiding the wives and families of men of all branches of the Land and Sea Forces of the United Kingdom. The want of any such organisation, as was then stated, had been most felt where troops are suddenly ordered on active service, when, in many cases, their wives and families became homeless; but the Association also undertook this charge in time of peace, and up to the outbreak of the War had aided with money grants alone ten thousand families with twenty-one thousand children.

Anticipating that war in South Africa was inevitable, the following letter was addressed to the Press on the 9th September 1899 by the Chairman of the Association, and subsequently, after the Declaration of War, the letter dated 13th October 1899:—

9th September 1899.

On the eve of embarcation of the first contingent of troops for South Africa, will you allow me to state through the medium of your columns that, where the names and addresses of the local office bearers of the Soldiers' and Sailors' Families Association are not known, these can be obtained by application to the secretary of the same at this office?

The object of the Association is to befriend at all times the wives and families of men of the land and sea forces of the United Kingdom, whether married "on" or "off the strength"; but especially so when their husbands or fathers are on active or foreign service.

The help and co-operation of all interested in the Services will be gladly welcomed.

13th October 1899.

On no previous occasion of the despatch of a large Expeditionary Force from this country has there been a complete organization, consisting of over three thousand ladies and gentlemen throughout the kingdom, voluntarily undertaking to befriend the wives and families of our Soldiers and Sailors during their absence on active service.

Additional funds are all that is now required to meet the extra demands which must of necessity fall on the Association at the present time.

It is needless to add that while those "on" the strength are equally helped by the Association with those "not on the strength," the needs and wants of the latter are far in excess of those of the former.

The wives and families of the Reserves, while serving with the Colours, are helped equally with those of the standing forces.

Her Royal Highness the President and the Council with confidence therefore appeal to the public, as well as to all interested in the Services at home and abroad to help in this great National work.

The Funds placed in the hands of the Association and the magnitude of the work carried out by its voluntary representatives, increased to over 12,000 during the War, throughout the Kingdom, in India, and the King's Dominions beyond the Seas, can best be seen in the summary of a Statement of Receipts and Payments at the bottom of this notice, covering the period of the War to the 31st December 1901. The keynote of the Association has, from its initiation, been decentralisation, Funds raised locally being locally retained and administered. Grants to supplement the same are, as needs arise, made by the Central General Fund, which, for the period under notice, amounted to £415,259 19s. 10d.

The administration of relief is carried out personally under the direction of the local Committees, the leading principle being that of helping those who help themselves, subject in time of war to a special scale of weekly allowances to be given or withheld (and for which no right or claim can be made) at the discretion of the local Committee, according to the merits of each individual case.

The scale of relief initiated by the Association, and which was almost universally adopted by the local independent Funds throughout the Kingdom, was to make up the income of the family from all sources to two-thirds of that of the breadwinner when at home; and as no Government separation allowance was granted to wives "not on" the strength, to supplement this loss by placing them in the same position, all circumstances being satisfactory, as those "on" the strength.

Fathers and mothers who were regularly dependent were also considered eligible for relief, although it was subsequently decided that such dependence before their sons left home gave them no claim for help, unless their sons made a regular voluntary allotment of their pay, which they were quite as well able to do as married men to their wives.

The wives living in the United Kingdom of men serving in the Colonial Corps were also considered eligible for help, as also those of the Imperial Yeomanry and Irregular Corps until the pay of these men was fixed at 5s. per day.

The help from the Association to wives becoming widows was continued until they received the first payment of their pension, but not after.

On the 1st of January 1901, the following Special Appeal (supplemented a few days later by a letter from Lord Roberts, *see* Appendix, page 172) was made by Her Majesty, then Princess of Wales, and is now known as Queen Alexandra's Appeal:—

" I desire, as President of the Soldiers' and Sailors' Families Association, to give a brief account of the work we have been carrying on since the commencement of the War, and of our position at the present time, and I ask—knowing that I shall not ask in vain—for your kind co-operation and support.

" By the munificence of the public, over £510,000 has been directly entrusted to our care, supplemented by £190,000 subscribed for wives and families to the Mansion House, and £50,000 received from the Lord Mayor's 'Discretionary' Fund. The whole of this sum, amounting to £750,000, is now nearly expended, the relief being given locally and personally through the voluntary services of our members, numbering not less than 12,000 ladies and gentlemen throughout the United Kingdom.

" By the last returns from our Branches there were over 80,000 families being then relieved, and notwithstanding the disembodiment of a large portion of the Militia, and of the return of some of the Troops, our numbers do not diminish to the extent which might be expected, from the fact of Local Funds working independently, although in co-operation, becoming exhausted, and the cases being handed over to the Association. The amount now being given in relief is not less than £50,000 per month.

" The task which was imposed upon us by a generous people was the maintenance of the family in the same position as when the breadwinner was at home. As the circumstances vary to such an extent, it was decided that this position would be secured if the income of the family were made up to about two-thirds of what it was previous to separation, the difference representing the amount which may be fairly attributed to the breadwinner's expenses.

" This principle has been almost universally adopted and acted upon by the various Funds throughout the Kingdom, which are being administered independently of the Association.

" Old fathers and mothers have also been largely aided to the extent of the help received from their sons before rejoining the Colours.

" Hundreds of letters have been received by our workers showing the gratitude of our Soldiers and Sailors for what has been done for their families during their absence; of the anxieties from which they have been relieved during the hardships they themselves were undergoing; and of the joy with which they are looking forward to find their homes intact on their return.

" Without further funds these homes must be broken up, and all that we have been doing for the last twelve months will be undone. This will be especially felt during the winter months, when coals and other necessaries of life have increased in price. I therefore very earnestly appeal for help to enable us to keep these homes together until the breadwinners return, as I cannot contemplate the effect, not only upon the families, but upon the men themselves, of the withdrawal of our aid.

" I take this opportunity of offering my grateful thanks to the Press generally throughout the Country, who have so generously supported the Association; to the Public, who have so liberally provided us with Funds; to the employers of labour, and working men themselves, who have for many months set aside part of their weekly earnings; and to the ladies and gentlemen who have devoted so much time and labour to carry on this great National work, which I have so much at heart.

" I may add that the Association exists for all times, Peace or War, and that its objects are the care of the Wives and Families of Soldiers and Sailors of the Queen, without any distinction, and in whatsoever part of the world they may be serving.

" The Lord Mayor has kindly consented to receive on our account subscriptions sent to the Mansion House for this object, and I would invite the co-operation of Lords Lieutenant of Counties, and of Lord Mayors, Provosts and Mayors, throughout the Kingdom, to help me in the same way.

" Subscriptions will also be received by our Local Branches in each County, and by our Treasurer, Colonel James Gildea, C.B., at 23, Queen Anne's Gate, Westminster, S.W.

" ALEXANDRA,
" Princess of Wales.

" *Marlborough House,*
" 31st *December* 1900."

The response to Her Majesty's Appeal amounted to over £300,000, half of which was subscribed within one month. The number of cases and amount given in relief during the War was as follows :—

			£ s. d.	
1899	{ Wives and Dependent Relatives	24,971 } = 41,361 13 1	
	{ Children	25,514 }	
1900	{ Wives and Dependent Relatives	93,429 } = 680,379 9 4	= £1,075,232 0 5
	{ Children	107,266 }	
1901	{ Wives and Dependent Relatives	59,129 } = 353,490 18 0	
	{ Children	68,979 }	

SUMMARY OF RECEIPTS AND PAYMENTS.

CENTRAL OFFICE, LONDON.

1ST JANUARY, 1899 TO 31ST DECEMBER, 1901.

RECEIPTS.			PAYMENTS.		
		£ s. d.			£ s. d.
To Balance, 1 January, 1899		548 19 5	By Cases relieved direct		255 17 4
,, Interest on Investments and Deposit		5,412 13 4	,, Advertising, Expenses, &c.		5,929 16 10
,, Contributions, &c.		501,775 14 9	,, Grants to Branches		415,259 19 10
,, Grants from Branches		2,763 3 7	,, Grants to Nursing Branch, &c.		2,158 6 0
			,, Investment (Legacy)		*1,599 3 10
			,, Balance, 31 December, 1901—		
			At Bank	£5,297 7 3	
			,, Deposit	80,000 0 0	85,297 7 3
		510,500 11 1			510,500 11 1

* £984 15s. 3d. of this amount was invested in 1899, before the War.

GENERAL SUMMARY OF RECEIPTS AND PAYMENTS

THROUGHOUT THE ASSOCIATION.

1ST JANUARY, 1899 TO 31ST DECEMBER, 1901.

N.B.—The following statement excludes all cross entries from and to the Council by the several Branches.

RECEIPTS.			PAYMENTS.		
		£ s. d.			£ s. d.
To Balance, 1 January, 1899—			By Cases relieved—		
The Council	£548 19 5		The Council	255 17 4	
Branches	10,964 10 10		Branches	1,074,976 3 1	
		11,513 10 3			1,075,232 0 5
,, Interest on Investments and Deposit—			,, Advertising and Expenses—		
The Council	5,412 13 4		The Council	5,929 16 10	
Branches	4,799 4 0		Branches	15,589 1 11	
		10,211 17 4			21,518 18 9
,, Contributions, &c.—			,, Grants to Nursing Branch, &c.—		
The Council	501,775 14 9		The Council	2,158 6 0	
Branches	808,243 12 2		Branches	463 12 6	
		1,310,019 6 11			2,621 18 6
			,, Investments (Legacies)—		
			The Council	1,599 3 10	
			Branches	797 12 11	
					2,396 16 9
			,, Balance on 31 December, 1901—		
			The Council	85,297 7 3	
			Branches	144,677 12 10	
					229,975 0 1
		1,331,744 14 6			1,331,744 14 6

23, Queen Anne's Gate, Westminster, S.W.

OFFICERS' FAMILIES FUND.

The necessity for helping the families of Officers having early in the War become apparent, a joint appeal was made through the Press in November 1899 by Lady Lansdowne and Lady Wolseley, the wives of the then Secretary of State for War and the Commander-in-Chief, who, for this object allied themselves with the Soldiers' and Sailors' Families Association, who had had for some years an Officers' Branch for the benefit of widows and children of Officers, and in connection with which a special Branch for this purpose was opened.

The approval of the public and those connected with the Services was soon made manifest from the fact, that over £23,000 was subscribed in one month, and an additional £53,000 in the following year.

A General and an Executive Committee (the latter consisting of two Ladies and two Officers, with Mrs. Edward Hope as Honorary Secretary) was formed, the adjudication of the claims being entrusted to the latter; Lansdowne House, by the wish of Lord Lansdowne, was made the headquarters of the Fund, so that no expenses on this head should be incurred; and the Chairman of the Soldiers' and Sailors' Families Association undertook to act as Honorary Treasurer.

It may be stated that what was most felt by Officers proceeding on active service was, not only the cost of extra outfit, but the increased war risk on their life insurance, as well as the loss of quarters and allowances to their families, necessitating in many cases the breaking up of the home, the removal and storage of furniture and effects, and in some cases a hurried sale.

Every effort was made to impress upon the ladies, for whose benefit the Fund was raised, that it partook in no way of the nature of a charity; but was the response of the country to the natural feeling that they should undergo no unnecessary hardships or privations during the absence of their husbands or relatives; and, although informed that references were required and full information as to their exact resources was necessary, every application would be treated in the strictest confidence, and would be only known to the Executive Committee and Lady Lansdowne, who had shared in their duties throughout. In connection with this it may be added that a large number of the beneficiaries have expressed their gratitude, not only for the assistance they have received, but also for the manner in which it has been rendered.

Indirect assistance has also been rendered, owing to the kind co-operation of those engaged in educational work, by which many sons and daughters have been provided for, some entirely free, and some at reduced fees; whilst numerous offers were made for the loan of houses and hospitality.

Altogether, 769 families of Officers of every rank and from every branch of the Service, have enjoyed the benefits of the Fund, among whom have been 64 Widows, pending the receipt of their pensions and the arrangement of their affairs.

Committees representing the Fund were also formed at the Cape, in Natal, New Zealand, Tasmania, and India, to whom grants amounting to £4,600 were entrusted.

SUMMARY OF RECEIPTS AND PAYMENTS.
1st December, 1899 to 31st December, 1901.

RECEIPTS	£	s.	d.	PAYMENTS	£	s.	d.	£	s.	d.
To Contributions	81,452	13	4	By Grants				49,305	7	9
,, Interest	1,184	3	1	,, Grants to Colonies—						
				Natal	£1,800	0	0			
				The Cape	1,500	0	0			
				New Zealand	500	0	0			
				Tasmania	500	0	0			
				India	300	0	0			
								4,600	0	0
				,, Advertising, &c.				696	4	1
				,, Balance				28,035	4	7
	82,636	16	5					82,636	16	5

The Accounts from which this Summary and that of the Central Office on the previous page are made, have been audited and certified as correct by Messrs. Drury, Thurgood & Co., *Chartered Accountants*, 11, Queen Victoria Street, E.C.

COUNTY AND BOROUGH FUNDS.
TABULAR STATEMENT.

INDEX TO COUNTIES, &c.

ENGLAND.

	Page
Bedford	17
Berks	17
Bucks	18
Cambridge	18
Chester	19
Cornwall	20
Cumberland	21
Derby	21
Devon	21
Dorset	22
Durham	23
Essex	24
Gloucester	24
Hereford	25
Hertford	25
Huntingdon	25
Kent	26
Lancaster	28
Leicester	30
Lincoln	31
London	31
Middlesex	33
Monmouth	33
Norfolk	34
Northampton	34
Northumberland	35
Nottingham	36
Oxford	37
Rutland	37
Salop	38
Somerset	38
Southampton (Hants)	39

ENGLAND—cont.

	Page
Stafford	40
Suffolk	42
Surrey	42
Sussex	43
Warwick	45
Westmoreland	45
Wilts	46
Worcester	47
Yorks	47

WALES.

	Page
Anglesey	51
Brecon	51
Cardigan	51
Carmarthen	52
Carnarvon	52
Denbigh	52
Flint	53
Glamorgan	53
Merioneth	54
Montgomery	54
Pembroke	54
Radnor	54

SCOTLAND.

	Page
Aberdeen	55
Argyll	56
Ayr	56
Banff	56
Berwick	57
Bute	57

SCOTLAND—cont.

	Page
Caithness	57
Clackmannan	58
Dumbarton	58
Dumfries	58
Edinburgh	58
Elgin	59
Fife	59
Forfar	60
Haddington	61
Inverness	61
Kincardine	61
Kinross	61
Kirkcudbright	61
Lanark	62
Linlithgow	62
Nairn	63
Orkney and Shetland	63
Peebles	63
Perth	63
Renfrew	63
Ross and Cromarty	64
Roxburgh	64
Selkirk	65
Stirling	65
Sutherland	65
Wigtown	65

	Page
IRELAND	66
ISLE OF MAN	70
CHANNEL ISLANDS	70
FOREIGN	71

TRANSVAAL WAR FUNDS.
1899 TO 1901.
COUNTIES—COUNTY BOROUGHS AND BOROUGHS.
ENGLAND.

Lord Mayors are distinguished by having L.M. after the name of the Borough; County Boroughs by having a * prefixed; and Towns, &c., which are not "County" Boroughs or Boroughs, by being printed in *italics*.—M.H. signifies The Mansion House Fund.—L.L. Fund, The Lord Lieutenant's Fund.—S. & S.F.A., The Soldiers' and Sailors' Families Association.—S. & S.H.S., The Soldiers' and Sailors' Help Society.—The Lansdowne Fund, Officers' Wives and Families.—The Abercorn Fund, Officers' Surgical and Medical Aid.—The Dudley Fund, Sick and Wounded Officers.—Y. and V. Equipment, Yeomanry and Volunteer Equipment.—Y. Hospital, Yeomanry Hospital; and a § in S. & S.F.A. column of Relief, that particulars of Relief in that Town or Borough are included in the Relief by the S. & S.F.A. at the head of the County.

Origin of Fund.	S. & S.F.A. Subscriptions Raised in County (a) including County Balances previous to the War. Grants from the Council (b).	Total Amount Received.	Expenditure in Relief, &c. By S. & S.F.A.	By Independent Committee.	Remitted to other Funds.		Balance.	Wives and Dependent Relatives.	Children.	Widows.	Men.	Remarks.
	£ s. d.	£ s. d.	£ s. d.	£ s. d.		£ s. d.	£ s. d.					
BEDFORDSHIRE.	(a) 5,965 0 10 (b) 500 0 0	6,465 0 10	5,291 6 3		...		1,173 14 7	720	601	—	—	
LORD LIEUTENANT'S FUND (EARL COWPER.)		... ...			... ...	...		...	...	...	...	No L.L. Fund.
Bedford		497 17 3	§		To M.H. (not earmarked)	350 0 0						
					„ „ Refugees' Fund	147 17 3						
						497 17 3						
Dunstable		125 0 0	§	20 0 0	„ The Dudley Fund	100 0 0	5 0 0	5	20	—	—	
Luton		916 18 3	§	28 0 0	„ S. & S.F.A. (local)	680 13 0		5	13			
					„ M.H. No. 1 Patriotic Fund	100 0 0						
					„ Red Cross Society	50 0 0						
					„ *Daily Telegraph*	25 0 0						
					„ *Daily Mail*	1 0 0						
					„ Men's extra comforts	5 5 10						
					„ M.H. Refugees' Fund	17 12 0						
					„ Expenses	7 6 6						
						886 17 4	2 0 11	—	—	—	—	
BERKSHIRE.	(a) 9,049 16 4 (b) 4,175 0 0	13,224 16 4	11,360 6 0		...		1,864 10 4	970	1,128	—	—	
LORD LIEUTENANT'S FUND (LORD WANTAGE) deceased. (JAMES H. BENYON, Esq.)		6,590 0 0		...	To Y. & V. Equipment	6,590 0 0						
Abingdon		573 0 0	§		„ M.H. (not earmarked)	323 0 0						
					„ S. & S.F.A. (local)	250 0 0						
						573 0 0						
Maidenhead		2,213 0 0	§	84 0 0	„ M.H. (not earmarked)	1,360 0 0		10	14	9	—	
					„ S. & S.F.A. (central)	250 0 0						
					„ „ „ (local)	58 0 0						
					„ L.L. Y. & V. Equipment	150 0 0						
					„ S. & S.H.S.	42 0 0						
					„ Expenses	34 0 0						
						1,894 0 0	235 0 0	—	—	—	—	
Newbury		450 0 0	§		„ S. & S.F.A. (local)	208 0 0						
					„ L.L. Y. & V. Equipment	160 0 0						
					„ M.H. Refugees	82 0 0						
						450 0 0						
*Reading		3,510 6 3	§	881 1 5	„ M.H. No. 1 Patriotic Fund	571 16 2		35	40	60	35	
					„ „ No. 2 Red Cross Society	192 3 4						
					„ „ Refugees' Fund	39 9 0						
					„ S. & S.F.A. (local)	1,687 15 10						
					„ Expenses	138 0 6						
						2,629 4 10						

TRANSVAAL WAR FUNDS, 1899 TO 1901. COUNTIES—COUNTY BOROUGHS AND BOROUGHS. ENGLAND—cont.

Lord Mayors are distinguished by having L.M. after the name of the Borough; County Boroughs by having a * prefixed; and Towns, &c., which are not "County" Boroughs or Boroughs, by being printed in *italics*.—M.H. signifies The Mansion House Fund.—L.L. Fund, The Lord Lieutenant's Fund.—S. & S.F.A., The Soldiers' and Sailors' Families Association.—S. & S.H.S., The Soldiers' and Sailors' Help Society.—The Lansdowne Fund, Officers' Wives and Families.—The Abercorn Fund, Officers' Surgical and Medical Aid.—The Dudley Fund, Sick and Wounded Officers.—Y. and V. Equipment, Yeomanry and Volunteer Equipment.—Y. Hospital, Yeomanry Hospital; and a § in S. & S.F.A. column of Relief, that particulars of Relief in that Town or Borough are included in the Relief by the S. & S.F.A. at the head of the County.

Origin of Fund.	S. & S.F.A. Subscriptions Raised in County (a) including County Balances previous to the War. Grants from the Council (b).	Total Amount Received.	Expenditure in Relief, &c. By S. & S.F.A.	Expenditure in Relief, &c. By Independent Committee.	Remitted to other Funds.		Balance.	Number of Cases Relieved. Wives and Dependent Relatives.	Children.	Widows.	Men.	Remarks.
	£ s. d.	£ s. d.	£ s. d.	£ s. d.		£ s. d.	£ s. d.					
BERKSHIRE—cont.												
Wallingford		213 0 0	§		To M.H. (not earmarked)	135 0 0						
					„ Red Cross Society	67 0 0						
					„ M.H. Refugees' Fund	11 0 0						
						213 0 0		—	—	—	—	
Windsor		6,100 0 0	§		To Red Cross Society	6,100 0 0		—	—	—	—	
Wokingham		667 0 0	§		To M.H. No. 1 Patriotic Fund	16 0 0						
					„ „ No. 2 Red Cross Society.	22 0 0						
					„ „ No. 3 Lloyd's Patriotic.	2 0 0						
					„ „ No. 4 S. & S.F.A.	56 0 0						
					„ S. & S.F.A. (local)	150 0 0						
					„ S. & S.H.S. (local)	55 0 0						
					„ L.L. Y. & V. Equipment	358 0 0						
					„ Expenses	8 0 0						
						667 0 0		—	—	—	—	
Hungerford		397 0 0	§		To M.H. No. 1 Patriotic Fund	14 2 0						
					„ „ No. 2 Red Cross Society.	9 12 9						
					„ „ No. 3 Lloyd's Patriotic.	9 11 3						
					„ „ No. 4 S. & S.F.A.	2 6 3						
					„ S. & S.F.A. (local)	65 0 0						
					„ M.H. Refugees' Fund	2 1 0						
					„ Y. Hospital	50 0 0						
					„ Mafeking Fund	13 0 0						
						165 13 3	231 6 9	—	—	—	—	
BUCKINGHAMSHIRE.	(a) 5,635 8 1	6,285 8 1	5,094 15 2		...		1,190 12 11	569	614			
	(b) 600 0 0											
LORD LIEUTENANT'S FUND (LORD ROTHSCHILD.)		7,634 4 11			To M.H. (not earmarked)	240 3 1						
					„ „ No. 1 Patriotic Fund	461 8 11						
					„ „ No. 2 Red Cross Society.	395 18 9						
					„ „ No. 3 Lloyd's Patriotic.	112 16 1						
					„ „ No. 4 S. & S.F.A.	195 9 1						
					„ Y. Equipment	5,259 16 6						
					„ V. Equipment	963 12 6						
						7,634 4 11		—	—	—	—	
NORTH BUCKS FUND		1,163 6 6	§	1,067 0 0	To S. & S.F.A. (local)	40 6 6		102	172	3	7	
					„ Expenses	61 0 0						
						101 6 6						
Buckingham		415 1 3	§		To M.H. (not earmarked)	208 7 6						
					„ S. & S.F.A. (local)	206 13 9						
						415 1 3		—	—	—	—	
High Wycombe		315 0 0	§		To S. & S.F.A. (local)	315 0 0		—	—	—	—	
CAMBRIDGESHIRE.	(a) 3,675 3 2	3,775 3 2	2,337 15 6		To S. & S.F.A. (central)	197 2 6	1,240 5 2	348	405	—		
	(b) 100 0 0											
LORD LIEUTENANT'S FUND (A. PECKOVER, ESQ.)		...	...		...	...	...	...	...	...		No L.L. Fund.
Cambridge		2,795 7 2	§	1,658 12 0	To M.H. (not earmarked)	343 8 0		158	83	2	—	
					„ M.H. No. 2 Red Cross Society.	151 0 0						
					Carried Forward	494 8 0						

TRANSVAAL WAR FUNDS, 1899 TO 1901. COUNTIES—COUNTY BOROUGHS AND BOROUGHS. ENGLAND—cont.

Lord Mayors are distinguished by having L.M. after the name of the Borough; County Boroughs by having a * prefixed; and Towns, &c., which are not "County" Boroughs or Boroughs, by being printed in *italics*.—M.H. signifies The Mansion House Fund.—L.L. Fund, The Lord Lieutenant's Fund.—S. & S.F.A., The Soldiers' and Sailors' Families Association.—S. & S.H.S., The Soldiers' and Sailors' Help Society.—The Lansdowne Fund, Officers' Wives and Families.—The Abercorn Fund, Officers' Surgical and Medical Aid.—The Dudley Fund, Sick and Wounded Officers.—Y. and V. Equipment, Yeomanry and Volunteer Equipment.—Y. Hospital, Yeomanry Hospital; and a § in S. & S.F.A. column of Relief, that particulars of Relief in that Town or Borough are included in the Relief by the S. & S.F.A. at the head of the County.

Origin of Fund.	S. & S.F.A. Subscriptions Raised in County (a) including County Balances previous to the War. Grants from the Council (b).	Total Amount Received.	Expenditure in Relief, &c. By S. & S.F.A.	Expenditure in Relief, &c. By Independent Committee.	Remitted to other Funds.		Balance.	Wives and Dependent Relatives.	Children.	Widows.	Men.	Remarks.
CAMBRIDGESHIRE—*cont.*	£ s. d.	£ s. d.	£ s. d.	£ s. d.		£ s. d.	£ s. d.					
Cambridge—*cont.*					Brought forward ...	494 8 0						
					To M.H. Queen Alexandra's Fund.	270 7 2						
					,, S. & S.F.A. (local)	335 0 0						
					,, Expenses	37 0 0						
						1,136 15 2	—	—	—	—	—	
Cambridge University		2,709 0 0		...	To M.H. (not earmarked) ...	2,709 0 0	—	—	—	—	—	
President of Queens'		165 6 5			To M.H. No. 1 Patriotic Fund	165 6 5	—	—	—	—	—	
Wisbech		713 0 0	§	474 0 0	To M.H. (not earmarked) ...	200 0 0		35	70	—	—	
					,, Expenses	4 0 0						
						204 0 0	35 0 0					
Ely (Isle of) (Lord de Ramsey.)		50 0 0	§		To Yeomanry Hospital ...	50 0 0	—	—	—	—	—	
CHESHIRE.	(a) 11,972 8 4	12,362 8 4	9,144 6 3				3,218 2 1	548	604	—	—	
	(b) 390 0 0											
Lord Lieutenant's Fund (Earl of Egerton and Tatton.)		17,043 19 10			To Patriotic Fund ...	398 19 9						
					,, Red Cross Society	303 8 1						
					,, Lloyd's Patriotic	450 15 1						
					,, S. & S.F.A. (central) ...	509 1 6						
					,, S. & S.F.A. (local) ...	1,996 2 1						
					,, The Lansdowne Fund...	400 0 0						
					,, Stockport War Fund ...	200 0 0						
					,, South African Graves...	100 0 0						
					,, S. & S.H.S (local)	1,000 0 0						
					,, Y. Hospital Bed ...	50 0 0						
					,, Y. & V. Equipment ...	5,234 0 0						
					,, Men's extra comforts ...	1,601 0 0						
					,, Expenses	48 9 7						
						12,291 16 1	4,752 3 9					
*Birkenhead		8,053 0 0	§	5,183 0 0	To S. & S.F.A. (local)	1,997 0 0		340	320	—	—	
					,, L.L. Y. Equipment ...	528 0 0						
					,, Expenses	345 0 0						
						2,870 0 0	—					
*Chester		2,800 0 0	§	2,000 0 0	...		800 0 0	...	...	...	...	No particulars supplied.
Congleton		586 0 0	§	302 16 6	To S. & S.F.A. (local)	280 0 0	...	14	5	—	—	
					,, Men's extra comforts ...	2 0 0						
					,, Expenses	1 3 6						
						283 3 6	—					
Crewe		2,543 0 0	§	2,365 0 0	To *Daily Telegraph*...	50 0 0	128 0 0	171	260	7	2	
Dukinfield		907 0 0	§	907 0 0				35	40	—	—	
Hyde		1,861 0 0	§	1,861 0 0	...			187	93	2	43	
Macclesfield		1,900 0 0	§	1,870 0 0	...		30 0 0	156	272	3	—	
Macclesfield Courier		1,000 0 0			To M.H. (not earmarked)...	1,000 0 0	—	—	—	—	—	
Stalybridge		1,811 7 8	§	1,703 2 6	To Expenses ...	15 5 0	93 0 2	101	108	3	—	
*Stockport		7,047 6 4	§	6,905 6 11	To S. & S.F.A. (local)	141 19 5		570	550	—	—	
Advertiser and Daily Echo		2,325 14 11			To Stockport Fund ...	2,325 14 11						

TRANSVAAL WAR FUNDS, 1899 TO 1901. COUNTIES—COUNTY BOROUGHS AND BOROUGHS. ENGLAND—cont.

Lord Mayors are distinguished by having L.M. after the name of the Borough; County Boroughs by having a * prefixed; and Towns, &c., which are not "County" Boroughs or Boroughs, by being printed in *italics*.—M.H. signifies The Mansion House Fund.—L.L. Fund, The Lord Lieutenant's Fund.—S. & S.F.A., The Soldiers' and Sailors' Families Association.—S. & S.H.S., The Soldiers' and Sailors' Help Society.—The Lansdowne Fund, Officers' Wives and Families.—The Abercorn Fund, Officers' Surgical and Medical Aid.—The Dudley Fund, Sick and Wounded Officers.—Y. and V. Equipment, Yeomanry and Volunteer Equipment.—Y. Hospital, Yeomanry Hospital; and a § in S. & S.F.A. column of Relief, that particulars of Relief in that Town or Borough are included in the Relief by the S. & S.F.A. at the head of the County.

Origin of Fund.	S. & S.F.A. Subscriptions Raised in County (a) including County Balances previous to the War. Grants from the Council (b).	Total Amount Received.	Expenditure in Relief, &c. By S. & S.F.A.	By Independent Committees.	Remitted to other Funds.		Balance.	Wives and Dependent Relatives.	Children.	Widows.	Men.	Remarks.
	£ s. d.	£ s. d.	£ s. d.	£ s. d.		£ s. d.	£ s. d.					
CHESHIRE—*cont.*												
Northwich		2,085 0 0	§	138 0 0	To S. & S.F.A. (local)	885 0 0		...	1	1	21	
					„ Y. Hospital	50 0 0						
					„ S. & S.H.S. (local)	12 0 0						
					„ Men's extra comforts, etc.	245 0 0						
						1,192 0 0	755 0 0	—	—	—	—	
Runcorn		1,699 8 1	§	9 10 0	To L.L. Fund	650 0 0						
					„ S. & S.F.A. (local)	400 0 0						
					„ Expenses	10 5 4						
						1,060 5 4	629 12 9	—	—	—	—	
CORNWALL.	(a) 9,558 1 0	9,658 1 0	4,383 3 10		...	...	5,274 17 2	457	733	—	—	
	(b) 100 0 0											
Lord Lieutenant's Fund (Earl of Mount-Edgcumbe.)		3,880 18 10			To Y. and V. Equipment	2,402 3 10						
					„ Expenses	23 15 2						
						2,425 19 0	1,454 19 10	—	—	—	—	
		(c) 1,015 8 4			To Reception, etc.	347 7 4		...	...	...	...	(c) Recognition Fund.
					„ Expenses	39 19 5						
						387 6 9	628 1 7	—	—	—	—	
Bodmin		31 6 5	§		To M.H. No. 1 Patriotic Fund	23 14 0						
					„ Western Morning News (d)	7 12 5		...	...	...	...	(d) See Devonshire.
						31 6 5	—					
Falmouth		211 0 0	§	56 0 0	To M.H. (not earmarked)	85 0 0	70 0 0					
Helston		261 3 4	§		To S. & S.F.A. (local)	261 3 4	—					
Launceston		40 0 0	§		To Prince Christian Victor Memorial	40 0 0	—					
Liskeard		375 0 0	§		To S. & S.F.A. (local)	300 0 0						
					„ L.L. Recognition Fund	75 0 0						
						375 0 0	—					
Lostwithiel		...	§		...	...		...	...	...	...	No particulars supplied.
Penrhyn		141 19 0	§		To M.H. (not earmarked)	141 19 0	—					
Penzance		1,907 9 4	§		To M.H. No. 1 Patriotic Fund	380 5 6						
					„ „ No. 2 Red Cross Society	153 17 4						
					„ „ No. 3 Lloyd's Patriotic	168 0 10						
					„ „ No. 4 S. & S.F.A.	112 7 8						
					„ „ Refugees	5 10 0						
					„ S. & S.F.A. (local)	11 9 9						
					„ Men's Extra Comforts	67 18 3						
					„ L.L. Y. & V. Equipment	966 18 0						
					„ „ Recognition Fund	41 2 0						
						1,907 9 4	—					
St. Ives		575 9 6	§		To S. & S.F.A. (local)	100 0 0						
					„ Prince Christian Victor Memorial	100 0 0						
						200 0 0	375 9 6	—	—	—	—	
Saltash *		146 9 6	§		To S. & S.F.A. (local)	146 9 6	—					
Truro		1,006 4 1	§	723 14 6	To M.H. (not earmarked)	100 0 0		...	...	...	...	Particulars of cases not supplied.
					„ S. & S.F.A. (local)	100 0 0						
						200 0 0	82 9 7					

TRANSVAAL WAR FUNDS, 1899 TO 1901. COUNTIES—COUNTY BOROUGHS AND BOROUGHS. ENGLAND—cont.

Lord Mayors are distinguished by having L.M. after the name of the Borough; County Boroughs by having a * prefixed; and Towns, &c., which are not "County" Boroughs or Boroughs, by being printed in *italics*.—M.H. signifies The Mansion House Fund.—L.L. Fund, The Lord Lieutenant's Fund.—S. & S.F.A., The Soldiers' and Sailors' Families Association.—S. & S.H.S., The Soldiers' and Sailors' Help Society.—The Lansdowne Fund, Officers' Wives and Families.—The Abercorn Fund, Officers' Surgical and Medical Aid.—The Dudley Fund, Sick and Wounded Officers.—Y. and V. Equipment, Yeomanry and Volunteer Equipment.—Y. Hospital, Yeomanry Hospital; and a § in S. & S.F.A. column of Relief, that particulars of Relief in that Town or Borough are included in the Relief by the S. & S.F.A. at the head of the County.

Origin of Fund.	S. & S.F.A. Subscriptions Raised in County (a) including County Balances previous to the War, Grants from the Council (b).	Total Amount Received.	Expenditure in Relief, &c. By S. & S.F.A.	By Independent Committee.	Remitted to other Funds.		Balance.	Wives and Dependent Relatives.	Children.	Widows.	Men.	Remarks.
	£ s. d.	£ s. d.	£ s. d.	£ s. d.		£ s. d.	£ s. d.					
CUMBERLAND.	(a) 4,893 4 1	4,993 4 1	4,102 2 8		To S & S.F.A. (Central)	341 11 4	549 10 1	335	525	—	—	
	(b) 100 0 0											
Lord Lieutenant's Fund (Lord Muncaster.)		13,372 5 11		8,028 4 0	To Y. Equipment	1,168 15 4		692	1,200	8	—	
					„ V. Equipment	187 12 8						
						1,356 8 0	3,987 13 11	—	—	—	—	
Carlisle		...	§	...	...	...	...	...	...	...	...	Funds raised in conjunction with the Lord Lieutenant's Fund.
Whitehaven		2,066 17 0	§	*...	To L.L. Fund	2,042 12 2		...	...	...	...	* Funds supplied for relief of local cases, and included in £8,028 4s.; and number of cases relieved.
					„ Expenses	24 4 10						
						2,066 17 0	—	—	—	—	—	
Workington		2,008 15 3	§	2,005 11 8	To Expenses	0 8 0	2 15 7	86	183	1	3	
DERBYSHIRE.	(a) 8,915 5 11	9,015 5 11	7,949 5 6				1,066 0 5	451	510	—	—	
	(b) 100 0 0											
Lord Lieutenant's Fund (Duke of Devonshire.)		21,357 10 0		2,517 0 0	To M.H. No 1 Patriotic Fund	406 1 1		357	496	—	—	
					„ „ No. 2 Red Cross Society.	83 3 8						
					„ „ No. 3 Lloyd's Patriotic.	123 16 7						
					„ „ No. 4 S & S.F.A.	280 14 7						
					„ S. & S.F.A. (local)	4,594 0 0						
					„ M.H. Refugees' Fund	13 15 0						
					„ Y. Equipment	4,838 10 0						
					„ V. Equipment	870 0 0						
						11,210 0 11	7,630 9 1	—	—	—	—	
Chesterfield		4,823 13 10	§		To S & S.F.A. (local)	4,069 18 6						
					„ M.H. No. 2 Red Cross Society.	100 0 0						
					„ The Lansdowne Fund	100 0 0						
					„ Expenses	104 7 0						
						4,374 5 6	449 8 4	—	—	—	—	
*Derby		8,186 0 0	§	7,340 0 0	To M.H. (not earmarked)	200 0 0		370	559	5	—	
					" Refugees' Fund	200 0 0						
						400 0 0	446 0 0	—	—	—	—	
Glossop		1,805 2 1	§	1,358 11 11	To Men's Extra Comforts	50 0 10		96	67	...	3	
					„ Indian Famine Fund	1 14 0						
					„ Expenses	6 7 10						
						58 2 8	388 7 6	—	—	—	—	
Ilkeston		901 18 6	§	901 18 6	...	...	...	...	...	...	...	No particulars supplied.
DEVONSHIRE.	(a) 16,906 4 2	23,366 4 2	21,935 9 5		...	...	1,430 14 9	2,831	3,961			
	(b) 6,460 0 0											
Lord Lieutenant's Fund (Lord Clinton.)		7,564 0 0			To Y. & V. Equipment, etc.	7,459 0 0						
					„ Y. Hospital	105 0 0						
						7,564 0 0	—	—	—	—	—	
Barnstaple		563 5 5	§	16 17 0	To M.H. No 1 Patriotic Fund	55 1 9						
					„ „ No. 2 Red Cross Society.	23 19 6						
					„ „ No. 3 Lloyd's Patriotic.	4 5 0						
					„ Refugees' Fund	24 13 0						
					„ S. & S.F.A. (local)	178 0 0						
					„ The Lansdowne Fund	2 2 0						
					„ Yeomanry Bed	74 11 9						
					„ Expenses	3 3 7						
						365 16 7	180 11 10	—	—	—	—	

Lord Mayors are distinguished by having L.M. after the name of the Borough; County Boroughs by having a * prefixed; and Towns, &c., which are not "County" Boroughs or Boroughs, by being printed in *italics*.—M.H. signifies The Mansion House Fund.—L.L. Fund, The Lord Lieutenant's Fund.—S. & S.F.A., The Soldiers' and Sailors' Families Association.—S. & S.H.S., The Soldiers' and Sailors' Help Society.—The Lansdowne Fund, Officers' Wives and Families.—The Abercorn Fund, Officers' Surgical and Medical Aid.—The Dudley Fund, Sick and Wounded Officers.—Y. and V. Equipment, Yeomanry and Volunteer Equipment.—Y. Hospital, Yeomanry Hospital; and a § in S. & S.F.A. column of Relief, that particulars of Relief in that Town or Borough are included in the Relief by the S. & S.F.A. at the head of the County.

Origin of Fund.	S. & S.F.A. Subscriptions Raised in County (a) including County Balances previous to the War. Grants from the Council (b).	Total Amount Received.	Expenditure in Relief, &c. By S. & S.F.A.	By Independent Committee.	Remitted to other Funds.		Balance.	Number of Cases Relieved. Wives and Dependent Relatives.	Children.	Widows.	Men.	Remarks.
	£ s. d.	£ s. d.	£ s. d.	£ s. d.		£ s. d.	£ s. d.					
DEVONSHIRE—*cont.*												
Bideford ...		686 2 4	§		To M.H. No. 1 Patriotic Fund	328 5 0						
					,, ,, No. 2 Red Cross Society.	39 16 0						
					,, ,, No. 3 Lloyd's Patriotic.	63 18 4						
					,, ,, No. 4 S. & S.F.A.	249 3 0						
						686 2 4	—	—	—	—	—	
Dartmouth ...		203 7 5	§		To M.H. (not earmarked) ...	170 16 6						
					,, Imperial War Fund ...	25 0 0						
					,, *Daily Mail* (London) ...	6 3 5						
					,, Expenses ...	1 7 6						
						203 7 5						
*Devonport ...		249 5 1	§	23 19 0	...	...	225 6 1	...	...	3	5	
*Exeter ...		... ...	§		...					...	...	No Mayor's Fund.
Great Torrington			§		...					...	...	No Mayor's Fund.
Honiton ...		294 11 4	§		To M.H. No. 1 Patriotic Fund	88 4 2						
					,, ,, No. 2 Red Cross Society.	11 3 10						
					,, ,, No. 3 Lloyd's Patriotic.	50 3 5						
					,, ,, No. 4 S. & S.F.A.	13 3 3						
					,, ,, Refugees' Fund ...	15 10 0						
					,, Expenses ...	2 5 11						
						180 10 7	114 0 9	—		—		
Okehampton ...			§		...					...	...	No Mayor's Fund.
*Plymouth ...		... ...	§		...					...	...	No Mayor's Fund.
Western Morning News		13,946 17 9		...	To S & S.F.A. (local) (c) ...	10,760 18 5				...	...	(c) Also S. & S.F.A., Cornwall.
					,, Y. Hospital	100 0 0						
					,, Mafeking Fund ...	100 0 0						
						10,960 18 5	2,985 19 4	—	—	—	—	
South Molton ...		60 0 0	§		To M.H. (not earmarked) ...	60 0 0	—					
Tiverton ...		... ...	§		...					...	...	No Mayor's Fund.
Torquay ...		3,094 0 0	§		To Syracuse Convalescent Home.	3,002 0 0						
					,, Y. Hospital ...	50 0 0						
					,, M.H. Refugees' Fund ...	42 0 0						
						3,094 0 0	—					
Totnes ...		311 15 8	§		To M.H. (not earmarked) ...	311 15 8	—					
DORSETSHIRE.	(a) 4,251 2 6	7,551 2 6	6,883 9 5		...	...	667 13 1	914	1,051			
	(b) 3,300 0 0											
LORD LIEUTENANT'S FUND ... (EARL OF ILCHESTER.)		1,892 8 2			To M.H. (not earmarked) ...	530 12 1						
					,, ,, No. 1 Patriotic Fund	488 9 3						
					,, ,, No. 2 Red Cross Society.	235 6 2						
					,, ,, No. 3 Lloyd's Patriotic.	258 1 8						
					,, ,, No. 4 S. & S.F.A.	357 13 4						
					,, Refugees' Fund ...	11 16 5						
					,, The Lansdowne Fund...	6 6 0						
					,, Expenses ...	4 3 3						
						1,892 8 2	—	—	—	—	—	
Do. do.		8,795 6 11			To Y. & V. Equipment ...	4,955 1 10						
					,, Miscellaneous ...	2,093 15 3						
					,, Insurance...	1,508 5 1						
					,, Y. Hospital ...	100 0 0						
					,, Expenses ...	138 4 9						
						8,795 6 11	—					

TRANSVAAL WAR FUNDS, 1899 TO 1901. COUNTIES—COUNTY BOROUGHS AND BOROUGHS. ENGLAND—cont.

Lord Mayors are distinguished by having L.M. after the name of the Borough; County Boroughs by having a * prefixed; and Towns, &c., which are not "County" Boroughs or Boroughs, by being printed in *italics*.—M.H. signifies The Mansion House Fund.—L.L. Fund, The Lord Lieutenant's Fund.—S. & S.F.A., The Soldiers' and Sailors' Families Association.—S. & S.H.S., The Soldiers' and Sailors' Help Society.—The Lansdowne Fund, Officers' Wives and Families.—The Abercorn Fund, Officers' Surgical and Medical Aid.—The Dudley Fund, Sick and Wounded Officers.—Y. and V. Equipment, Yeomanry and Volunteer Equipment.—Y. Hospital, Yeomanry Hospital; and a § in S. & S.F.A. column of Relief, that particulars of Relief in that Town or Borough are included in the Relief by the S. & S.F.A. at the head of the County.

Origin of Fund.	S. & S.F.A. Subscriptions Raised in County (a) including County Balances previous to the War. Grants from the Council (b).	Total Amount Received.	Expenditure in Relief, &c. By S. & S.F.A.	Expenditure in Relief, &c. By Independent Committee.	Remitted to other Funds.		Balance.	Number of Cases Relieved. Wives and Dependent Relatives.	Children.	Widows.	Men.	Remarks.
DORSETSHIRE—*cont*.	£ s. d.	£ s. d.	£ s. d.	£ s. d.		£ s. d.	£ s. d.					
Blandford	...	45 17 6	§		To M.H. No. 1 Patriotic Fund	45 17 6	—	—	—	—	—	
Bridport	...	195 0 0	§		To M.H. (not earmarked) ...	195 0 0	—	—	—	—	—	
Dorchester	...	652 0 0	§		To M.H. No. 3 Lloyd's Patriotic.	640 0 0						
					„ *Daily Mail* (London) ...	12 0 0						
						652 0 0	—	—	—	—	—	
Lyme Regis	...	165 0 0	§		To M.H. (not earmarked) ...	165 0 0	—	—	—	—	—	
Poole	...	719 1 7	§		To M.H. (not earmarked) ...	513 0 9						
					„ S. & S.F.A. (local)	198 13 6						
					„ Expenses ...	7 7 4						
						719 1 7	—	—	—	—	—	
Shaftesbury	...	116 10 0	§		To M.H. (not earmarked) ...	116 10 0	—	—	—	—	—	
Wareham	...	263 13 11	§		To M.H. (not earmarked) ...	263 13 11	—	—	—	—	—	
Weymouth	...	1,202 0 0	§		To M.H. (not earmarked) ...	1,202 0 0	—	—	—	—	—	
DURHAM.	(a) 24,733 6 3	24,933 6 3	20,073 18 8		...	...	4,859 7 7	1,447	1,627	—	—	
	(b) 200 0 0											
LORD LIEUTENANT'S FUND (THE EARL OF DURHAM.)		28,631 0 0		2,721 0 0	To Sunderland Fund	500 0 0		...	...	...	...	Number of cases relieved not supplied.
					„ S. & S.F.A. (local)	930 0 0						
					„ Y. & V. Equipment	16,527 0 0						
						17,957 0 0	7,953 0 0	—	—	—	—	
Darlington	...		§					...	...	...	...	No Mayor's Fund.
Durham	...	...	§		...	...		...	...	...	...	L.L. Fund.
*Gateshead	...	5,883 0 0	§	*...	To Northumberland and Tyneside Reservists' Fund.	5,883 0 0		*...	*...	*...	...	Amount expended and cases relieved included in N. & T. Reservists' Fund, of which this is a branch.
Hartlepool	...	1,155 0 0	§		To M.H. (not earmarked) ...	848 0 0						
					„ S. & S.F.A. (local)	50 0 0						
					„ Mayor West Hartlepool	26 0 0						
					„ Expenses ...	45 0 0						
						969 0 0	186 0 0	—	—	—	—	
Northern Daily Mail	...	81 0 0		...	To Mayor of Hartlepool ...	81 0 0	—	—	—	—	—	
Jarrow-on-Tyne	...	3,296 19 10	§	3,249 10 4			47 9 6	...				Number of cases relieved not supplied.
South Shields	...	4,328 0 0	§	2,842 0 0			1,486 0 0	89	115	—	—	
Stockton-on-Tees	...	2,942 0 0	§		To L.L. Fund ...	200 0 0						
					„ M.H. (not earmarked) ...	112 0 0						
					„ Y. Hospital	100 0 0						
					„ Men's Extra Comforts ...	260 0 0						
					„ L.L.Y. and V.Equipment	2,270 0 0						
						2,942 0 0	—	—	—	—	—	
Sunderland	...	13,342 7 2	§	12,429 17 6	To S. & S.F.A (local) ...	912 9 8		631	593		7	
West Hartlepool	...	9,514 0 0	§	5,125 0 0	To M.H. No. 1 Patriotic Fund	1,000 0 0		110	198	68	2	
					„ No. 2 Red Cross Society.	1,025 0 0						
					„ No. 3 Lloyd's Patriotic.	1,025 0 0						
					„ S. & S.F.A. (local)	50 0 0						
					„ Pietermaritzburg Hospital.	15 0 0						
					„ Expenses ...	152 0 0						
						3,267 0 0	1,122 0 0					

TRANSVAAL WAR FUNDS, 1899 TO 1901. COUNTIES—COUNTY BOROUGHS AND BOROUGHS. ENGLAND—cont.

Lord Mayors are distinguished by having L.M. after the name of the Borough; County Boroughs by having a * prefixed; and Towns, &c., which are not "County" Boroughs or Boroughs, by being printed in *italics*.—M.H. signifies The Mansion House Fund.—L.L. Fund, The Lord Lieutenant's Fund.—S. & S.F.A., The Soldiers' and Sailors' Families Association.—S. & S.H.S., The Soldiers' and Sailors' Help Society.—The Lansdowne Fund, Officers' Wives and Families.—The Abercorn Fund, Officers' Surgical and Medical Aid.—The Dudley Fund, Sick and Wounded Officers.—Y. and V. Equipment, Yeomanry and Volunteer Equipment.—Y. Hospital, Yeomanry Hospital; and a § in S. & S.F.A. column of Relief, that particulars of Relief in that Town or Borough are included in the Relief by the S. & S.F.A. at the head of the County.

Origin of Fund.	S. & S.F.A. Subscriptions Raised in County (a) including County Balances previous to the War, Grants from the Council (b).	Total Amount Received.	Expenditure in Relief, &c.		Remitted to other Funds.		Balance.	Number of Cases Relieved.				Remarks.
			By S. & S.F.A.	By Independent Committee.				Wives and Dependent Relatives.	Children.	Widows.	Men.	
DURHAM—*cont.*	£ s. d.	£ s. d.	£ s. d.	£ s. d.		£ s. d.	£ s. d.					
Western Daily Mail		1,313 0 0			To Mayor West Hartlepool	1,313 0 0	—	—	—	—	—	
Northern Guardian		670 0 0			To Mayor West Hartlepool	670 0 0	—	—	—	—	—	
ESSEX.	(a) 12,471 3 9 (b) 14,910 0 0	27,381 13 9	25,985 3 10				1,396 9 11	3,408	4,698	—	—	
LORD LIEUTENANT'S FUND (LORD RAYLEIGH) Resigned. (EARL OF WARWICK.)		8,068 13 2		100 0 0	To S. & S.F.A. (local) „ S. & S.H.S. (local) „ Y. & V. Equipment „ Expenses	3,350 0 0 300 0 0 644 4 7 94 9 4 4,388 13 11	3,579 19 3	1	...	...	1	
Chelmsford		647 10 3	§		To M.H. (not earmarked)	647 10 3	—	—	—	—	—	
Colchester		1,650 3 3	§		To S. & S.F.A. (local) „ Expenses	1,635 0 0 15 3 3 1,650 3 3	—	—	—	—	—	
Harwich		251 12 8	§		To M.H. Refugees' Fund „ M.H. No. 1 Patriotic Fund	16 14 6 234 18 2 251 12 8	—	—	—	—	—	
Maldon		315 17 5	§		To M.H. (not earmarked)	315 17 5	—	—	—	—	—	
Saffron Walden		208 18 3	§		To M.H. No. 1 Patriotic Fund „ „ Refugees' Fund	178 5 6 30 12 9 208 18 3	—	—	—	—	—	
Southend-on-Sea		1,039 15 9	§	1,029 13 3	To Expenses	10 2 6	—	60	120	—	—	
*West Ham		210 6 5	§		To M.H. No. 1 Patriotic Fund „ „ No. 2 Red Cross Society. „ „ No. 3 Lloyd's Patriotic. „ „ No. 4 S. & S.F.A.	171 6 11 1 1 0 23 4 5 14 14 1 210 6 5	—	—	—	—	—	
Essex County Chronicle		4,327 9 7			To S. & S.F.A. (local) „ S. & S.H.S. (local) „ Essex Regiment (Mrs. Stephenson). „ Expenses	3,749 15 0 384 16 6 119 3 6 73 14 7 4,327 9 7	—	—	—	—	—	
GLOUCESTERSHIRE.	(a) 26,831 13 2 (b) 183 0 0	27,014 13 2	24,474 2 8				2,540 10 6	2,864	3,109	—	—	
LORD LIEUTENANT'S FUND (EARL OF DUCIE.)		5,204 1 4			To Y. Equipment „ V. Equipment „ Expenses	3,441 13 0 1,596 5 10 166 2 6 5,204 1 4	—	—	—	—	—	
*Bristol, L.M.		23,081 0 0	§	2,551 0 0	To S. & S.F.A. (local) „ Red Cross Society „ Men's Extra Comforts „ V. Equipment „ M.H. Refugees' Fund	12,444 0 0 500 0 0 343 0 0 1,018 0 0 1,375 0 0 15,680 0 0	4,850 0 0	...	113	94	110	
Cheltenham		340 14 5	§		To S. & S.F.A. (local)	340 14	—	—	—	—	—	
The Echo		504 4 3			To S. & S.F.A. (local)	504 4 3	—	—	—	—	—	

TRANSVAAL WAR FUNDS, 1899 TO 1901. COUNTIES—COUNTY BOROUGHS AND BOROUGHS. ENGLAND—cont.

Lord Mayors are distinguished by having L.M. after the name of the Borough; County Boroughs by having a * prefixed; and Towns, &c., which are not "County" Boroughs or Boroughs, by being printed in *italics*.—M.H. signifies The Mansion House Fund.—L.L. Fund, The Lord Lieutenant's Fund.—S. & S.F.A., The Soldiers' and Sailors' Families Association.—S. & S.H.S., The Soldiers' and Sailors' Help Society.—The Lansdowne Fund, Officers' Wives and Families.—The Abercorn Fund, Officers' Surgical and Medical Aid.—The Dudley Fund, Sick and Wounded Officers.—Y. and V. Equipment, Yeomanry and Volunteer Equipment.—Y. Hospital, Yeomanry Hospital; and a § in S. & S.F.A. column of Relief, that particulars of Relief in that Town or Borough are included in the Relief by the S. & S.F.A. at the head of the County.

Origin of Fund.	S. & S.F.A. Subscriptions Raised in County (a) including County Balances previous to the War. Grants from the Council (b).	Total Amount Received	Expenditure in Relief, &c. By S. & S.F.A.	Expenditure in Relief, &c. By Independent Committee.	Remitted to other Funds		Balance.	Number of Cases Relieved. Wives and Dependant Relatives.	Children.	Widows.	Men.	Remarks.
GLOUCESTERSHIRE—*cont.*	£ s. d.	£ s. d.	£ s. d.	£ s. d.		£ s. d.	£ s. d.					
*Gloucester		2,638 7 10	§	64 12 5	To S. & S.F.A. (local)	2,507 0 0		6	6	—	—	
					„ Expenses	53 11 8						
						2,560 11 8	13 3 9	—	—	—	—	
Atlas Employees		351 4 0		338 14 0	No Expenses	...	12 10 0	7	15			
Gloucester Railway Works		185 5 3		177 16 6	No Expenses	...	7 8 9	11	20			
Tewkesbury			§		...		...	...	...	...	...	No Mayor's Fund.
HEREFORDSHIRE.	(a) 3,755 1 1	4,955 1 1	4,696 14 1				258 7 0	595	787	—	—	
	(b) 1,200 0 0											
LORD LIEUTENANT'S FUND (LORD BATEMAN) deceased. (J. H. ARKWRIGHT, ESQ.)		581 18 0			To S. & S.F.A. (local)	497 5 9	84 12 3	—	—			
Hereford		1,319 6 4	§		To M.H. No. 1 Patriotic Fund	100 0 0						
					„ No. 2 Red Cross Society.	100 0 0						
					„ No. 3 Lloyd's Patriotic.	90 0 0						
					„ S. & S.F.A. (local)	300 0 0						
					„ Y. & V. Equipment	541 6 4						
					„ M.H. Refugees' Fund	184 0 0						
					„ Expenses	4 0 0						
						1,319 6 4						
Leominster		163 3 8	§		To S. & S.F.A. (local)	163 3 8						
					„ The Lansdowne Fund	5 0 0						
						168 3 8	—	—	—	—	—	
HERTFORDSHIRE.	(a) 12,319 17 1	12,419 17 1	10,500 7 8			...	1,919 9 5	906	994	—	—	
	(b) 100 0 0											
LORD LIEUTENANT'S FUND (EARL OF CLARENDON.)		3,588 13 6			To Y. Equipment	3,588 13 6						
Hemel Hempsted		255 11 6	§	233 7 10	...	...	22 3 8	9	20			
Hertford		413 13 11	§		To M.H. No. 1 Patriotic Fund	240 17 0						
					„ S. & S.F.A. (local)	148 13 5						
					„ M.H. Refugees' Fund	24 3 6						
						413 13 11	—	—	—	—	—	
St. Albans		1,360 6 6	§		To M.H. No. 1 Patriotic Fund	1,168 13 5						
					„ S. & S.F.A. (local)	137 19 10						
					„ Expenses	53 13 3						
						1,360 6 6	—	—	—	—	—	
Barnet		436 15 8	§		To S. & S.F.A. (local)	436 15 8	—					
Waltham Cross		442 0 1	§	414 17 0	...	...	27 3 1	14	15			
Watford Observer		132 19 0			To S. & S.F.A. (local)	132 19 0	—					
HUNTINGDONSHIRE.	(a) 490 19 10	790 19 10	579 0 11			...	211 18 11	128	216	—	—	
	(b) 300 0 0											
LORD LIEUTENANT'S FUND (EARL OF SANDWICH.)		232 0 0			To M.H. No. 1 Patriotic Fund	82 0 0						
					„ „ No. 2 Red Cross Society.	12 0 0						
					„ „ No. 3 Lloyd's Patriotic.	32 0 0						
					„ „ No. 4 S. & S.F.A.	56 0 0						
					„ S. & S.F.A. (Central)	50 0 0						
						232 0 0						

TRANSVAAL WAR FUNDS, 1899 TO 1901. COUNTIES—COUNTY BOROUGHS AND BOROUGHS. ENGLAND—cont.

Lord Mayors are distinguished by having L.M. after the name of the Borough; County Boroughs by having a * prefixed; and Towns, &c., which are not "County" Boroughs or Boroughs, by being printed in *italics*.—M.H. signifies The Mansion House Fund.—L.L. Fund, The Lord Lieutenant's Fund.—S. & S.F.A., The Soldiers' and Sailors' Families Association.—S. & S.H.S., The Soldiers' and Sailors' Help Society.—The Lansdowne Fund, Officers' Wives and Families.—The Abercorn Fund, Officers' Surgical and Medical Aid.—The Dudley Fund, Sick and Wounded Officers.—Y and V. Equipment, Yeomanry and Volunteer Equipment.—Y. Hospital, Yeomanry Hospital; and a § in S. & S.F.A. column of Relief, that particulars of Relief in that Town or Borough are included in the Relief by the S. & S.F.A. at the head of the County.

Origin of Fund.	S. & S.F.A. Subscriptions Raised in County (a) including County Balances previous to the War. Grants from the Council (b).	Total Amount Received.	Expenditure in Relief, &c.		Remitted to other Funds.		Balance.	Number of Cases Relieved.				Remarks.
			By S. & S.F.A.	By Independent Committee.				Wives and Dependent Relatives.	Children.	Widows.	Men.	
	£ s. d.	£ s. d.	£ s. d.	£ s. d.		£ s. d.	£ s. d.					
HUNTINGDONSHIRE—*cont.*												
Godmanchester ...		38 7 9	§		To S. & S.F.A. (local) ...	38 7 9		—	—	—	—	
Huntingdon ...		1,538 14 3	§		To M.H. No. 1 Patriotic Fund	377 17 9		—	—	—	—	
					„ „ No. 2 Red Cross Society	377 17 9						
					„ „ No. 3 Lloyd's Patriotic.	377 17 9						
					„ „ No. 4 S. & S.F.A.	377 17 9						
					„ „ Refugees' Fund ...	27 3 3						
						1,538 14 3						
St. Ives ...		197 0 0	§		To L.L. Fund... ...	182 0 0		—	—	—	—	
					„ Princess Christian Hospital.	9 0 0						
					„ Mafeking Fund ...	6 0 0						
						197 0 0						
KENT.	(a)16,371 10 11 (b)20,350 0 0	36,721 10 11	33,724 12 0			...	2,996 18 11	3,833	5,273	—	—	
Lord Lieutenant's Fund ... (Earl Stanhope.)		10,097 8 8			To Yeomanry Hospital ...	1,250 0 0		—	—	—	—	
					„ Y. Equipment } „ V. Equipment } ...	8,608 11 10						
					„ S. & S.H.S. ...	238 16 10						
						10,097 8 8						
*Canterbury ...		1,251 2 9	§		To M.H. (not earmarked) ...	359 9 0		—	—	—	—	
					„ „ No. 1 Patriotic Fund	597 3 4						
					„ „ No. 2 Red Cross Society.	73 4 0						
					„ „ No. 3 Lloyd's Patriotic.	37 11 1						
					„ „ No. 4 S. & S.F.A. ...	183 15 4						
						1,251 2 9						
Chatham... ...		1,145 2 7	§		To M.H. No. 1 Patriotic Fund	830 3 3		—	—	—	—	
					„ „ No. 4 S. & S.F.A. ...	171 8 4						
					„ S. & S.F.A. (local) ...	143 11 0						
						1,145 2 7						
Chatham Dockyard ...		1,214 0 0		644 0 0			570 0 0	129	205	4	—	
Chatham, etc., Observer ...		149 15 6			To S. & S.F.A. (local)	149 15 6		—	—	—	—	
Deal		...	§		...	...		...	...	...	...	No Mayor's Fund.
Dover		2,241 0 0	§	2,234 0 0	To Expenses ...	7 0 0		336	620	...	1	
Faversham ...		493 12 4	§		To M.H. (not earmarked) ...	108 1 6		—	—	—	—	
					„ S. & S.F.A. (local) ...	385 10 10						
						493 12 4						
Folkestone ...		1,007 0 0	§		To S. & S.F.A. (local)	775 0 0		—	—	—	—	
					„ Christmas Gifts, etc. ...	152 0 0						
					„ S. & S.H.S. (local)	50 0 0						
						977 0 0	30 0 0					
Gravesend ...		1,298 0 7	§	730 12 3	To M.H. (not earmarked) ...	333 11 0		24	51	3	—	
					„ S. & S.F.A. (local)	129 12 10						
					„ The Dudley Fund	50 0 0						
					„ *Daily Telegraph*...	50 0 0						
					„ *Daily Mail*	4 4 6						
						567 8 4						

TRANSVAAL WAR FUNDS, 1899 TO 1901. COUNTIES—COUNTY BOROUGHS AND BOROUGHS. ENGLAND—cont.

Lord Mayors are distinguished by having L.M. after the name of the Borough; County Boroughs by having a * prefixed; and Towns, &c., which are not "County" Boroughs or Boroughs, by being printed in *italics*.—M.H. signifies The Mansion House Fund.—L.L. Fund, The Lord Lieutenant's Fund.—S. & S.F.A., The Soldiers' and Sailors' Families Association.—S. & S.H.S., The Soldiers' and Sailors' Help Society.—The Lansdowne Fund, Officers' Wives and Families.—The Abercorn Fund, Officers' Surgical and Medical Aid.—The Dudley Fund, Sick and Wounded Officers.—Y. and V. Equipment, Yeomanry and Volunteer Equipment.—Y. Hospital, Yeomanry Hospital; and a § in S. & S.F.A. column of Relief, that particulars of Relief in that Town or Borough are included in the Relief by the S. & S.F.A. at the head of the County.

| Origin of Fund. | S. & S.F.A. Subscriptions Raised in County (a) including County Balances previous to the War, Grants from the Council (b). | Total Amount Received. | Expenditure in Relief, &c. | | Remitted to other Funds. | | Balance. | Number of Cases Relieved. | | | | Remarks. |
			By S. & S.F.A.	By Independent Committee.				Wives and Dependent Relatives.	Children.	Widows.	Men.	
KENT—*cont.*	£ s. d.	£ s. d.	£ s. d.	£ s. d.		£ s. d.	£ s. d.					
Hythe	...	496 0 0	§		To M.H. No. 1 Patriotic Fund	210 0 0						
					,, ,, No. 2 Red Cross Society.	70 0 0						
					,, ,, No. 3 Lloyd's Patriotic.	106 0 0						
					,, ,, No. 4 S. & S.F.A.	110 0 0						
						496 0 0	—	—	—	—	—	
Lydd		43 2 3	§		To M.H. (not earmarked) ...	43 2 3	—	—	—	—	—	
Maidstone		2,353 11 2	§		To M.H. No. 1 Patriotic Fund	1,372 5 3						
					,, ,, No. 2 Red Cross Society.	203 17 10						
					,, ,, No. 3 Lloyd's Patriotic.	100 15 11						
					,, ,, No. 4 S. & S.F.A.	165 18 9						
					,, S. & S.F.A. (local) ...	102 11 4						
					,, M.H. Refugees' Fund ...	325 3 5						
					,, Expenses ...	82 18 8						
						2,353 11 2	—	—	—	—	—	
Margate	...	1,083 11 11	§	1,024 16 7	To Mafeking Fund ...	50 0 0		37	58	1	2	
					,, Expenses ...	8 15 4						
						58 15 4	—	—	—	—	—	
New Romney	...	112 0 1	§		To M.H. No. 2 Red Cross Society.	37 6 9						
					,, ,, No. 3 Lloyd's Patriotic.	37 6 8						
					,, ,, No. 4 S. & S.F.A.	37 6 8						
						112 0 1	—	—	—	—	—	
Queenborough	...	56 17 9	§		To M.H. (not earmarked) ...	53 10 3						
					,, *Daily Mail* Fund ...	3 7 6						
						56 17 9	—	—	—	—	—	
Ramsgate		777 14 10	§	66 12 6	To M.H. No. 1 Patriotic Fund	600 0 0		...	...	...	...	No particulars of cases supplied.
					,, Y. Hospital ...	56 5 6						
					,, L.L. Y. Equipment Fund	25 14 6						
					,, Expenses ...	19 2 9						
						701 2 9	9 19 7	—	—	—	—	
Rochester		2,179 1 4	§		To S. & S.F.A. (Central) ...	2,179 1 4	—	—	—	—	—	
Sandwich		219 0 0	§		To M.H. (not earmarked) ...	100 0 0						
					,, S. & S.F.A. (local) ...	19 0 0						
					,, *Daily Telegraph* ...	100 0 0						
						219 0 0	—	—	—	—	—	
Tenterden		92 6 8	§		To M.H. No. 1 Patriotic Fund	92 6 8	—	—	—	—	—	
Tunbridge Wells		3,669 12 3	§	...	To M.H. No. 1 Patriotic Fund	1,636 18 4						
					,, ,, No. 2 Red Cross Society.	208 6 10						
					,, ,, No. 3 Lloyd's Patriotic.	203 2 1						
					,, ,, No. 4 S. & S.F.A.	460 6 6						
					,, S. & S.F.A. (Central) ...	60 6 0						
					,, S. & S.F.A. (local) ...	142 7 0						
					,, Y. Hospital ...	50 0 0						
					,, L.L. Y. & V. Equipment	220 0 0						
					,, M.H. Refugees' Fund ...	581 6 9						
					,, Mafeking Fund ...	2 10 6						
					,, Expenses ...	54 8 3						
						3,669 12 3	—	—	—	—	—	

TRANSVAAL WAR FUNDS, 1899 TO 1901. COUNTIES—COUNTY BOROUGHS AND BOROUGHS. ENGLAND—cont.

Lord Mayors are distinguished by having L.M. after the name of the Borough; County Boroughs by having a * prefixed; and Towns, &c., which are not "County" Boroughs or Boroughs, by being printed in *italics*.—M.H. signifies The Mansion House Fund.—L.L. Fund, The Lord Lieutenant's Fund.—S. & S.F.A., The Soldiers' and Sailors' Families Association.—S. & S.H.S., The Soldiers' and Sailors' Help Society.—The Lansdowne Fund, Officers' Wives and Families.—The Abercorn Fund, Officers' Surgical and Medical Aid.—The Dudley Fund, Sick and Wounded Officers.—Y. and V. Equipment, Yeomanry and Volunteer Equipment.—Y. Hospital, Yeomanry Hospital; and a § in S. & S.F.A. column of Relief, that particulars of Relief in that Town or Borough are included in the Relief by the S. & S.F.A. at the head of the County.

Origin of Fund.	S. & S.F.A. Subscriptions Raised in County (a) including County Balances previous to the War. Grants from the Council (b).	Total Amount Received.	Expenditure in Relief, &c.		Remitted to other Funds.		Balance.	Number of Cases Relieved.				Remarks.
			By S. & S.F.A.	By Independent Committee.				Wives and Dependent Relatives.	Children.	Widows.	Men.	
KENT—*cont.*	£ s. d.	£ s. d.	£ s. d.	£ s. d.		£ s. d.	£ s. d.					
Gillingham		554 7 2	§	5 5 0	To M.H. (not earmarked) ...	394 16 5		1	—	—	—	
					„ S. and S.F.A. (local)	146 0 0						
					„ Expenses ...	8 5 9						
						549 2 2		—	—	—	—	
Northfleet		346 0 0	§	82 0 0	To M.H. No. 1 Patriotic Fund	55 11 5		21	20	—	—	
					„ „ No. 4 S. & S.F.A.	27 11 4						
					„ Mafeking Fund ...	5 0 0						
					„ Expenses ...	13 17 3						
						102 0 0	161 0 0	—	—	—	—	
Walmer		131 3 2	§		To M.H. (not earmarked) ...	131 3 2		—	—	—	—	
LANCASHIRE.	(a)18,581 19 7	41,965 17 1	38,497 5 0		...		3,463 12 1	4,000	3,093			
	(b)23,383 17 6											
LORD LIEUTENANT'S FUND (THE EARL OF DERBY.)					...			...	...	...		No L.L. Fund.
Accrington		3,918 0 0	§	2,967 0 0	To Men's Extra Comforts...	45 0 0		...	...	...	...	Number of cases not supplied.
					„ Expenses ...	100 0 0						
						145 0 0	806 0 0					
Ashton-under-Lyne		3,327 0 0	§	3,319 0 0	To Expenses ...	8 0 0		185	257			
Bacup		1,016 10 6	§		To S. & S.F.A. (local)	850 0 0						
					„ V. Insurance	120 18 8						
					„ Expenses ...	42 4 1						
						1,013 2 9	3 7 9	—	—	—	—	
*Barrow-in-Furness		3,842 0 0	§	2,764 0 0	To M.H. No. 1 Patriotic Fund	400 0 0		128	135	1	3	
					„ „ No. 3 Lloyd's Patriotic.	100 0 0						
					„ „ No. 4 S. & S.F.A.	300 0 0						
						800 0 0	273 0 0					
*Blackburn		9,278 0 0	§	8,476 0 0	To Expenses ...	306 0 0	496 0 0	485	1,255	1	1	
Blackpool		2,127 4 9	§	1,084 0 0	To M.H. No. 2 Red Cross Society.	200 0 0		64		4		
					„ „ No. 4 S. & S.F.A.	275 0 0						
					„ Expenses ...	11 0 0						
						486 0 0	(c)557 4 9	...	...	...	...	(c) £400 set aside for Widows.
*Bolton		11,245 3 3	§	11,245 3 3	...		...	563	619	40	567	
*Bootle		2,750 0 0	§	1,719 0 0	...		1,031 0 0	109	91	...	1	
*Burnley		4,156 0 0	§	3,395 0 0	To Men's Extra Comforts...	761 0 0		318	585	—	—	
Burnley Express		489 0 0			To Mayor of Burnley	489 0 0		—	—	—	—	
*Bury		4,853 0 0	§	4,041 0 0	To Expenses ...	106 0 0	706 0 0	283	451	77	27	
Chorley		1,142 17 8	§	6 10 0	To M.H. No. 4 S. & S.F.A.	1,011 7 10						
					„ Insurance, &c., of Volunteers.	124 19 10						
						1,136 7 8		—	—	—	—	
Clitheroe		228 16 3	§	47 5 0	To M.H. No. 1 Patriotic Fund	50 0 0		2	4			
					„ „ No. 2 Red Cross Society.	5 0 0						
					„ „ (not earmarked) ...	109 10 3						
					„ S. & S.F.A. (local)	11 11 0						
					To *Daily Mail*	5 10 0						
						181 11 3		—	—	—	—	

TRANSVAAL WAR FUNDS, 1899 TO 1901. COUNTIES—COUNTY BOROUGHS AND BOROUGHS. **ENGLAND**—*cont.*

Lord Mayors are distinguished by having L.M. after the name of the Borough; County Boroughs by having a * prefixed; and Towns, &c., which are not "County" Boroughs or Boroughs, by being printed in *italics*.—M.H. signifies The Mansion House Fund.—L.L. Fund, The Lord Lieutenant's Fund.—S. & S.F.A., The Soldiers' and Sailors' Families Association.—S. & S.H.S., The Soldiers' and Sailors' Help Society.—The Lansdowne Fund, Officers' Wives and Families.—The Abercorn Fund, Officers' Surgical and Medical Aid.—The Dudley Fund, Sick and Wounded Officers.—Y. and V. Equipment, Yeomanry and Volunteer Equipment.—Y. Hospital, Yeomanry Hospital; and a § in S. & S.F.A. column of Relief, that particulars of Relief in that Town or Borough are included in the Relief by the S. & S.F.A. at the head of the County.

Origin of Fund.	S. & S.F.A. Subscriptions Raised in County (a) including County Balances previous to the War. Grants from the Council (b).	Total Amount Received.	Expenditure in Relief, &c. By S. & S.F.A.	Expenditure in Relief, &c. By Independent Committee.	Remitted to other Funds.		Balance.	Number of Cases Relieved. Wives and Dependent Relatives.	Children.	Widows.	Men.	Remarks.
LANCASHIRE—*cont.*		£ s. d.	£ s. d.	£ s. d.		£ s. d.	£ s. d.					
Colne		802 14 4	§	769 16 1	To Expenses ...	2 18 3	30 0 0	38	43	5	3	
Darwen ...		2,134 0 0	§	1,823 0 0	To M.H. No. 1 Patriotic Fund	25 0 0		78	64	1	—	
					" " No. 2 Red Cross Society.	25 0 0						
					" " No. 3 Lloyd's Patriotic.	25 0 0						
					" " o. 4 S. & S.F.A...	25 0 0						
						100 0 0	211 0 0					
Eccles			§			...	...	...	...	...	...	Included in Manchester.
Haslingden		976 10 0	§	935 0 0	To S. & S.F.A. (local)	9 0 0		41	3	...	5	
					" Expenses ...	32 10 0						
						41 10 0	—					
Heywood		1,504 0 0	§	1,009 0 0		...	495 0 0	63	110	—	—	
Kirkham ...		230 0 0	§	138 10 0	To S. & S.F.A. (local)	10 0 0		20				
					" Expenses ...	1 10 0						
						11 10 0	80 0 0					
Lancaster								...	...	...	...	Information refused.
Leigh		2,533 17 7	§	1,543 10 11	To V. Equipment ...	80 0 0	910 6 8	90	9	3	3	
*Liverpool, L.M. ...		52,695 0 0	§	622 0 0	To The Patriotic Fund	500 0 0		...	...	...	...	Information refused. Particulars given were those supplied to Mansion House Council.
(Queen Alexandra's Appeal)		1,293 10 3			" S. & S.F.A. (Central) ...	4,132 8 11						
		53,988 10 3			" " (Queen Alexandra Appeal).	1,293 10 3						
					" The Lansdowne Fund ...	20 0 0						
					" Red Cross Society	50 0 0						
					" Lloyd's Patriotic ...	5,152 0 0						
					" Imperial War Fund	500 0 0						
					" Expenses ...	394 0 0						
						12,041 19 2	41,324 11 1	—	—	—	—	
—		1,750 0 0			To Refugees' Fund (Sir A. Milner).	1,750 0 0	—					
Liverpool Daily Post ...		10,000 0 0			To L.M. Liverpool ...	10,000 0 0	—					
The Courier Express ...		36,680 0 0		36,200 0 0	No Expenses ...		480 0 0	...	...	...	...	No particulars of cases given.
*Manchester, L.M.		76,552 6 1	§	71,927 6 11			4,624 19 2	3,553	...	12	10	
Middleton			§		...			...	...	...	...	Included in Manchester.
Mossley ...		359 0 0	§	311 0 0	To Life Insurance & Expenses	15 0 0	33 0 0	16	30	—	—	
Nelson ...		1,548 0 6	§	1,520 4 8	To Expenses ...	27 15 10	...	66	97	1	5	
*Oldham ...		11,945 8 1	§	6,538 2 2	To Red Cross Society	400 0 0		500	984	—	—	
					" Insurance... ...	937 1 0						
					" Purchase of Annuity ...	143 9 2						
					" Expenses ...	392 18 3						
						1,873 8 5	3,533 17 6	—	—			
*Preston ...		5,061 1 7	§	...	To M.H. No. 1 Patriotic Fund.	925 0 0						
					" " No. 4 S. & S.F.A...	4,003 7 5						
					" " Refugees' Fund ...	55 0 0						
					" Expenses	77 14 2						
						5,061 1 7	—					

TRANSVAAL WAR FUNDS, 1899 TO 1901. COUNTIES—COUNTY BOROUGHS AND BOROUGHS. ENGLAND—cont.

Lord Mayors are distinguished by having L.M. after the name of the Borough; County Boroughs by having a * prefixed; and Towns, &c., which are not "County" Boroughs or Boroughs, by being printed in italics.—M.H. signifies The Mansion House Fund.—L.L. Fund, The Lord Lieutenant's Fund.—S. & S.F.A., The Soldiers' and Sailors' Families Association.—S. & S.H.S., The Soldiers' and Sailors' Help Society.—The Lansdowne Fund, Officers' Wives and Families.—The Abercorn Fund, Officers' Surgical and Medical Aid.—The Dudley Fund, Sick and Wounded Officers.—Y. and V. Equipment, Yeomanry and Volunteer Equipment.—Y. Hospital, Yeomanry Hospital; and a § in S. & S.F.A. column of Relief, that particulars of Relief in that Town or Borough are included in the Relief by the S. & S.F.A. at the head of the County.

Origin of Fund.	S. & S.F.A. Subscriptions Raised in County (a) including County Balances previous to the War. Grants from the Council (b).	Total Amount Received.	Expenditure in Relief, &c.		Remitted to other Funds.		Balance.	Number of Cases Relieved.				Remarks.
			By S. & S.F.A.	By Independent Committee.				Wives and Dependent Relatives.	Children.	Widows.	Men.	
LANCASHIRE.—cont.	£ s. d.	£ s. d.	£ s. d.	£ s. d.		£ s. d.	£ s. d.					
Rawtenstall ...		1,162 5 6	§	12 2 0	To S. & S.F.A. (local)	1,000 0 0			4	1		
					„ Expenses ...	29 11 1						
						1,029 11 1	120 12 5	—	—	—	—	
*Rochdale ...		5,514 0 0	§	4,721 0 0	To Insurance and Expenses	503 0 0	290 0 0	214	316	6	7	
Rochdale Observer ...		200 0 0		...	To Mayor of Rochdale ...	200 0 0	—					
*St. Helens ...		7,869 0 0	§		To S. & S.F.A. (central) ...	2,000 0 0						
					„ S. & S.F.A. (local)	3,800 0 0						
					„ Expenses ...	13 0 0						
						5,813 0 0	2,056 0 0					
*Salford ...		...	§		...		...	...	...		...	Included in Manchester.
Southport ...		2,425 0 0	§	250 0 0	To M.H. No.1 Patriotic Fund	75 0 0		...	...		...	Number of cases not supplied.
					„ No.2 Red Cross Society.	75 0 0						
					„ No. 3 Lloyd's Patriotic.	75 0 0						
					„ No. 4 S. & S.F.A.	75 0 0						
						300 0 0	1,875 0 0	—	—	—	—	
*Warrington ...		7,362 0 0	§	4,704 0 0	To M.H. (not earmarked) ...	50 0 0		250	164	9	6	
					„ Y. Hospital	150 0 0						
					„ V. Equipment ...	390 0 0						
					„ Men's extra comforts ...	243 0 0						
					„ L.M. Manchester	75 0 0						
					„ Expenses ...	279 0 0						
						1,187 0 0	1,471 0 0					
Widnes ...		3,696 16 11	§		To S. & S.F.A. (local)	3,696 16 11	—					
*Wigan ...		10,391 11 2		4,606 1 9	To Red Cross Society	300 0 0		335	420			
					„ S. & S.F.A. (local)	250 0 0						
					„ Y. Hospital	50 0 0						
					„ V. Life Insurance	136 15 9						
					„ V. Equipment ...	32 18 0						
					„ Expenses ...	82 14 9						
						852 8 6	4,933 0 11	—	—	—	—	
LEICESTERSHIRE.	(a) 4,738 18 10	8,588 18 10	7,401 13 9		...		1,187 5 1	709	1,197	—	—	
	(b) 3,850 0 0											
LORD LIEUTENANT'S FUND* ... (MARQUESS OF GRANBY.) Title: THE LEICESTER AND LEICESTERSHIRE PATRIOTIC FUND.	...	12,884 0 0		1,103 0 0	To M.H. No. 1. Patriotic Fund	594 0 0		181	300	24	44	* Conjointly with the Mayor of Leicester.
					„ No. 2 Red Cross Society.	136 0 0						
					„ No. 3 Lloyd's Patriotic.	122 0 0						
					„ M.H. Church Collections	450 0 0						
					„ S. & S.F.A. (local) ...	1,942 0 0						
					„ Loughborough Committee.	1,400 0 0						
					„ Leicester Reservist Fund	252 0 0						
					„ Melton Committee ...	210 0 0						
					„ St. John's Ambulance (local).	25 0 0						
					„ Y. & V. Equipment ...	3,622 0 0						
					„ Expenses...	177 0 0						
						8,930 0 0	2,851 0 0	—	—	—	—	
Leicester ...		(c) 4,095 2 10	§	4,095 2 10			...	415	...	...	...	(c) Includes £252 from Leicestershire Patriotic Fund.

TRANSVAAL WAR FUNDS, 1899 TO 1901.   COUNTIES—COUNTY BOROUGHS AND BOROUGHS.   **ENGLAND**—*cont.*

Lord Mayors are distinguished by having L.M. after the name of the Borough; County Boroughs by having a * prefixed; and Towns, &c., which are not "County" Boroughs or Boroughs, by being printed in *italics*.—M.H. signifies The Mansion House Fund.—L.L. Fund, The Lord Lieutenant's Fund.—S. & S.F.A., The Soldiers' and Sailors' Families Association.—S. & S.H.S., The Soldiers' and Sailors' Help Society.—The Lansdowne Fund, Officers' Wives and Families.—The Abercorn Fund, Officers' Surgical and Medical Aid.—The Dudley Fund, Sick and Wounded Officers.—Y. and V. Equipment, Yeomanry and Volunteer Equipment.—Y. Hospital, Yeomanry Hospital; and a § in S. & S.F.A. column of Relief, that particulars of Relief in that Town or Borough are included in the Relief by the S. & S.F.A. at the head of the County.

Origin of Fund.	S. & S.F.A. Subscriptions Raised in County (a) including County Balances previous to the War. Grants from the Council (b).	Total Amount Received.	Expenditure in Relief, &c.		Remitted to other Funds.		Balance.	Number of Cases Relieved.				Remarks.
			By S. & S.F.A.	By Independent Committee.				Wives and Dependent Relatives.	Children.	Widows.	Men.	
LEICESTERSHIRE—*cont.*	£ s. d.	£ s. d.	£ s. d.	£ s. d.		£ s. d.	£ s. d.					
Loughborough ...		(d)1,791 0 0	§	1,549 0 0	To Patriotic Fund ... 127 0 0			97	135	2	4	(d) Includes £1,400 from Leicestershire Patriotic Fund.
					„ S. & S.F.A. (local) 100 0 0							
					„ Expenses ... 15 0 0							
					242 0 0		—	—	—	—	
Malton ...		(e) 360 0 0	§	325 0 0	To Expenses ... 5 0 0		30 0 0	8	...	1	...	(e) Includes £210 from Leicestershire Patriotic Fund.
LINCOLNSHIRE.	(a) 7,039 0 9	7,109 0 9	5,538 5 0		...		1,570 15 9	509	595	—	—	
	(b) 70 0 0											
LORD LIEUTENANT'S FUND ... (EARL BROWNLOW.)		446 6 0			To V. Equipment ... 446 6 0							
Boston ...		977 4 7	§		To M.H. (not earmarked) ... 815 7 0							
					„ „ No. 1 Patriotic Fund 5 0 0							
					„ „ No. 2 Red Cross Society. 5 0 0							
					„ „ No. 3 Lloyd's Patriotic. 5 0 0							
					„ „ No. 4 S. & S.F.A. 5 0 0							
					„ S. & S.F.A. (Central) 105 2 4							
					„ M.H. Refugees' Fund 36 15 3							
					977 4 7							
Grantham ...		1,158 0 0	§	...	To M.H. No. 1 Patriotic Fund 840 0 0							
					„ „ No. 2 Red Cross Society. 51 0 0							
					„ „ No. 3 Lloyd's Patriotic. 169 0 0							
					„ „ No. 4 S. & S.F.A. 98 0 0							
					1,158 0 0							
*Grimsby ...		3,098 2 3	§	3,087 3 6	To Expenses ... 10 18 9			128	110	2	1	
*Lincoln ...		1,715 9 7	§		To M.H. No. 1 Patriotic Fund 1,397 16 10							
					„ „ Refugees' Fund 317 12 9							
					1,715 9 7			—	—	—	—	
Working Men's Fund ...		470 4 8		460 0 6	To Expenses ... 10 4 2			...	...	...	...	Number of cases not supplied.
Louth ...		248 16 5	§		To M.H. (not earmarked) ... 248 16 5							
Stamford ...		548 15 11	§		To M.H. No. 1 Patriotic Fund 223 7 5							
					„ „ No. 2 Red Cross Society. 104 14 2							
					„ „ No. 3 Lloyd's Patriotic. 104 14 2							
					„ „ No. 4 S. & S.F.A. 116 0 2							
					548 15 11			—	—	—	—	
LONDON.												
North ...	(a) 3,523 11 8	61,188 1 8	56,570 18 2		...		4,617 3 6	6,146	5,776	—	—	
	(b) 57,664 10 0											
South ...	(a) 3,783 3 7	37,428 3 7	35,604 4 2		...		1,823 19 5	3,640	3,701	—	—	
	(b) 33,645 0 0											
East ...	(a) 6,717 0 1	33,417 0 1	30,543 3 3				2,873 16 10	3,184	3,616	—	—	
	(b) 26,700 0 0											
West ...	(a) 5,038 4 4	34,633 4 4	31,776 11 4				2,856 13 0	3,513	3,666	—	—	
	(b) 29,595 0 0											
LORD LIEUTENANT'S FUND ... (DUKE OF FIFE.)					...			...	...	...	...	No L.L. Fund.
City L.M. ...			§					...	...	...	...	See M.H. Fund, page 1, also C.I.V. Fund, page 132.
Battersea ...		1,250 0 0	§		To *Daily Telegraph* ... 1,250 0 0			...	...	...	...	Carnival.

Lord Mayors are distinguished by having L.M. after the name of the Borough; County Boroughs by having a * prefixed; and Towns, &c., which are not "County" Boroughs or Boroughs, by being printed in *italics*.—M.H. signifies The Mansion House Fund.—L.L. Fund, The Lord Lieutenant's Fund.—S. & S.F.A., The Soldiers' and Sailors' Families Association.—S. & S.H.S., The Soldiers' and Sailors' Help Society.—The Lansdowne Fund, Officers' Wives and Families.—The Abercorn Fund, Officers' Surgical and Medical Aid.—The Dudley Fund, Sick and Wounded Officers.—Y. and V. Equipment, Yeomanry and Volunteer Equipment.—Y. Hospital, Yeomanry Hospital; and a § in S. & S.F.A. column of Relief, that particulars of Relief in that Town or Borough are included in the Relief by the S. & S.F.A. at the head of the County.

Origin of Fund.	S. & S.F.A. Subscriptions Raised in County (a) including County Balances previous to the War, Grants from the Council (b).	Total Amount Received.	Expenditure in Relief, &c.		Remitted to other Funds.		Balance.	Number of Cases Relieved.				Remarks.
			By S. & S.F.A.	By Independent Committee.				Wives and Dependent Relatives.	Children.	Widows.	Men.	
LONDON—*cont.*	£ s. d.	£ s. d.	£ s. d.	£ s. d.		£ s. d.	£ s. d.					
Bermondsey	...	1,970 0 0	§		To S. & S.F.A. (local)	1,300 0 0						
					„ *Daily Telegraph*	650 0 0		...	...	...	...	Carnival.
						1,950 0 0	—					
Bethnal Green	...		§		...	...						
Camberwell	...	2,248 0 0	§		To *Daily Telegraph*	2,248 0 0		...	...	...	...	Carnival.
Chelsea	...	500 0 0	§		To *Daily Telegraph*	500 0 0		...	...	...	...	Carnival.
Deptford	...	1,022 13 6	§		To *Daily Telegraph*	1,022 13 6		...	...	...	...	Carnival.
Finsbury	...		§				—					
Fulham	...	633 16 2	§		To M.H. (not earmarked)	50 0 0						
					„ *Daily Telegraph*	583 16 2		...	...	...	...	Carnival.
						633 16 2	—					
Greenwich	...	1,022 0 0	§		To *Daily Telegraph*	1,022 0 0		...	...	...	...	Carnival.
Hackney	...	1,108 3 2	§	1,081 1 6	To Expenses	17 2 6		250	300			
					„ S. & S.F.A. (local)	9 19 2						
						27 1 8						
Hammersmith	...	1,783 19 4	§		To *Daily Telegraph*	1,783 19 4		...	...	...	...	Carnival.
—		912 7 0	§		To *Daily Telegraph*	903 7 0	...	...	...	...	...	Carnival.
					„ *Daily Mail*	9 0 0						
						912 7 0	—					
Hampstead	...	2,938 6 6	§		To *Daily Telegraph*	2,938 6 6		...	...	...	...	Carnival.
Holborn	...		§		...							
Islington	...	4,287 6 8	§		To S. & S.F.A. (local)	47 6 9						
					„ *Daily Telegraph*	4,239 19 11		...	...	...	...	Carnival.
						4,287 6 8	—					
Kensington (Royal)	...	1,000 0 0	§		To *Daily Telegraph*	1,000 0 0		...	...	...	...	Carnival.
Lambeth	...		§				—					
Lewisham	...	1,554 16 2	§		To *Daily Telegraph*	1,554 16 2		...	...	...	...	Carnival.
St. Marylebone	...	2,542 11 1	§		To *Daily Telegraph*	2,389 15 0		...	...	...	...	Carnival.
					„ M.H. No. 1 Patriotic Fund	32 14 1						
					„ „ No. 2 Red Cross Society.	100 0 0		...	...	...	...	Gymnastic Display.
					„ *Daily Mail*	20 2 0						
						2,542 11 1	—					
Paddington	...		§		...	...						
St. Pancras	...	6,059 4 10	§		To *Daily Telegraph*	6,059 4 10		...	...	...	...	Carnival.
Poplar	...	1,052 10 0	§		To *Daily Telegraph*	1,052 10 0		...	...	...	...	Carnival.
Shoreditch	...		§				—					
Southwark	...		§				—					
Stepney	...		§				—					
Stoke Newington	...		§				—					

TRANSVAAL WAR FUNDS, 1899 TO 1901. COUNTIES—COUNTY BOROUGHS AND BOROUGHS. ENGLAND—cont.

Lord Mayors are distinguished by having L.M. after the name of the Borough; County Boroughs by having a * prefixed; and Towns, &c., which are not "County" Boroughs or Boroughs, by being printed in *italics*.—M.H. signifies The Mansion House Fund.—L.L. Fund, The Lord Lieutenant's Fund.—S. & S.F.A., The Soldiers' and Sailors' Families Association.—S. & S.H.S., The Soldiers' and Sailors' Help Society.—The Lansdowne Fund, Officers' Wives and Families.—The Abercorn Fund, Officers' Surgical and Medical Aid.—The Dudley Fund, Sick and Wounded Officers.—Y. and V. Equipment, Yeomanry and Volunteer Equipment.—Y. Hospital, Yeomanry Hospital; and a § in S. & S.F.A. column of Relief, that particulars of Relief in that Town or Borough are included in the Relief by the S. & S.F.A. at the head of the County.

Origin of Fund.	S. & S.F.A. Subscriptions Raised in County (a) including County Balances previous to the War. Grants from the Council (b).	Total Amount Received.	Expenditure in Relief, &c. By S. & S.F.A.	Expenditure in Relief, &c. By Independent Committee.	Remitted to other Funds.		Balance.	Wives and Dependent Relatives.	Children.	Widows.	Men.	Remarks.
	£ s. d.	£ s. d.	£ s. d.	£ s. d.		£ s. d.	£ s. d.					
LONDON—*cont.*												
Wandsworth		100 0 0	§		To *Daily Telegraph*...	100 0 0	—	...	...	...	...	Carnival.
Westminster, City of...		1,300 0 0			To M.H. (not earmarked)...	1,300 0 0	—	—	—	—	—	
		400 0 0			" *Daily Telegraph*...	400 0 0	—	—	—	—	—	Carnival.
Woolwich		1,366 0 0	§		To S. & S.F.A. (local)	1,366 0 0	—	—	—	—	—	
Royal Arsenal Reservists		6,949 10 5	...	6,865 13 2	To R. Carriage Dept. Fund	20 0 0	...	414	587	...	...	
					" Expenses	51 1 11						
						71 1 11	12 15 4					
Royal Laboratory		303 1 10		299 18 0	...	...	3 3 10	15	16	...	...	
Royal Carriage Factory		2,168 0 0		2,100 0 0	...	...	68 0 0	78	102	3	—	
Plumstead		1,580 0 0	§		To S. & S.F.A. (local)	1,580 0 0	—	—	—	—	—	
City Police		1,087 17 7	...	(c) 888 5 11	To M.H. (not earmarked)...	199 11 8	...	26	17	...	...	(c) Allowance from Corporation, City of London.
South Metropolitan Gas Co.		6,000 7 8		5,289 17 11	...	...	710 9 9	113	192	6	—	
North Metropolitan Tramways.		4,629 18 9		4,541 4 7	...	...	88 14 2	135	149	7	—	
London Road Car Co.		1,602 0 0		1,392 0 0	To M.H. No. 1 Patriotic Fund	105 0 0	...	...	...	...	...	Number of cases not supplied.
					" Refugees' Fund	105 0 0						
						210 0 0						
London General Omnibus Co.		3,456 1 2		3,206 1 2	To M.H. (not earmarked)...	250 0 0	...	101	108	—	—	
Tillings Limited		305 10 0		305 10 0	...	...	...	15	...	...	...	
Projectile Company		822 0 9		771 2 6	...	...	50 18 3	20	10	2	1	
Scruttons Limited Employees		618 15 6		583 15 9	To M.H. No. 4 S. & S.F.A...	5 9 0	29 10 9	14	18	—	—	
MIDDLESEX.	(a) 7,491 1 9 (b) 21,400 0 0	28,891 1 9	27,784 1 7		...	...	1,107 0 2	2,287	3,089	—	—	
LORD LIEUTENANT'S FUND... (DUKE OF BEDFORD.)		2,254 0 0	...		To Y. Equipment and Soldiers' extra comforts.	1,160 0 0	—	—	—	—	—	
					" Expenses	10 12 7						
						1,170 12 7						
					Returned to subscribers	1,083 7 5						
						2,254 0 0						
Ealing		1,067 0 0		817 0 0	To Expenses	28 0 0	222 0 0	75	91	...	1]	
Southgate		732 9 1	§		To M.H. (not earmarked)...	682 12 1						
					" Men's extra comforts	25 0 0						
					" Expenses	24 17 0						
						732 9 1						
MONMOUTHSHIRE.	(a) 8,810 6 11 (b) 2,295 0 0	11,105 6 11	10,510 4 7		...	...	595 2 4	950	1,255	—	—	
LORD LIEUTENANT'S FUND... (LORD TREDEGAR.)	...	3,273 5 11	...	25 7 6	To M.H. No. 1 Patriotic Fund	109 18 9		1	—	—	—	
					" Red Cross Society	20 19 0						
					" Lloyd's Patriotic	55 2 0						
					" S. & S.F.A. (local)	1,350 0 0						
					" Expenses	291 17 3						
						1,827 17 0	1,420 1 5	—	—	—	—	
Abergavenny		508 10 11	§	...	To S. & S.F.A. (local)	316 0 0						
					" Expenses	3 8 6						
						319 8 6	189 2 5	—	—	—	—	

TRANSVAAL WAR FUNDS, 1899 TO 1901. COUNTIES—COUNTY BOROUGHS AND BOROUGHS. ENGLAND—cont.

Lord Mayors are distinguished by having L.M. after the name of the Borough; County Boroughs by having a * prefixed; and Towns, &c., which are not "County" Boroughs or Boroughs, by being printed in *italics*.—M.H. signifies The Mansion House Fund.—L.L. Fund, The Lord Lieutenant's Fund.—S & S.F.A., The Soldiers' and Sailors' Families Association.—S. & S.H.S., The Soldiers' and Sailors' Help Society.—The Lansdowne Fund, Officers' Wives and Families.—The Abercorn Fund, Officers' Surgical and Medical Aid.—The Dudley Fund, Sick and Wounded Officers.—Y. and V. Equipment, Yeomanry and Volunteer Equipment.—Y. Hospital, Yeomanry Hospital; and a § in S. & S.F.A. column of Relief, that particulars of Relief in that Town or Borough are included in the Relief by the S. & S.F.A. at the head of the County.

Origin of Fund.	S. & S.F.A. Subscriptions Raised in County (a) including County Balances previous to the War. Grants from the Council (b).	Total Amount Received.	Expenditure in Relief, &c. By S. & S.F.A.	By Independent Committee.	Remitted to other Funds.		Balance.	Wives and Dependent Relatives.	Children.	Widows.	Men.	Remarks.
MONMOUTHSHIRE—*cont.*	£ s. d.	£ s. d.	£ s. d.	£ s. d.		£ s. d.	£ s. d.					
Monmouth	...	...	§		... ...	... ...	...	...	...	...	...	No Mayor's Fund.
Monmouthshire Beacon	...	154 15 0			To *Daily Telegraph* ...	154 15 0	—	—	—	—	—	
Nantyglo and Blaina	...	694 0 8	§	538 3 8	To L.L. Fund ...	90 0 0		32	50			
					„ S. & S.F.A. (local)	64 7 9						
					„ Expenses ...	1 9 3						
						155 17 0						
*Newport	...	2,694 0 0	§	2,694 0 0	...	...		349	1,047			
South Wales Argus	...	1,228 14 10			To Mayor of Newport ...	1,104 4 4						
					„ L.L. Fund ...	103 18 6						
					„ M.H. (not earmarked) ...	5 5 0						
						1,213 7 10	15 7 0					
NORFOLK.	(a) 8,207 11 2	13,457 11 2	12,869 11 3			...	587 19 11	1,628	1,853	—	—	
	(b) 5,250 0 0											
LORD LIEUTENANT'S FUND (EARL OF LEICESTER.)		4,087 10 0			To M.H. No. 1 Patriotic Fund	1,919 0 0						
					„ S. & S.F.A. (local) ...	2,062 0 0						
					„ Expenses ...	94 19 0						
						4,075 19 0	11 11 0	—	—	—	—	
King's Lynn	...	1,328 5 2	§		To M.H (not earmarked) ...	979 0 5						
					„ S. & S.F.A. (local)	313 0 0						
					„ Expenses ...	36 4 9						
						1,328 5 2	—	—	—	—	—	
*Norwich	...	4,631 14 7	§		To M.H. (not earmarked) ...	52 11 6						
					„ „ No. 1 Patriotic Fund	2,060 18 7						
					„ „ No. 2 Red Cross Society.	596 0 0						
					„ „ No. 3 Lloyd's Patriotic.	618 0 0						
					„ „ No. 4 S. & S.F.A. ...	1,173 0 0						
					„ S. & S.F.A (local) ...	131 4 6						
						4,631 14 7	—	—	—	—	—	
Thetford	...	331 0 0	§		To M.H. No. 1 Patriotic Fund	168 0 0						
					„ „ No. 2 Red Cross Society.	16 0 0						
					„ „ No. 4 Lloyd's Patriotic.	31 0 0						
					„ S. & S.F.A. (local)	98 0 0						
					„ *Daily Mail* (London) ...	8 0 0						
					„ Y. Hospital ...	9 0 0						
					„ M.H. Refugees' Fund ...	1 0 0						
						331 0 0						
*Yarmouth (Great)	...	1,459 0 0	§		To M.H. No. 1 Patriotic Fund	486 6 8						
					„ „ No. 2 Red Cross Society.	486 6 8						
					„ „ No. 4 S. & S.F.A. ...	486 6 8						
						1,459 0 0	—	—	—	—	—	
Yarmouth Mercury	...	564 0 0	...		To Mayor of Yarmouth ...	564 0 0	—	—	—	—	—	
NORTHAMPTONSHIRE.	(a) 6,515 6 1	8,535 6 1	8,267 11 9		...	...	267 14 4	755	1,181			
	(b) 2,020 0 0											
LORD LIEUTENANT'S FUND (EARL SPENCER.)		7,146 6 6		...	To M.H. No. 1 Patriotic Fund	784 0 0						
					„ „ No. 2 Red Cross Society.	94 0 0						
					„ S. & S.F.A. (local) ...	4,816 0 0						
					„ St. John Ambulance (local).	68 0 0		...	...	...	...	Equipment.
					Carried forward ...	5,762 0 0						

TRANSVAAL WAR FUNDS, 1899 TO 1901. COUNTIES—COUNTY BOROUGHS AND BOROUGHS. ENGLAND—cont.

Lord Mayors are distinguished by having L.M. after the name of the Borough; County Boroughs by having a * prefixed; and Towns, &c., which are not "County" Boroughs or Boroughs, by being printed in *italics*.—M.H. signifies The Mansion House Fund.—L.L. Fund, The Lord Lieutenant's Fund.—S. & S.F.A., The Soldiers' and Sailors' Families Association.—S. & S.H.S., The Soldiers' and Sailors' Help Society.—The Lansdowne Fund, Officers' Wives and Families.—The Abercorn Fund, Officers' Surgical and Medical Aid.—The Dudley Fund, Sick and Wounded Officers.—Y. and V. Equipment, Yeomanry and Volunteer Equipment.—Y. Hospital, Yeomanry Hospital; and a § in S. & S.F.A. column of Relief, that particulars of Relief in that Town or Borough are included in the Relief by the S. & S.F.A. at the head of the County.

Origin of Fund.	S. & S.F.A. Subscriptions Raised in County (a) including County Balances previous to the War, Grants from the Council (b).	Total Amount Received.	Expenditure in Relief, &c.		Remitted to other Funds.		Balance.	Number of Cases Relieved.				Remarks
			By S. & S.F.A.	By Independent Committee.				Wives and Dependent Relatives.	Children.	Widows.	Men.	
NORTHAMPTONSHIRE—*cont.*	£ s. d.	£ s. d.	£ s. d.	£ s. d.		£ s. d.	£ s. d.					
					Brought forward ...	5,762 0 0						
					To Yeomanry Hospital ...	400 0 0						
					„ S. & S.H.S. (local) ...	72 0 0						
					„ County Borough Fund	500 0 0						
					„ Expenses ...	209 6 6						
						6,943 6 6	203 0 0	—	—	—	—	
Duke of Grafton's Fund ...		978 17 0			To St. John Ambulance (local).	220 0 0		...	...	...	...	Equipment.
					„ Y. Equipment ...	71 0 0						
					„ V. Equipment ...	425 0 0						
					„ Men's extra comforts ...	50 0 0						
					„ Expenses ...	19 7 11						
						785 7 11	193 9 1					
Brackley ...		226 4 7	§		To L.L. Fund	226 4 7	—	—	—	—	—	
Daventry ...		56 16 6	§		To S. & S.F.A. (local) ...	56 16 6	—	—	—	—	—	
Daventry Reservists ...		122 0 0		122 0 0	...			28	52	3	1	
Higham Ferrers ...		108 0 0	§		To L.L. Fund ...	108 0 0	—	—	—	—	—	
*Northampton ...		3,871 16 2 } *500 0 0 }	§	4,371 16 2	...			432	732	...	...	* From L.L. Fund.
Peterborough ...		1,632 9 11	§		To M.H. No. 1 Patriotic Fund	435 8 4						
					„ „ No. 2 Red Cross Society.	100 0 0						
					„ „ No. 3 Lloyd's Patriotic.	100 0 0						
					„ „ No. 4 S. & S.F.A. (local).	840 0 0						
					„ S. & S.F.A. (central) ...	154 19 7						
					„ M.H. Refugees' Fund ...	2 2 0						
						1,632 9 11	—	—	—	—	—	
Kettering ...		797 0 0	§	737 10 0	To Expenses ...	59 10 0		52	120	16	—	
Wellingborough ...		1,353 12 2	§	1,109 15 1	To Men's extra comforts ...	150 0 0		38	60	—	—	
					„ Expenses ...	22 7 0						
						172 7 0	71 10 1					
NORTHUMBERLAND.	(a) 6,707 3 1 } (b) 690 0 0 }	7,397 3 1	4,561 1 2		...		2,836 1 11	356	371	—	—	
Lord Lieutenant's Fund ... (Earl Grey.)		42,977 16 1			To Northumberland and Tyneside Reservists' Fund.	1,345 7 1						
					„ S. & S.F.A. (local) ...	36 15 7						
					„ Y. Hospital ...	2,500 0 0						
					„ Convalescent Home, Southampton.	250 0 0						
					„ Y. & V. Equipment ...	33,558 0 0						
						37,690 2 8	5,287 13 5	—	—	—	—	
Berwick-on-Tweed ...		570 0 0	§		To The Patriotic Fund	100 0 0						
					„ S. & S.F.A. (local)	200 0 0						
					„ *Daily Telegraph*	50 0 0						
					„ Northumberland & Tyneside Fund.	220 0 0						
						570 0 0	—	—	—	—	—	
Morpeth ...		736 1 11	§	335 17 0	To V. Equipment ...	30 0 0		14	30			
					„ Men's extra comforts ...	139 2 10						
						169 2 10	231 2 1	—	—			

TRANSVAAL WAR FUNDS, 1899 TO 1901. COUNTIES—COUNTY BOROUGHS AND BOROUGHS. ENGLAND—cont.

Lord Mayors are distinguished by having L.M. after the name of the Borough; County Boroughs by having a * prefixed; and Towns, &c., which are not "County" Boroughs or Boroughs, by being printed in *italics*.—M.H. signifies The Mansion House Fund.—L.L. Fund, The Lord Lieutenant's Fund.—S. & S.F.A., The Soldiers' and Sailors' Families Association.—S. & S.H.S., The Soldiers' and Sailors' Help Society.—The Lansdowne Fund, Officers' Wives and Families.—The Abercorn Fund, Officers' Surgical and Medical Aid.—The Dudley Fund, Sick and Wounded Officers.—Y. and V. Equipment, Yeomanry and Volunteer Equipment.—Y. Hospital, Yeomanry Hospital; and a § in S. & S.F.A. column of Relief, that particulars of Relief in that Town or Borough are included in the Relief by the S. & S.F.A. at the head of the County.

Origin of Fund.	S. & S.F.A. Subscriptions Raised in County (a) including County Balances previous to the War, Grants from the Council (b).	Total Amount Received.	Expenditure in Relief, &c. By S. & S.F.A.	Expenditure in Relief, &c. By Independent Committee.	Remitted to other Funds.		Balance.	Number of Cases Relieved. Wives and Dependent Relatives.	Children.	Widows.	Men.	Remarks.
NORTHUMBERLAND—*cont*.	£ s. d.	£ s. d.	£ s. d.	£ s. d.		£ s. d.	£ s. d.					
*Newcastle-on-Tyne		*52,840 4 5	§	*48,047 16 9	To Expenses	312 19 3	4,479 8 5	*2,595	*5,200	...	...	* Includes Gateshead, county Durham.
Title: *Northumberland and Tyneside Reservists Fund.*												
Tynemouth		3,286 11 4	§	2,525 13 9	To M.H. (not earmarked)	127 3 0		85	253	1		
					,, Expenses	29 8 2						
						156 11 2	604 6 5	—	—	—	—	
NOTTINGHAMSHIRE.	(a) 946 10 3	1,144 8 3	370 6 7				774 1 8	261	298	—	—	
	(b) 197 18 0											
Lord Lieutenant's Fund (Duke of Portland.)		4,239 15 6			To Y. & V. Equipment	4,239 15 6	—					
Lady Belper's Fund		521 0 0			To Y. Hospital	521 0 0	—					
County Reservists		4,307 18 11		3,834 13 9	To Expenses	32 11 10	440 13 4	349	497	—		
Mansfield		944 0 0	§		To L.L. Fund	174 0 0						
					,, M.H. (not earmarked)	636 0 0						
					,, Y. Hospital	106 0 0						
					,, Mafeking Fund	20 0 0						
					,, Expenses	8 0 0						
						944 0 0						
Newark		1,366 0 0	§		To City of Nottingham Fund	1,210 0 0						
					,, S. & S.F.A. (local)	84 0 0						
					,, Y. Hospital	72 0 0						
						1,366 0 0		—	—	—	—	
Newark Advertiser		710 0 0			To Mayor of Newark	710 0 0	—	—	—	—	—	
*Nottingham (City)		(c)14,478 6 7		13,838 18 7	To Expenses	434 11 1	204 16 11	883	1,261			(c) £4,218 2s. 3d. received from the Mansion House.
Daily Express		1,997 12 9			To Nottingham City Fund	1,997 12 9	—	—	—	—	—	
Daily Guardian		10,138 0 0		373 0 0	To M.H. (not earmarked)	9,645 0 0		...	...	...	...	Number of cases not supplied.
					,, ,, No. 2 Red Cross Society.	20 0 0						
					,, ,, No. 3 Lloyd's Patriotic.	15 0 0						
					,, ,, No. 4 S. & S.F.A.	50 0 0						
					,, Mafeking Fund	35 0 0						
						9,765 0 0	—					
Raleigh Cycle Co.		405 14 0		405 14 0	No Expenses	...		17	17	—	—	
Retford		1,510 0 0	§		To S. & S.F.A. (local)	400 0 0						
					,, Lloyd's Patriotic	300 0 0						
					,, Portland Hospital	200 0 0						
					,, S. & S.H.S. (central)	200 0 0						
					,, Y. Hospital	150 0 0						
					,, the Lansdowne Fund	100 0 0						
					,, Notts Reservists Fund	100 0 0						
					,, Sherwood Rangers Hospital.	60 0 0						
						1,510 0 0						

TRANSVAAL WAR FUNDS, 1899 TO 1901. COUNTIES—COUNTY BOROUGHS AND BOROUGHS. ENGLAND—cont.

Lord Mayors are distinguished by having L.M. after the name of the Borough; County Boroughs by having a * prefixed; and Towns, &c., which are not "County" Boroughs or Boroughs, by being printed in *italics*.—M.H. signifies The Mansion House Fund.—L.L. Fund, The Lord Lieutenant's Fund.—S. & S.F.A., The Soldiers' and Sailors' Families Association.—S. & S.H.S., The Soldiers' and Sailors' Help Society.—The Lansdowne Fund, Officers' Wives and Families.—The Abercorn Fund, Officers' Surgical and Medical Aid.—The Dudley Fund, Sick and Wounded Officers.—Y. and V. Equipment, Yeomanry and Volunteer Equipment.—Y. Hospital, Yeomanry Hospital; and a § in S. & S.F.A. column of Relief, that particulars of Relief in that Town or Borough are included in the Relief by the S. & S.F.A. at the head of the County.

Origin of Fund.	S. & S.F.A. Subscriptions Raised in County (a); including County Balances previous to the War. Grants from the Council (b).	Total Amount Received.	Expenditure in Relief, &c. By S. & S.F.A.	By Independent Committee.	Remitted to other Funds.		Balance.	Wives and Dependent Relatives.	Children.	Widows.	Men.	Remarks.
NOTTINGHAMSHIRE—*cont.*	£ s. d.	£ s. d.	£ s. d.	£ s. d.		£ s. d.	£ s. d.					
Worksop		1,201 6 9	§	...	To Lloyd's Patriotic	300 0 0						
					„ The Lansdowne Fund	260 0 0						
					„ S. & S.F.A. (local)	200 0 0						
					„ Portland Hospital	200 0 0						
					„ Y. Hospital	160 0 0						
					„ Notts. Reservists' Fund	77 9 8						
					„ Expenses	3 17 1						
						1,201 6 9						
OXFORDSHIRE.	(a) 3,065 15 4	5,764 5 4	4,754 6 8	...		...	1,009 18 8	535	619	—	—	
	(b) 2,698 10 0											
LORD LIEUTENANT'S FUND (THE EARL OF JERSEY.)		7,490 6 0			To M.H. No. 1 Patriotic Fund	1,732 18 2						
					„ „ No. 2 Red Cross Society.	528 9 5						
					„ „ No. 3 Lloyd's Patriotic.	600 14 1						
					„ „ No. 4 S. & S.F.A.	1,195 17 0						
					„ Y. & V. Equipment	3,392 8 1						
					„ Expenses	39 19 3						
						7,490 6 0						
Banbury		714 7 5	§	714 7 5		...		...	...	...	...	Number of cases not supplied.
Chipping Norton		409 5 10	§		To L.L. Fund	309 5 10	100 0 0	—	—	—	—	
Henley-on-Thames		740 0 0	§		To L.L. Fund	540 0 0						
					„ S. & S.F.A. (local)	140 0 0						
					„ Men's Extra Comforts	60 0 0						
						740 0 0						
*Oxford		5,444 17 4	§		To M.H. No. 1 Patriotic Fund	1,000 0 0						
					„ „ No. 2 Red Cross Society.	1,000 0 0						
					„ „ No. 3 Lloyd's Patriotic	1,000 0 0						
					„ „ No. 4 S & S.F.A.	1,500 0 0						
					„ S. & S.F.A. (local)	450 0 0						
					„ *Daily Mail* (London)	100 0 0						
					„ Expenses	62 14 6						
						5,112 14 6	332 2 10	—	—	—	—	
Woodstock		207 19 0	§		To L.L. Fund	200 0 0	7 19 0					
RUTLAND.	(a) 307 2 2	757 2 2	564 3 6			...	192 18 8	39	19	—	—	
	(b) 450 0 0											
LORD LIEUTENANT'S FUND (EARL OF DYSART.)		1,392 0 0			To M.H. No. 1 Patriotic Fund	600 18 1						
					„ „ No. 2 Red Cross Society.	9 6 9						
					„ „ No. 3 Lloyd's Patriotic.	35 11 1						
					„ „ No. 4 S. & S.F.A.	600 18 1						
					„ Expenses	145 6 0						
						1,392 0 0						

TRANSVAAL WAR FUNDS, 1899 TO 1901. COUNTIES—COUNTY BOROUGHS AND BOROUGHS. ENGLAND—cont.

Lord Mayors are distinguished by having L.M. after the name of the Borough; County Boroughs by having a * prefixed; and Towns, &c., which are not "County" Boroughs or Boroughs, by being printed in *italics*.—M.H. signifies The Mansion House Fund.—L.L. Fund, The Lord Lieutenant's Fund.—S. & S.F.A., The Soldiers' and Sailors' Families Association.—S. & S.H.S., The Soldiers' and Sailors' Help Society.—The Lansdowne Fund, Officers' Wives and Families.—The Abercorn Fund, Officers' Surgical and Medical Aid.—The Dudley Fund, Sick and Wounded Officers.—Y. and V. Equipment, Yeomanry and Volunteer Equipment.—Y. Hospital, Yeomanry Hospital; and a § in S. & S.F.A. column of Relief, that particulars of Relief in that Town or Borough are included in the Relief by the S. & S.F.A. at the head of the County.

Origin of Fund.	S. & S.F.A. Subscriptions Raised in County (a) including County Balances previous to the War, Grants from the Council (b).	Total Amount Received.	Expenditure in Relief, &c. By S. & S.F.A.	Expenditure in Relief, &c. By Independent Committee.	Remitted to other Funds.		Balance.	Wives and Dependent Relatives.	Children.	Widows.	Men.	Remarks.
	£ s. d.	£ s. d.	£ s. d.	£ s. d.		£ s. d.	£ s. d.					
SHROPSHIRE.	(a) 9,357 17 3	9,457 17 3	7,236 19 5		To S. & S.F.A. (central)	110 0 0	2,110 17 10	634	652	—	—	
	(b) 100 0 0											
LORD LIEUTENANT'S FUND (EARL OF POWIS.)		5,149 0 0			To Y. Equipment	2,490 0 0						
					„ V. Equipment	426 0 0						
					„ Men's extra comforts	200 0 0						
					„ Expenses	30 0 0						
						3,146 0 0	2,003 0 0	—	—	—	—	
Countess of Powis		149 5 10			To Men's extra comforts	149 5 10	—					
Bishops Castle		260 3 7	§		To S. & S.F.A. (local)	231 13 7						
					„ L.L. Y. Equipment Fund	28 10 0						
						260 3 7	—					
Bridgnorth		...	§		...	...	...	...	...	...	...	No Mayor's Fund.
Ludlow		572 9 8	§		To S. & S.F.A. (local)	572 9 8	—					
Oswestry		1,155 0 0		837 0 0	...		318 0 0	72	83			
Shrewsbury		2,240 17 0	§		To S. & S.F.A. (local)	200 0 0						
					„ Expenses	17 18 2						
						217 18 2	2,022 18 10	—	—	—	—	
Wenlock			§		...							No Mayor's Fund.
SOMERSETSHIRE.	(a) 13,705 15 7	13,894 15 7	9,114 17 11		...		4,779 17 8	1,212	1,456	—	—	
	(b) 189 0 0											
LORD LIEUTENANT'S FUND (EARL OF CORK AND ORRERY.)		1,450 0 0	...		To Y. Equipment	1,450 0 0	—					
*Bath		2,475 0 0	§		To M.H. (not earmarked)	1,820 0 0						
					„ S. & S.F.A. (local)	536 0 0						
					„ Convalescent Home	50 0 0						
					„ *Bath Chronicle* Fund	69 0 0						
						2,475 0 0	—					
		2,500 0 0			To Convalescent Home, Combe Down.	2,500 0 0	—					
Bath Chronicle		890 7 4		715 2 0	No Expenses		175 5 4	102	—			
Bridgwater		...	§		... ...		...	...	...	...	...	No Mayor's Fund.
Somerset County Gazette and Bridgwater Mercury.		663 9 0			To S. & S.F.A. (local)	663 9 0	—					
Bridgwater Mercury		208 5 7			To Mafeking Relief Fund	208 5 7	—					
Chard		307 11 10	§		To M.H. (not earmarked)	150 0 0						
					„ „ No. 2 Red Cross Society.	40 9 8						
					„ S. & S.F.A. (local)	50 0 0						
					„ M.H. Refugees	16 0 0						
					„ Expenses	1 2 2						
						257 11 10	50 0 0					
Glastonbury			§		...		...	...				No Mayor's Fund.
Taunton		509 10 3	§	40 5 0	To M.H. (not earmarked)	77 3 2		...	11	8	—	
					„ Men's extra comforts	320 16 4						
						397 19 6	71 5 9					

TRANSVAAL WAR FUNDS, 1899 TO 1901. COUNTIES—COUNTY BOROUGHS AND BOROUGHS. ENGLAND—cont.

Lord Mayors are distinguished by having L.M. after the name of the Borough; County Boroughs by having a * prefixed; and Towns, &c., which are not "County" Boroughs or Boroughs, by being printed in *italics*.—M.H. signifies The Mansion House Fund.—L.L. Fund, The Lord Lieutenant's Fund.—S. & S.F.A., The Soldiers' and Sailors' Families Association.—S. & S.H.S., The Soldiers' and Sailors' Help Society.—The Lansdowne Fund, Officers' Wives and Families.—The Abercorn Fund, Officers' Surgical and Medical Aid.—The Dudley Fund, Sick and Wounded Officers.—Y. and V. Equipment, Yeomanry and Volunteer Equipment.—Y. Hospital, Yeomanry Hospital; and a § in S. & S.F.A. column of Relief, that particulars of Relief in that Town or Borough are included in the Relief by the S. & S.F.A. at the head of the County.

Origin of Fund.	S. & S.F.A. Subscriptions Raised in County (a) including County Balances previous to the War. Grants from the Council (b).	Total Amount Received.	Expenditure in Relief, &c. By S. & S.F.A.	Expenditure in Relief, &c. By Independent Committee.	Remitted to other Funds.		Balance.	Wives and Dependent Relatives.	Children.	Widows.	Men.	Remarks.
	£ s. d.	£ s. d.	£ s. d.	£ s. d.		£ s. d.	£ s. d.					
SOMERSETSHIRE—cont.												
Wells		494 9 3	§		To M.H. No. 1 Patriotic Fund	239 0 0						
					" " No. 2 Red Cross Society.	101 0 0						
					" " No. 3 Lloyd's Patriotic.	47 0 0						
					" S. & S.F.A. (local)	77 9 3						
					" M.H. Refugees' Fund	8 0 0						
					" Mafeking Fund	22 0 0						
						494 9 3	—	—	—	—	—	
Yeovil		625 0 0	§	11 0 0	To M.H. No. 1 Patriotic Fund	128 0 0		1	1	—	—	
					" " No. 2 Red Cross Society.	7 0 0						
					" " No. 4 S. & S.F.A.	22 0 0						
					" " Refugees' Fund	9 0 0						
					" S. & S.F.A. (local)	358 0 0						
					" *Daily Mail* (London)	1 0 0						
					" Expenses	9 0 0						
						534 0 0	80 0 0					
Brackwell Village		286 0 0	§	8 0 0	To M.H. (not earmarked)	17 0 0		—	—	—	—	
					" " No. 2 Red Cross Society.	20 0 0						
					" S. & S.F.A. (local)	119 0 0						
					" M.H. Refugees' Fund	25 0 0						
						181 0 0	97 0 0					
SOUTHAMPTON (HANTS).	(a) 34,203 1 11 (b) 18,680 0 0	52,883 1 11	46,994 8 1		...		5,888 13 10	6,189	8,932	—	—	
LORD LIEUTENANT'S FUND (THE EARL OF NORTHBROOK.)		9,768 0 0			To S. & S.F.A. (local)	780 0 0						
					" O.C. 37th Reg. District	179 0 0		...	...	...	...	For Widows, &c.
					" S. & S.H.S. (local)	204 0 0						
					" Men's extra comforts	1,185 0 0		...	...	...	...	£1,100 to S. Africa.
					" Y. Equipment and Insurance.	2,226 0 0						Single men insured for £100, married men £200.
					" V. Equipment and Insurance.	2,151 0 0						
					" Expenses	177 0 0						
						6,902 0 0	2,866 0 0	—	—	—	—	
Andover		6 7 0	§		To S. & S.F.A. (local)	6 7 0	—	—	—	—	—	
Andover Advertiser		204 15 4			To M.H. No. 1 Patriotic Fund	175 10 6						
					" " No. 2 Red Cross Society.	6 4 2						
					" " No. 3 Lloyd's Patriotic.	1 1 0						
					" " No. 4 S. & S.F.A.	2 12 0						
					" S. & S.F.A. (local)	19 7 8						
						204 15 4	—	—	—	—	—	
Basingstoke		281 13 0	§		To S. & S.F.A. (local)	167 13 6						
					" *Daily Telegraph*	50 0 0						
					" O.C. 37th Reg. District	61 4 3		...	...	...	...	For Widows, &c.
					" Expenses	2 15 3						
						281 13 0	—	—	—	—	—	
Bournemouth		2,747 1 10	§		To M.H. No. 1 Patriotic Fund	769 14 5						
					" " No. 2 Red Cross Society.	401 16 1						
					" " No. 3 Lloyd's Patriotic.	456 15 5						
					" " No. 4 S. & S.F.A.	543 17 3						
					Carried forward	2,172 3 2						

TRANSVAAL WAR FUNDS, 1899 TO 1901. COUNTIES—COUNTY BOROUGHS AND BOROUGHS. ENGLAND—cont.

Lord Mayors are distinguished by having L.M. after the name of the Borough; County Boroughs by having a * prefixed; and Towns, &c., which are not "County" Boroughs or Boroughs, by being printed in *italics*.—M.H. signifies The Mansion House Fund.—L.L. Fund, The Lord Lieutenant's Fund.—S. & S.F.A., The Soldiers' and Sailors' Families Association.—S. & S.H.S., The Soldiers' and Sailors' Help Society.—The Lansdowne Fund, Officers' Wives and Families.—The Abercorn Fund, Officers' Surgical and Medical Aid.—The Dudley Fund, Sick and Wounded Officers.—Y. and V. Equipment, Yeomanry and Volunteer Equipment.—Y. Hospital, Yeomanry Hospital; and a § in S. & S.F.A. column of Relief, that particulars of Relief in that Town or Borough are included in the Relief by the S. & S.F.A. at the head of the County.

Origin of Fund.	S. & S.F.A. Subscriptions Raised in County (a) including County Balances previous to the War. Grants from the Council (b).	Total Amount Received.	Expenditure in Relief, &c. By S. & S.F.A.	By Independent Committee.	Remitted to other Funds.		Balance.	Number of Cases Relieved.				Remarks.
								Wives and Dependent Relatives.	Children.	Widows.	Men.	
SOUTHAMPTON (HANTS)—cont.	£ s. d.	£ s. d.	£ s. d.	£ s. d.		£ s. d.	£ s. d.					
					Brought forward ...	2,172 3 2						
					To M.H. Refugees' Fund ...	203 4 3						
					,, L.L. Fund	18 11 0						
					,, Y. Hospital	*56 0 0		...	...	...	...	*Bournemouth Bed.
					,, Expenses ...	79 8 4						
						2,529 6 9	217 15 1	—	—	—	—	
Christchurch ...	...	730 0 0	§		To M.H. No. 1 Patriotic Fund	110 0 0						
					,, ,, No. 2 Red Cross Society.	30 0 0						
					,, ,, No. 3 Lloyd's Patriotic.	75 0 0						
					,, ,, No. 4 S. & S.F.A. ...	90 0 0						
					,, S. & S.F.A. (local)	257 0 0						
					,, Men's extra comforts ...	5 0 0						
					,, L.L. Y. & V. Equipment	127 0 0						
					,, M.H. Refugees' Fund ...	36 0 0						
						730 0 0		—	—	—	—	
Lymington ...	...	479 4 3	§		To M.H. (not earmarked) ...	479 4 3		—	—	—	—	
*Portsmouth ...	...	8,525 0 0	§	495 0 0	To S. & S.F.A. (local) ...	6,740 0 0		21	48	32	16	
					,, Expenses ...	246 9 7						
						6,986 9 7	1,043 10 5	—	—	—	—	
Romsey ...	...	... ...	§		...	...		...	...	...	...	No Mayor's Fund.
*Southampton ...	...	2,378 2 9	§		To M.H. No. 1 Patriotic Fund	701 7 10						
					,, S. & S.F.A. (local)	1,006 2 8						
					,, Ambulance Corps	670 12 3						
						2,378 2 9		—	—	—	—	
Winchester ...	...	587 0 0	§		To Men's extra comforts ...	350 0 0						
					,, Mafeking Fund ...	20 0 0						
						370 0 0	217 0 0					
SOUTHAMPTON (ISLE OF WIGHT).	(a) 2,834 18 1 (b) 300 0 0	3,134 18 1	2,866 0 9		...		268 17 4	380	527	—	—	
THE GOVERNOR'S FUND		*2,005 0 0		5 0 0	To S. & S.F.A. (local) ...	2,000 0 0				1	...	*No further particulars as to full extent of Fund supplied.
STAFFORDSHIRE—	(a) 40,045 19 5 (b) 4,050 0 0	44,095 19 5	41,491 12 8		...		2,604 6 9	3,439	3,602	—	—	
LORD LIEUTENANT'S FUND (THE EARL OF DARTMOUTH).		9,696 14 7			To M.H. No. 1 Patriotic Fund	504 18 4						
					,, ,, No. 2 Red Cross Society.	283 16 10						
					,, ,, No. 3 Lloyd's Patriotic.	174 11 3						
					,, S. & S.F.A. (local) ...	4,625 5 10						
					,, Y. & V. Equipment ...	3,690 0 0						
					,, Y. Hospital ...	250 0 0						
					,, Men's extra comforts ...	48 0 0						
					,, Expenses ...	120 2 4						
						9,696 14 7		—	—	—	—	
Burslem ...		152 1 2	§		To S. & S.F.A. (local)	152 1 2		...	...	...	...	No particulars supplied by the Mayor.
*Burton-on-Trent ...		6,261 4 0	§		To M.H. (not earmarked) ...	3,388 3 1						
					,, ,, Queen Alexandra's Appeal.	1,000 0 0						
					,, S. & S.F.A. (local) ...	1,873 0 11						
						6,261 4 0		—	—	—	—	
Burton Daily Mail ...		570 0 0			To S. & S.F.A. (local)	520 0 0						
					,, ,, (Derbyshire)	50 0 0						
						570 0 0						

TRANSVAAL WAR FUNDS, 1899 TO 1901. COUNTIES—COUNTY BOROUGHS AND BOROUGHS. **ENGLAND**—cont.

Lord Mayors are distinguished by having L.M. after the name of the Borough; County Boroughs by having a * prefixed; and Towns, &c., which are not "County" Boroughs or Boroughs, by being printed in *italics*.—M.H. signifies The Mansion House Fund.—L.L. Fund, The Lord Lieutenant's Fund.—S. & S.F.A., The Soldiers' and Sailors' Families Association.—S. & S.H.S., The Soldiers' and Sailors' Help Society.—The Lansdowne Fund, Officers' Wives and Families.—The Abercorn Fund, Officers' Surgical and Medical Aid.—The Dudley Fund, Sick and Wounded Officers.—Y. and V. Equipment, Yeomanry and Volunteer Equipment.—Y. Hospital, Yeomanry Hospital; and a § in S. & S.F.A. column of Relief, that particulars of Relief in that Town or Borough are included in the Relief by the S. & S.F.A. at the head of the County.

Origin of Fund.	S. & S.F.A. Subscriptions Raised in County (a) including County Balances previous to the War. Grants from the Council (b).	Total Amount Received.	Expenditure in Relief, &c. By S. & S.F.A.	Expenditure in Relief, &c. By Independent Committee.	Remitted to other Funds.		Balance.	Wives and Dependent Relatives.	Children.	Widows.	Men.	Remarks.
STAFFORDSHIRE—*cont.*	£ s. d.	£ s. d.	£ s. d.	£ s. d.		£ s. d.	£ s. d.					
*Hanley		2,848 0 0	§	2,848 0 0	...	...	... ...	151	216	—	—	
Lichfield		1,095 18 9	§	28 19 0	To M.H. Refugees' Fund	18 3 0						
					„ S. & S.F.A. (local)	315 0 0						
					„ Welcome Home, &c.	490 14 9						
					„ Expenses	9 16 4						
						833 14 1	233 5 8	—	—	—	—	
Longton		1,960 0 0	§		To S. & S.F.A. (local)	1960 0 0	—					
Newcastle-under-Lyme		864 0 4	§		To Patriotic Fund	83 8 4						
					„ Red Cross Society	60 15 9						
					„ Lloyd's Patriotic Fund	16 3 9						
					„ S. & S.F.A. (local)	701 6 10						
					„ Expenses	2 5 8						
						864 0 4	—	—	—	—	—	
Smethwick	...	2,716 13 3	§	2,405 15 10			310 17 5	144	153	—	—	
Stafford		1,129 4 9	§	...	To L.L. Fund	984 2 1						
					„ S. & S.F.A. (local)	92 7 0						
					„ Expenses	52 15 8						
						1,129 4 9	—	—	—	—	—	
Stoke-upon-Trent		1,596 1 6	§		To S. & S.F.A. (local)	1,213 6 5	382 15 1					
Tamworth		1,128 16 10	§	34 13 0	To S. & S.F.A. (local)	825 0 0						
					„ „ (Warwickshire)	250 0 0						
					„ Expenses	2 11 8						
						1,077 11 8	16 12 2	—	—	—	—	
*Walsall		5,560 14 5	§	5,407 1 7	To S. & S.F.A. (local)	153 12 10		256	275	...	9	
Wednesbury		2,078 17 0	§		To S. & S.F.A. (local)	1,580 0 0						
					„ Expenses	130 12 6						
						1,710 12 6	368 4 6	—	—	—	—	
*West Bromwich		4,085 14 7	§		To S. & S.F.A. (local)	2,971 0 0						
					„ M.H. Refugees'	200 0 0						
					„ L.L.Y & V. Equipment	100 0 0						
					„ St. John Ambulance	50 0 0						
					„ Natal Volunteers	20 0 0						
					„ Expenses	188 3 6						
						3,529 3 6	556 11 1	—	—	—	—	
*Wolverhampton		11,337 0 0	§	11,171 0 0	...	...	166 0 0	549	522	—	—	
Bilston		1,121 0 0	§	24 0 0	To M.H. (not earmarked)	36 0 0		2	7	1	3	
					„ S. & S.F.A. (local)	650 0 0						
					„ Send-off of Reservists	56 0 0		...	...	...	...	56 Reservists £1 each.
					„ Men's extra comforts	14 0 0						
						756 0 0	341 0 0	—	—	—	—	
Bucknall		53 7 6	§		To S. & S.F.A. (local)	53 7 6	—					
Coseley		300 0 0	§	...	To S. & S.F.A. (local)	300 0 0	—					
Darlaston		1,477 0 0	§	1,266 0 0	To S. & S.F.A. (local)	50 0 0						
					„ V. Equipment	46 0 0						
					„ Expenses	22 0 0						
						118 0 0	93 0 0	56	74	—	—	
Fenton		250 0 0	§	...	To S. & S.F.A. (local)	250 0 0	—					

TRANSVAAL WAR FUNDS, 1899 TO 1901. COUNTIES—COUNTY BOROUGHS AND BOROUGHS. ENGLAND—cont.

Lord Mayors are distinguished by having L.M. after the name of the Borough; County Boroughs by having a * prefixed; and Towns, &c., which are not "County" Boroughs or Boroughs, by being printed in *italics*.—M.H. signifies The Mansion House Fund.—L.L. Fund, The Lord Lieutenant's Fund.—S. & S.F.A., The Soldiers' and Sailors' Families Association.—S. & S.H.S., The Soldiers' and Sailors' Help Society.—The Lansdowne Fund, Officers' Wives and Families.—The Abercorn Fund, Officers' Surgical and Medical Aid.—The Dudley Fund, Sick and Wounded Officers.—Y. and V. Equipment, Yeomanry and Volunteer Equipment.—Y. Hospital, Yeomanry Hospital; and a § in S. & S.F.A. column of Relief, that particulars of Relief in that Town or Borough are included in the Relief by the S. & S.F.A. at the head of the County.

Origin of Fund.	S. & S.F.A. Subscriptions Raised in County (a) including County Balances previous to the War. Grants from the Council (b).	Total Amount Received.	Expenditure in Relief, &c.		Remitted to other Funds.		Balance.	Number of Cases Relieved.				Remarks.
			By S. & S.F.A.	By Independent Committee.				Wives and Dependent Relatives.	Children.	Widows.	Men.	
	£ s. d.	£ s. d.	£ s. d.	£ s. d.		£ s. d.	£ s. d.					
STAFFORDSHIRE—*cont.*												
Kidsgrove		73 18 9	§		To S. & S.F.A. (local)	73 18 9	—	—	—	—	—	
Kingswinford		86 11 6	§	86 11 6				29	30			
Leek		392 3 4	§	392 3 4	...	...	...	11	6	...	2	
Rowley Regis		1,427 0 0	§		To S. & S.F.A. (local)	950 0 0						
					„ Red Cross Society	100 0 0						
					„ Lloyd's Patriotic	100 0 0						
						1,150 0 0	277 0 0	—	—	—	—	
Silverdale		174 15 6	§		To S. & S.F.A. (local)	174 15 6	—	—	—	—	—	
Tipton		212 3 3	§		To S. & S.F.A. (local)	212 3 3	—	—	—	—	—	
Tunstall		776 10 0	§		To S. & S.F.A. (local)	776 10 0	—	—	—	—	—	
Willenhall		876 0 0	§		To S. & S.F.A. (local)	876 0 0	—	—	—	—	—	
SUFFOLK.	(a) 5,258 17 5	9,338 17 5	6,617 8 0				...	2,721 9 5	1,263	1,385	—	
	(b) 4,080 0 0											
Lord Lieutenant's Fund (Marquess of Bristol.)		6,000 0 0			To M.H. No. 1 Patriotic Fund	1,150 0 0						
					„ No. 2 Red Cross Society.	550 0 0						
					„ No. 3 Lloyd's Patriotic.	550 0 0						
					„ No. 4 S. & S.F.A.	3,750 0 0						
						6,000 0 0	—	—	—	—	—	
Aldeburgh		302 6 8	§		To L.L. Fund	302 6 8	—	—	—	—	—	
Beccles		214 17 10	§		To M.H. (not earmarked)	214 17 10	—	—	—	—	—	
Bury St. Edmunds		979 1 5	§	641 6 0	To M.H. No. 1 Patriotic Fund	250 13 2		8	...		1	
					„ Men's Extra Comforts	60 0 0						
					„ Expenses	0 16 0						
						311 9 2	26 6 3					
Eye		120 1 7	§		To M.H. No. 1 Patriotic Fund	112 7 3						
					„ No. 2 Red Cross Society.	3 17 2						
					„ No. 4 S. & S.F.A.	3 17 2						
						120 1 7	—	—	—	—	—	
*Ipswich		2,333 0 0	§	38 0 0	To S. & S.F.A. (local)	1,751 0 0		1	...	3	10	
					„ Mafeking Fund	15 0 0						
					„ Expenses	11 0 0						
						1,777 0 0	518 0 0	—	—	—	—	
Lowestoft		1,615 2 9	§		To M.H. (not earmarked)	1,615 2 9	—	—	—	—	—	
Southwold		113 7 8	§		To M.H. (not earmarked)	113 7 8	—	—	—	—	—	
Sudbury		408 0 0	§		To M.H. (not earmarked)	408 0 0	—	—	—	—	—	
SURREY.	(a)31,562 4 11	34,662 4 11	29,628 6 3				...	5,033 18 8	2,456	2,863	—	
	(b) 3,100 0 0											
Lord Lieutenant's Fund (Viscount Midleton.)		7,600 0 0			To Y. & V. Equipment	7,600 0 0	—	—	—	—	—	
*Croydon		2,764 19 7	§	(a) 45 13 8	To L.L. Y. & V. Equipment	1,000 0 0		...	...	...	...	(a) Men's Insurance, &c.
					„ S. & S.F.A. (local)	500 0 0						
					„ Expenses	101 16 10						
						1,601 16 10	1,117 9 1	—	—	—	—	

TRANSVAAL WAR FUNDS, 1899 TO 1901. COUNTIES—COUNTY BOROUGHS AND BOROUGHS. ENGLAND—cont.

Lord Mayors are distinguished by having L.M. after the name of the Borough; County Boroughs by having a * prefixed; and Towns, &c., which are not "County" Boroughs or Boroughs, by being printed in *italics*.—M.H. signifies The Mansion House Fund.—L.L. Fund, The Lord Lieutenant's Fund.—S. & S.F.A., The Soldiers' and Sailors' Families Association.—S. & S.H.S., The Soldiers' and Sailors' Help Society.—The Lansdowne Fund, Officers' Wives and Families.—The Abercorn Fund, Officers' Surgical and Medical Aid.—The Dudley Fund, Sick and Wounded Officers.—Y. and V. Equipment, Yeomanry and Volunteer Equipment —Y. Hospital, Yeomanry Hospital; and a § in S. & S.F.A. column of Relief, that particulars of Relief in that Town or Borough are included in the Relief by the S. & S.F.A. at the head of the County.

Origin of Fund.	S. & S.F.A. Subscriptions Raised in County (a) including County Balances previous to the War, Grants from the Council (b).	Total Amount Received.	Expenditure in Relief, &c.		Remitted to other Funds.		Balance.	Number of Cases Relieved.				Remarks.
			By S. & S.F.A.	By Independent Committee.				Wives and Dependent Relatives.	Children.	Widows.	Men.	
SURREY—cont.	£ s. d.	£ s. d.	£ s. d.	£ s. d.		£ s. d.	£ s. d.					
Chamber of Commerce		271 3 0			To M.H. (not earmarked)	21 0 0						
					" S. & S.F.A. (local)	250 3 0						
						271 3 0	—	—	—	—	—	
Croydon Guardian		512 10 0		...	To S. & S.F.A. (local)	512 10 0	—	—	—	—	—	
Godalming		964 7 1	§	602 0 6	To M.H. No. 1 Patriotic Fund	105 0 0		97	116	—	—	
					" " Refugees' Fund	105 0 0						
					" Expenses	9 16 3						
						219 16 3	142 10 4	—	—	—	—	
Guildford		... ...	§	... ...	... ...	... ...		...	...	...	...	No Mayor's Fund.
Kingston-on-Thames		706 8 2	§		To V. Equipment	706 8 2	—					
Reigate		1,236 15 6	§	31 19 7	To S. & S.F.A. (local)	1,035 12 0		50	60	—		
					" Expenses	10 18 0						
						1,046 10 0	158 5 11	—	—	—	—	
Richmond		588 11 10	§		To V. Equipment	573 5 0						
					" Expenses	15 6 10						
						588 11 10	—					
Dorking		732 0 0	§	6 6 0 0	To Expenses	14 0 0	72 0 0	48	35	2	2	
Mitcham and Morden		673 14 2	§	647 8 1	To Expenses	9 1 6	17 4 7	42	40	—	—	
Surrey Advertiser		2,800 0 0			To S. & S.F.A. (local)	2,800 0 0	—					
Surrey Comet		2,107 19 9			To S. & S.F.A. (local)	2,107 19 9	—					
Richmond and Twickenham Times.		1,046 2 8			To S. & S.F.A. (local)	1,046 2 8	—					
Surrey Mirror		258 15 3			To S. & S.F.A. (local)	258 15 3	—					
Surrey Times		85 0 0			To S. & S.F.A. (local)	85 0 0	—					
SUSSEX.	(a) 14,080 0 6	18,509 9 11	16,870 3 2		...	...	1,639 6 9	1,559	2,049			
	(b) 4,429 9 5											
LORD LIEUTENANT'S FUND (MARQUESS OF ABERGAVENNY).		5,890 0 0			To M.H. No. 1 Patriotic Fund	820 0 0						
					" " No. 2 Red Cross Society.	144 0 0						
					" " No. 3 Lloyd's Patriotic.	178 0 0						
					" " No. 4 S. & S.F.A.	380 0 0						
					" Y. Equipment	1,060 0 0						
					" V. Equipment	3,308 0 0						
						5,890 0 0						
Arundel		381 16 2	§	31 0 6	To S. & S.F.A. (local)	200 0 0		...	...	1	10	
					" Daily Telegraph	100 0 0						
						300 0 0	50 15 8	—	—	—	—	
*Brighton		5,321 19 0	§	12 0 0	To Patriotic Fund	1,000 0 0		3	—	—	—	
					" S. & S.F.A. (local)	2,072 17 11						
					" Lloyd's Patriotic	800 0 0						
					" S. & S.H.S. (local)	50 0 0						
					" Daily Mail (London)	27 11 11						
					" Mafeking Fund	155 4 3						
					" M.H. Refugees' Fund	597 12 8						
					" Expenses	153 17 10						
						4,857 4 7	452 14 5	—	—	—	—	

Lord Mayors are distinguished by having L.M. after the name of the Borough; County Boroughs by having a * prefixed; and Towns, &c., which are not "County" Boroughs or Boroughs, by being printed in *italics*.—M.H. signifies The Mansion House Fund.—L.L. Fund, The Lord Lieutenant's Fund.—S. & S.F.A., The Soldiers' and Sailors' Families Association.—S. & S.H.S., The Soldiers' and Sailors' Help Society.—The Lansdowne Fund, Officers' Wives and Families.—The Abercorn Fund, Officers' Surgical and Medical Aid.—The Dudley Fund, Sick and Wounded Officers.—Y. and V. Equipment, Yeomanry and Volunteer Equipment.—Y. Hospital, Yeomanry Hospital; and a § in S. & S.F.A. column of Relief, that particulars of Relief in that Town or Borough are included in the Relief by the S. & S.F.A. at the head of the County.

Origin of Fund.	S. & S.F.A. Subscriptions Raised in County (a) including County Balances previous to the War. Grants from the Council (b).	Total Amount Received.	Expenditure in Relief, &c. By S. & S.F.A.	Expenditure in Relief, &c. By Independent Committee.	Remitted to other Funds.		Balance.	Wives and Dependent Relatives.	Children.	Widows.	Mem.	Remarks.
SUSSEX—*cont.*	£ s. d.	£ s. d.	£ s. d.	£ s. d.		£ s. d.	£ s. d.					
Chichester		607 1 3	§	...	To M.H. No. 1 Patriotic Fund	607 1 3	—	—	—	—	—	
Eastbourne		3,222 0 0	§		To M.H. No. 1 Patriotic Fund	1,125 0 0						
					,, S. & S.F.A. (local)	1,459 0 0						
					,, M.H. Refugees' Fund	134 0 0						
					,, Expenses	64 0 0						
						2782 0 0	440 0 0	—	—	—	—	
*Hastings		1,671 15 4	§		To M.H. (not earmarked)	516 0 0						
					,, ,, S. & S.F.A.	336 0 0						
					,, S. & S.F.A. (local)	243 0 0						
					,, *Daily Mail*	7 1 8						
					,, Lloyd's Patriotic	130 0 0						
					,, Y. Hospital	100 0 0						
					,, V. Equipment	244 13 8						
					,, M.H. Refugees'	35 0 0						
					,, Mafeking Fund	50 0 0						
					,, Expenses	10 0 0						
						1,671 15 4	—	—	—	—	—	
Hastings Rifle Volunteers		297 3 9		246 13 0	To Concert to Volunteers	19 5 2		15	32	—	—	
					,, Expenses	12 2 6						
						31 7 8	19 3 1					
Hove		3,695 0 0	§		To M.H. (not earmarked)	3,000 0 0		—	—	—	—	
					,, V. Equipment	409 0 0						
						3,409 0 0	286 0 0					
The Mayoress Fund		459 8 4		337 8 0	...	...	122 0 4	37	41	1		
Lewes		838 0 0	§		To M.H. (not earmarked)	310 0 0						
					,, ,, No. 1 Patriotic Fund	10 0 0						
					,, ,, No. 2 Red Cross Society.	10 0 0						
					,, ,, No. 3 Lloyd's Patriotic.	10 0 0						
					,, ,, No. 4 S. & S.F.A.	10 0 0						
					,, S. & S.F.A. (local)	295 0 0						
					,, *Daily Mail*	18 0 0						
					,, V. Equipment	21 0 0						
					,, M.H. Refugees'	154 0 0						
						838 0 0	—	—	—	—	—	
Rye		200 0 0	§		To M.H. (not earmarked)	200 0 0	—	—	—	—	—	
Winchelsea		35 0 0	§		To M.H. (not earmarked)	35 0 0	—	—	—	—	—	
Worthing		1,429 2 3	§	896 12 9	To M.H. No. 1 Patriotic Fund	100 0 0		71	95	—	—	
					,, ,, No. 2 Red Cross Society.	50 0 0						
					,, ,, No. 3 Lloyd's Patriotic.	50 0 0						
					,, ,, No. 4 S. & S.F.A.	50 0 0						
					,, Mafeking Relief Fund	42 0 0						
					,, Expenses	39 13 8						
						331 13 8	200 15 10	—	—	—	—	

TRANSVAAL WAR FUNDS, 1899 TO 1901. COUNTIES—COUNTY BOROUGHS AND BOROUGHS. ENGLAND—cont.

Lord Mayors are distinguished by having L.M. after the name of the Borough; County Boroughs by having a * prefixed; and Towns, &c., which are not "County" Boroughs or Boroughs, by being printed in *italics*.—M.H. signifies The Mansion House Fund.—L.L. Fund, The Lord Lieutenant's Fund.—S. & S.F.A., The Soldiers' and Sailors' Families Association.—S & S.H.S., The Soldiers' and Sailors' Help Society.—The Lansdowne Fund, Officers' Wives and Families.—The Abercorn Fund, Officers' Surgical and Medical Aid.—The Dudley Fund, Sick and Wounded Officers.—Y. and V. Equipment, Yeomanry and Volunteer Equipment.—Y. Hospital, Yeomanry Hospital; and a § in S. & S.F.A. column of Relief, that particulars of Relief in that Town or Borough are included in the Relief by the S. & S.F.A. at the head of the County.

Origin of Fund.	S. & S.F.A. Subscriptions Raised in County (a) including County Balances previous to the War. Grants from the Council (b).	Total Amount Received.	Expenditure in Relief, &c.		Remitted to other Funds.		Balance.	Number of Cases Relieved.				Remarks.
			By S. & S.F.A.	By Independent Committee.				Wives and Dependent Relatives.	Children.	Widows.	Men.	
	£ s. d.	£ s. d.	£ s. d.	£ s. d.		£ s. d.	£ s. d.					
WARWICKSHIRE.	(a) 9,543 13 6	12,993 13 6	12,040 8 10	...			953 4 8	1,339	1,716	—	—	
	(b) 3,450 0 0											
LORD LIEUTENANT'S FUND (LORD LEIGH.)		16,638 0 0		...	To M.H. No. 1 Patriotic Fund	7,726 0 0						
					" " No. 2 Red Cross Society.	2,032 0 0						
					" " No. 3 Lloyd's Patriotic.	2,745 0 0						
					" " No. 4 S. & S.F.A.	4,156 0 0						
					" Expenses	29 0 0						
						16,638 0 0		—	—	—	—	
Marquis of Hertford's Fund		2,701 11 0			To Y. Equipment, etc.	2,701 11 0		—	—	—	—	
*Birmingham, L.M.		15,855 17 9	§		To M.H. No. 1 Patriotic Fund	4,620 1 6						
					" " No. 2 Red Cross Society.	1,040 12 0						
					" " No. 3 Lloyd's Patriotic.	1,284 16 2						
					" " No. 4 S. & S.F.A.	1,512 4 11						
					" " Refugees' Fund	7,137 4 8						
					" Expenses	260 18 6						
						15,855 17 9		—	—	—	—	
Daily Mail Fund		54,592 1 6	53,597 16 5	...	...	...	994 5 1	...	...	...	...	See Page 73.
Daily Post Fund		2,141 16 0			To V. Equipment	2,141 16 0		—				
Daily Argus Fund		353 0 0			To Mafeking Fund	353 0 0		—				
*Coventry		1,525 0 0	§		To L.L. Fund	958 0 0						
					" Midland Daily Telegraph Fund	400 0 0						
						1,358 0 0	167 0 0	—	—	—	—	
Midland Daily Telegraph		5,972 0 0	5,589 0 0		...	...	383 0 0	181	221	6	—	
Leamington		1,870 8 11	§	1 10 0	To L.L. Fund	1,311 19 1						
					" S. & S.F.A. (local)	261 13 11						
					" M.H. National Church Collection.	134 0 11						
					" The Lansdowne Fund	50 0 0						
					" Daily Telegraph	41 7 0						
					" M.H. Refugees' Fund	0 5 0						
						1,799 5 11	69 13 0	—	—	—	—	
Spa Courier		470 13 10			To S. & S.F.A. (local)	470 13 10		—				
Stratford-on-Avon		228 11 1	§	129 11 3	...	...	98 19 10	14	18			
Sutton Coldfield		498 18 11	§		To L.L. Fund	257 1 5						
					" M.H. Refugees' Fund	89 1 6						
					" Birmingham Refugees' Fund.	152 16 0						
						498 18 11		—	—	—	—	
Warwick		362 18 6			To L.L. Fund	362 18 6		—				
WESTMORELAND.	(a) 474 2 11	1,274 2 11	1,053 14 9		... ...	...	220 8 2	66	90	—	—	
	(b) 800 0 0											
LORD LIEUTENANT'S FUND (LORD HOTHFIELD.)		... ...	...	...				...	...	...	...	No L.L. Fund.
Appleby		629 18 8	§		To M.H. No. 1 Patriotic Fund	66 1 9						
					" " No. 2 Red Cross Society.	20 0 0						
					" " No. 3 Lloyd's Patriotic.	228 9 10						
					" " No. 4 S. & S.F.A.	286 19 10						
					" The O.C. Border Regiment.	24 3 2						
					" Expenses	4 4 1						
						629 18 8		—	—			

TRANSVAAL WAR FUNDS, 1899 TO 1901. COUNTIES—COUNTY BOROUGHS AND BOROUGHS. ENGLAND—cont.

Lord Mayors are distinguished by having L.M. after the name of the Borough; County Boroughs by having a * prefixed; and Towns, &c., which are not "County" Boroughs or Boroughs, by being printed in *italics*.—M.H. signifies The Mansion House Fund.—L.L. Fund, The Lord Lieutenant's Fund.—S. & S.F.A., The Soldiers' and Sailors' Families Association.—S. & S.H.S., The Soldiers' and Sailors' Help Society.—The Lansdowne Fund, Officers' Wives and Families.—The Abercorn Fund, Officers' Surgical and Medical Aid.—The Dudley Fund, Sick and Wounded Officers.—Y. and V. Equipment, Yeomanry and Volunteer Equipment.—Y. Hospital, Yeomanry Hospital; and a § in S. & S.F.A. column of Relief, that particulars of Relief in that Town or Borough are included in the Relief by the S. & S.F.A. at the head of the County.

Origin of Fund.	S. & S.F.A. Subscriptions Raised in County (a) including County Balances previous to the War. Grants from the Council (b).	Total Amount Received.	Expenditure in Relief, &c. By S. & S.F.A.	Expenditure in Relief, &c. By Independent Committee.	Remitted to other Funds.		Balance.	Wives and Dependent Relatives.	Children.	Widows.	Men.	Remarks.
WESTMORELAND—*cont.*	£ s. d.	£ s. d.	£ s. d.	£ s. d.		£ s. d.	£ s. d.					
Kendal		3,714 8 10	§	(d) 28 19 8	To M.H. No. 1 Patriotic Fund	836 3 5	...	1	1	1	...	(d) Special Grants.
					„ „ No. 2 Red Cross Society.	114 15 8						
					„ „ No. 3 Lloyd's Patriotic.	136 2 1						
					„ „ No. 4 S. & S.F.A.	714 3 2						
					„ S. & S.F.A. (local)	400 0 0						
					„ Portland Hospital	543 12 6						
					„ Men's Extra Comforts	(e) 137 4 11		...	...	...		(e) Border Regiment Christmas Gifts, etc.
					„ Trustees' Border Regiment.	636 13 7						
					„ Expenses	102 10 0						
						3,621 5 4	64 3 10	—	—	—	—	
Kirkby Stephen		228 9 10	§		To M.H. No. 2 Red Cross Society.	62 13 4						
					„ „ No. 3 Lloyd's Patriotic.	62 13 4						
					„ „ No. 4 S. & S.F.A.	62 13 4						
					„ S. & S.H.S. (National Bazaar).	15 0 0						
					„ Portland Hospital	25 0 0						
					„ Expenses	0 9 10						
						228 9 10		—	—	—	—	
WILTSHIRE.	(a) 6,905 11 2	7,980 11 2	5,934 5 4	...	...		2,046 5 10	873	1,212	—	—	
	(b) 1,075 0 0											
LORD LIEUTENANT'S FUND (MARQUESS OF LANSDOWNE.)		2,831 0 0			To M.H. (not earmarked)	1,363 0 0						
					„ „ No. 1 Patriotic Fund	638 0 0						
					„ „ No. 2 Red Cross Society.	222 0 0						
					„ „ No. 3 Lloyd's Patriotic.	162 0 0						
					„ „ No. 4 S. & S.F.A.	399 0 0						
					„ S. & S.F.A. (local)	29 0 0						
					„ The Patriotic Fund	9 0 0						
					„ Expenses	9 0 0						
						2,831 0 0						
Calne		42 19 6	§		To M.H. No. 1 Patriotic Fund	31 19 6						
					„ *Daily Mail* (London)	11 0 0						
						42 19 6		—				
Chippenham		... ...	§		... ...	...		...	...	...		No Mayor's Fund.
Devizes		488 8 4	§		To S. & S.F.A. (local)	488 8 4						
Malmesbury		129 15 10	§		To M.H. No. 1 Patriotic Fund	109 18 6						
					„ „ Refugees' Fund	19 17 4						
						129 15 10		—				
Marlborough		... ...	§		... ...	...						No Mayor's Fund.
Salisbury		863 1 6	§		To L.L. Fund	863 1 6						
Swindon		3,770 0 0	§	3,770 0 0	...			240	320			
Wilton		393 2 6	§		To M.H. No. 1 Patriotic Fund	15 0 0						
					„ „ No. 2 Red Cross Society.	15 0 0						
					„ „ No. 3 Lloyd's Patriotic.	30 0 0						
					„ S. & S.F.A. (local)	333 2 6						
						393 2 6						

TRANSVAAL WAR FUNDS, 1899 TO 1901. COUNTIES—COUNTY BOROUGHS AND BOROUGHS. ENGLAND—cont.

Lord Mayors are distinguished by having L.M. after the name of the Borough; County Boroughs by having a * prefixed; and Towns, &c., which are not "County" Boroughs or Boroughs, by being printed in *italics*.—M.H. signifies The Mansion House Fund.—L.L. Fund, The Lord Lieutenant's Fund.—S. & S.F.A., The Soldiers' and Sailors' Families Association.—S. & S.H.S., The Soldiers' and Sailors' Help Society.—The Lansdowne Fund, Officers' Wives and Families.—The Abercorn Fund, Officers' Surgical and Medical Aid.—The Dudley Fund, Sick and Wounded Officers.—Y. and V. Equipment, Yeomanry and Volunteer Equipment.—Y. Hospital, Yeomanry Hospital; and a § in S. & S.F.A. column of Relief, that particulars of Relief in that Town or Borough are included in the Relief by the S. & S.F.A. at the head of the County.

Origin of Fund.	S. & S.F.A. Subscriptions Raised in County (a) including County Balances previous to the War. Grants from the Council (b).	Total Amount Received.	Expenditure in Relief, &c.		Remitted to other Funds.	Balance.	Number of Cases Relieved.				Remarks.
			By S. & S.F.A.	By Independent Committee.			Wives and Dependent Relatives.	Children.	Widows.	Men.	
	£ s. d	£ s. d.	£ s. d.	£ s. d.	£ s. d.	£ s. d.					
WORCESTERSHIRE.	(a) 6,719 6 9	7,819 6 9	6,124 9 7		...	1,694 17 2	875	1,026	—	—	
	(b) 1,100 0 0										
LORD LIEUTENANT'S FUND (EARL OF COVENTRY.)		4,214 8 10			To M.H. No. 1 Patriotic Fund 15 3 0						
					,, S. & S.F.A. (local) 2,726 9 10						
					,, The Lansdowne Fund 3 3 0						
					,, *Daily Telegraph* 1 1 0						
					,, Red Cross Society 14 11 2						
					,, Lloyd's Patriotic 2 2 0						
					,, S. & S.H.S. (London) 24 3 0						
					,, Men's extra comforts 171 8 0						
					,, British Refugee Fund 17 0 0						
					,, Lady G. Vernon's Home 50 0 0						
					,, Expenses 61 0 9						
					3,086 1 9	1,128 7 1	—	—	—	—	
LORD WINDSOR'S FUND		2,494 5 0			To Y. & V. Equipment 2,494 5 0	—	—	—	—	—	
Bewdley		...	§	...	...	...	...	...	...	...	No Mayor's Fund.
Droitwich		166 0 0	§		To S. & S.F.A. (local) 73 0 0						
					,, *Daily Telegraph* 63 0 0						
					,, *Daily Mail* 30 0 0						
					166 0 0	—	—	—	—	—	
*Dudley		2,902 0 0	§	2,856 0 0	To S. & S.F.A. (local) 46 0 0		212	294	4		
Evesham		167 16 10	§		To M.H. (not earmarked) 167 16 10	—					
Kidderminster		1,700 7 10	§	1,279 12 11	To S. & S.F.A. (local) 150 0 0						
					,, M.H. Refugees' Fund 124 6 6						
					274 6 6	146 8 5	—	—	—	—	
*Worcester		2,216 4 1	§	2,134 12 2	To Expenses 81 11 11		237	410	11		
YORKSHIRE (NORTH RIDING).	(a) 7,528 8 6	9,728 8 6	7,954 14 7		...	1,773 13 11	601	748	—	—	
	(b) 2,200 0 0										
LORD LIEUTENANT'S FUND (MARQUESS OF RIPON).		*7,653 13 1			To M.H. (not earmarked) 1,608 18 9						*Includes £3,188 7s. 6d., an apportioned sum of £16,920 6s. 4d., a joint Yeomanry and Volunteer Equipment Fund raised in the 3 Ridings.
					,, ,, No. 1 Patriotic Fund 1,639 0 6						
					,, ,, No. 2 Red Cross Society. 518 11 9						
					,, ,, No. 3 Lloyd's Patriotic. 333 13 4						
					,, ,, No. 4 S. & S.F.A. 314 0 3						
					,, ,, Refugees' Fund 1 1 0						
					,, V. and Y. Equipment 3,188 7 6						
					7,653 13 1						
*Middlesbrough		3,622 4 1	§	2,301 15 3	To M.H. (not earmarked) 467 17 2	852 11 8	...	...	...	...	Number of cases not supplied.
Richmond		630 7 1	§		To M H. No. 1 Patriotic Fund 92 7 1						
					,, ,, No. 2 Red Cross Society. 57 0 0						
					,, ,, No. 3 Lloyd's Patriotic. 72 0 0						
					,, ,, No. 4 S. & S.F.A. 459 0 0						
					630 7 1	—	—	—	—	—	
Scarborough		1,587 0 0	§		To M.H. (not earmarked) 1,587 0 0	—	—	—	—	—	
Thornaby-on-Tees		1,255 4 7		1,086 10 6	To M.H. (not earmarked) 100 0 0	68 14 1	39	121	—	—	
Whitby		146 16 7	§	123 1 9	...	23 14 10	20	29	1	1	

Lord Mayors are distinguished by having L.M. after the name of the Borough; County Boroughs by having a * prefixed; and Towns, &c., which are not "County" Boroughs or Boroughs, by being printed in *italics*.—M.H. signifies The Mansion House Fund.—L.L. Fund, The Lord Lieutenant's Fund.—S. & S.F.A., The Soldiers' and Sailors' Families Association.—S. & S.H.S., The Soldiers' and Sailors' Help Society.—The Lansdowne Fund, Officers' Wives and Families.—The Abercorn Fund, Officers' Surgical and Medical Aid.—The Dudley Fund, Sick and Wounded Officers.—Y. and V. Equipment, Yeomanry and Volunteer Equipment.—Y. Hospital, Yeomanry Hospital; and a § in S. & S.F.A. column of Relief, that particulars of Relief in that Town or Borough are included in the Relief by the S. & S.F.A. at the head of the County.

Origin of Fund.	S. & S.F.A. Subscriptions Raised in County (a) including County Balances previous to the War. Grants from the Council (b).	Total Amount Received.	Expenditure in Relief, &c. By S. & S.F.A.	Expenditure in Relief, &c. By Independent Committee.	Remitted to other Funds.		Balance.	Number of Cases Relieved. Wives and Dependent Relatives.	Number of Cases Relieved. Children.	Number of Cases Relieved. Widows.	Number of Cases Relieved. Men.	Remarks.
	£ s. d.	£ s. d.	£ s. d.	£ s. d.		£ s. d.	£ s. d.					
YORKSHIRE (EAST RIDING)	(a) 6,789 5 7 (b) 4,962 10 6	11,751 16 1	10,702 14 9		...		1,049 1 4	820	1,081	—	—	
LORD LIEUTENANT'S FUND (LORD HERRIES).		*4,702 11 7			To M.H. (not earmarked) ...	59 4 6		...	...	...	...	*Includes £3,995 16s. 6d., an apportioned sum of £16,920 6s. 4d., a joint Yeomanry and Volunteer Equipment Fund raised in the 3 Ridings.
					" Patriotic Fund ...	270 7 7						
					" Red Cross Society ...	23 16 0						
					" Men's extra comforts ...	353 7 0						
					" Y. and V. Equipment ...	3,995 16 6						
						4,702 11 7		—	—	—	—	
Beverley ...		373 1 0	§		To M.H. No. 3 Lloyd's Patriotic.	2 0 0						
					" No. 4 S. & S.F.A. ...	290 0 0						
						292 0 0	81 1 0	—	—	—	—	
Bridlington		717 0 0	§		To M.H. (not earmarked) ...	478 0 0						
					" S. & S.F.A. (local)	154 0 0						
					" V. Reception ...	85 0 0						
						717 0 0		—	—	—	—	
Hedon ...		52 6 7	§		To M.H. (not earmarked) ...	51 3 7						
					" British Refugee Fund ...	1 3 0						
						52 6 7		—	—	—	—	
Hull ...		12,279 0 0	§	2,400 0 0	To M.H. No. 1 Patriotic Fund	3,553 0 0		441	877	—	—	
					" No. 2 Red Cross Society.	1,073 0 0						
					" No. 3 Lloyd's Patriotic.	1,758 0 0						
					" No. 4 S. & S.F.A. ...	3,437 0 0						
					" S. & S.F.A. (local)	53 0 0						
					" *Daily Mail* (London) ...	5 0 0						
						9,879 0 0						
YORKSHIRE (WEST RIDING).	(a) 59,545 2 4 (b) 1,232 10 0	60,777 12 4	55,969 13 10		To S. & S.F.A. (central) ...	(c) 5 0 0	4,802 18 6	4,824	5,340	—	—	(c) Officers' Branch.
LORD LIEUTENANT'S FUND (EARL OF SCARBROUGH).		*14,457 4 2			To M.H. No. 1. Patriotic Fund	291 2 2		...	...	...	...	* Includes £9,736 2s. 4d. an apportioned sum of £16,920 6s. 4d., a joint Yeomanry and Volunteer Equipment Fund raised in the 3 Ridings.
					" No. 2 Red Cross Society.	370 9 6						
					" No. 3 Lloyd's Patriotic.	84 7 4						
					" S. & S.F.A. (local) ...	2,025 2 10						
					" Y. Hospital ...	1,900 0 0						
					" S. & S.H.S. (local) ...	50 0 0						
					" Y. & V. Equipment ...	9,736 2 4						
						14,457 4 2		—	—	—	—	
Barnsley ...		6,379 10 1	§	4,128 4 4	To M.H. (not earmarked) ...	700 0 0		...	...	...	...	Number of cases not supplied.
					" Expenses ...	400 10 1						
						1,100 10 1	1,150 15 8	—	—	—	—	
Whitworth Collieries ...		1,140 12 11		951 10 10		...	189 2 1	...	...	...	...	Number of cases not supplied.
Batley ...		612 0 0	§	76 0 0	To M.H. (not earmarked) ...	200 0 0		45	—	—	—	
					" *Dewsbury Reporter* Fund	200 0 0						
					" Expenses ...	9 0 0						
						409 0 0	127 0 0					
* Bradford		15,527 4 5	§	10,063 8 6	To Expenses ...	458 15 11	5,000 0 0	445	620	22	24	

TRANSVAAL WAR FUNDS, 1899 TO 1901. COUNTIES—COUNTY BOROUGHS AND BOROUGHS. ENGLAND—cont.

Lord Mayors are distinguished by having L.M. after the name of the Borough; County Boroughs by having a * prefixed; and Towns, &c., which are not "County" Boroughs or Boroughs, by being printed in *italics*.—M.H. signifies The Mansion House Fund.—L.L. Fund, The Lord Lieutenant's Fund.—S. & S.F.A., The Soldiers' and Sailors' Families Association.—S. & S.H.S., The Soldiers' and Sailors' Help Society.—The Lansdowne Fund, Officers' Wives and Families.—The Abercorn Fund, Officers' Surgical and Medical Aid.—The Dudley Fund, Sick and Wounded Officers.—Y. and V. Equipment, Yeomanry and Volunteer Equipment.—Y. Hospital, Yeomanry Hospital; and a § in S. & S.F.A. column of Relief, that particulars of Relief in that Town or Borough are included in the Relief by the S. & S.F.A. at the head of the County.

Origin of Fund.	S. & S.F.A. Subscriptions Raised in County (a) including County Balances previous to the War, Grants from the Council (b).	Total Amount Received.	Expenditure in Relief, &c.		Remitted to other Funds.		Balance.	Number of Cases Relieved.				Remarks.
			By S. & S.F.A.	By Independent Committee.				Wives and Dependent Relatives.	Children.	Widows.	Men.	
	£ s. d.	£ s. d.	£ s. d.	£ s. d.		£ s. d.	£ s. d.					
YORKSHIRE (WEST RIDING)—cont.												
Daily Argus	...	1,222 12 0			To Mayor of Bradford	1,222 12 0	—	—	—	—	—	
Observer	...	633 12 0			To Mayor of Bradford	633 12 0	—	—	—	—	—	
Brighouse		711 0 0	§	543 0 0	To M.H. (not earmarked)	150 0 0	18 0 0	9	21	2	9	
Dewsbury		1,084 13 9	§		To M.H. No. 1 Patriotic Fund	200 0 0						
					,, ,, No. 2 Red Cross Society.	50 0 0						
					,, ,, No. 3 Lloyd's Patriotic.	150 0 0						
					,, S. & S.F.A. (local)	379 14 6						
						779 14 6	304 19 3	—	—	—	—	
Dewsbury Reporter	...	1,526 17 1		1,512 3 6	To Expenses	14 5 9		123	112			
					,, S. & S.F.A. (local)	0 7 10						
						14 13 7	—					
Doncaster		1,683 14 6	§	1,608 10 9	To Expenses	23 8 0	51 15 9	65	66	2	1	
* Halifax		6,571 0 0	§	5,313 0 0	To M.H. (not earmarked)	32 0 0		301	299	9	9	
					,, ,, No. 1 Patriotic Fund	250 0 0						
					,, ,, No. 2 Red Cross Society.	250 0 0						
					,, ,, No. 3 Lloyd's Patriotic.	250 0 0						
					,, ,, No. 4 S. & S.F.A.	250 0 0						
					,, Expenses	226 0 0						
						1,258 0 0	—					
Halifax Courier		3,062 0 0			To M.H. (not earmarked)	280 0 0						
					,, Mayor of Halifax	2,782 0 0						
						3,062 0 0	—					
Harrogate		3,507 0 0	§	1,497 13 6	To Red Cross Society	20 15 5		28	39	14	2	
					,, Lloyd's Patriotic	55 6 5						
					,, Knaresborough Committee.	220 0 0						
						296 1 10	1,713 4 8	—	—	—	—	
* Huddersfield		6,645 0 0	§	226 0 0	To M.H. (not earmarked)	856 0 0		7	10	...	7	
					,, S. & S.F.A. (local)	3,621 0 0						
					,, M.H. Refugees' Fund	28 0 0						
					,, Natal Fund	150 0 0						
					,, Pretoria Prisoners' Fund	10 0 0						
					,, V. Insurance and Expenses.	913 0 0						
						5,578 0 0	841 0 0	—	—	—	—	
Huddersfield Examiner		121 4 11		...	To Mayor of Huddersfield	121 4 11	—					
Keighley		4,607 0 0	...	3,825 0 0	To M.H. Refugees' Fund	250 0 0		181	165	...	4	
					,, Men's Extra Comforts	5 0 0						
					,, Y. Equipment	22 0 0						
					,, V. Insurance	207 0 0						
					,, British Refugees'	50 0 0						
					,, Mafeking Fund	50 0 0						
					,, Pretoria Prisoners' Fund	10 0 0						
					,, Expenses	23 0 0						
						617 0 0	165 0 0	—	—	—	—	

G

Lord Mayors are distinguished by having L.M. after the name of the Borough; County Boroughs by having a * prefixed; and Towns, &c., which are not "County" Boroughs or Boroughs, by being printed in *italics*.—M.H. signifies The Mansion House Fund.—L.L. Fund, The Lord Lieutenant's Fund.—S. & S.F.A., The Soldiers' and Sailors' Families Association.—S. & S.H.S., The Soldiers' and Sailors' Help Society.—The Lansdowne Fund, Officers' Wives and Families.—The Abercorn Fund, Officers' Surgical and Medical Aid.—The Dudley Fund, Sick and Wounded Officers.—Y. and V. Equipment, Yeomanry and Volunteer Equipment.—Y. Hospital, Yeomanry Hospital; and a § in S. & S.F.A. column of Relief, that particulars of Relief in that Town or Borough are included in the Relief by the S. & S.F.A. at the head of the County.

Origin of Fund.	S. & S.F.A. Subscriptions Raised in County (a) including County Balances previous to the War, Grants from the Council (b).	Total Amount Received.	Expenditure in Relief, &c.		Remitted to other Funds.		Balance.	Number of Cases Relieved.				Remarks.
			By S. & S.F.A.	By Independent Committee.				Wives and Dependent Relatives.	Children.	Widows.	Men.	
YORKSHIRE (WEST RIDING)—*cont.*	£ s. d.	£ s. d.	£ s. d.	£ s. d.		£ s. d.	£ s. d.					
*Leeds, L.M.	...	18,706 19 3	§	63 0 0	To S. & S.F.A. (local) ...	13,000 0 0						
					" The Patriotic Fund	93 0 1						
					" Red Cross Society ...	1,500 0 0						
					" Lloyd's Patriotic	89 9 8						
					" *Daily Mail*	38 0 0						
					" Refugees (Lord Milner)	3,590 0 0						
					" Expenses	304 0 9						
						18,614 10 6	29 8 9	—	—	—	—	
Morley	...	740 0 0	§	580 0 0	...		160 0 0	30	40	2	—	
Ossett	...	605 0 0	§	360 0 0	To V. Insurance ...	95 0 0	150 0 0	12	21	1	—	
Pontefract	...	169 17 6	§		To M H. No. 1 Patriotic Fund	169 17 6	—					
Pudsey ...	...	554 12 2	§	233 11 1	To L.L. Fund...	100 0 0		13	20	...	6	
					" Expenses	27 6 0						
						127 6 0	193 15 1	—	—	—	—	
Ripon	...	928 8 3	§	80 0 0	To M.H. (not earmarked) ...	500 0 0		20	30			
					" S. & S.F.A. (local)	59 6 6						
					" Men's Extra Comforts ...	111 7 3						
					" Expenses ...	37 0 9						
						707 14 6	140 13 9	—	—	—	—	
*Rotherham	...	4,121 0 0	§	3,406 0 0	To Men's Extra Comforts...	10 0 0		148	203	—	—	
					" Y. & V. Equipment	60 0 0						
					" Expenses ...	76 0 0						
						146 0 0	569 0 0	—	—	—	—	
*Sheffield, L.M. ...	...	23,670 0 0	§	23,420 0 0	To *Daily Telegraph* ...	250 0 0		1,022	1,174	—	—	
Sheffield Daily Telegraph	...	5,880 14 0			To Lord Mayor of Sheffield	5,880 14 0	—					
Todmorden	...	1,194 0 0	§	438 0 0	To Men's Extra Comforts...	20 0 0		28	40	—	—	
					" V. Insurance ...	37 0 0						
						57 0 0	699 0 0	—	—	—	—	
Wakefield	...	4,597 2 11	§	559 8 7	To S. & S.F.A. (local) ...	3,087 4 8		...	8	7	107	Lives of 103 men Insured.
					" Lansdowne Fund	52 11 6						
					" Expenses ...	44 0 6						
						3,183 16 8	853 17 8					
Altofts	...	125 8 7		52 2 9			73 5 10	3	5	—	—	
Normanton	...	226 13 10		188 13 0			38 0 10	12	20	—	—	
*York, L.M.	...	1,733 19 8	§		To M.H. No. 1 Patriotic Fund	776 7 8						
					" " No. 2 Red Cross Society.	79 7 0						
					" " No. 3 Lloyd's Patriotic.	74 16 1						
					" " No. 4 S. & S.F.A....	113 0 9						
					" Refugees' Fund ...	286 3 8						
					" Expenses	52 15 1						
						1,382 10 3	351 9 5	—	—	—	—	
Yorkshire Herald	...	1,645 0 0			To S. & S.F.A. (local) ...	1,645 0 0	—	—	—	—	—	

TRANSVAAL WAR FUNDS.
1899 TO 1901.
COUNTIES—COUNTY BOROUGHS AND BOROUGHS.
WALES.

County Boroughs are distinguished by having a * prefixed; and Towns, &c., which are not "County" Boroughs or Boroughs, by being printed in *italics*.—M.H. signifies The Mansion House Fund.—L.L. Fund, The Lord Lieutenant's Fund.—S. & S.F.A., The Soldiers' and Sailors' Families Association.—S. & S.H.S., The Soldiers' and Sailors' Help Society.—The Lansdowne Fund, Officers' Wives and Families.—The Abercorn Fund, Officers' Surgical and Medical Aid.—The Dudley Fund, Sick and Wounded Officers.—Y. and V. Equipment, Yeomanry and Volunteer Equipment.—Y. Hospital, Yeomanry Hospital; and a § in S. & S.F.A. column of Relief, that particulars of Relief in that Town or Borough are included in the Relief by the S. & S.F.A. at the head of the County.

Origin of Fund.	S. & S.F.A. Subscriptions Raised in County (a) including County Balances previous to the War. Grants from the Council (b).	Total Amount Received.	Expenditure in Relief, &c. By S. & S.F.A.	By Independent Committee.	Remitted to other Funds.	Balance.	Wives and Dependent Relatives.	Children.	Widows.	Men.	Remarks.
	£ s. d.	£ s. d.	£ s. d.	£ s. d.	£ s. d.	£ s. d.					
ANGLESEY—	(a) 65 6 6 (b) 100 0 0	165 6 6	124 16 2			40 10 4	20	32	—	—	
LORD LIEUTENANT'S FUND (SIR R. H. WILLIAMS BULKELEY, BT.).							...	...	...	...	No. L.L. Fund.
HIGH SHERIFF'S FUND		354 4 8			To Life Insurance ... 290 12 6 " Equipment 40 0 3 " Expenses ... 4 6 9 334 19 6	19 5 2	—	—	—	—	
Beaumaris		119 16 5	§	8 10 6	To M.H. (not earmarked) ... 88 0 0 " Y. Equipment ... 11 11 0 " Welsh Hospital ... 5 5 0 " Expenses ... 4 10 2 109 6 2	1 19 9	4	8	—	—	
BRECKNOCKSHIRE—	(a) 1,368 2 0 (b) 100 0 0	1,468 2 0	1,272 14 6		...	195 7 6	113	171	—	—	
LORD LIEUTENANT'S FUND (LORD GLANUSK.)		1,614 0 9			To S. & S.F.A. (local) 332 12 0	1,281 8 9	—	—	—	—	
CARDIGANSHIRE—	(a) 680 5 4 (b) 50 0 0	730 5 4	532 13 8		...	197 11 8	44	26	—	—	
LORD LIEUTENANT'S FUND (H. DAVIES-EVANS, ESQ.).		1,295 6 5			To M.H. (not earmarked) ... 511 7 9 " Patriotic Fund ... 7 6 0 " Red Cross Society 16 2 0 " Lloyd's Patriotic 18 14 6 " S. & S.F.A. (local) 370 9 0 " *Daily Telegraph* ... 127 19 0 " Welsh Hospital ... 225 15 0 " Men's extra comforts ... 17 13 2 1,295 6 5		—	—	—	—	
Aberystwith		500 0 0	§		To L.L. Fund... ... 500 0 0	—	—	—	—	—	
Cardigan...		278 0 11	§		To M.H. No. 1 Patriotic Fund 136 15 8 " " No. 2 Red Cross Society 68 7 9 " " No. 4 S. & S.F.A.... 68 7 9 " Expenses ... 4 9 9 278 0 11		—	—	—	—	
Lampeter		36 0 0	§		To L.L. Fund... ... 36 0 0		—	—	—	—	

TRANSVAAL WAR FUNDS, 1899 TO 1901. COUNTIES—COUNTY BOROUGHS AND BOROUGHS. WALES—cont.

County Boroughs are distinguished by having a * prefixed; and Towns, &c., which are not "County" Boroughs or Boroughs, by being printed in *italics*.—M.H. signifies The Mansion House Fund.—L.L. Fund, The Lord Lieutenant's Fund.—S. & S.F.A., The Soldiers' and Sailors' Families Association.—S. & S.H.S., The Soldiers' and Sailors' Help Society.—The Lansdowne Fund, Officers' Wives and Families.—The Abercorn Fund, Officers' Surgical and Medical Aid.—The Dudley Fund, Sick and Wounded Officers.—Y. and V. Equipment, Yeomanry and Volunteer Equipment.—Y. Hospital, Yeomanry Hospital; and a § in S. & S.F.A. column of Relief, that particulars of Relief in that Town or Borough are included in the Relief by the S. & S.F.A. at the head of the County.

Origin of Fund.	S. & S.F.A. Subscriptions Raised in County (a) including County Balances previous to the War. Grants from the Council (b).	Total Amount Received.	Expenditure in Relief, &c.		Remitted to other Funds.		Balance.	Number of Cases Relieved.				Remarks.
			By S. & S.F.A.	By Independent Committee.				Wives and Dependent Relatives.	Children.	Widows.	Men.	
	£ s. d.	£ s. d.	£ s. d.	£ s. d.		£ s. d.	£ s. d.					
CARMARTHENSHIRE—	(a) 2,601 15 0 (b) 50 0 0	2,651 15 0	1,078 14 0				1,573 1 0	57	37	—	—	
LORD LIEUTENANT'S FUND (SIR J. H. WILLIAMS-DRUMMOND, BT.).		1,322 5 10			To S. & S.F.A. (local) ... 1,322 5 10		—	—	—	—	—	
Carmarthen		670 10 10	§	8 0 0	To L.L. Fund... 642 10 10 „ Men's extra comforts 10 0 0 „ Mafeking Relief Fund 10 0 0 662 10 10			1	—	—	—	
Kidwelly		51 13 2	§		To L.L. Fund... 51 13 2		—	—	—	—	—	
Llandovery		356 6 5	§		To L.L. Fund... 356 6 5		—	—	—	—	—	
Llanelly		780 0 8	§		To S. & S.F.A. (local) ... 780 0 8		—	—	—	—	—	
CARNARVONSHIRE—	(a) 577 7 5 (b) 150 0 0	727 7 5	274 18 5				452 9 0	91	180	—	—	
LORD LIEUTENANT'S FUND (J. ERNEST GREAVES, ESQ.).		5,215 0 0		3,059 0 0	To Y. Hospital ... 10 0 0 „ Welsh Hospital ... 20 0 0 „ Men's extra comforts 10 0 0 „ Y. Equipment 450 0 0 „ Expenses ... 50 0 0 540 0 0		1,616 0 0	129	131	2	4	
Bangor		788 19 4	§		To L.L. Fund... 619 0 7 „ Mafeking Fund ... 164 13 9 „ Men's extra comforts 5 5 0 788 19 4		—	—	—	—	—	
Carnarvon		335 1 0	§		To L.L. Fund... 335 1 0		—	—	—	—	—	
Conway		296 1 9	§		To L.L. Fund... 279 5 6 „ V. Insurance 11 11 3 „ Expenses ... 5 5 0 296 1 9		—	—	—	—	—	
Pwllheli		89 0 0	§		To L.L. Fund... 89 0 0		—	—	—	—	—	
DENBIGHSHIRE.	(a) 1,131 11 3 (b) 235 9 11	1,367 1 2	1,091 15 1				275 6 1	188	223	—	—	
LORD LIEUTENANT'S FUND (COL. W. CORNWALLIS WEST.)		2,000 0 0			To Y. & V. Equipment ... 2,000 0 0		...	...			...	For Denbighshire, Carnarvonshire, and Flintshire Y. & V.
Denbigh		91 13 6	§	38 4 6	To S. & S.F.A. (local) 53 9 0		—	—	—	—	—	
Denbighshire Free Press		122 13 0			To M.H. (not earmarked) ... 76 4 6 „ S. & S.F.A. (London) ... 44 18 6 „ *Daily Mail* (London) ... 1 10 0 122 13 0		—	—	—	—	—	
Ruthin		297 0 0	§		To M.H. (not earmarked) ... 105 0 0 „ „ No. 1 Patriotic Fund 10 0 0 „ „ No. 3 Lloyd's Patriotic. 5 0 0 „ S. & S.F.A. (local) 150 0 0 „ Welsh Hospital ... 16 0 0 „ Expenses ... 11 0 0 297 0 0		—	—	—	—	—	

TRANSVAAL WAR FUNDS, 1899 TO 1901. COUNTIES—COUNTY BOROUGHS AND BOROUGHS. WALES—cont. 53

County Boroughs are distinguished by having a * prefixed; and Towns, &c., which are not "County" Boroughs or Boroughs, by being printed in *italics*.—M.H. signifies The Mansion House Fund.—L.L. Fund, The Lord Lieutenant's Fund.—S. & S.F.A., The Soldiers' and Sailors' Families Association.—S. & S.H.S., The Soldiers' and Sailors' Help Society.—The Lansdowne Fund, Officers' Wives and Families.—The Abercorn Fund, Officers' Surgical and Medical Aid.—The Dudley Fund, Sick and Wounded Officers.—Y. and V. Equipment, Yeomanry and Volunteer Equipment.—Y. Hospital, Yeomanry Hospital; and a § in S. & S.F.A. column of Relief, that particulars of Relief in that Town or Borough are included in the Relief by the S. & S.F.A. at the head of the County.

Origin of Fund.	S. & S.F.A. Subscriptions Raised in County (a) including County Balances previous to the War. Grants from the Council (b).	Total Amount Received.	Expenditure in Relief, &c.		Remitted to other Funds.		Balance.	Number of Cases Relieved.				Remarks.
			By S. & S.F.A.	By Independent Committee.				Wives and Dependent Relatives.	Children.	Widows.	Men.	
DENBIGHSHIRE—cont.	£ s. d.	£ s. d.	£ s. d.	£ s. d.		£ s. d.	£ s. d.					
Wrexham		4,940 1 6	§	4,319 14 2	To Expenses	180 0 0	440 7 4	260	367	2	2	
Llanrwst		117 0 0	§		To M.H. No 1 Patriotic Fund	52 0 0						
					„ „ No. 4 S. & S.F.A.	26 0 0						
					„ S. & S.F.A. (local)	39 0 0						
						117 0 0						
FLINTSHIRE.	(a) 1,740 15 11	2,140 15 11	1,844 11 2		...	...	296 4 9	155	163	—	—	
	(b) 400 0 0											
LORD LIEUTENANT'S FUND (Hugh R. Hughes, Esq.)					...	...	...	...	...	...		No L.L. Fund.
Flint		159 0 0	§	...	To M.H. No 1 Patriotic Fund	79 10 0						
					„ „ No. 4 S. & S.F.A.	79 10 0						
						159 0 0						
GLAMORGANSHIRE.	(a) 37,574 15 3	38,874 15 3	33,859 17 9		...	...	5,014 17 6	2,516	2,551	—	—	
	(b) 1,300 0 0											
LORD LIEUTENANT'S FUND (Lord Windsor.)		7,171 13 0			To Y. Equipment	7,171 13 0						
Aberavon		350 0 0	§		To S. & S.F.A. (local)	350 0 0						
*Cardiff		987 0 0	§		To Daily Mail	50 0 0						
					„ Welsh Hospital	500 0 0						
					„ Men's Extra Comforts	220 0 0						
					„ V. Equipment	140 0 0						
					„ Refugees' Fund	20 0 0						
					„ Mafeking Fund	57 0 0						
						987 0 0						
Cowbridge		297 7 8	§		To M.H. (not earmarked)	170 0 0						
					„ S. & S.F.A. (local)	100 0 0						
					„ Expenses	5 3 2						
						275 3 2	22 4 6	—	—	—	—	
Neath		1,811 0 0	§		To S. & S.F.A. (local)	1,300 0 0						
					„ Welsh Hospital	50 0 0						
					„ Men's Extra Comforts	12 0 0						
						1,362 0 0	449 0 0	—	—	—	—	
*Swansea		6,049 13 9	§		To S. & S.F.A. (local)	5,636 14 7						
					„ Welsh Hospital	100 0 0						
					„ Refugees' Fund	129 1 2						
					„ Mafeking Fund	14 18 0						
						5,880 13 9	169 0 0	—	—	—	—	
South Wales Daily Post		2,303 1 7			To Mayor of Swansea	2,303 1 7	—	—	—	—	—	
Barry Town Fund		500 0 0			To S. & S.F.A.	500 0 0	—	—	—	—	—	
Briton Ferry		350 0 0	...		To S. & S.F.A.	350 0 0	—	—	—	—	—	

TRANSVAAL WAR FUNDS, 1899 TO 1901. COUNTIES—COUNTY BOROUGHS AND BOROUGHS. WALES—cont.

County Boroughs are distinguished by having a * prefixed; and Towns, &c., which are not "County" Boroughs or Boroughs, by being printed in *italics*.—M.H. signifies The Mansion House Fund.—L.L. Fund, The Lord Lieutenant's Fund.—S. & S.F.A., The Soldiers' and Sailors' Families Association.—S. & S.H.S., The Soldiers' and Sailors' Help Society.—The Lansdowne Fund, Officers' Wives and Families.—The Abercorn Fund, Officers' Surgical and Medical Aid.—The Dudley Fund, Sick and Wounded Officers.—Y. and V. Equipment, Yeomanry and Volunteer Equipment.—Y. Hospital, Yeomanry Hospital; and a § in S. & S.F.A. column of Relief, that particulars of Relief in that Town or Borough are included in the Relief by the S. & S.F.A. at the head of the County.

Origin of Fund.	S. & S.F.A. Subscriptions Raised in County (a) including County Balances previous to the War. Grants from the Council (b).	Total Amount Received.	Expenditure in Relief, &c.		Remitted to other Funds.		Balance.	Number of Cases Relieved.				Remarks.
			By S. & S.F.A.	By Independent Committee.				Wives and Dependent Relatives.	Children.	Widows.	Men.	
	£ s. d.	£ s. d.	£ s. d.	£ s. d.		£ s. d.	£ s. d.					
MERIONETHSHIRE.	(a) 1,107 11 11 (b) 50 0 0	1,157 11 11	584 13 8		To S. & S.F.A. (central)	300 0 0	272 18 3	54	73	—	—	
Lord Lieutenant's Fund... (Wm. Maurice R. Wynne, Esq.)		1,113 0 0			To S. & S.F.A. (local) „ S. & S.F.A. (central) „ Welsh Hospital „ Sundries	500 0 0 100 0 0 20 0 0 10 0 0 630 0 0	483 0 0					
MONTGOMERYSHIRE.	(a) 259 13 4 (b) 50 0 0	309 13 4	126 7 9		...	...	183 5 7	27	8	—	—	
Lord Lieutenant's Fund... (Sir H. L. W. Williams-Wynn, Bart.).		2,863 0 0		583 0 0	To Y. Equipment „ Mayor of Welshpool	2,108 0 0 177 0 0 2,285 0 0	—	56	63	...	1	
Llanfyllin		50 0 0	§		To S. & S.F.A. (local) „ Men's Extra Comforts	35 0 0 15 0 0 50 0 0	—					
Llanidloes		101 0 0	§		To L.L. Fund „ M.H. (not earmarked) „ „ No. 4 S. & S.F.A. „ S. & S.F.A. (central)	15 0 0 58 0 0 8 0 0 20 0 0 101 0 0	—					
Montgomery		132 3 10	§	10 10 0	To M.H. No. 4 S. & S.F.A. „ Welsh Hospital „ M.H. Refugees' Fund „ Expenses	95 3 1 10 0 0 10 0 0 6 10 9 121 13 10	—	1				
Welshpool		474 0 0	§	474 0 0	...	...		31	45	—	—	
Newtown...		359 7 10		333 5 9	...	...	26 2 1	14	13	—	—	
PEMBROKESHIRE.	(a) 2,825 4 3 (b) 800 0 0	3,625 4 3	2,385 14 11		To S. & S.F.A. (central)	600 0 0	639 9 4	235	362	—	—	
Lord Lieutenant's Fund... (Earl Cawdor.)		1,177 0 0			To Y. & V. Equipment	1,177 0 0	—					
Haverfordwest... (Sir C. E. Gregg Philipps.)		383 0 0	§	76 0 0	...	...	307 0 0	5				
Pembroke		104 12 10	§		To S. & S.F.A. (local)	104 12 10	—	—	—	—	—	
Tenby			§		...			...			...	No Mayor's Fund.
RADNORSHIRE.	(a) 323 15 11 (b) 0 0 0	323 15 11	160 14 1		...		163 1 10	9	18	—	—	
Lord Lieutenant's Fund... (Sir Powlett Milbank, Bart.)		1,152 7 2			To M.H. No. 1 Patriotic Fund „ „ No. 2 Red Cross Society. „ „ No. 3 Lloyd's Patriotic. „ S. & S.F.A. (local) „ Expenses	326 10 8 219 3 3 294 6 9 311 13 2 0 13 4 1,152 7 2	—					
Elan Valley Army Relief Fund		267 0 11			To S. & S.F.A. (central) „ Expenses	266 16 2 0 4 9 267 0 11	—	—	—	—	—	

TRANSVAAL WAR FUNDS,
1899 TO 1901.
COUNTIES—ROYAL BURGHS AND BURGHS.
SCOTLAND.

Lord Provosts are distinguished by having L.P. after the name of their Burghs; Royal Burghs by having a * prefixed; and Towns, &c., which are not Royal Burghs or Burghs, by being printed in *italics*.—M.H. signifies The Mansion House Fund.—L.L. Fund, The Lord Lieutenant's Fund.— S. & S.F.A., The Soldiers' and Sailors' Families Association.—S. & S.H.S., The Soldiers' and Sailors' Help Society.—The Lansdowne Fund, Officers' Wives and Families.—The Abercorn Fund, Officers' Surgical and Medical Aid.—The Dudley Fund, Sick and Wounded Officers.—Y. and V. Equipment, Yeomanry and Volunteer Equipment.—Y. Hospital, Yeomanry Hospital; and a § in S. & S.F.A. column of Relief, that particulars of Relief in that Town or Burgh are included in the Relief by the S. & S.F.A. at the head of the County.

THE SOLDIERS' AND SAILORS' FAMILIES ASSOCIATION.
EAST SCOTTISH BRANCH (EDINBURGH).
Treasurer's Account, 1899 to 1901.

RECEIPTS.	£ s. d.	PAYMENTS.	£ s. d.
To Balance, 1st January, 1899	938 0 8	By Cases relieved direct	178 11 8
„ Received from Contributions	9,711 1 4	„ Expenses, etc.	1,160 13 11
„ „ „ Divisions	33,975 9 9	„ Grants to Divisions	42,271 14 1
„ „ „ London Council	1,164 5 0	„ Balance, 31st December, 1901	2,485 17 4
„ „ „ Interest	308 0 3		
	46,096 17 0		46,096 17 0

WEST SCOTTISH BRANCH (GLASGOW).
Treasurer's Account, 1899 to 1901.

RECEIPTS.	£ s. d.	PAYMENTS.	£ s. d.
To Balance, 1st January, 1899	972 9 3	By Cases relieved direct	0 0 0
„ Received from Contributions	6,422 17 4	„ Expenses	465 10 7
„ „ „ Divisions	1,489 14 11	„ Grants to Divisions	1,100 0 0
„ „ „ London Council	1,113 5 0	„ Investments	797 12 11
„ „ „ Interest	316 16 11	„ Balance, 31st December, 1901	7,951 19 11
	10,315 3 5		10,315 3 5

Origin of Fund.	S. & S.F.A. Subscriptions Raised in County (a) including County Balances previous to the War. Grants from the Council (b).	Total Amount Received.	Expenditure in Relief, &c. By S. & S.F.A.	Expenditure in Relief, &c. By Independent Committee.	Remitted to other Funds.	Balance.	Wives and Dependent Relatives.	Children.	Widows.	Men.	Remarks.
ABERDEENSHIRE. (East Scotland.)	(a) 5,365 15 9 (b) 80 0 0	5,445 15 9	4,162 17 11		To Head Office, Edinburgh 1,040 16 6	242 1 4	432	460	—	—	
The Lord Provost of Aberdeen.		2,280 0 6			To M.H. (not earmarked) ... 2,041 12 9						
					„ „ Refugees' Fund ... 231 17 0						
					„ Expenses ... 6 10 9						
					2,280 0 6	—					
*Aberdeen		... ...	§		... ...	... ...	...	...	...	...	Lord Provost's Fund.
*Inverurie		148 10 1	§		To S. & S.F.A. (local) ... 82 1 3						
					„ Scottish Hospital & Bed 66 8 10						
					148 10 1	—					
*Kintore		...	§		... ...	... ...	...	...	...	...	No Provost's Fund.
Peterhead		281 0 0	§		To M.H. (not earmarked) ... 175 0 0						
					„ „ Refugees' Fund ... 25 0 0						
					„ S. & S.F.A. (local) ... 81 0 0						
					281 0 0	—					
Aberdeen Journal		4,986 1 10		12 13 11	To S. & S.F.A. (local) ... 3,969 16 2						
					„ *Daily Mail* (London) ... 1,000 0 0						
					„ Expenses ... 3 11 9						
					4,973 7 11	—	—	—	—	—	

TRANSVAAL WAR FUNDS, 1899 TO 1901. COUNTIES—ROYAL BURGHS AND BURGHS. SCOTLAND—cont.

Lord Provosts are distinguished by having L.P. after the name of their Burghs; Royal Burghs by having a * prefixed; and Towns, &c., which are not Royal Burghs or Burghs, by being printed in *italics*.—M.H. signifies The Mansion House Fund.—L.L. Fund, The Lord Lieutenant's Fund.—S. & S.F.A., The Soldiers' and Sailors' Families Association.—S. & S.H.S., The Soldiers' and Sailors' Help Society.—The Lansdowne Fund, Officers' Wives and Families.—The Abercorn Fund, Officers' Surgical and Medical Aid.—The Dudley Fund, Sick and Wounded Officers.—Y. and V. Equipment, Yeomanry and Volunteer Equipment.—Y. Hospital, Yeomanry Hospital; and a § in S. & S.F.A. column of Relief, that particulars of Relief in that Town or Burgh are included in the Relief by the S. & S.F.A. at the head of the County.

Origin of Fund.	S. & S.F.A. Subscriptions Raised in County (a) including County Balances previous to the War. Grants from the Council (b).	Total Amount Received.	Expenditure in Relief, &c.		Remitted to other Funds.		Balance.	Number of Cases Relieved.				Remarks.
			By S. & S.F.A.	By Independent Committee.				Wives and Dependent Relatives.	Children.	Widows.	Men.	
	£ s. d.	£ s. d.	£ s. d.	£ s. d.		£ s. d.	£ s. d.					
ARGYLLSHIRE. (West Scotland.)	(a) 2,065 0 11 (b) 0 0 0	2,065 0 11	633 9 10				1,431 11 1	339	505	—	—	
Lord Lieutenant's Fund... (The Duke of Argyll.)		... ...			... ...			...	...	...	...	No L.L. Fund.
*Campbeltown		1,159 0 0	§		To S. & S.F.A. (local)	479 0 0						
					„ The Lansdowne Fund	50 0 0						
					„ *The Daily Telegraph*	75 0 0						
					„ Red Cross Society	130 0 0						
					„ Lloyd's Patriotic	130 0 0						
					„ Scottish Hospital	177 0 0						
					„ Men's extra comforts	89 0 0						
						1,130 0 0	29 0 0	—	—	—	—	
*Inveraray		36 13 0	§		To S. & S.F.A. (local)	18 6 6						
					„ S. & S.H.S. (local)	18 6 6						
						36 13 0	—					
Oban		80 13 5	§		To S. & S.F.A. (local)	50 12 11						
					„ Argyll & S. Highlanders	30 0 6						
						80 13 5	—					
Oban Times		429 18 0	394 18 1		...	...	34 19 11	33	...	58	—	
AYRSHIRE. (West Scotland.)	(a) 12,320 9 1 (b) 0 0 0	12,320 9 1	8,814 11 6		...		3,505 17 7	872	1,288	—	—	
Lord Lieutenant's Fund... (Earl of Eglinton.)		8,708 0 0		329 0 0	To S. & S.F.A. (local)	5,228 0 0	3,151 0 0	11	38	10	2	
		2,829 13 2			To Y. & V. Equipment	2,161 11 3	668 1 11	—	—	—	—	
		3,344 0 0			To Scottish Hospital	3,344 0 0	—					
		3,119 14 2			To Y. Hospital	3,119 14 2	—					
*Ayr		...	§		... ...			...			...	No Provost's Fund.
*Irvine		200 0 0	§		To Scottish National Hospital	200 0 0	—					
Irvine Herald		78 12 0		1 10 0	To Dundonald Home	25 0 0					3	
					„ Expenses	8 17 6						
						33 17 6	43 4 6	—	—	—		
Kilmarnock		2,063 5 5	§		To S. & S.F.A. (local)	2,063 5 5	—					
Troon		404 18 6		...	To L.L. Fund	331 11 0						
					„ Scottish National Hospital	73 7 6						
						404 18 6						
BANFFSHIRE (East Scotland).	(a) 867 13 9 (b) 251 0 0	1,118 13 9	686 4 6		To Head Office, Edinburgh	422 13 9	9 15 6	57	32	—	—	
Lord Lieutenant's Fund... (Duke of Richmond.)		1,799 14 0			To M.H. (not earmarked)	574 8 3						
					„ S. & S.F.A. (local)	400 15 9						
					„ Red Cross Society	155 15 9						
					„ Scottish Hospital	(c) 383 10 7		...	...	...	...	(c) Raised by Lady Caroline Gordon Lennox.
					„ Lloyd's Patriotic	133 15 8						
					„ V. Equipment	151 8 0						
						1,799 14 0	—	—	—	—		

TRANSVAAL WAR FUNDS, 1899 TO 1901. COUNTIES—ROYAL BURGHS AND BURGHS. **SCOTLAND**—*cont.*

Lord Provosts are distinguished by having L.P. after the name of their Burghs; Royal Burghs by having a * prefixed; and Towns, &c., which are not Royal Burghs or Burghs, by being printed in *italics*.—M.H. signifies The Mansion House Fund.—L.L. Fund, The Lord Lieutenant's Fund.—S. & S.F.A., The Soldiers' and Sailors' Families Association.—S. & S.H.S., The Soldiers' and Sailors' Help Society.—The Lansdowne Fund, Officers' Wives and Families.—The Abercorn Fund, Officers' Surgical and Medical Aid.—The Dudley Fund, Sick and Wounded Officers.—Y. and V. Equipment, Yeomanry and Volunteer Equipment.—Y. Hospital, Yeomanry Hospital; and a § in S. & S.F.A. column of Relief, that particulars of Relief in that Town or Burgh are included in the Relief by the S. & S.F.A. at the head of the County.

Origin of Fund.	S. & S.F.A. Subscriptions Raised in County (a) including County Balances previous to the War. Grants from the Council (b).	Total Amount Received.	Expenditure in Relief, &c. By S. & S.F.A.	Expenditure in Relief, &c. By Independent Committee.	Remitted to other Funds.		Balance.	Wives and Dependent Relatives.	Children.	Widows.	Men.	Remarks.
BANFFSHIRE (East Scotland) —*cont.*	£ s. d.	£ s. d.	£ s. d.	£ s. d.		£ s. d.	£ s. d.					
*Banff		186 15 6	§		To M.H. No. 1 Patriotic Fund	130 10 6						
					,, ,, No. 2 Red Cross Society.	21 14 6						
					,, ,, No. 3 Lloyd's Patriotic.	12 16 6						
					,, ,, No. 4 S. & S.F.A.	21 14 0						
						186 15 6	—	—	—	—	—	
*Cullen		26 17 7	§		To L.L. Fund	2 14 3						
					,, M.H. No. 4 S. & S.F.A.	24 3 4						
						26 17 7	—	—	—	—	—	
Buckie		79 18 1		56 16 10	To M.H. Refugees' Fund	21 0 6	2 0 9	2	...	1	1	
Gardenstown		20 18 3			To L.L. Fund	20 18 3	—					
Keith		249 13 2			To M.H. No. 1 Patriotic Fund	56 6 8						
					,, ,, No. 2 Red Cross Society.	12 18 6						
					,, ,, No. 3 Lloyd's Patriotic.	17 5 9						
					,, S. & S.F.A. (local)	105 5 7						
					,, S. & S.H.S. (local)	10 0 0						
					,, Scottish Hospital	27 13 2						
						229 9 8	20 3 6	—	—	—	—	
BERWICKSHIRE (East Scotland).	(a) 1,780 3 0 (b) 360 0 0	2,140 3 0	1,157 18 7		To Head Office, Edinburgh	979 13 2	2 11 3	—	—	—	—	
LORD LIEUTENANT'S FUND (LORD BINNING.)		75 0 0			To Y. Equipment	(c) 75 0 0		...	...	...	...	(c) To L.L. Haddingtonshire.
*Lauder		79 16 11	§		To S. & S.F.A. (local)	60 7 2						
					,, *Scotsman*	13 1 9						
					,, Men's extra comforts	6 8 0						
						79 16 11	—					
BUTESHIRE (West Scotland).	(a) 204 7 6 (b) 0 0 0	204 7 6	129 14 4		To Head Office, Glasgow	6 0 0	68 13 2	13	10	—	—	
LORD LIEUTENANT'S FUND (RT. HON. A. G. MURRAY.)					...	...		...	...	...	...	No L.L. Fund.
*Rothesay		720 9 9	§	370 6 3	To S. & S.F.A. (local)	100 0 0		22	10	—	—	
					,, *Daily Telegraph*	90 0 0						
					,, Scottish Hospital	100 0 0						
					,, S. & S.H.S. (London)	24 0 0						
						314 0 0	36 3 6					
Rothesay Express		113 5 0			To Provost of Rothesay	113 5 0	—					
CAITHNESS (East Scotland).	(a) 1,099 3 8 (b) 88 0 0	1,187 3 8	322 5 8		To Head Office, Edinburgh	862 7 10	2 10 2	25	28	—	—	
LORD LIEUTENANT'S FUND (DUKE OF PORTLAND.)					...	...		...	...	...	...	No L.L. Fund.
*Wick		255 5 7			To S. & S.F.A. (local)	205 5 7						
					,, Scottish Hospital	50 0 0						
						255 5 7	—					

TRANSVAAL WAR FUNDS, 1899 TO 1901. COUNTIES—ROYAL BURGHS AND BURGHS. **SCOTLAND**—cont.

Lord Provosts are distinguished by having L.P. after the name of their Burghs; Royal Burghs by having a * prefixed; and Towns, &c., which are not Royal Burghs or Burghs, by being printed in *italics*.—M.H. signifies The Mansion House Fund.—L.L. Fund, The Lord Lieutenant's Fund.—S. & S.F.A., The Soldiers' and Sailors' Families Association.—S. & S.H.S., The Soldiers' and Sailors' Help Society.—The Lansdowne Fund, Officers' Wives and Families.—The Abercorn Fund, Officers' Surgical and Medical Aid.—The Dudley Fund, Sick and Wounded Officers.—Y. and V. Equipment, Yeomanry and Volunteer Equipment.—Y. Hospital, Yeomanry Hospital; and a § in S. & S.F.A. column of Relief, that particulars of Relief in that Town or Burgh are included in the Relief by the S. & S.F.A. at the head of the County.

Origin of Fund.	S. & S.F.A. Subscriptions Raised in County (a) including County Balances previous to the War. Grants from the Council (b).	Total Amount Received.	Expenditure in Relief, &c. By S. & S.F.A.	By Independent Committee.	Remitted to other Funds.		Balance.	Wives and Dependent Relatives.	Children.	Widows.	Men.	Remarks.
	£ s. d.	£ s. d.	£ s. d.	£ s. d.		£ s. d.	£ s. d.					
CLACKMANNAN (East Scotland).	(a) 1,330 2 7 (b) 226 0 0	1,556 2 7	1,073 5 4		To Head Office, Edinburgh	477 17 2	5 0 1	65	72	—	—	
Lord Lieutenant's Fund... (Earl of Mar and Kellie.)		2,045 6 3			To S. & S.F.A. (local)	1,212 14 3						
					„ Scottish Hospital	300 0 0						
					„ V. Equipment	532 12 0						
						2,045 6 3	—	—	—	—	—	
DUMBARTONSHIRE (West Scotland.)	(a) 5,410 9 4 (b) 0 0 0	5,410 9 4	3,591 18 6		...	...	1,818 10 10	265	302	—	—	
Lord Lieutenant's Fund... (Sir James Colquhoun, Bt.)					...		...	...	...	...	...	No L.L. Fund.
*Dumbarton		2,739 0 0	§	1,144 0 0	...		1,595 0 0	58	56	—	—	
Helensburgh		1,513 13 11	§	10 0 0	To S. & S.F.A. (local)	1,000 0 0		...	...	1	...	
					„ Princess Christian Hospital	45 0 0						
					„ Scottish Hospital	300 0 0						
						1,345 0 0	158 13 11					
DUMFRIESSHIRE (West Scotland).	(a) 3,123 1 6 (b) 0 0 0	3,123 1 6	2,312 7 9		...		810 13 9	223	333	—	—	
Lord Lieutenant's Fund... (Duke of Buccleuch.)					...		...	...	...	...	...	No L.L. Fund.
*Annan		226 0 0	§		To S. & S.F.A. (local)	226 0 0	—	—	—	—	—	
*Dumfries		2,899 0 0	§	90 0 0	To M.H. No. 1 Patriotic Fund	261 0 0		...	19	2	1	
					„ No. 3 Lloyd's Patriotic.	237 0 0						
					„ S. & S.F.A. (local)	1,524 0 0						
					„ *Scotsman* Fund	250 0 0						
					„ M.H. Refugees' Fund	16 0 0						
						2,288 0 0	521 0 0	—	—	—	—	
*Lochmaben		28 9 0	§		To S. & S.F.A. (local)	28 9 0	—	—	—	—	—	
*Sanquhar		303 9 6	§		To S. & S.F.A. (local)	303 9 6	—	—	—	—	—	
Moffat		522 0 0	§		To M.H. (not earmarked)	6 0 0						
					„ No. 1 Patriotic Fund	261 0 0						
					„ No. 2 Red Cross Society.	79 0 0						
					„ No. 3 Lloyd's Patriotic.	43 0 0						
					„ No. 4 S. & S.F.A.	98 0 0						
					„ *Scotsman* Fund	35 0 0						
						522 0 0	—					
EDINBURGH (East Scotland.)	(a) 6,198 8 9 (b) 13,232 4 11	19,430 13 8	17,548 18 1		To Head Office, Edinburgh	1,701 11 7	180 4 0	1,764	2,188	—	—	
Lord Lieutenant's Fund... (The Earl of Rosebery.)		...			...		...	...	...	...	...	No L.L. Fund.
Edinburgh L.P.		53,775 7 4	§		To the Patriotic Fund	14,000 0 0						
					„ S. & S.F.A. (local)	14,192 6 11						
					„ Compassionate Fund	150 0 0						
					„ S. & S.H.S.	148 16 0						
					„ Refugees' Fund, Lord Milner.	5,655 19 0						
					„ *Scotsman* Fund	2,000 0 0						
					„ Volunteers' Insurance	(c) 31 10 0		...	...	...	...	(c) 10 Volunteers.
					„ Scottish Hospital	13,249 9 7						
					„ Expenses	1,488 0 2						
						50,916 1 8	2,859 5 8	—	—	—	—	

TRANSVAAL WAR FUNDS, 1899 TO 1901. COUNTIES—ROYAL BURGHS AND BURGHS. **SCOTLAND**—*cont.*

Lord Provosts are distinguished by having L.P. after the name of their Burghs; Royal Burghs by having a * prefixed; and Towns, &c., which are not Royal Burghs or Burghs, by being printed in *italics*.—M.H. signifies The Mansion House Fund.—L.L. Fund, The Lord Lieutenant's Fund.—S. & S.F.A., The Soldiers' and Sailors' Families Association.—S. & S.H.S., The Soldiers' and Sailors' Help Society.—The Lansdowne Fund, Officers' Wives and Families.—The Abercorn Fund, Officers' Surgical and Medical Aid.—The Dudley Fund, Sick and Wounded Officers.—Y. and V. Equipment, Yeomanry and Volunteer Equipment.—Y. Hospital, Yeomanry Hospital; and a § in S. & S.F.A. column of Relief, that particulars of Relief in that Town or Burgh are included in the Relief by the S. & S.F.A. at the head of the County.

Origin of Fund.	S. & S.F.A. Subscriptions Raised in County (a) including County Balances previous to the War. Grants from the Council (b).	Total Amount Received.	Expenditure in Relief, &c. By S. & S.F.A.	Expenditure in Relief, &c. By Independent Committee.	Remitted to other Funds.		Balance.	Wives and Dependent Relatives.	Children.	Widows.	Men.	Remarks.
	£ s. d.	£ s. d.	£ s. d.	£ s. d.		£ s. d.	£ s. d.					
EDINBURGH (East Scotland)—*cont.*		189 5 0	...	...	To V. Equipment	189 5 0	—	—	—	—	—	
Leith	...	...	§	...	...	...	...	...	...	...	...	No Provost's Fund.
Musselburgh	...	...	§	...	...	...	...	...	...	...	...	No Provost's Fund.
The Scotsman Shilling Fund		54,683 18 6		8,783 11 8	To *Daily Telegraph* (London)	45,699 18 0	200 8 10	—	54	31	—	
ELGINSHIRE. (East Scotland.)	(a) 952 11 1 (b) 0 0 0	952 11 1	522 18 11		To Head Office, Edinburgh	109 18 6	319 13 8	56	30	—	—	
LORD LIEUTENANT'S FUND (DUKE OF FIFE.)		...	...	...	...	...	...	...	...	...	...	No L.L. Fund.
*Elgin		551 0 0	§	464 0 0	...	...	87 0 0	46	42	2	2	
*Forres		200 0 0	§		To S. & S.F.A. (local)	125 0 0						
					„ *The Scotsman* Fund	35 0 0						
						160 0 0	40 0 0	—	—	—	—	
Lossiemouth	...	92 0 0		60 0 0	...	...	32 0 0	5	12	—	—	
FIFESHIRE. (East Scotland.)	(a) 5,754 6 6 (b) 1,429 0 0	7,183 6 6	3,797 19 1		To Head Office, Edinburgh	3,379 19 3	5 8 2	315	393	—	—	
LORD LIEUTENANT'S FUND (EARL OF ELGIN.)		6,603 10 6			To S. & S.F.A. (local)	1,750 0 0						
					„ *The Scotsman* Fund	253 12 6						
					„ Y. Equipment	2,800 8 6						
					„ Y. Hospital	847 13 1						
					„ Expenses	8 19 7						
						5,660 13 8	942 16 10	—	—	—	—	
*Anstruther Easter	...		§		...	...	...	...	...	...	...	No Provost's Fund.
*Anstruther Wester	...	...	§		...	...	...	...	...	...	...	No Provost's Fund.
*Burntisland		48 4 4	§		To *The Scotsman* Fund	48 4 4	—	—	—	—	—	
*Crail	...	125 14 6	§		To M.H. (not earmarked)	65 9 6						
					„ *The Scotsman* Fund	7 17 0						
					„ *The Daily Mail* (London)	2 8 0						
					„ Yeomanry Hospital	50 0 0						
						125 14 6	—	—	—	—	—	
*Culross	...	...	§	...	...	...	...	...	...	...	...	No Provost's Fund.
*Cupar-Fife		341 1 9	§	37 7 8	To *Scotsman* Fund	145 0 0		5	—	—	—	
					„ S. & S.F.A. (local)	60 0 0						
					„ Scottish Red Cross	50 0 0						
						255 0 0	48 14 1	—	—	—	—	
*Dunfermline		1,852 0 0	§		To M.H. No. 1 Patriotic Fund	507 0 0						
					„ „ No. 4 S. & S.F.A.	1,150 0 0						
					„ S. & S.F.A. (local)	165 0 0						
					„ Expenses	30 0 0						
						1,852 0 0	—	—	—	—	—	
Dunfermline Journal		15 10 0			To Provost Fund	5 0 0						
					„ S. & S.F.A. (local)	5 5 0						
					„ S. & S.H.S. (local)	5 5 0						
						15 10 0	—	—	—	—	—	
*Dysart		88 5 9	§		To *Scotsman* Fund	86 5 9						
					„ Expenses	2 0 0						
						88 5 9	—	—	—	—	—	

TRANSVAAL WAR FUNDS, 1899 TO 1901. COUNTIES—ROYAL BURGHS AND BURGHS. SCOTLAND—cont.

Lord Provosts are distinguished by having L.P. after the name of their Burghs; Royal Burghs by having a * prefixed; and Towns, &c., which are not Royal Burghs or Burghs, by being printed in *italics*.—M.H. signifies The Mansion House Fund.—L.L. Fund, The Lord Lieutenant's Fund.—S. & S.F.A., The Soldiers' and Sailors' Families Association.—S. & S.H.S., The Soldiers' and Sailors' Help Society.—The Lansdowne Fund, Officers' Wives and Families.—The Abercorn Fund, Officers' Surgical and Medical Aid.—The Dudley Fund, Sick and Wounded Officers.—Y. and V. Equipment, Yeomanry and Volunteer Equipment.—Y. Hospital, Yeomanry Hospital; and a § in S. & S.F.A. column of Relief, that particulars of Relief in that Town or Burgh are included in the Relief by the S. & S.F.A. at the head of the County.

Origin of Fund.	S. & S.F.A. Subscriptions Raised in County (a) including County Balances previous to the War. Grants from the Council (b).	Total Amount Received.	Expenditure in Relief, &c. By S. & S.F.A.	Expenditure in Relief, &c. By Independent Committee.	Remitted to other Funds.		Balance.	Wives and Dependent Relatives.	Children.	Widows.	Men.	Remarks.
	£ s. d.	£ s. d.	£ s. d.	£ s. d.		£ s. d.	£ s. d.					
FIFESHIRE (East Scotland)—*cont.*												
*Inverkeithing	...	148 1 9	§		To M.H. (not earmarked)	148 1 9	—	—	—	—	—	
*Kilrenny	...	...	§			...		...	...	...	...	No Provost's Fund.
*Kinghorn	...	66 9 11	§		To *Scotsman* Fund	66 9 11						
*Kirkcaldy	...	2,568 0 0	§	20 0 0	To S. & S.F.A. (local)	925 0 0		...	...	...	...	Number of cases not supplied.
					,, *Scotsman* Fund	1,254 0 0						
					,, Scottish Red Cross	50 0 0						
					,, Black Watch Fund	8 0 0						
					,, M.H. Refugees' Fund	200 0 0						
					,, Expenses	7 0 0						
						2,444 0 0	104 0 0	—	—	—	—	
*Pittenween	...	35 0 0	§		To *Scotsman* Fund	35 0 0	—					
*St. Andrews	...	966 19 10	§		To S. & S.F.A. (local)	550 0 0						
					,, *Scotsman* Fund	250 0 1						
					,, S & S.H.S. (local)	25 0 1						
					,, Christmas Gifts	25 5 1						
					,, Expenses	1 9 8						
						851 14 11	115 4 11	—	—	—	—	
FORFARSHIRE (East Scotland.)	(a) 6,556 5 2 (b) 6,235 5 11	12,791 11 1	12,062 6 8		To Head Office, Edinburgh	520 15 8	208 8 9	1,146	450	—	—	
LORD LIEUTENANT'S FUND (EARL OF STRATHMORE.)		2,154 0 0			To Scottish Hospital	496 0 0						
					,, Y. & V. Equipment	1,383 0 0						
						1,879 0 0	275 0 0	—	—	—	—	
*Arbroath	...	752 0 0		573 0 0	...		179 0 0	55				
*Brechin	...	309 3 9	§		To Men's extra comforts	304 10 0						
					,, Expenses	4 13 9						
						309 3 9	—					
*Dundee	...	2,625 0 1			To M.H. Refugees' Fund	54 9 11						
					,, S. & S.F.A. (local)	1,773 10 0						
					,, *Scotsman* Fund	750 0 0						
					,, Expenses	47 0 2						
						2,625 0 1	—					
People's Journal Fund	...	1,058 0 0		948 0 0	...		110 0 0	193	—	—	—	
*Forfar	...	570 6 6	§		To S. & S.F.A. (local)	377 12 10						
					,, Men's extra comforts	149 15 6						
						527 8 4	42 18 2	—	—	—	—	
*Montrose	...	500 2 8	§	57 12 0	To S. & S.F.A. (local)	100 0 0						
					,, *Daily Telegraph*	250 0 0						
					,, Black Watch Fund	25 0 0						
					,, Gordon Highlanders	25 0 0						
					,, Expenses	9 14 6						
						409 14 6	32 16 2	—	—	—	—	
Montrose Standard	...	211 6 10			To Provost of Montrose	211 6 10	—					

TRANSVAAL WAR FUNDS, 1899 TO 1901. COUNTIES—ROYAL BURGHS AND BURGHS. **SCOTLAND**—*cont.*

Lord Provosts are distinguished by having L.P. after the name of their Burghs; Royal Burghs by having a * prefixed; and Towns, &c., which are not Royal Burghs or Burghs, by being printed in *italics*.—M.H. signifies The Mansion House Fund.—L.L. Fund, The Lord Lieutenant's Fund.—S. & S.F.A., The Soldiers' and Sailors' Families Association.—S. & S.H.S., The Soldiers' and Sailors' Help Society.—The Lansdowne Fund, Officers' Wives and Families.—The Abercorn Fund, Officers' Surgical and Medical Aid.—The Dudley Fund, Sick and Wounded Officers.—Y. and V. Equipment, Yeomanry and Volunteer Equipment.—Y. Hospital, Yeomanry Hospital; and a § in S. & S.F.A. column of Relief, that particulars of Relief in that Town or Burgh are included in the Relief by the S. & S.F.A. at the head of the County.

Origin of Fund.	S. & S.F.A. Subscriptions Raised in County (a) including County Balances previous to the War. Grants from the Council (b).	Total Amount Received.	Expenditure in Relief, &c. By S. & S.F.A.	By Independent Committee.	Remitted to other Funds.		Balance.	Wives and Dependent Relatives.	Children.	Widows.	Men.	Remarks.
	£ s. d.	£ s. d.	£ s. d.	£ s. d.		£ s. d.	£ s. d.					
HADDINGTONSHIRE (East Scotland.)	(a) 551 18 2 (b) 223 0 0	774 18 2	601 6 8	...	To Head Office, Edinburgh	165 7 1	8 4 5	43	55	—	—	
LORD LIEUTENANT'S FUND ... (EARL OF HADDINGTON.)		... ...	...	...	...	...	...	...	...	...	...	No L.L. Fund.
*Dunbar		94 0 0	§		To S. & S.F.A. (local)	94 0 0	—	—	—	—	—	
*Haddington		414 0 0	§		To *Scotsman* Fund	414 0 0	—	—	—	—	—	
*North Berwick... ...		259 0 0	§		To Patriotic Fund ...	178 0 0	—	—	—	—	—	
					„ *The Scotsman* ...	54 0 0						
					„ Y. Hospital ...	14 0 0						
					„ Scottish Hospital ...	13 0 0						
						259 0 0						
INVERNESS-SHIRE (East Scotland.)	(a) 2,224 9 2 (b) 1,503 7 11	3,727 17 1	3,364 7 4	...	To Head Office, Edinburgh	354 14 2	8 15 7	524	563	—	—	
LORD LIEUTENANT'S FUND ... (DONALD CAMERON OF LOCHIEL.)		... ...	...	...	...	...	...	...	...	...	...	No L.L. Fund.
*Inverness		1,105 13 6	§		To M.H. (not earmarked)...	503 13 6	—	—	—	—	—	
					„ „ Refugees' Fund...	80 0 0						
					„ „ Men's extra comforts ...	522 0 0						
						1,105 13 6						
Grantown-on-Spey ...		105 1 11	...	...	To S. & S.F.A. (local)	48 16 0	—	—	—	—	—	
					„ *Scotsman*	35 0 0						
					„ V. Insurance	21 5 11						
						105 1 11						
Lochmaddy		66 9 8			To M.H. No. 1 Patriotic Fund	36 9 8	—	—	—	—	—	
					„ Lovat's Scouts ...	30 0 0						
						66 9 8						
KINCARDINESHIRE (East Scotland.)	(a) 1,217 11 7 (b) 0 0 0	1,217 11 7	166 16 3	...	To Head Office, Edinburgh	934 17 6	115 17 10	15	15	—	—	
LORD LIEUTENANT'S FUND ... (SIR A. BAIRD OF URIE BART.)		265 0 0			To Scottish Hospital	213 0 0	—	—	—	—	—	
					„ St. Andrew's Ambulance	52 0 0						
						265 0 0						
*Bervie		54 4 2	§		To *The Scotsman* Fund ...	54 4 2	—	—	—	—	—	
KINROSS.	(a) 0 0 0 (b) 0 0 0	...	...	...	...	...	...	...	...	...	...	*See* Clackmannan.
LORD LIEUTENANT'S FUND ... (LORD MONCREIFF.)		250 0 0	...	...	To Imperial War Fund ...	200 0 0	—	—	—	—	—	
					„ Scottish Hospital ...	50 0 0						
						250 0 0						
KIRKCUDBRIGHTSHIRE (West Scotland.)	(a) 2,078 14 9 (b) 0 0 0	2,078 14 9	906 7 5	...	To Head Office, Glasgow ...	500 0 0	672 7 4	77	74	—	—	
LORD LIEUTENANT'S FUND ... (LORD HERRIES.)		...	...	...	...	...	...	...	...	...	...	No L.L. Fund.
*Kirkcudbright		...	§	...	...	...	...	...	...	...	...	No Provost's Fund.
*New Galloway ...		...	§	...	...	...	...	...	...	...	...	No Provost's Fund.

TRANSVAAL WAR FUNDS, 1899 TO 1901. COUNTIES—ROYAL BURGHS AND BURGHS. SCOTLAND—cont.

Lord Provosts are distinguished by having L.P. after the name of their Burghs; Royal Burghs by having a * prefixed; and Towns, &c., which are not Royal Burghs or Burghs, by being printed in *italics*.—M.H. signifies The Mansion House Fund.—L.L. Fund, The Lord Lieutenant's Fund.—S. & S.F.A., The Soldiers' and Sailors' Families Association.—S & S.H.S., The Soldiers' and Sailors' Help Society.—The Lansdowne Fund, Officers' Wives and Families.—The Abercorn Fund, Officers' Surgical and Medical Aid.—The Dudley Fund, Sick and Wounded Officers.—Y. and V. Equipment, Yeomanry and Volunteer Equipment.—Y. Hospital, Yeomanry Hospital; and a § in S. & S.F.A. column of Relief, that particulars of Relief in that Town or Burgh are included in the Relief by the S. & S.F.A. at the head of the County.

Origin of Fund.	S. & S.F.A. Subscriptions Raised in County (a) including County Balances previous to the War. Grants from the Council (b).	Total Amount Received.	Expenditure in Relief, &c. By S. & S.F.A.	Expenditure in Relief, &c. By Independent Committee.	Remitted to other Funds.		Balance.	Number of Cases Relieved. Wives and Dependent Relatives.	Children.	Widows.	Men.	Remarks.
	£ s. d.	£ s. d.	£ s. d.	£ s. d.		£ s. d.	£ s. d.					
LANARKSHIRE. (West Scotland.)	(a) 89,215 19 4 (b) 920 0 0	90,135 19 4	85,646 7 5	...		...	4,489 11 11	6,637	7,952	—	—	
Lord Lieutenant's Fund (Earl of Home.)		10,588 0 0		...	To Patriotic Fund	33 0 0						
					„ Red Cross Society	105 0 0						
					„ Lloyd's Patriotic	68 0 0						
					„ S. & S.F.A. (local)	5,533 0 0						
					„ The Lansdowne Fund	66 0 0						
					„ Men's extra comforts	93 0 0						
					„ Y. Equipment	4,189 0 0						
					„ V. Equipment	405 0 0						
					„ Expenses	96 0 0						
						10,588 0 0						
Airdrie		1,470 0 0	§	16 0 0	To S. & S.F.A. (local)	957 0 0	497 0 0	—	—	—	—	
Coatbridge		2,833 0 0	§		To S. & S.F.A. (local)	2,120 0 0						
					„ *Daily Telegraph*	100 0 0						
					„ Red Cross Society	100 0 0						
						2,320 0 0	513 0 0	—	—	—	—	
Glasgow, L.P.		98,002 0 0	§	206 0 0	To S. & S.F.A. (Glasgow)	65,064 0 0	...	...	...	106	212	
					„ „ (local)	3,251 0 0						
					„ Patriotic Fund	25 0 0						
					„ Red Cross Society	55 0 0						
					„ Lloyd's Patriotic	25 0 0						
					„ M.H. Refugees' Fund	20,299 0 0						
					„ Expenses on Refugees' Fund.	189 0 0						
					„ Expenses on War Fund	1,020 0 0						
						89,928 0 0	7,868 0 0	—	—			
The Glasgow Herald		7,450 0 0		2,000 0 0	To Lord Provost (Glasgow)	2,000 0 0		...		200		
					„ S. & S.F.A. (local)	1,500 0 0						
						3,500 0 0	1,950 0 0					
The Glasgow Evening Citizen		3,904 10 9		(c) 2,533 9 0	To S. & S.F.A. (local)	500 0 0	871 1 9			...	700	(c) Administered by G.O.C. Scottish District, Edinburgh.
Hamilton		407 4 4	§		To S. & S.F.A. (local)	400 7 9						
					„ Expenses	6 16 7						
						407 4 4	—	—	—	—	—	
*Lanark		107 14 6			To S. & S.F.A. (local)	107 14 6	—	—	—	—	—	
*Rutherglen		250 0 0	§		To S. & S.F.A. (local)	250 0 0	—	—	—	—	—	
Cambuslang		666 0 0		585 0 0	...		81 0 0	20	48	4	—	
Thornliebank		169 14 1		96 18 6	To S. & S.F.A. (local)	68 0 0						
					„ Expenses	0 6 6						
						68 6 6	4 9 1	—	—	—	—	
LINLITHGOWSHIRE (East Scotland.)	(a) 2,095 12 9 (b) 444 10 6	2,540 3 3	1,294 12 0		To Head Office, Edinburgh	1,251 18 11	*6 7 8	221	253	...	...	*Deficit.
Lord Lieutenant's Fund. (Earl of Rosebery.)				...	...			...		...	...	No L.L. Fund.
*Linlithgow				§	...			...		...	...	No Provost's Fund.
*Queensferry				§	...			...		...	...	No Provost's Fund.

TRANSVAAL WAR FUNDS, 1899 TO 1901. COUNTIES—ROYAL BURGHS AND BURGHS. **SCOTLAND**—cont.

Lord Provosts are distinguished by having L.P. after the name of their Burghs; Royal Burghs by having a * prefixed; and Towns, &c., which are not Royal Burghs or Burghs, by being printed in *italics*.—M.H. signifies The Mansion House Fund.—L.L. Fund, The Lord Lieutenant's Fund.—S. & S.F.A., The Soldiers' and Sailors' Families Association.—S. & S.H.S., The Soldiers' and Sailors' Help Society.—The Lansdowne Fund, Officers' Wives and Families.—The Abercorn Fund, Officers' Surgical and Medical Aid.—The Dudley Fund, Sick and Wounded Officers.—Y. and V. Equipment, Yeomanry and Volunteer Equipment.—Y. Hospital, Yeomanry Hospital; and a § in S. & S.F.A. column of Relief, that particulars of Relief in that Town or Burgh are included in the Relief by the S. & S.F.A. at the head of the County.

Origin of Fund.	S. & S.F.A. Subscriptions Raised in County (a) including County Balances previous to the War. Grants from the Council (b).	Total Amount Received.	Expenditure in Relief, &c. By S. & S.F.A.	Expenditure in Relief, &c. By Independent Committee.	Remitted to other Funds.		Balance.	Wives and Dependent Relatives.	Children.	Widows.	Men.	Remarks.
	£ s. d.	£ s. d.	£ s. d.	£ s. d.		£ s. d.	£ s. d.					
NAIRNSHIRE (East Scotland.)	(a) 442 5 11 (b) 30 0 0	472 5 11	100 9 6		To Head Office, Edinburgh	365 5 11	6 10 6	16	20	—	—	
LORD LIEUTENANT'S FUND. (MAJOR JAMES ROSE.)								...	...	...	...	No Provost's Fund.
Nairn		179 0 0	§		To M.H (not earmarked)	50 0 0						
					„ Red Cross Society	20 0 0						
					„ *Scotsman* Fund	50 0 0						
					„ Gordon Highlanders' Fund	5 0 0						
					„ Seaforth Highlanders' Fund	54 0 0						
						179 0 0						
ORKNEY AND SHETLAND (East Scotland).	(a) 986 19 5 (b) 71 0 0	1,057 19 5	347 4 6		To Head Office, Edinburgh	709 10 2	1 4 9	20	6	—	—	
LORD LIEUTENANT'S FUND. (M. A. LAING, Esq.)												
Orkney		246 0 0	§		To Red Cross Society	347 14 9						
Shetland		116 0 0	§		„ Expenses	14 5 3						
		362 0 0				362 0 0						
*Kirkwall		600 0 3	§	...	To S. & S.F.A., Edinburgh	600 0 3	—					
PEEBLESSHIRE (East Scotland).	(a) 823 15 6 (b) 45 0 0	868 15 6	153 7 8		To Head Office, Edinburgh	688 15 6	26 12 4	13	5	—	—	
LORD LIEUTENANT'S FUND (LORD ELIBANK.)		1,190 0 0			To M.H. No. 4 S. & S.F.A.	54 0 0						
					„ S. & S.F.A., Edinburgh	646 0 0						
					„ *Scotsman* Fund	200 0 0						
					„ Scottish Hospital	147 0 0						
					„ S. & S.H.S. (local)	10 0 0						
					„ Men's extra comforts	87 0 0						
						1,144 0 0	46 0 0	—	—	—	—	
Peebles			§		...			...	...	...	...	Included with L. L. Fund.
PERTHSHIRE (East Scotland).	(a) 1,518 3 9 (b) 147 10 3	1,665 14 0	59 19 5		To Head Office, Edinburgh	1,605 14 7	—	—	—	—	—	
LORD LIEUTENANT'S FUND (DUKE OF ATHOLL)				...	...	...		...	...	...	...	No L.L. Fund.
*Perth		5,447 0 0	§	4,427 0 0	To *Scotsman* Fund	215 0 0		194	225	9	20	
					„ *Glasgow Herald*	25 0 0						
					„ *People's Journal*	25 0 0						
					„ Expenses	45 0 0						
						310 0 0	710 0 0	—	—	—	—	
RENFREWSHIRE. (West Scotland.)	(a) 15,389 11 4 (b) 0 0 0	15,389 11 4	11,747 14 5	...	...		3,641 16 11	1,077	1,321	—	—	
LORD LIEUTENANT'S FUND (SIR M. R. SHAW STEWART, BT.)		1,325 0 0			To Red Cross Society	1,325 0 0	—					
Greenock		2,138 0 0	§		To S. & S.F.A. (local)	1,614 0 0						
					„ Red Cross Society	115 0 0						
					„ Argyll & S. Highlanders	250 0 0						
					„ V. Equipment	159 0 0						
						2,138 0 0						

TRANSVAAL WAR FUNDS, 1899 TO 1901. COUNTIES—ROYAL BURGHS AND BURGHS. SCOTLAND—cont.

Lord Provosts are distinguished by having L.P. after the name of their Burghs; Royal Burghs by having a * prefixed; and Towns, &c., which are not Royal Burghs or Burghs, by being printed in *italics*.—M.H. signifies The Mansion House Fund.—L.L. Fund, The Lord Lieutenant's Fund.—S. & S.F.A., The Soldiers' and Sailors' Families Association.—S. & S.H.S., The Soldiers' and Sailors' Help Society.—The Lansdowne Fund, Officers' Wives and Families.—The Abercorn Fund, Officers' Surgical and Medical Aid.—The Dudley Fund, Sick and Wounded Officers.—Y. and V. Equipment, Yeomanry and Volunteer Equipment.—Y. Hospital, Yeomanry Hospital; and a § in S. & S.F.A. column of Relief, that particulars of Relief in that Town or Burgh are included in the Relief by the S. & S.F.A. at the head of the County.

Origin of Fund.	S. & S.F.A. Subscriptions Raised in County (a) including County Balances previous to the War. Grants from the Council (b).	Total Amount Received.	Expenditure in Relief, &c. By S. & S.F.A.	Expenditure in Relief, &c. By Independent Committee.	Remitted to other Funds.		Balance.	Wives and Dependent Relatives.	Children.	Widows.	Men.	Remarks.
	£ s. d.	£ s. d.	£ s. d.	£ s. d.		£ s. d.	£ s. d.					
RENFREWSHIRE (West Scotland)—*cont.*												
Greenock Telegraph ...	...	1,250 0 0			To Provost of Greenock ...	1,250 0 0	—	—	—	—	—	
Paisley ...	...	1,211 0 0	§		To Scottish Red Cross ...	1,211 0 0	—	—	—	—	—	
Port Glasgow ...	...	1,197 2 7	§		To S. & S.F.A. (local) ...	1,197 2 7	—	—	—	—	—	
*Renfrew ...	...	50 0 0	§		To Agent-Gen., Natal ...	50 0 0	—	—	—	—	—	
ROSS AND CROMARTY.	(a) 1,245 6 2	3,141 18 7	3,246 7 1		To Head Office, Edinburgh	251 18 7	*356 7 1	448	82	...		*Deficit.
	(b) 1,896 12 5											
LORD LIEUTENANT'S FUND ... (SIR HECTOR MUNRO, BT.)		963 0 0			To S. & S.F.A. (local) ...	25 0 0						
					„ St. Andrew's Ambulance	50 0 0						
						75 0 0	888 0 0	—	—	—	—	
Cromarty ...		326 0 0	§		To Red Cross Society	120 0 0						
					„ *Scotsman* Fund ...	26 0 0						
					„ Gifts to Volunteers, etc.	80 0 0						
						326 0 0	—	—	—	—	—	
*Dingwall...	...	120 0 0	§		To L.L. Fund ...	60 0 0						
					„ S. & S.F.A. (local)	60 0 0						
						120 0 0						
*Fortrose ...	...	228 0 0	§	...	To S. & S.F.A. (local)	39 0 0						
					„ S. & S.H.S. (local)	2 0 0						
					„ *Scotsman* Fund	21 0 0						
					„ Men's extra comforts ...	166 0 0						
						228 0 0						
*Tain	...	65 1 10	§		To M.H. No. 1 Patriotic Fund	45 1 10						
					„ „ Refugees' Fund ...	20 0 0						
						65 1 10						
ROXBURGHSHIRE (East Scotland.)	(a) 1,647 12 2	1,896 12 2	673 10 8		To Head Office, Edinburgh	1,215 7 9	7 13 9	71	50			
	(b) 249 0 0											
LORD LIEUTENANT'S FUND ... (LORD REAY.)		1,440 0 0			To The Patriotic Fund ...	354 0 0						
					„ Red Cross Society	79 0 0						
					„ Lloyd's Patriotic	44 0 0						
					„ S. & S.F.A. (local)	588 0 0						
					„ *Scotsman* Fund	354 0 0						
					„ Men's extra comforts ...	21 0 0						
						1,440 0 0						
Hawick ...	...	550 1 7	§	10 5 0	To S. & S.F.A. (local)	124 0 0						
					„ *Scotsman* Fund	284 6 3						
					„ Scottish Red Cross ...	50 0 0						
					„ Scottish Hospital	10 0 0						
					„ V. Life Premiums ...	14 10 0						
					„ Men's extra comforts ...	26 3 0						
					„ Expenses	30 17 4						
						539 16 7	—	—	—	—	—	
*Jedburgh	...	80 0 0	§		To Scottish Hospital	50 0 0						
					„ Volunteers	30 0 0						
						80 0 0						

TRANSVAAL WAR FUNDS, 1899 TO 1901. COUNTIES—ROYAL BURGHS AND BURGHS. **SCOTLAND**—cont.

Lord Provosts are distinguished by having L.P. after the name of their Burghs; Royal Burghs by having a * prefixed; and Towns, &c., which are not Royal Burghs or Burghs, by being printed in *italics*.—M.H. signifies The Mansion House Fund.—L.L. Fund, The Lord Lieutenant's Fund.—S. & S.F.A., The Soldiers' and Sailors' Families Association.—S. & S.H.S., The Soldiers' and Sailors' Help Society.—The Lansdowne Fund, Officers' Wives and Families.—The Abercorn Fund, Officers' Surgical and Medical Aid.—The Dudley Fund, Sick and Wounded Officers.—Y. and V. Equipment, Yeomanry and Volunteer Equipment.—Y. Hospital, Yeomanry Hospital; and a § in S. & S.F.A. column of Relief, that particulars of Relief in that Town or Burgh are included in the Relief by the S. & S.F.A. at the head of the County.

Origin of Fund.	S. & S.F.A. Subscriptions Raised in County (a) including County Balances previous to the War. Grants from the Council (b).	Total Amount Received.	Expenditure in Relief, &c. By S. & S.F.A.	By Independent Committee.	Remitted to other Funds.		Balance.	Number of Cases Relieved. Wives and Dependent Relatives.	Children.	Widows.	Men.	Remarks.
	£ s. d.	£ s. d.	£ s. d.	£ s. d.		£ s. d.	£ s. d.					
SELKIRKSHIRE (East Scotland.)	(a) 967 14 3 (b) 85 0 0	1,052 14 3	579 18 6		To Head Office, Edinburgh	460 3 6	12 12 3	11	9	—	—	
LORD LIEUTENANT'S FUND (LORD POLWARTH.)		311 0 0			To S. & S.F.A. (local)	311 0 0	—					
Galashiels		270 5 4	§	25 6 6	To V. Life Insurance, etc.	226 5 2		—	—	—	—	
					„ Scottish Hospital	18 10 0						
					„ Expenses	0 3 8						
						244 18 10						
Selkirk		582 14 5	§		To S. & S.F.A. (local)	296 18 9						
					„ *Scotsman* Fund	161 10 0						
					„ Men's extra comforts	124 5 8						
						582 14 5						
STIRLINGSHIRE (West Scotland.)	(a) 5,371 19 0 (b) 0 0 0	5,371 19 0	3,840 16 4		...	...	1,531 2 8	416	561	—	—	
LORD LIEUTENANT'S FUND (DUKE OF MONTROSE.)		...	...		...	...	...	...	...	...	...	No L.L. Fund.
Falkirk		... ...	§	... ...	...	...	...	...	...	...	...	No Provost's Fund.
Falkirk Herald		2,548 0 0		2,320 0 0	To S. & S.F.A. (local)	10 0 0		170	231	—	—	
					„ *Daily Telegraph*	100 0 0						
					„ Expenses	26 0 0						
						136 0 0	92 0 0	—	—	—	—	
*Stirling		880 0 0	§		To S. & S.F.A. (local)	630 0 0						
					„ Argyll & S. Highlanders	250 0 0						
						880 0 0						
SUTHERLANDSHIRE (East Scotland.)	(a) 635 2 5 (b) 60 0 0	695 2 5	166 15 6		To Head Office Edinburgh	515 2 5	13 4 6	13	15	—	—	
LORD LIEUTENANT'S FUND (DUKE OF SUTHERLAND.)		727 1 8			To S. & S.F.A. (local)	368 14 9						
					„ Red Cross Society	358 6 11						
						727 1 8	—					
*Dornoch		93 3 0	§		To S. & S.F.A. (local)	93 3 0	—					
WIGTOWNSHIRE (West Scotland.)	(a) 1,294 9 3 (b) 0 0 0	1,294 9 3	624 10 1		...	...	669 19 2	97	52	—	—	
LORD LIEUTENANT'S FUND (EARL OF STAIR.)		...			...		...	...	...	...	...	No L.L. Fund.
*Stranraer		... ...	§	... ...	...	...	...	...	...	...	...	No Provost's Fund.
*Whithorn		19 3 6	§		To *Scotsman* Fund	19 3 6	—					
*Wigtown		57 5 4			To S. & S.F.A. (local)	50 7 0						
					„ *Daily Mail* (London)	3 10 0						
					„ Princess Christian Hospital.	2 6 0						
					„ Men's extra comforts	1 2 4						
						57 5 4	—					

TRANSVAAL WAR FUNDS,
1899 TO 1901.
COUNTIES—PARLIAMENTARY BOROUGHS AND BOROUGHS.
IRELAND.

Lord Mayors are distinguished by having L.M. after the name of the Borough; Parliamentary Boroughs by having a * prefixed; and Towns, &c., which are not Parliamentary Boroughs or Boroughs, by being printed in *italics*.—M.H. signifies The Mansion House Fund.—H.M.L. Fund, His Majesty's Lieutenant's Fund.—S. & S.F.A., The Soldiers' and Sailors' Families Association.—S. & S.H.S., The Soldiers' and Sailors' Help Society.—The Lansdowne Fund, Officers' Wives and Families.—The Abercorn Fund, Officers' Surgical and Medical Aid.—The Dudley Fund, Sick and Wounded Officers.—Y. and V. Equipment, Yeomanry and Volunteer Equipment.—Y. Hospital, Yeomanry Hospital; and a § in S. & S.F.A. column of Relief, that particulars of Relief in that Town or Borough are included in the Relief by the S. & S.F.A. at the head of the County.

THE SOLDIERS' AND SAILORS' FAMILIES ASSOCIATION.
IRISH BRANCH (DUBLIN).
Treasurer's Account, 1899 to 1901.

RECEIPTS.	£	s.	d.	PAYMENTS.	£	s.	d.
At Head Office, Dublin	17,823	3	0	By Expenditure	122	2	9
From Districts	16	15	6	„ Grants to Districts	99,349	8	8
From the London Council	82,650	0	0	„ Balance, 31st December, 1901	1,018	7	1
	100,489	18	6		100,489	18	6

District.	Subscriptions Raised in District (a) including District Balances previous to the War. Grants from Branch Treasurer (b).			Total Amount Received.			Expenditure in Relief, &c.			Balance, 31st December, 1901.		
	£	s.	d.	£	s.	d.	£	s.	d.	£	s.	d.
Dublin	(a) 5,374	1	11	71,577	6	5	68,003	6	0	3,574	0	5
	(b) 66,203	4	6									
Ulster	(a) 24,695	4	3	32,624	12	11	30,040	17	8	2,583	15	3
	(b) 7,929	8	8									
Cork	(a) 5,680	8	5	30,888	3	4	30,107	14	8	780	8	8
	(b) 25,207	14	11									

Origin of Fund.	S. & S.F.A. Subscriptions Raised in County (a) including County Balances previous to the War. Grants from the Council (b).	Total Amount Received.	Expenditure in Relief, &c.		Remitted to other Funds.		Balance.	Number of Cases Relieved.				Remarks.
			By S. & S.F.A.	By Independent Committee.				Wives and Dependent Relatives.	Children.	Widows.	Men.	
	£ s. d.	£ s. d.	£ s. d.	£ s. d.		£ s. d.	£ s. d.					
ANTRIM (Ulster District.)	(a) 3,237 7 1	13,409 3 0	13,223 7 9		...		185 15 3	1,979	2,330	—	—	
	(b) 10,171 15 11											
H.M. Lieutenant's Fund (Sir F. E. W. Macnaghten, Bart.)	...				...			...	...	...	...	No H.M.L. Fund.
*Belfast, L.M.		11,717 2 9	§	578 9 8	To S. & S.F.A. (local)	10,250 0 0						No particulars of cases supplied.
					„ Men's extra comforts	175 19 11						
					„ S. & S.H.S. (local)	25 0 0						
					„ Expenses	549 15 3						
						11,000 15 2	137 17 11	—	—	—	—	
		1,547 1 4			To Refugees (Lord Milner)	1,450 0 0						
					„ Expenses	55 2 0						
						1,505 2 0	41 19 4	—	—	—	—	
Lisburn		543 0 0	§	15 0 0	To S. & S.F.A. (local)	315 0 0	213 0 0	2				
Ballymena		409 15 2	§		To S. & S.F.A. (local)	409 15 2	—	—	—	—	—	
ARMAGH (Ulster District.)	(a) 1,475 7 0	3,213 11 9	3,118 18 7				94 13 2	787	984	—	—	
	(b) 1,738 4 9											
H.M. Lieutenant's Fund (Earl of Gosford.)			...		...			...	...	...	...	No H.M.L. Fund.
*Armagh			§		...			...	...	...	...	No Mayor's Fund.

TRANSVAAL WAR FUNDS, 1899 TO 1901. COUNTIES—PARLIAMENTARY BOROUGHS AND BOROUGHS. IRELAND—cont.

Lord Mayors are distinguished by having L.M. after the name of the Borough; Parliamentary Boroughs by having a * prefixed; and Towns, &c., which are not Parliamentary Boroughs or Boroughs, by being printed in *italics*.—M.H. signifies The Mansion House Fund.—H.M.L. Fund, His Majesty's Lieutenant's Fund.—S. & S.F.A., The Soldiers' and Sailors' Families Association.—S. & S.H.S., The Soldiers' and Sailors' Help Society.—The Lansdowne Fund, Officers' Wives and Families.—The Abercorn Fund, Officers' Surgical and Medical Aid.—The Dudley Fund, Sick and Wounded Officers.—Y. and V. Equipment, Yeomanry and Volunteer Equipment.—Y. Hospital, Yeomanry Hospital; and a § in S. & S.F.A. column of Relief, that particulars of Relief in that Town or Borough are included in the Relief by the S. & S.F.A. at the head of the County.

Origin of Fund.	S. & S.F.A. Subscriptions Raised in County (a) including County Balances previous to the War. Grants from the Council (b).	Total Amount Received.	Expenditure in Relief, &c. By S. & S.F.A.	By Independent Committee.	Remitted to other Funds.		Balance.	Number of Cases Relieved. Wives and Dependent Relatives.	Children.	Widows.	Men.	Remarks.
	£ s. d.	£ s. d.	£ s. d.	£ s. d.		£ s. d.	£ s. d.					
CARLOW (Dublin District.)	(a) 312 15 0 (b) 1,400 0 0	1,712 15 0	1,698 0 0	...	...		14 15 0	383	109	—	—	
H.M. LIEUTENANT'S FUND (LORD RATHDONNELL.)	...	...	...	...	...		...	...	...	...	...	No H.M.L. Fund.
*Carlow		140 19 1	§	...	To St. John Ambulance 85 16 1 „ Y. Hospital 55 3 0 140 19 1							
CAVAN (Ulster District.)	(a) 346 8 4 (b) 900 0 0	1,246 8 4	1,201 8 3				45 0 1	340	164	—	—	
H.M. LIEUTENANT'S FUND (COLONEL SAUNDERSON.)	...	...	...				...	...	...	...	...	No H.M.L. Fund.
CLARE (Cork District.)	(a) 358 14 11 (b) 390 0 0	748 14 11	746 12 1	...	...		2 2 10	182	80	—	—	
H.M. LIEUTENANT'S FUND (CAPTAIN VANDELEUR.)		...	...				...	...	...	...	...	No H.M.L. Fund.
Ennis		...	§									No Mayor's Fund.
CORK (Cork District.)	(a) 1,227 9 5 (b) 13,629 10 2	14,856 19 7	14,755 17 5	...	...		101 2 2	2,154	1,721	—	—	
H.M. LIEUTENANT'S FUND (EARL OF BANDON.)	...	...	...	...	...		...	...	...	...	...	No H.M.L. Fund.
Bandon	...	...	§	§...			...					No Mayor's Fund.
*Cork, L.M.	...	...	§	...	...		...					No Lord Mayor's Fund.
Cork Constitution	...	3,162 17 9	...		To M.H. (not earmarked) 3,077 9 2 „ S. & S.F.A. (local) 79 2 7 „ Daily Telegraph 6 6 0 3,162 17 9							
Kinsale	...	...	§	...	...							No Mayor's Fund.
Youghal	...	...	§	...	...							No Mayor's Fund.
DONEGAL (Ulster District.)	(a) 183 15 11 (b) 191 3 11	374 19 10	347 1 6	...	...		27 18 4	30	24	—	—	
H.M. LIEUTENANT'S FUND (DUKE OF ABERCORN.)	...	...	...	...	...		...	...	...	...	...	No H.M.L. Fund.
DOWN (Ulster District.)	(a) 2,420 16 5 (b) 2,139 18 4	4,560 14 9	4,307 16 10	...	...		252 17 11	633	729	—	—	
H.M. LIEUTENANT'S FUND (MARQUESS OF DUFFERIN, deceased. MARQUESS OF LONDONDERRY.)	...	...	...	...	...		...	...	...	...	...	No H.M.L. Fund.
DUBLIN (Dublin District.)	(a) 1,058 10 0 (b) 42,765 0 0	43,823 10 0	41,945 11 4	...	...		1,877 18 8	4,582	3,960	—	—	
H.M. LIEUTENANT'S FUND (EARL OF MEATH.)	...	...	...	...	...		...	...	...	...	...	No H.M.L. Fund.
*Dublin, L.M.		2,345 0 0	§	...	To M.H, Refugees' Fund 1,486 0 0 „ Irish Regiments 738 0 0 „ Mafeking Relief Fund 121 0 0 2,345 0 0							
Irish Times Fund	...	14,740 8 10	...	(c) 8,898 15 8	To Expenses 416 2 8		5,425 10 6		412	263	...	(c) Includes £2,500 paid for *Daily Telegraph* Annuities for 47 widows.

TRANSVAAL WAR FUNDS, 1899 TO 1901. COUNTIES—PARLIAMENTARY BOROUGHS AND BOROUGHS. IRELAND—cont.

Lord Mayors are distinguished by having L.M. after the name of the Borough; Parliamentary Boroughs by having a * prefixed; and Towns, &c., which are not Parliamentary Boroughs or Boroughs, by being printed in *italics*.—M.H. signifies The Mansion House Fund.—H.M.L. Fund, His Majesty's Lieutenant's Fund.—S. & S.F.A., The Soldiers' and Sailors' Families Association.—S. & S.H.S., The Soldiers' and Sailors' Help Society.—The Lansdowne Fund, Officers' Wives and Families.—The Abercorn Fund, Officers' Surgical and Medical Aid.—The Dudley Fund, Sick and Wounded Officers.—Y. and V. Equipment, Yeomanry and Volunteer Equipment.—Y. Hospital, Yeomanry Hospital; and a § in S. & S.F.A. column of Relief, that particulars of Relief in that Town or Borough are included in the Relief by the S. & S.F.A. at the head of the County.

Origin of Fund.	S. & S.F.A. Subscriptions Raised in County (a) including County Balances previous to the War. Grants from the Council (b).	Total Amount Received.	Expenditure in Relief, &c.		Remitted to other Funds.	Balance.	Number of Cases Relieved.				Remarks.
			By S. & S.F.A.	By Independent Committee.			Wives and Dependent Relatives.	Children.	Widows.	Men.	
	£ s. d.	£ s. d.	£ s. d.	£ s. d.	£ s. d.	£ s. d.					
FERMANAGH (Ulster District).	(a) 367 8 9 (b) 1,720 0 0	2,087 8 9	2,129 14 3	...	...	*42 5 6	426	107	...	...	*Deficit.
H.M. LIEUTENANT'S FUND (EARL OF ERNE)	...	...	...	...	...	...	...	...	...	...	No H.M.L. Fund.
Enniskillen	... ...	... ...	§	...	... ...	...	...	...	...	...	No Mayor's Fund.
Fermanagh Times	... ...		197 7 0	... ...	...	To Inniskilling Fusiliers Fund 197 7 0	—	—	—	—	—	
GALWAY (Dublin District.)	(a) 134 7 0 (b) 2,923 15 4	3,058 2 4	2,968 1 5	...	...	90 0 11	394	440	—	—	
H.M. LIEUTENANT'S FUND (LORD CLONBROOK.)	...	...	...	...	...	...	...	...	...	...	No H.M.L. Fund.
Galway	... ...	...	§	...	...	...	...	...	...	...	No Mayor's Fund.
KERRY (Cork District.)	(a) 454 8 11 (b) 2,270 0 0	2,724 8 11	2,682 0 4	...	...	42 8 7	333	292	—	—	
H.M. LIEUTENANT'S FUND (EARL OF KENMARE.)	...	...	...	...	...	...	...	...	...	...	No H.M.L. Fund.
Tralee	... ...	... ...	...	...	...	...	...	...	...	...	No Mayor's Fund.
KILDARE (Dublin District.)	(a) 829 10 7 (b) 4,014 15 11	4,844 6 6	4,707 14 10	...	...	136 11 8	614	589	—	—	
H.M. LIEUTENANT'S FUND (ROBERT KENNEDY, Esq.)	...	...	...	...	...	...	...	...	...	...	No H.M.L. Fund.
KILKENNY (Dublin District.)	(a) 515 18 6 (b) 450 0 0	965 18 6	953 12 6	...	...	12 6 0	275	239	—	—	
H.M. LIEUTENANT'S FUND (MARQUESS OF ORMONDE.)	...	...	...	...	...	...	...	...	...	...	No H.M.L. Fund.
Kilkenny	... ...	...	...	...	...	...	...	...	...	...	No Mayor's Fund.
KING'S COUNTY (Dublin District.)	(a) 139 0 3 (b) 3,175 0 0	3,314 0 3	3,266 13 4	...	...	47 6 11	351	474	—	—	
H.M. LIEUTENANT'S FUND (EARL OF ROSSE.)	...	...	...	...	...	...	...	...	...	...	No H.M.L. Fund.
LEITRIM (Dublin District.)	(a) 50 16 4 (b) 630 0 0	680 16 4	672 13 3	...	...	8 3 1	434	45	—	—	
H.M. LIEUTENANT'S FUND (LORD HARLECH.)	...	...	...	...	...	...	...	...	...	...	No H.M.L. Fund.
LIMERICK (Cork District.)	(a) 1,207 12 4 (b) 2,260 0 0	3,467 12 4	3,436 8 3	...	...	31 4 1	1,024	221	—	—	
H.M. LIEUTENANT'S FUND (EARL OF DUNRAVEN.)	...	...	...	...	...	...	...	...	...	...	No H.M.L. Fund.
Limerick	... ...	...	§	...	...	...	...	...	...	...	No Mayor's Fund.
LONDONDERRY. (Ulster District.)	(a) 908 19 3 (b) 500 0 0	1,408 19 3	1,401 12 3	...	...	7 7 0	255	198	—	—	
H.M. LIEUTENANT'S FUND (SIR H. H. BRUCE, BART.)	...	...	...	...	...	...	...	...	...	...	No H.M.L. Fund.
Coleraine	... ...	191 0 0	§	...	To S. & S.F.A. (local) 150 0 0 ,, Expenses ... 1 0 0 151 0 0	40 0 0	—	—	—	—	
Londonderry	... ...	...	§	...	...	...	...	...	...	...	No Mayor's Fund.

TRANSVAAL WAR FUNDS, 1899 TO 1901. COUNTIES—PARLIAMENTARY BOROUGHS AND BOROUGHS. IRELAND—cont.

Lord Mayors are distinguished by having L.M. after the name of the Borough; Parliamentary Boroughs by having a * prefixed; and Towns, &c., which are not Parliamentary Boroughs or Boroughs, by being printed in *italics*.—M.H. signifies The Mansion House Fund.—H.M.L. Fund, His Majesty's Lieutenant's Fund.—S. & S.F.A., The Soldiers' and Sailors' Families Association.—S. & S.H.S., The Soldiers' and Sailors' Help Society.—The Lansdowne Fund, Officers' Wives and Families.—The Abercorn Fund, Officers' Surgical and Medical Aid.—The Dudley Fund, Sick and Wounded Officers.—Y. and V. Equipment, Yeomanry and Volunteer Equipment.—Y. Hospital, Yeomanry Hospital; and a § in S. & S.F.A. column of Relief, that particulars of Relief in that Town or Borough are included in the Relief by the S. & S.F.A. at the head of the County.

Origin of Fund.	S. & S.F.A. Subscriptions Raised in County (a) including County Balances previous to the War. Grants from the Council (b).	Total Amount Received.	Expenditure in Relief, &c. By S. & S.F.A.	Expenditure in Relief, &c. By Independent Committee.	Remitted to other Funds.	Balance.	Wives and Dependent Relatives.	Children.	Widows.	Men.	Remarks.
	£ s. d.	£ s. d.	£ s. d.	£ s. d.	£ s. d.	£ s. d.					
LONGFORD (Dublin District.)	(a) 91 9 3 (b) 2,850 0 0	2,941 9 3	2,821 2 9	...	...	120 6 6	371	361	—	—	
H.M. LIEUTENANT'S FUND (EARL OF LONGFORD.)	...	...	...	...	...	...	...	...	...	...	No H.M.L. Fund.
LOUTH. (Ulster District.)	(a) 361 10 6 (b) 1,635 0 0	1,996 10 6	1,977 5 1	...	...	19 5 5	334	344	—	—	
H.M. LIEUTENANT'S FUND (LORD BELLEW.)	...	248 0 0	...	...	To M.H. (not earmarked)... 248 0 0	—	...	...	...	...	
Drogheda	...	...	§	...	...	...	...	...	...	...	No Mayor's Fund.
Dundalk	...	...	§	...	...	...	...	...	...	...	No Mayor's Fund.
MAYO (Dublin District.)	(a) 207 11 1 (b) 1,175 0 0	1,382 11 1	1,329 1 4	...	...	53 9 9	334	436	—	—	
H.M. LIEUTENANT'S FUND (EARL OF ARRAN, *deceased*. EARL OF LUCAN.)	...	1,300 0 0	...	...	To Connaught Rangers' Fund. 1,300 0 0	—	...	...	...	...	
MEATH (Dublin District.)	(a) 288 10 0 (b) 1,950 0 0	2,238 10 0	2,208 17 11	...	...	29 12 1	562	190	—	—	
H.M. LIEUTENANT'S FUND (SIMSON MANGAN, ESQ.)	...	...	...	...	...	...	...	...	...	...	No H.M.L. Fund.
MONAGHAN (Ulster District.)	(a) 679 14 5 (b) 250 0 0	929 14 5	915 19 1	...	...	13 15 4	118	12	—	—	
H.M. LIEUTENANT'S FUND (LORD ROSSMORE.)	...	...	...	...	...	...	...	...	...	...	No H.M.L. Fund.
Newry	...	...	§	...	...	...	...	...	...	...	No Mayor's Fund.
QUEEN'S COUNTY (Dublin District.)	(a) 469 16 10 (b) 610 0 0	1,079 16 10	1,067 5 1	...	...	12 11 9	186	138	—	—	
H.M. LIEUTENANT'S FUND (SIR ALGERNON COOTE, Bart.)	...	...	...	...	...	...	...	...	...	...	No H.M.L. Fund.
ROSCOMMON (Dublin District.)	(a) 55 7 0 (b) 373 4 6	428 11 6	396 5 11	...	...	32 5 7	100	47	—	—	
H.M. LIEUTENANT'S FUND (THE O'CONNOR DON.)	...	...	...	...	...	...	...	...	...	...	No H.M.L. Fund.
SLIGO (Dublin District.)	(a) 257 14 2 (b) 301 10 0	559 4 2	507 1 7	...	...	52 2 7	100	29	—	—	
H.M. LIEUTENANT'S FUND (RIGHT HON. E. H. COOPER, *deceased*.)	...	...	...	...	...	...	...	...	...	...	No H.M.L. Fund.
Sligo	...	...	§	...	...	...	...	...	...	...	No Mayor's Fund.
TIPPERARY (Cork District.)	(a) 1,113 10 10 (b) 4,325 0 0	5,438 10 10	5,239 11 3	...	...	198 19 7	815	899	—	—	
H.M. LIEUTENANT'S FUND (EARL DE MONTALT.)	...	...	...	...	...	...	...	...	...	...	No H.M.L. Fund.
Cashel	...	...	§	...	...	...	...	...	...	...	No Mayor's Fund.
Clonmel	...	...	§	...	...	...	...	...	...	...	No Mayor's Fund.

TRANSVAAL WAR FUNDS, 1899 TO 1901. COUNTIES—PARLIAMENTARY BOROUGHS AND BOROUGHS. IRELAND, &c.—cont.

Lord Mayors are distinguished by having L.M. after the name of the Borough; Parliamentary Boroughs by having a * prefixed; and Towns, &c., which are not Parliamentary Boroughs or Boroughs, by being printed in *italics*.—M.H. signifies The Mansion House Fund.—H.M.L. Fund, His Majesty's Lieutenant's Fund.—S. & S.F.A., The Soldiers' and Sailors' Families Association.—S. & S.H.S., The Soldiers' and Sailors' Help Society.—The Lansdowne Fund, Officers' Wives and Families.—The Abercorn Fund, Officers' Surgical and Medical Aid.—The Dudley Fund, Sick and Wounded Officers.—Y. and V. Equipment, Yeomanry and Volunteer Equipment.—Y. Hospital, Yeomanry Hospital; and a § in S. & S.F.A. column of Relief, that particulars of Relief in that Town or Borough are included in the Relief by the S. & S.F.A. at the head of the County.

Origin of Fund.	S. & S.F.A. Subscriptions Raised in County (a) including County Balances previous to the War. Grants from the Council (b).	Total Amount Received.	Expenditure in Relief, &c. By S. & S.F.A.	Expenditure in Relief, &c. By Independent Committee.	Remitted to other Funds.	Balance.	Number of Cases Relieved. Wives and Dependent Relatives.	Children.	Widows.	Men.	Remarks.
	£ s. d.	£ s. d.	£ s. d.	£ s. d.	£ s. d.	£ s. d.					
TYRONE (Ulster District.)	(a) 1,455 0 7 (b) 100 0 0	1,555 0 7	1,379 15 4	...	...	175 5 3	333	314	—	—	
H.M. Lieutenant's Fund (Earl of Belmore.)	...	...	...	...	...	...	...	...	...	...	No H.M.L. Fund.
Dungannon	...	...	§	...	...	...	...	...	...	...	No Mayor's Fund.
WATERFORD (Cork District.)	(a) 650 13 6 (b) 1,657 1 10	2,307 15 4	2,297 11 9	...	...	10 3 7	678	714	—	—	
H.M. Lieutenant's Fund (Duke of Devonshire.)	...	...	...	...	...	...	...	...	...	...	No H.M.L. Fund.
Dungarvan	...	...	§	...	...	...	...	...	...	...	No Mayor's Fund.
*Waterford	...	...	§	...	...	...	...	...	...	...	No Mayor's Fund.
WESTMEATH (Dublin District.)	(a) 286 8 9 (b) 2,335 0 0	2,621 8 9	2,588 17 8	...	...	32 11 1	375	353	—	—	
H.M. Lieutenant's Fund (Lord Castlemaine.)	...	...	...	...	...	...	...	...	...	...	No H.M.L. Fund.
WEXFORD. (Cork District.)	(a) 531 7 0 (b) 0 0 0	531 7 0	257 9 9	...	...	273 17 3	93	40	—	—	
H.M. Lieutenant's Fund (Lord Stopford.)	...	...	...	...	...	...	...	...	...	...	No H.M.L. Fund.
Wexford	...	...	§	...	...	...	...	...	...	...	No Mayor's Fund.
WICKLOW. (Dublin District.)	(a) 545 15 7 (b) 520 0 0	1,065 15 7	845 19 10	...	...	219 15 9	165	108	—	—	
H.M. Lieutenant's Fund (Earl of Carysford.)	...	...	...	...	...	...	...	...	...	...	No H.M.L. Fund.
ISLE OF MAN Lieutenant Governor (Lord Henniker.)	(a) 51 10 10 (b) 300 0 0	351 10 10	285 17 2	...	...	65 13 8	28	42	—	—	
Castletown	...	182 0 0	§	...	To M.H. (not earmarked) ... 155 0 0	27 0 0	—	—	—	—	
Douglas	...	1,401 0 0	§	...	To M.H. (not earmarked) ... 1,000 0 0 „ S. & S.F.A. (local) ... 50 0 0 „ Convalescent Home ... 50 0 0 1,100 0 0	301 0 0	—	—	—	—	
Peel	...	190 0 0	§	...	To M.H. (not earmarked) ... 190 0 0	—	—	—	—	—	
Ramsey	...	246 0 0	§	...	To M.H. (not earmarked) ... 221 0 0	25 0 0	—	—	—	—	
JERSEY Lieutenant Governor (Major-General Abadie.)	(a) 126 7 8 (b) 1,850 0 0	1,976 7 8 2,922 8 8	1,929 5 4	...	... To M.H. No. 1 Patriotic Fund 800 0 0 „ „ No. 2 Red Cross Society. 100 0 0 „ „ No. 3 Lloyd's Patriotic. 1,014 0 0 „ „ No. 4 S. & S.F.A. 1,000 0 0 „ Expenses ... 8 8 8 2,922 8 8	47 2 4	204	478	—	—	

Origin of Fund.	S. & S.F.A. Subscriptions Raised in County (a) including County Balances previous to the War. Grants from the Council (b).	Total Amount Received.	Expenditure in Relief, &c. By S. & S.F.A.	Expenditure in Relief, &c. By Independent Committee.	Remitted to other Funds.		Balance.	Number of Cases Relieved. Wives and Dependent Relatives.	Number of Cases Relieved. Children.	Number of Cases Relieved. Widows.	Number of Cases Relieved. Men.	Remarks.
	£ s. d.	£ s. d.	£ s. d.	£ s. d.		£ s. d.	£ s. d.					
GUERNSEY	(a) 780 3 11	1,730 3 11	1,646 19 0				83 4 11	137	196	—	—	
	(b) 950 0 0											
Lieutenant Governor (Major-General Saward.)		2,502 8 2			To M.H. No. 1 Patriotic Fund	1,227 10 10						
					,, ,, No. 2 Red Cross Society.	122 8 11						
					,, ,, No. 3 Lloyd's Patriotic.	262 5 10						
					,, ,, No. 4 S. & S.F.A.	73 19 10						
					,, S. & S.F.A. (local)	691 2 9						
					,, Mens' extra comforts	125 0 0						
						2,502 8 2		—	—	—	—	
CANADA	(a) 339 0 0	339 0 0	139 17 6		...		199 2 6	42	79	...	...	See also Part VI. Page 140.
	(b) 0 0 0											
CAPE COLONY (Lieut.-Gen. Sir F. Forestier Walker.)	(a) 577 4 10	7,577 4 10	6,360 19 6		...	...	1,216 5 4	628	1,012	...	...	See also Part VI. Page 141.
	(b) 7,000 0 0											
CHINA (Hong Kong)		7,500 0 0			To M.H. No. 4 S. & S.F.A.	7,500 0 0	—	—	—	—	—	
EGYPT	(a) 307 3 10	507 3 10	327 18 3	...	...	...	179 5 7	210	430			
	(b) 200 0 0											
Lord Cromer		4,700 0 0	?		To M.H. (not earmarked)	4,700 0 0	—	—	—	—	—	
Gen. Talbot		600 0 0			To M.H. (not earmarked)	400 0 0						
					,, The Lansdowne Fund	200 0 0						
						600 0 0						
GIBRALTAR	(a) 382 6 2	382 6 2	351 12 1		...	...	30 14 1	52	72	—	—	
	(b) 0 0 0											
Governor (General Sir R. Biddulph.)		1,581 6 0			To M.H. No 1 Patriotic Fund	310 3 4						
					,, ,, No. 2 Red Cross Society.	58 6 0						
					,, ,, No. 3 Lloyd's Patriotic.	393 5 9						
					,, ,, No. 4 S. & S.F.A.	340 1 8						
					,, ,, (not earmarked)	479 9 3						
						1,581 6 0						
MALTA	(a) 1,014 9 5	1,214 9 5	780 11 10			...	433 17 7	238	411	—	—	
	(b) 200 0 0											
Governor (General Sir F. Grenfell.)		795 0 0			To S. & S.F.A. (local)	445 0 0						
					,, M.H. No. 1 Patriotic Fund	300 0 0						
					,, Y. Hospital	50 0 0						
						795 0 0		—	—	—	—	
NATAL	(a) 48 16 11	1,198 16 11	1,153 13 3		...	...	45 3 8	142	269	...	...	See also Part VI. Page 143.
Governor. (Hon. Sir W. F. Hely Hutchinson.)	(b) 1,150 0 0											
WEST INDIES (Barbadoes.)	(a) 30 0 0	30 0 0	21 10 10	...	...	...	8 9 2	4	6	—	—	
	(b) 0 0 0											

TRANSVAAL WAR FUNDS, 1899 TO 1901. REGIMENTS AND CORPS.

Regiment or Corps.	Approximate Amount Subscribed for the War.	Expended in Relief.	Expended in Extra Comforts.	Balance.	Wives, Widows, &c.	Children.	Men.	Remarks.
	£ s. d.	£ s. d.	£ s. d.	£ s. d.				
Royal Horse Guards ...	1,387 8 11	1,329 5 8	...	58 3 3	73	66		Further subscriptions have been promised until the conclusion of the War, but are only called upon as required.
4th Royal Irish Dragoon Guards ...	340 0 0	To M.H. (not earmarked). 40 0 0 „ Prince Christian Victor Memorial Fund. 300 0 0						
		340 0 0						Remitted from India.
Royal Artillery...	*1,711 0 0	992 0 0	90 0 0	629 0 0	224	10	13	* Includes £230 received from *Daily Telegraph* for purchase of Annuity for one Widow, and sundry grants from Imperial War Fund.
Royal Engineers ...	612 0 0	...	...	*571 0 0	41 0 0	...		* Extra comforts additional to value of £796.
Grenadier Guards ...	2,800 0 0	373 12 0	1,400 0 0 *126 8 0	900 0 0	32	96		* To Lady E. Cecil, Cape Town Hospital.
Coldstream Guards ...	2,161 0 0	222 0 0	1,178 0 0	761 0 0	42	112	51	Generally it may be stated that the Brigade of Guards entirely undertook the care and relief of all families on the married strength.
Scots Guards ...	1,107 0 0 *79 0 0	696 0 0	500 0 0		64	86	16	* From Regimental Funds.
Irish Guards	...	...	...	...	...	...	...	No special Fund.
The Queens (Royal West Surrey Regiment), (2nd Battalion).	625 0 0	*322 0 0	153 0 0	150 0 0	* *2	* ...	20 *11	* To S. & S.F.A. (local), £200. * Relieved in India to the amount of £25.
The Royal Fusiliers (City of London Regiment), (2nd Battalion).	3,100 0 0	924 0 0	676 0 0	1,500 0 0	306		20	
Somersetshire Light Infantry (Prince Albert's), (2nd Battalion).	320 0 0	...	...	320 0 0	—	—	—	
The Royal Irish Regiment (1st Battalion)	353 8 0	*65 0 0	288 8 0		*	*		* To S. & S.F.A. (local), £65.
The Royal Scots Fusiliers (2nd Battalion)	76 18 11	10 0 0	...	66 18 11	—	—		
Miss E. Gaffney's Fund ...	101 8 0	...		101 8 0	...	...		Daughter of a Pensioner Serjeant.
Countess of Eglinton's Fund ...	463 13 11	...	...	429 1 4	34 12 7			Also for Service Companies of 1st and 2nd Volunteer Battalions and the Ayrshire Imperial Yeomanry.
The Cheshire Regiment (2nd Battalion) ...	217 18 0	...	...	...	...			To S. & S.F.A. (local), £217 18s.
The Royal Inniskilling Fusiliers (1st Battalion).	1,635 0 0	975 0 0	190 0 0	470 0 0	202	210	10	
The Duke of Cornwall's Light Infantry (2nd Battalion).	659 0 0	...	500 0 0	159 0 0	—	—	—	
The Border Regiment (1st Battalion) ...	...	...	...	...				Particulars not supplied.
The Royal Sussex Regiment (2nd Battalion).	83 0 0	To M.H. (not earmarked). 13 0 0 „ Cape of Good Hope Society. 70 0 0						Remitted from India.
		83 0 0						
The Hampshire Regiment (2nd Battalion)	477 9 5	117 1 7	166 4 7	194 3 3	6	17	8	
The South Staffordshire Regiment (1st Battalion).	550 0 0	...	...	550 0 0	—	—	—	
The Black Watch (Royal Highlanders) (2nd Battalion).	915 9 0	581 10 6		333 18 6	49	2	12	
The Essex Regiment (1st Battalion) ...	194 12 9	90 13 10	*	103 18 11	7	3		Mrs. Stephenson's Fund for Widows and Orphans. * Extra comforts to the value of £1,180.
The Derbyshire Regiment (Sherwood Foresters), (1st Battalion)	875 0 0	200 0 0	670 0 0	5 0 0	—	—	—	
The Royal Berkshire Regiment (2nd Battalion).	348 0 0	...	...	348 0 0	—	—	—	
The Highland Light Infantry (1st Battalion).	60 0 0	...	...	60 0 0	—	—	—	
The Gordon Highlanders (1st and 2nd Battalions).	999 17 2	173 9 0		826 8 2	26		14	
	517 11 1	...	...	450 19 6	66 11 7	—	—	
The Connaught Rangers (1st Battalion) ...	1,313 0 0	1,313 0 0			35	12	30	
The Princess Louise's (Argyle and Sutherland Highlanders), (1st Battalion).	1,850 0 0	190 0 0	260 0 0	1,400 0 0	59	3	12	
The Royal Dublin Fusiliers...	486 0 0	311 0 0		175 0 0	180		20	
The Riflemen's Aid Society (King's Royal Rifles and Rifle Brigade).	3,442 0 0	208 0 0		3,134 0 0	73	136	10	To 31st March, 1901.
The Royal Army Medical Corps ...	2,500 0 0	...	2,300 0 0					To Bisley Homes, £200.

NOTE.—The above particulars are somewhat incomplete through many Regiments not having supplied the information asked for. It may be stated, however, that where there were no Special Funds raised regimentally, in most, if not in all cases, extra comforts have been subscribed for and forwarded by old officers, ladies, and others, specially interested in some particular Regiment or Corps.

BIRMINGHAM "DAILY MAIL" RESERVISTS' FUND.

(Communicated.)

On October 15th, 1899, the Birmingham *Daily Mail* opened a Fund to assist the families of Army Reservists from Birmingham and the district, who had been called upon to re-join the Colours. Among the first subscribers were Lord Roberts, who had previously been associated with the Editor, Mr. W. C. Sullivan, in forming an association for helping the Crimean Veterans in the City, and Mr. Joseph Chamberlain. Realising the magnitude of his task, the Editor invited the Lord Mayor to call a Town's Meeting to organise the distribution of the Fund, when the following officers were appointed, viz.—Chairman, Charles G. Beale, Lord Mayor; Hon. Treasurer, W. C. Sullivan, up to his death, when the position was filled by John R. H. Smyth; Honorary Secretaries, Cecil Crosskey and Charles Hyde. The City was divided into its Parliamentary Divisions, each having a Divisional Hon. Secretary, who appointed helpers to assist in the work of relief. It was decided to draw no hard and fast lines in administering the Fund, and that each case should be relieved on its merits. The system being to make up as far as possible the deficiency in the weekly income during the absence of the breadwinner, after allowing for what money was coming in.

The great feature in connection with the Fund has been the support given to it by the working classes, nearly every firm in the City and district having organised weekly collections, which varied from one penny to as much as three-pence per week from each employee. One firm, the Birmingham Small Arms, has contributed over £1,200, two-thirds of the whole Fund having been contributed by the working classes.

In the early part of 1901 the Committee decided that when the Fund reached £50,000, they would not make any further appeal to the workpeople, but when this total was reached on May 4th it was found that the funds in hand were not sufficient, and a "Special Appeal" was made to the more wealthy citizens. This appeal, however, did not meet with sufficient response and the workpeople again came to help the Fund.

The whole of the amount collected, with the Bank interest, is spent in relief, the Proprietor of the *Mail* paying the entire cost of administration.

In February, 1900, the Hon. Secretaries received through Sir Arthur Bigge the following message from Her late Majesty Queen Victoria:—

"I have brought to the Queen's notice the fact that your Fund amounted to over £20,000, and Her Majesty was much gratified to hear of this substantial proof of the patriotism and sympathy of the Citizens of Birmingham."

The following extract from a letter was also received from Lord Roberts, when the Fund had reached £50,000:—

"The good that such patriotic movements do, and the benefit that is derived from them by the families of our gallant soldiers, who are serving in South Africa, cannot be estimated."

In the early days of the Fund a donation of £1,000 was received from the Kipling Poem Fund, and other interesting contributions include a collection from the British working men in Warsaw (Russia), a day's pay from the Officers, N.C.O's., and Men of the Warwickshire Militia; and £400 from a raffle of a bicycle for penny tickets. From nearly every country in the world where Warwickshire men are living contributions have been received.

Although the Fund was originally formed to help the families of Reservists; the Militia, Volunteers and Imperial Yeomen were afterwards included. At one time there were over two thousand families on the books receiving assistance.

The care of the widows and orphans, and to assist in obtaining their pensions, has been one of the chief features of the work of the Fund, and great satisfaction was felt when the Government gave notice of their intention to form the Navy and Army Pension Boards.

In addition to raising such a magnificent Fund, the *Birmingham Mail* has awakened the interest taken in the "Soldier" in Birmingham, and has brought out the patriotism and generosity of the working classes who have made so many sacrifices to help to keep together the homes of those who are fighting for their King and Country.

STATEMENT OF RECEIPTS AND PAYMENTS.

13th October, 1899 to 29th March, 1902.

RECEIPTS.	£	s.	d.	PAYMENTS.	£	s.	d.
To Contributions	54,182	1	3	By Grants to dependents	53,597	16	5
,, Bank Interest	410	0	3	,, Balance	994	5	1
	54,592	1	6		54,592	1	6

Joseph Lewis,
Bloomer & Ford, } *Chartered Accountants and Hon. Auditors.*

THE WAR EMPLOYMENT BUREAU.

The War Employment Bureau was established in October, 1899, in connection with the War in South Africa, by Mr. H. C. W. Gilson, and Mr. S. H. Benson, late Royal Navy, who, from its initiation, have acted as Honorary Secretaries, to find employment for wives and dependent relatives of soldiers and sailors employed on active service, and so to assist them as far as possible to maintain their homes during the absence of the breadwinner.

By the generosity of the late Mr. J. Lawson Johnston the expenses of the Organisation were, during his lifetime, defrayed without the issue of any appeals to the public, and the payments made to the women for work done, and the employment found have been of invaluable use, partly by supplementing the pecuniary aid rendered by the Soldiers' and Sailors' Families Association, but mainly by their being taught and encouraged to help themselves.

The Bureau had two distinct departments, the Registry Department for obtaining employment, and the Needlework Department for the supply of work to be done at their own homes.

The Registry Department was open to receive and deal with an unlimited number of applicants for charwomen, caretakers, and outwork of similar description; but though from time to time it had on its books women willing to enter domestic service, these were the exception, and as a rule the field of work in this direction was very small.

The Needlework Department was open two days in the week, when work was issued to the women on application, and the work completed returned. Lady visitors attended to inspect and pass the work for payment. The earnings varied from 7s. to 14s. per week. Women, whose husbands had returned from South Africa, were entered on a temporary list for three months, after which time, unless for some exceptional circumstances, their names were removed.

From the commencement of the War work has been found for over 1,800 women, 1,100 of whom have been employed at Needlework at their own homes.

Orders were received for every description of plain needlework, such for instance as 500 petticoats for a well-known charity; parcels of cholera belts and shirts for private despatch to the troops, charity garments for winter distribution to the poor, and even shirts and higher class work for private orders; but the chief work has been the making of shirts and other garments under contract with the Army Clothing Department from whom orders have been received for 400,000 garments.

STATEMENT OF RECEIPTS AND PAYMENTS.

October, 1899 to 31st March, 1902.

RECEIPTS.	£	s.	d.	PAYMENTS.	£	s.	d.
To Contribution by the late Mr. J. Lawson Johnston, and Payments by the War Office and other persons for Needlework done, etc.	11,393	0	0	By Payments to Reservists' wives, etc., for work done, and finding situations, office expenses, etc.	11,100	0	0
				,, Balance	293	0	0
	11,393	0	0		11,393	0	0

42, Shoe Lane, E.C.

SUMMARY

OF

APPROXIMATE AMOUNT SUBSCRIBED.

NOTE.—To arrive at an approximate estimate of Funds subscribed, it has been necessary to "delete" amounts passing through different hands, and to account for them only in the hands of the Administrators.

EXAMPLE.—Subscriptions raised by the Mayor of a Borough for the Mansion House Fund, and sent direct, or through the Lord Lieutenant of the County, earmarked for Widows and Orphans, are only here accounted for in the total amount received by the Patriotic Commissioners for administration.

PART I.

WIDOWS AND ORPHANS.

	£	s.	d.	£	s.	d.
The Mansion House Fund.						
Total amount received	1,135,015	0	0			
Less allocated to objects under various headings in this Record	1,098,368	0	0	*36,647	0	0
The Patriotic Fund.						
Received from the Mansion House	440,600	0	0			
,, ,, other sources	25,753	2	1	466,353	2	1
The Daily Telegraph Fund...				254,800	0	6
The Imperial War Fund.						
Received from the Mansion House	2,600	0	0			
,, ,, other sources	3,088	19	9			
	5,688	19	9			
Less included in other Funds	2,290	0	0	3,398	19	9
				761,199	2	4

WIVES AND FAMILIES.

The Soldiers' and Sailors' Families Association.						
Received from the Mansion House General Fund	194,827	0	0			
,, ,, ,, ,, Discretionary Fund	110,000	0	0			
,, ,, ,, ,, Queen Alexandra's Appeal	62,261	0	0			
,, ,, other sources	953,143	4	3	1,320,231	4	3
Officers' Families Fund				82,636	16	5
County and Borough Funds under this Part				668,125	0	0
Regimental Funds				32,361	15	2
The Birmingham Daily Mail Reservists' Fund				54,592	1	6
The War Employment Bureau				11,393	0	0
				2,930,538	19	8

	£	s.	d.
* Allocated to objects, such as Grants to Schools for Orphans, etc., having no place in this Record	26,870	0	0
Balance at Mansion House and in Consols on 31st December, 1901	9,777	0	0
	36,647	0	0

PART II.

SICK AND WOUNDED.
HOSPITAL SHIPS AND TRAINS.
PRIVATE HOSPITALS.

CONTENTS.

	PAGE
THE CENTRAL BRITISH RED CROSS COMMITTEE	79
NATIONAL SOCIETY FOR AID TO SICK AND WOUNDED IN WAR ...	80
THE CENTRAL BRITISH RED CROSS COMMITTEE'S WORK IN SOUTH AFRICA ...	81
ST. JOHN AMBULANCE ASSOCIATION	82
ST. JOHN AMBULANCE BRIGADE	82
ARMY NURSING SERVICE RESERVE	83
QUEEN ALEXANDRA'S IMPERIAL MILITARY NURSING SERVICE	83
HOSPITAL SHIPS { THE PRINCESS OF WALES	84
AMERICAN SHIP "MAINE" ...	86
HOSPITAL TRAINS { THE "PRINCESS CHRISTIAN"	88
"No. 4" ...	88
PRIVATE HOSPITALS { THE PORTLAND ...	89
THE LANGMAN ...	90
THE VAN ALEN ...	90
THE IRISH	91
THE "PRINCESS CHRISTIAN"	91
THE WELSH	92
THE EDINBURGH AND EAST OF SCOTLAND	92
THE SCOTTISH NATIONAL RED CROSS	93
THE IMPERIAL YEOMANRY	94
SUMMARY OF APPROXIMATE AMOUNTS SUBSCRIBED ...	95

THE CENTRAL BRITISH RED CROSS COMMITTEE.

The Central British Red Cross Committee, of which Her Majesty Queen Alexandra (then Princess of Wales) graciously accepted the appointment of Honorary President, and of which the late Lord Wantage was appointed Chairman,* and Major Macpherson Hon. Secretary, may be stated to have been definitely constituted and officially recognised in a letter of the 19th January, 1899, received from Lord Lansdowne, then Secretary of State for War.

The Committee was formed of representatives of the National Society for Aid to Sick and Wounded in War;—of the St. John Ambulance Association;—of the Army Nursing Service Reserve;—and of the Secretary of State for War.

The general object for which the Committee was formed was to maintain amongst voluntary aid societies in time of peace an organisation which would enable them to render prompt and efficient aid in time of war to sick and wounded, in the manner best suited to supplement the Army Medical Service.

It was understood that the Committee would have no control over, or take any part in the work and objects of the societies represented on it, except so far as these were concerned in providing and organising assistance for the relief of the sick and wounded in wars in which British troops were engaged; and, further, that the assistance of other voluntary aid societies, or of individuals desirous of working under the Red Cross, would be accepted only through one or other of the societies represented on the Committee, or through District Committees which it was proposed should be organised.

Regulations defining the method in which the voluntary aid resources of the country might be utilised to supplement the Army Medical Service in time of war were prepared and submitted for the sanction of the Secretary of State for War; but it was not until hostilities were imminent in South Africa that they were definitely accepted and printed for general information.

At a meeting of the Committee held on the 19th September, 1899, it was agreed:—

(1) That all subscriptions received from the public on behalf of sick and wounded should be handed over to the general funds of the National Aid Society.

(2) That all contributions of articles of clothing and other Hospital comforts should be sent to a central depôt in London to be packed and despatched to South Africa, the depôt to be under the direction of the St. John Ambulance Association.

(3) That a Red Cross Commissioner should be appointed to proceed to South Africa and make such preparations locally as might seem necessary for the reception and distribution of the articles sent from this country, with full power to enter into any expenditure on the spot, within the limits of the funds available, in whatever way might seem, in co-operation with the Principal Medical Officer of the Field Force, most suitable for adding to the well-being and comfort of the sick and wounded.

(4) That two hospital trains and a hospital ship should be fitted out with the funds which the National Aid Society could at once place at the disposal of the Committee, the sum available at that date being £20,000.

(5) That all offers of personal assistance as nursing sisters, and applications for employment as such, should be referred to the Army Nursing Service Reserve, and that the Committee should not in any way use their influence to obtain the employment of nurses whose qualifications did not entitle them to employment in the Reserve.

(6) That all offers of male assistance or applications for appointment as hospital workers should be referred to the St. John Ambulance Brigade, arrangements having been already made with the War Office by the Commissioner of the Brigade to supply any supplementary aid that might be required in this direction.

(7) That all offers of qualified medical aid or applications for appointment as Doctors, etc., under the Red Cross, should be referred to the Director-General of the Army Medical Service, he having a full list of civil surgeons, from whom to select, much in excess of possible requirements.

Such were the arrangements made for dealing with existing resources in anticipation of hostilities (see page 81).

---

* Lord Wantage, having died on 10th June, 1891, was succeeded by Viscount Knutsford.

THE NATIONAL SOCIETY FOR AID TO SICK AND WOUNDED IN WAR.

This Society, of which the late Lord Wantage was virtually the Founder, was the initiation of all such work in England, and was formed, upon the Rules laid down by the Geneva Convention in 1864, at a Public Meeting held at Willis's Rooms on the 4th August, 1870, with the object of rendering aid and assistance in the first instance to the sick and wounded of British and Imperial troops when engaged in war; and, secondly, in giving similar aid impartially to the sick and wounded of belligerent armies in case of England's neutrality.

A Branch of the Society was formed in February, 1885, by Queen Alexandra (then Princess of Wales), and known as "The Princess of Wales's Branch," for the purpose of sending to the sick and wounded of British, Indian, and Australian troops in Egypt and the Soudan, medical and other luxuries, and of providing troops with amusements, games, books, and extra comforts.

In anticipation of the outbreak of hostilities in South Africa, and with a view of enabling the Central British Red Cross Committee to meet any sudden demands, the late Lord Wantage, in his dual capacity of Chairman of the above Society and of the Red Cross Committee, issued an appeal to the public through the press on 28th September, 1899. By the Regulations of the Red Cross Committee, referred to on the previous page, it will be seen that all contributions for Red Cross work should be handed over to the National Aid Society; but, as regards the South African Campaign, it was agreed that all subscriptions resulting from this appeal should be utilised for carrying out the various schemes in connection with the War. This appeal was subsequently supported by the Lord Mayor of London, including amongst the four objects of the Mansion House Fund that under No. 2 for Sick and Wounded.

The contributions from this latter source amounted to £96,759, with an addition of £5,000 from the Lord Mayor's Discretionary Fund, whilst the response to the appeal of Lord Wantage amounted to £77,191, making together £178,950.

In addition £9,000 was received from Queen Alexandra towards the special equipment of Her Majesty's Hospital Ship *The Princess of Wales*, and £8,750 from the Mayor of Windsor, The Princess Christian's Windsor Fund for the construction of Her Royal Highness's Hospital Train; the former, and £650 of the latter, being balances of "The Princess of Wales's Branch" of this Society above referred to.

The Society, after the outbreak of hostilities, obtained various concessions on behalf of Red Cross work. The Castle Line Steamship Company allowed all stores to be shipped to South Africa at half rates. The Eastern Telegraph Company arranged for the free transmission of all telegrams between London and Cape Town. The Standard Bank remitted the Commission charges on the large sums that were cabled to the Society's Agents; whilst Messrs. Barnes & Co., of Tooley Street, gave the free use of one of their large store-rooms (placed under the direction of the St. John Ambulance Association) for the reception of "material," previous to its despatch.

THE CENTRAL BRITISH RED CROSS COMMITTEE'S WORK IN SOUTH AFRICA.

The twelve months' work of the Central British Red Cross Committee at the seat of war, which commenced on the 14th November, 1899, and ended on the 10th November, 1900, was chiefly that of organization and supervision through its commissioners and agents sent out from England, and may be shortly summarised as follows:—

In addition to *The Princess of Wales* Hospital Ship (see page 84) and "The Princess Christian" Hospital Train (see page 88), sent out from England, the commissioners prepared another Hospital Train ("No. 4," see also page 88) in South Africa;—a Hospital Hut offered by the Princess of Wales, the gift of the Portable Buildings Company, handed over to the principal Medical Officer and erected at Naauwpoort in January, 1900;—and a second Hospital Hut, planned, erected, and equipped at Green Point, in the name of the Actors and Actresses of London (who provided the chief part of the funds).

At the first outbreak of enteric fever in February, De Aar Hospital was furnished with 200 beds and bedding. Over 100 beds and bedding were provided at Maitland, and similar help was given in Natal. At Bloemfontein, during the great epidemic, large quantities of supplies and clothing were provided. At the relief of Kimberley the British Red Cross Stores were the first to reach the sick and wounded of the garrison, and entered Ladysmith with a large supply three days after its relief; "The Princess Christian" Hospital Train being also the first train to reach Ladysmith after the siege, the temporary trestle bridge over the Tugela being inaugurated by the passage of the train over it. Finally, aid was also given at the relief of Mafeking.

In the early days of the campaign the Committee's provision of clothing to home-returning invalids met an urgent need, and, in combination with "The Good Hope Society,"* it supplied some 20,000 hospital kits to the Hospital Trains for the comfort of the sick and wounded passengers. Throughout South Africa it gave help to over 200 hospitals up to the furthest point of the lines of communication, and distributed over 13,000 bales and cases received from England, the Colonies, and abroad, to the value of £30,000. In addition it expended in South Africa the sum of £40,000, of which £3,238 was after much difficulty got into Pretoria for the relief of the sick and wounded prisoners in the hands of the Boers.

The commissioners were also able to obtain the following privileges and concession: The Cape Government gave free carriage for Red Cross stores, and free passes over its lines, to its agents. The Speaker and Clerk of the House of Assembly placed a large and convenient committee room in Parliament House for an office as well as providing a small packing store.

The Collector of Customs lent a large shed as a receiving store at the docks, and allowed the services of one of his officers as a storekeeper. The principal Naval Transport Officer granted free shipments for Red Cross stores on His Majesty's transports, and whenever necessary free passages to Durban and other ports. The Castle and Union lines, who had already agreed to bring out stores from England at half rates, made the same concession for the coast traffic, and subsequently remitted all charges; and lastly, Messrs. A. R. McKenzie, the largest shipping agents in Cape Town, agreed to clear, to store, and to carry all Red Cross stores at reduced rates. Similar privileges were also obtained in Natal.

---

* Part VI., Page 142.

THE ST. JOHN AMBULANCE ASSOCIATION.

The work of the Association, established in 1877 by the Order of St. John of Jerusalem, was chiefly devoted to preparing, collecting, and forwarding to appointed depôts in the field, clothing, medical and surgical materials, such as dressings, utensils, linen, bedding, hospital equipment, and medical comforts.

As stated in a previous article, a large store-room was placed at the disposal of the Association by Messrs. Barnes & Co.—Lieut.-Colonel Holbeche having undertaken the duty of Director of the Depôt, Mr. W. G. Barnes, Junior, devoting a great deal of his time gratuitously to superintending the sorting, re-packing and shipments of the stores. The total number of packages received from the public was 3,550. 7,216 special cases (which could be utilised on arrival) made with buckle-hinged lids, and strengthened with patent wire secured by staples instead of hoop iron, were sent out, the weight being about 500 tons; 300 of these were sent to Natal. In addition to this work, the Association supplied from their manufactory at Ashford 150 military stretchers and covers in connection with the fitting out of improvised hospital trains.

THE ST. JOHN AMBULANCE BRIGADE.

Two distinct classes of contingents were furnished from this Brigade, which is also a branch of the Order of St. John of Jerusalem, for service in South Africa, viz., 1st, men required as auxiliaries to the Royal Army Medical Corps;—Mr. Mosely's ("The Princess Christian") Hospital;—and for the Rhodesian Field Force Hospital, all of whom served immediately under the War Office; 2nd, men required for service in the private hospitals equipped under the auspices of the Central British Red Cross Committee. Under this head are included the Princess of Wales's Hospital Ship, the Portland Hospital, the Princess Christian's Hospital Train, the Langman Hospital, the American (Mr. Van Alen's) Section of a Field Hospital, the Imperial Yeomanry Hospital, the Imperial Yeomanry Field Hospital, and the *Maine* (American) Hospital Ship, the men in which categories served under contract with the Committees or providers of the Hospitals.

The men accepted for service were not enlisted in the army, but entered into a civil contract with the Secretary of State for War, or the several Committees, &c., to serve for not less than six months, and although not subject to the conditions of the Army Act, undertook in these contracts to submit to the usual rules of discipline, and were liable to dismissal at any time in case of misconduct. Each man had to provide himself with a personal outfit, which in some cases were paid by the volunteer himself, in some by the corps or division to which the man belonged, and in some by local public subscriptions. The cost of the field kit was advanced by the Order of St. John, or defrayed by the several Hospitals or Committees. Up to the month of March 1901, 39 contingents were despatched to South Africa under the above conditions, containing altogether 1,884 men. Since that time 50 men have been supplied to the South African Constabulary, and 112 have enlisted in the Royal Army Medical Corps, thus bringing up the total to 2,046 men, among whom 65 deaths have occurred.

A Special Fund in connection with the Brigade was raised, and the sum of £951 expended in the purchase of extra comforts, besides contributing large quantities of material in kind.

St. John's Gate, Clerkenwell, E.C.

ARMY NURSING SERVICE RESERVE.

THE work of the Army Nursing Service Reserve, in connection with the voluntary aid resources of the War, was confined to the selection and outfit of Nursing Sisters for duty, not only in the hospitals in South Africa, but also in the larger Military Hospitals at home, whose establishment of Nursing Sisters of the Regular Army Nursing Service had become depleted, the qualifications for enrolment in the Reserve being similar to that required for admission into the Army Nursing Service.

At the commencement of the War on 9th October, 1899, the number of Nursing Sisters on the list of the Army Nursing Service Reserve was 101, but between that date and the 10th May, 1901, 839 were added. Among these were twelve specially selected and sent to South Africa by Queen Alexandra, and called the "Princess of Wales's Nurses."

QUEEN ALEXANDRA'S IMPERIAL MILITARY NURSING SERVICE.*

BY a Royal Warrant issued on 27th March 1902 † it was enacted that an Imperial Military Nursing Service, to be designated the "Queen Alexandra's Imperial Military Nursing Service," and comprising the "Army Nursing Service," should be established under certain regulations as to pay, allowances, and pensions on retirement. To this new service Her Majesty Queen Alexandra was appointed President.

---

* Although not immediately connected with voluntary aid work during the War, the creation of this Service may be said to be the outcome of it, and may be of interest in the future as showing the time and circumstances under which it was established.

† Army Order (67) April, 1902.

"THE PRINCESS OF WALES" HOSPITAL SHIP.

AT a meeting of the Central British Red Cross Committee held on the 19th September, 1899, it was agreed to equip and send a Hospital Ship to South Africa in the event of the outbreak of hostilities, enquiries being at once set on foot to find a suitable vessel.

After several ships had been inspected, and War having been declared, *The Midnight Sun*, a yachting cruiser, was decided upon as being considered the most suitable, and the work of refitting at once put in hand. Her Majesty Queen Alexandra (then Princess of Wales), the Hon. President of the Central British Red Cross Committee, having expressed a wish to devote a sum of £9,000, part balance of the Princess of Wales's Branch of the National Aid Society, the ship was, with her gracious consent, re-named *The Princess of Wales*.

When refitted the ward accommodation consisted of 184 Cots, viz. :—

No. 1. "Princess Alexandra" (Surgical)	...	40 Cots.
No. 2. "Princess Louise" (General)	...	52 ,,
No. 3. "Princess Maud" (Medical)	...	30 ,,
No. 4. ,, ,, (Convalescents)		56 ,,
No. 5. "Princess Victoria" (Officers)	...	4 ,,
No. 6. (Isolation)	...	2 ,,

The Hospital establishment consisted of five medical officers, four nursing sisters, and 41 non-commissioned officers and men, about half of whom belonged to the Royal Army Medical Corps, and the remainder to the St. John Ambulance Brigade.

The ship's company consisted of 85 officers and men.

The Hospital Staff were appointed and paid by the War Office, but all other expenses, including the messing of the officers, victualling of the non-commissioned officers and men, dieting of invalids, coaling and other sailing expenses, were defrayed from Red Cross funds, with the exception of the coal supplied by the Naval Authorities in South Africa, payment for which was made by the War Office.

A large supply of Red Cross stores was shipped, besides a varied and plentiful assortment of wines, spirits, and mineral waters contributed by several firms and private individuals.

Her Majesty Queen Alexandra presented games of every description, as well as a large quantity of tobacco, pipes, and cigarettes for distribution to the patients.

There was also a piano and an excellent organ on board, as well as a library, largely supplemented by voluntary contributions.

The ship thus fully equipped was inspected at Tilbury on the 22nd November by His Majesty the King (then Prince of Wales) and Queen Alexandra, and sailed for South Africa, reaching Cape Town on the 8th January, 1900.

On the 31st of the same month she made her first homeward voyage with 174 invalids on board, arriving at Southampton on the 26th February, and after being visited by Queen Alexandra and the Prince of Wales (then Duke of York) disembarked her patients.

Previous to her despatch on a second voyage the ship was thoroughly overhauled, the whole of the electric wires and dynamos receiving special attention.

On the 12th of April she sailed again from Southampton after taking in a further supply of Red Cross stores, and reached Cape Town on the 10th May.

While awaiting the embarkation of invalids, the ship remained in Simon's Bay, and was eventually sent to East London to take on board a number of sick and wounded that had accumulated there and were waiting transfer to the Base Hospital at Cape Town or to England.

The ship arrived at East London on the 29th of May, took on board 178 invalids, and sailed on the 4th of June, reaching Cape Town two days later. Ninety-two invalids and one officer disembarked there, when their places were taken by other invalids who were being sent home.

The homeward voyage lasted from the 13th of June to the 9th of July—173 invalids being on board; Queen Alexandra again visiting the ship before they disembarked.

The ship sailed again from Southampton on her third and last voyage on the 23rd of August, arriving at Cape Town on the 16th of September, sailing again on the 24th of September for Durban, which she reached three days later, and remained at that port as a Stationary Hospital ship till the 5th of November. During this period four officers and 255 of other ranks were admitted for treatment in the wards.

The time of the ship's commission having nearly expired, she left Durban with 174 invalids, including three officers, for Cape Town, which was reached on the 8th of November, where four of the invalids were landed and six others taken on board, the ship eventually sailing, homeward bound, on the 12th of November, and reaching Southampton on the 8th of December, when Queen Alexandra again, for the third time, visited her before the disembarkation of the invalids.

One of the patients died on this voyage, being the only death during the whole period of the ship's employment as a Hospital ship.

The actual number of cases treated during the whole period of the ship's commission was 728, of whom 25 were men belonging to the hospital staff or ship's company, 133 were cases of enteric fever, and 33 of dysentery—the fatal case being one of enteric.

The distance covered during the ship's runs was over 40,000 miles.

It may be stated that in proportion to tonnage *The Princess of Wales* Hospital Ship afforded more ward accommodation and other hospital facilities than larger ships, from the fact that practically the whole of the main and lower deck space was available for hospital purposes.

The total expenditure on the Hospital Ship amounted to about £54,000.

The following will prove of special interest in connection with this ship :—

A Committee of Danish farmers having collected a quantity of the best Danish butter, and having asked the Princess of Wales to accept 12,000 boxes as a gift for the British soldiers, received the following telegram—

"SANDRINGHAM,

"*6th January*, 1900.

"My heart was deeply moved when I heard of the handsome and practical manner in which the Danish dairies are showing their sympathy for our gallant British soldiers by sending them 12,000 boxes of butter. In asking me to distribute this large and splendid gift among the sick and wounded in South Africa and on my Hospital Ship, you cause me the greatest pleasure, as I shall be able to say that it is a present from my beloved native country—Denmark.

"ALEXANDRA."

AMERICAN HOSPITAL SHIP "MAINE."

Mrs. Blow, an American lady long resident in South Africa, first originated the idea of a Hospital Ship for this War, Lady Randolph Churchill (Mrs. George Cornwallis West) carrying it out and forming a Committee. A Meeting was held on the 25th of October, 1899, at her house, when Lady Randolph Churchill was appointed Chairman, Mrs. Blow, Hon. Secretary, and Mrs. Ronalds, Hon. Treasurer, and the following resolution was proposed and carried:—

"That whereas Great Britain is now involved in a war affecting the rights and liberty of the Anglo-Saxon people in South Africa, and has under arms 70,000 troops to maintain such rights and liberty;

"And whereas 50,000 English and American men, women, and children have been expelled from the States now at war with Her Majesty's Government, and are congregated at Durban, Delagoa Bay, and Cape Town;

"And whereas, in consequence of the inevitable results of war, together with the congested conditions of these places of refuge, the dangers of approaching summer, and the dreaded African fever, there will be great need of medical attendance, nursing, and nourishing food, before and after the cessation of hostilities;

"And whereas the people of Great Britain have, by their sympathy and moral support, materially aided the people of the United States of America in the war in Cuba and the Philippine Islands: It is therefore resolved:—

"That the American women in Great Britain, whilst deploring the necessity for War, shall endeavour to raise, among their compatriots here and in America, a fund for the relief of the sick and wounded soldiers and refugees in South Africa. It is proposed to dispatch immediately a suitable Hospital Ship, fully equipped with medical stores and provisions, to accommodate 200 patients for three months, with a staff of four doctors, five nurses, and forty non-commissioned officers and orderlies."

The *Maine*, through Mr. Bernard Baker, the President of the Atlantic Transport Company, was offered to the Government, including the captain and crew, who were to be maintained at the Company's expense during the time she was in commission. The Admiralty, having taken no steps to alter her from a cattle boat to a Hospital Ship, when the Ladies' Committee was formed, the latter undertook to take her on the same terms and fit her up.

The Ship made three voyages (two to South Africa and one to China). Lady Randolph Churchill, as the Committee's representative went out on the first voyage. Before sailing on the 23rd of December, 1899, her late Majesty Queen Victoria presented the ship with a Union Jack, and deputed the Duke of Connaught to make the presentation, when His Royal Highness made the following speech:—

"In the name of Her Majesty the Queen, I present this Union Jack to the Hospital Ship *Maine* as a mark of her appreciation of the generosity of those who have found the money for this ship, and also as a mark of her appreciation of that charity which a large number of ladies and gentlemen have shown towards the soldiers of her kin speaking their own language, and who are now fighting gallantly in South Africa. It is a great pleasure to me to have been asked to perform what I believe is a unique ceremony. Never before has a ship sailed under the combined flags of the Union Jack and the Stars and Stripes, and it marks, I hope, an occasion which brings out that feeling of generosity and affection that the two countries have for each other. I cannot sufficiently thank those who have come forward in such a liberal manner for what they have done. As an officer in the English Army, I feel, I can assure you, most deeply what you all have done for us this day, and I am sure that the officers and men who may reap the advantage of this well-formed ship, will bless those who have done so much towards it. I should like to mention many names, but I am afraid it is impossible, and I will therefore ask Lady Randolph Churchill to accept, in the name of all those who have worked with her, the thanks both of the Sovereign, of our Country, and of all English men and English women for this splendid present, which has been made in aid of our Wounded Soldiers in South Africa."

During the *Maine's* absence Mrs. Adair (who had been appointed Vice-Chairman) proceeded to America in the interest of the Fund, and succeeded in enlisting the active co-operation of a number of ladies in New York and elsewhere.

The *Maine* arrived at Cape Town on the 23rd of January, and having proceeded to Durban, remained there from the 5th of February to the 17th of March, receiving on board and treating a large number of cases. She then sailed for England with 163 patients, and arrived at Southampton on the 23rd of April.

After refitting the ship sailed for South Africa on her second voyage on the 3rd of May, arriving at Cape Town on the 29th of the same month, sailing again homeward bound with 160 patients on the 8th of June, and arriving at Southampton on the 3rd of July, when her late Majesty sent a gracious message of welcome and Her Majesty's appreciation of this generous undertaking, through H.R.H. the Princess Louise, Duchess of Argyll, to the Hon. Treasurer, requesting that the same should be communicated to the Committee. H.R.H. the Princess Louise on this occasion visited the ship, and presented, on behalf of the Committee, to each patient as he left the ship (as had previously been done) a commemorative medal, tobacco, and a pipe.

The ship was again refitted for a third voyage, but the demand for China being more pressing than for South Africa, she sailed for the Far East on the 12th of July, 1900, arriving at Wei-hai-Wei on the 6th of September and Taku on the 21st of October, being employed in receiving and conveying sick and wounded between Yokohama, Nagasaki, and other ports until sailing for home again on the 9th of November, *viâ* Malta (where two officers and thirty-three men were taken on board); she arrived at Southampton on the 13th of January, 1901. The total number treated on this voyage was twenty-one officers and 333 men.

The ship was thus kept in commission for fifteen months, instead of three, as was originally intended, having been supported almost entirely by American money during that time.

At the conclusion of the third voyage, Mr. Bernard Baker, President of the Atlantic Transport Company, most generously presented the ship to the English Government, the Ladies' Committee giving all the hospital fittings and equipment, and the *Maine* is now attached to the Mediterranean Squadron as a permanent Hospital Ship.

It had been intended to offer Her late Majesty a medal and address as a souvenir in remembrance of the work done by the ship and of Her Majesty's great interest in the same. These were presented to His Majesty King Edward and were graciously accepted.

STATEMENT OF RECEIPTS AND PAYMENTS.

RECEIPTS.	£	s.	d.	PAYMENTS.	£	s.	d.
To Donations, subscriptions, etc.	41,597	13	2	By Construction, repairs, etc.	20,313	3	4
				,, Stores	5,923	12	10
				,, Equipment	5,093	1	2
				,, Staff	7,408	15	4
				,, Office, secretarial, etc.	2,562	13	2
				,, Balance	296	7	4
	£41,597	13	2		£41,597	13	2

THE "PRINCESS CHRISTIAN" HOSPITAL TRAIN.

On the initiative of the Princess Christian, the Central British Red Cross Committee agreed to supplement the Army Medical Service by the building and equipping of a complete Hospital Train, which was named "The Princess Christian Hospital Train;" more especially as Her Royal Highness had for so long identified herself with the Hospital work in general, and was taking so keen an interest in this scheme for the comfort of the sick and wounded. The train consisted of seven bogie "corridor" carriages, each about 36 feet long by eight feet wide, the passage through the centre being continuous. No. 1 carriage was divided into three compartments for linen and other stores, for two Nurses, and for two Invalid Officers respectively. No. 2 was divided also into three compartments, for two Medical Officers, a dining-room, and a Dispensary. Nos. 3, 4, 5, and 6, were each constructed to carry 18 invalids and four Hospital Orderlies. Each carriage was provided with a stove, a lavatory, and a closet. No. 7 contained the kitchen and pantry, berths for two cooks, divided by a compartment for the guard.

The Train was perfectly fitted with hygienic appliances for cooking; several large cisterns for cold water storage, two large filters, two refrigerators (one at each end of the train), and everything complete for 97 persons.

It had been intended to put the Train together at Cape Town, but on its arrival, early in February, 1900, Lord Roberts decided that it should be sent to Durban, and on the 18th March it commenced the work for which it was intended by its first journey to Ladysmith.

The following is a summary of the numbers carried by the Train in its 108 journeys of 42,115 miles, under Red Cross auspices, viz:—

Officers	321
Nursing Sisters	19
Non-commissioned Officers and Men	... 7,208

Total: 7,548

There were three deaths among sick carried, and three among Staff of Train.

In the month of June, 1901, the Train was formally presented by the British Central Red Cross Committee to the Secretary of State for War, on the understanding that it should retain the name of "The Princess Christian Hospital Train," and remain as a complete Hospital Train unit for the use of the Military Forces in South Africa.

No. 4 HOSPITAL TRAIN.

This may be stated to have been a "replica" of the above, and was made up (when in April, 1900, it was found there was great need for another Hospital Train) of carriages converted on the spot. It consisted of five coaches and a brake van, and, later on, two additional carriages, making up a total of 114 beds, including six in a separate compartment for officers. Two small vans were also added for soldiers' kits, pack stores, and guard. A continuous passage ran through the train, and each coach had a lavatory. Folding doors, one each side of every carriage, allowed the sick and wounded to be taken in and out on stretchers. The whole of the Train was painted white outside and green inside. The Train, in charge of a doctor, two nursing sisters, and 12 orderlies, with accommodation for 72 patients (subsequently increased to 114), left East London for Bloemfontein on the 10th June, 1900.

The whole of the expenses were defrayed by the British Central Red Cross Committee.

THE PORTLAND HOSPITAL.

THE suggestion of sending out Private Hospitals to the War originated in a letter written to *The Times* by Dr. George Stoker, on 15th October, 1899, advocating independent flying hospitals as the most useful form of voluntary aid, but on the recommendation of the British Central Red Cross Committee, stationary hospitals of 100 beds, to be attached to some of the larger Military Hospitals at the base or on the lines of communication, were generally adopted.

The credit of the establishment of the first of these Hospitals was due to the indefatigable zeal and energy of Captain and Mrs. Bagot and their friends, of whom Lord and Lady Henry Bentinck, in the preliminary stage, were the chief supporters. Subsequently the Duke of Portland made a generous donation, obviating the necessity for a public appeal, and was requested to allow the Hospital to bear his name.

The conditions under which this and similar Hospitals were accepted by the War Office were as follows, viz. :—

(1). The Officer in Charge to be an Officer of the Royal Army Medical Corps, who will be assisted by a Staff of two Non-Commissioned Officers of the same Corps.

(2). The Hospital to be attached to one of the General Hospitals in South Africa.

(3). The Hospital to be entirely at the disposal of the Military Authorities on its arrival in South Africa.

(4.) The War Office to convey the Hospital to South Africa, and when its services are no longer required to grant passages back to England.

The original number of beds for which it was organised was 104, but eventually it expanded in South Africa in times of pressure to 160.

The *personnel* consisted of an Army Medical Officer in charge, 4 Civil Surgeons, 6 Nursing Sisters of the Army Nursing Service Reserve, 2 Non-Commissioned Officers of the Royal Army Medical Corps, 26 Ambulance Officers and men of the St. John Ambulance Brigade, a Cook, an Assistant Cook, and 4 Servants.

Lord Henry Bentinck and Captain Jocelyn Bagot sailed with the Hospital for South Africa as Hon. Treasurer and Hon. Secretary respectively, and were accompanied by Lady Henry Bentinck and Mrs. Bagot in an unofficial capacity. These ladies remained with the Hospital nearly the whole period of its work, doing their part, as so many noble men and women have done, in helping to alleviate the suffering of the sick and wounded.

The Hospital and Staff arrived at Cape Town in the closing days of 1899 and was opened at Rondebosch on the 8th of January, 1900, being attached there to No. 3 General Hospital. It was subsequently transferred to Bloemfontein at the time of the enteric fever epidemic, and was opened there on the 19th of April, continuing to be used until the 12th of July, 1900, when it was closed.

The number of Patients who passed through the Wards amounted to 119 Officers and 890 Non-Commissioned Officers and men, of whom 303 were surgical cases. Two officers and 35 men died in the Hospital.

The voluntary subscriptions amounted to £13,647 10s. 3d., with a balance in hand, when the Hospital ceased its work, of £6,069 1s. 1d.

THE LANGMAN HOSPITAL.

The successful organisation of the Portland Hospital, and the interest which it excited among those who undertook its organisation, led Mr. Langman, who was its Honorary Treasurer, to offer to equip another hospital on similar lines at his own expense. The conditions with the War Office were that Mr. Langman was to provide 100 beds, in six 20 ft. by 20 ft. tents for ten beds each; five square bell tents for four beds each; seven tents for officers, one for an office, one for a dispensary, one bell tent as a mortuary, seven ordinary bell tents for orderlies, with one screen for a kitchen, and one screen for latrines. He also agreed to equip the Hospital with the necessary bedding, clothing, ward utensils, and medical supplies, and further undertook to pay and bear all the expenses of the staff, along with the upkeep of the Hospital for six months from the date of its embarkation till its return to England. The War Office undertook to supply the usual free ration to each individual of the Hospital *personnel*, and to supply the diet and extras of the patients under treatment. They further undertook to convey the *personnel* and equipment free of charge to South Africa, and also to pay the passages back to England.

The staff consisted of one officer of the Royal Army Medical Corps in charge, four civil physicians and surgeons, five medical students as dressers, one quartermaster, 26 subordinate ambulance officers and men, including cooks, clerks, dispensers, and storekeepers, and his son, Lieut. A. L. Langman, of the Middlesex Yeomanry, as Secretary and Treasurer. When the Hospital was expanded to 180 beds, four nurses and eight regimental orderlies were added.

The Hospital reached East London on 28th March, 1900, and was opened at Bloemfontein on 8th April, remaining there until 25th July, when it left for Pretoria, and where it was again opened on 2nd August. On 4th November, 1900, the whole of the Hospital material, tents, and equipment were presented as a free gift to the Government by the donor. The number of patients admitted was 1,211, of whom 58 died. The medical cases included 69 officers and 778 men; the surgical cases 27 officers and 337 men.

The special feature of this Hospital was that the whole equipment and *personnel* sailed in the same transport, and were never separated. Thus when the Hospital was moved from Bloemfontein to Pretoria at the time when there was immense pressure on the railway, and every truck was of great value, the whole equipment, tents, bedsteads, etc., including the stores for 100 beds, went up in five trucks. This was the first private Hospital to reach Bloemfontein.

THE VAN ALEN HOSPITAL.

Mr. Van Alen, an American citizen, obtained sanction to proceed to South Africa with a 25-bed section of a Field Hospital, to be called "The American Section of a Field Hospital." The conditions under which his offer was accepted were that it should be in charge of an officer of the Royal Army Medical Corps, and be attached to whatever Field Hospital the Military Authorities in South Africa might direct. Mr. Alen was to accompany the unit, and to provide at his own expense all necessary equipment and transport, the War Office agreeing to convey the Hospital to South Africa, and when no longer required give it passage back to England.

The staff consisted of one warrant officer of the Royal Army Medical Corps, nine men of the St. John Ambulance Brigade, seven drivers, and Mr. Murray Guthrie, M.P., as Secretary. The transport consisted of two riding horses, 22 mules, and three tortoise waggons.

On 10th March, 1900, a few days after its arrival at Cape Town, the Hospital was sent up to Kimberley, arriving there on 13th March, and commencing work in Newton Camp immediately after. On 3rd April it left Kimberley, and proceeded with Lord Methuen in his operations north and west of that town, and was eventually handed over to the Government at Paardekraal on 6th July, 1900.

THE IRISH HOSPITAL.

This Hospital was the gift of Lord Iveagh, who offered to equip the same as a Stationary Hospital of 100 beds, conditionally that he should be permitted to provide means of transport to accompany the Hospital, so as to enable it to occupy any position on the lines of communication that might be required from time to time by the local Military Authorities. The Staff consisted, in addition to one Officer of the Royal Army Medical Corps, four Civil Surgeons, four Nursing Sisters, two Non-commissioned Officers of the Royal Army Medical Corps, four Officers of the St. John Ambulance Brigade, 12 Ward Orderlies, 1st. grade, and 12 Ward Orderlies, 2nd grade, of the St. John Ambulance Brigade, six servants, including a cook and female servant, and a secretary and treasurer.

The transport consisted of 15 waggons, two carts, and harness for 80 mules.

Soon after the arrival of the Hospital at Cape Town on the 26th of February, 1900, it proceeded to Naauwport, where a detachment was detailed to accompany Lord Kitchener on an expedition to Prieska. The rest of the Hospital received orders to proceed to Bloemfontein at short notice, when a start was made on the 10th of April, and Bloemfontein reached on the 21st of April. On the 10th of May a portion of the Hospital, viz; 10 waggons, four large tortoise tents, and seven square bell-tents, left by route march to join Lord Roberts at Kroonstadt, where they were attached to the 11th Division; Pretoria being reached on the 6th of June. On the 14th of June the Palace of Justice was taken over by the Hospital and placed at the disposal of its Staff, who equipped it sufficiently to enable 83 patients to be admitted on the 19th of same month. On the 25th of June it had expanded to 260 beds; on the 10th of July to 365, and on the 26th of July to 500 beds; the section left behind at Bloemfontein rejoining at Pretoria on the 1st of July. No patients were admitted to the Hospital after the 30th September, and the Staff left for England on the 15th October, 1900.

The mules, waggons, harness, and tents, were disposed of by sale to the Government; the beds, bedding, and hospital equipment being given over as a free gift.

THE "PRINCESS CHRISTIAN" HOSPITAL.

At the request of Mr. Alfred Mosely, the donor, and with the permission of the Princess Christian, this Hospital was named "The Princess Christian Hospital."

The conditions under which the gift was accepted by the War Office, were, that Mr. Mosely should provide 100 beds in hut wards, two warehouses for storing goods, a fully equipped kitchen, and storehouses for linen, with all the necessary bedding, ward utensils, and medical supplies.

It was agreed that he should select four Civil Surgeons, six Nursing Sisters (to be enrolled in the Army Nursing Service Reserve), and two Dressers, paying all expenses. He also undertook to pay and cater for the Surgeons, Nurses, and Dressers, and bear all expenses connected with the up-keep of the Hospital for four months after its arrival in South Africa; the Government on their part undertaking to convey the *personnel* to Cape Town, and back again to England when their services were no longer required.

The Hospital arrived at Cape Town on the 10th March, 1900; but to the great disappointment of Mr. Mosely, whose associations were entirely with Cape Colony, it was immediately shipped to Durban, where it arrived on the 30th of March. Mr. Mosely, who remained with the Hospital himself through the period of its existence, was, however, able to obtain an exceptional healthy site for it at Pinetown Bridge, about 15 miles from Durban, where the Hospital was opened on the 19th April, 1900. During the pressure that arose, in consequence of the epidemic of enteric fever, immediately after the opening of the Hospital, the local authorities were anxious to expand the Hospital to 200 beds at the Government expense; but this Mr. Mosely himself most generously undertook. A large quantity of comforts were presented by the Princess Christian, and many articles of equipment by several manufacturers and personal friends of Mr. Mosely. The Hospital was closed as a Private Hospital on the 20th of July 1900, when the buildings and equipment were placed by Mr. Mosely at the disposal of Her Royal Highness, and by her presented to the Government.

THE WELSH HOSPITAL.

The funds for this Hospital were obtained by subscriptions from Welshmen in and connected with the Principality, and included £100 from Her late Majesty Queen Victoria, £50 from the King (then Prince of Wales), and £25 from the Duke of York, besides many substantial gifts of hospital supplies from Queen Alexandra (then Princess of Wales).

The Hospital was originally organised as a Stationary Hospital of 100 beds, or as a section of a General Hospital, although the number of beds was eventually increased to 150, and to 200 when it was eventually moved to Pretoria. The Staff consisted of three Senior Surgeons, two Assistant Surgeons, eight Medical Students as Dressers, ten Nursing Sisters, two maids, and forty-eight orderlies, cooks, and stretcher-bearers. Before leaving for South Africa the Staff were honoured by being inspected at Marlborough House by the King and Queen Alexandra.

The Hospital and Staff arrived at Cape Town on 3rd of May, 1900, and immediately on arrival the Surgeons and Dressers were sent to assist in the Bloemfontein Hospitals and in the Hospitals at Cape Town. Subsequently the Hospital was established as a complete unit, attached to No. 3 Hospital at Springfontein, and commenced to receive patients on the 7th of June. Here it had the misfortune to lose its Chief Surgeon, Professor Thomas Jones, and Assistant Surgeon Davies, and subsequently Professor Alfred Hughes, its chief organiser, who, in the emergency caused by the death of these two surgeons, volunteered at once to proceed to South Africa, and after remaining with the Hospital until it was closed, died of enteric fever soon after his return to England. On the 1st of August the Hospital was transferred to Pretoria, and was attached to No. 2 General Hospital there until the 15th of November, 1900, when the whole of the marquees, tents, material, equipment, and stores were handed over to the Government as a free gift.

The number of cases treated was 1,107, of whom only 10 died, a percentage of less than one.

The subscriptions received amounted to £12,539 9s. 7d. leaving a balance of £3,892 10s. 5d. for disposal after all liabilities had been met.

THE EDINBURGH AND EAST OF SCOTLAND HOSPITAL.

This Hospital was organised by the Lord Provost of Edinburgh, and was provided by subscriptions raised in Edinburgh and the East of Scotland.

The Committee agreed to provide 100 beds in specially-constructed huts, along with a warehouse for storing goods, a storehouse for linen, a fully-equipped kitchen and hutting for the Staff and *personnel*, and to equip these huts with the necessary beds, bedding, clothing, ward utensils, and all medical supplies. The War Office undertook to replenish the latter, when they became exhausted, at the public expense. The Committee were further permitted to select, for the professional staff, seven Civil Physicians and Surgeons, eight Dressers, and six Nursing Sisters of the Army Nursing Service Reserve, along with a Matron, and undertook to pay all the expenses connected with them and with any other hospital employé who might be drawn from civil sources. The patients and the whole of the *personnel* were to receive the usual Government ration free, but all extras beyond those included in the diet scales for patients in Military Hospitals were to be provided out of the funds of the Hospital. The equipment and *personnel* were to be conveyed to Cape Town free, and, when their services were no longer required, to be granted free passages home. The Hospital, which was intended to act as a separate and distinct unit on the lines of communication, arrived at Cape Town on the 10th of April, 1900, and was opened at Norval's Point on 2nd May, where it remained till the 14th of October. During the pressure of work at the time of its opening the Hospital was expanded to 150 beds.

The number of patients admitted was 507, of whom 334 were medical and 173 surgical cases. There were 14 deaths.

The subscriptions received amounted to £21,325 5s. 4d., a balance of £8,000 being left after all expenses had been met, which was disposed of as follows, viz.:—

To Queen Alexandra's Appeal for the Soldiers' and Sailors' Families Association	£6,000 0 0
To *The Scotsman*, for Widows and Orphans	2,000 0 0

The Hospital was presented as a free gift to the Government.

THE SCOTTISH NATIONAL RED CROSS HOSPITAL.
ST. ANDREW'S AMBULANCE ASSOCIATION.

The Central British Red Cross Committee having recognised the above Association as a Branch of Red Cross work in Scotland, a public meeting was held in March, 1900, in Glasgow, and an appeal made for funds with the object of sending out and establishing a Base Hospital at Cape Town or elsewhere in South Africa, as the Military Authorities should decide, to be known as the Scottish National Red Cross Hospital.

The Association undertook to provide all the Staff and equipment and to bear all the expenses connected with the up-keep of the Hospital for six months, the Government undertaking all expenses of transit out and home, and the issue of the usual field ration free.

The first equipment and stores were despatched on 13th April, the second on 11th May, and the third on 3rd July, 1900, the total number of beds being 520.

The *personnel* of the Hospital, when completed, consisted of a Deputy Surgeon-General, in command, 3 Surgeons, 15 Medical Officers, 3 Staff Officers (a Quartermaster, Secretary, and Sergeant-Major), 35 Nursing Sisters of the Army Nursing Reserve, 47 First Class Orderlies (all Medical Students), and 58 Second Class Orderlies, making a total *personnel* of 162.

The number of patients treated were 74 officers and 978 combatants and civilians, among whom there were only 18 deaths.

At the end of six months, the requirements of the Army being by that time amply met by the Government service, the equipment was offered to the Government as a gift, and gratefully accepted, and was handed over on the 14th October, 1900, several of the Staff electing to remain in South Africa, while the remainder returned in charge of two Hospital Ships, the first with 78 invalids, the second with 620.

Her Royal Highness the Princess Louise (Duchess of Argyll) who was President of the Hospital, presented their Army Nursing Reserve Badges to the Nurses.

This was the only Private Hospital which took, as part of its equipment, portable huts of the Doecker system, so widely known in connection with Red Cross work on the Continent of Europe. They are stated to have stood the work well, and to have been far more portable and more readily put up than the galvanised iron huts which were constructed for other Private Hospitals.

STATEMENT OF RECEIPTS AND PAYMENTS.

RECEIPTS.	£	s.	d.	PAYMENTS.	£	s.	d.
To Contributions, &c...	45,833	15	6	By Expenses	27,743	14	5
				„ Soldiers' and Sailors' Families Association (Scottish Branch)	8,000	0	0
				„ Funds for Relief of sick and wounded Soldiers	1,000	0	0
				„ Balance	9,090	1	1
	45,833	15	6		45,833	15	6

103, West Regent Street, Glasgow.

THE IMPERIAL YEOMANRY HOSPITAL.

The scheme of providing special hospitals for the Imperial Yeomanry originated with Lady Chesham and Lady Georgiana Curzon (now Countess Howe) when the movement to send Imperial Yeomanry to South Africa was first started.

After consultation with the Central British Red Cross Committee, it was decided to form on the lines of communication, or at the base, a Hospital that would afford *special* comforts to sick and wounded yeomen; the Authorities undertaking that every effort would be made to fill the Hospital with men from these corps. Subsequently, however, the action of the Committee was enlarged by the establishment of a Field Hospital and Bearer Company;—a branch Hospital at Pretoria;—and, later on, by three minor schemes, viz., a branch at Mackenzie's Farm of the Base Hospital at Cape Town;—a Convalescent Home for Officers at Johannesburg;—and a branch Hospital at Elandsfontein.

The Imperial Yeomanry Base Hospital was organised for 500 beds, but temporarily extended to 1,000 during the enteric epidemic. The *personnel* staff, with the additional reliefs sent out, consisted of 20 medical officers, two chaplains, 50 nurses, ten dressers, ten wardmaids, and 178 orderlies. The Hospital was opened at Deelfontein on 15th March, 1900, and from that date to 31st March, 1901, 6,093 patients were treated.

The Yeomanry Field Hospital (with a Bearer Company attached) was organised as a Military Field Hospital of 100 beds. The total staff of the Field Hospital and Bearer Company, who sailed from London on 12th March, 1900, numbered 168, and continued work in South Africa till 8th March, 1901, when the units returned to England. The Hospital staff estimate that they treated 2,692 patients in the field, as well as 265 Boer women and children temporarily, and 1,160 for more or less prolonged periods.

The Branch Hospital at Pretoria was opened on 18th August, 1900, originally organised for 400 beds, but subsequently increased to 530. The staff sent out numbered 139, with 68 subsequently added. Some transfers were also made from the Base Hospital at Deelfontein. The Hospital was maintained as a private Hospital until the end of September, 1901.

The above three Hospitals formed the main work of the Imperial Yeomanry Committee. The minor schemes were:—The Mackenzie Farm branch of the Base Hospital at Cape Town, established at Maitland Camp on 15th August for 100 beds, the staff being supplied from Deelfontein and Pretoria, and closed on 30th March, 1901, 1,066 patients having passed through the wards.

The "Chesham Home" for convalescent Officers at Johannesburg containing eight beds;—and the branch Hospital at Elandsfontein for 50 beds, subsequently increased to 88, opened on 29th June, 1901, and closed on 28th December of the same year.

The total number of the staff, including the reliefs employed in the five schemes, was 711. Number of beds, 1,926. Number of in-patients, 18,288; out-patients, 1,995.—Total, 20,283.

SUMMARY

OF

APPROXIMATE AMOUNT SUBSCRIBED.

PART II.

	£ s. d.	£ s. d.
The Central British Red Cross Committee	⎫	
National Society for Aid to Sick and Wounded in War	⎪	
The Central British Red Cross Committee's work in South Africa	⎬ 178,950 0 0	
St. John Ambulance Association	⎪	
St. John Ambulance Brigade	⎪	
Army Nursing Service Reserve	⎭	
Queen Alexandra Imperial Military Nursing Service	—	
Hospital Ships — The *Princess of Wales*	—	
Hospital Ships — American Ship *Maine*	41,597 13 2	
Hospital Trains — The "Princess Christian"	—	*750,000 0 0
Hospital Trains — "No. 4"	—	
Private Hospitals — The Portland	13,647 10 3	
Private Hospitals — The Langman	—	
Private Hospitals — The Van Alen	—	
Private Hospitals — The Irish	—	
Private Hospitals — The "Princess Christian"	—	
Private Hospitals — The Welsh	12,000 0 0	
Private Hospitals — The Edinburgh and East of Scotland	21,325 5 4	
Private Hospitals — The Scottish National Red Cross	45,833 15 6	
Private Hospitals — The Imperial Yeomanry	—	

* The Central British Red Cross Committee estimate the above voluntary aid work at "close on £1,000,000 sterling"; but in the absence in most cases of details, and with a desire, where such are not given, to under rather than over estimate what has been done, I have placed it at a less figure.   J. G.

PART III.

DISABLED OFFICERS AND MEN.
CONVALESCENT HOMES.

CONTENTS

	PAGE
Lloyd's Patriotic Fund	99
Georgina, Countess of Dudley's Fund	100
The Layard Home for Officers	100
Medical and Surgical Aid for Sick and Wounded Officers (The Duke of Abercorn's Fund)	101
The Incorporated Soldiers' and Sailors' Help Society	102
Regimental Cottage Homes	103
Their Majesties' Convalescent Home at Babingley	104
The Princess Louise's (Duchess of Argyll) Transfer Hospital, Roseneath	105
King Edward's Hospital (Misses Keyser)	106
The Earl of Sandwich's Home at Hinchingbrooke	107
Wounded Officers' Fund (Cannes)	107
Sir Alfred Cooper's Private Military Hospital, Surbiton	108
Glenearn Convalescent Home (Miss Ker Dunlop)	109
The Grosvenor Home, Dover (Miss L. Hardy)	109
Golder's Hill, Hampstead (Brigade of Guards)	109
Syracusa Convalescent Home, Torquay	110
Western Counties Convalescent Home, Combe Down, Bath	110
Convalescent Homes, Private Houses, &c. (Tabular Statement)	111
Summary of Approximate Amount Subscribed	114

LLOYD'S PATRIOTIC FUND. (*Established* 1803.)
SPECIAL TRANSVAAL WAR FUND.
(*Communicated.*)

In the appeal, which the Lord Mayor of London issued on the 21st October, 1899, on behalf of sufferers by the War in South Africa, he stated that, "All subscriptions for the benefit of soldiers disabled by wounds (for their benefit after they left the Service) would be handed over for disbursement to Lloyd's Patriotic Fund."

As the invalids from South Africa did not begin to arrive in England until the end of December, 1899, and then went to the various Naval and Military Hospitals for treatment, no cases came before the Trustees for assistance until the middle of March, 1900.

As at first there was no Fund for assisting the men "temporarily incapacitated and on sick furlough, pending return to their regiments," the Trustees of Lloyd's Patriotic Fund, with the sanction of the Lord Mayor, extended their assistance to this class of sufferers; but in July, 1900, the Soldiers' and Sailors' Help Society took over this branch of the work.

The Trustees decided that officers and men of all forces engaged (Imperial and Colonial) were eligible for relief, which has since been extended to the doolie-bearers and engine drivers of armoured trains.

As it was recognised that the bulk of Colonial cases must be dealt with in their own Colonies, grants in proportion to the strengths of the various contingents were made through the Agents-General for disbursement by the Committees of the War Funds in the different Colonies. This arrangement has, however, not prevented many Colonials being assisted in this country.

The burden of the work has been in connection with the soldiers in the United Kingdom (the Navy having from the nature of the War contributed few cases for relief), who have been assisted in various ways to the number of 4,053, which practically agrees with the official "Return" of men "discharged disabled" up to the 1st of January, 1902.

Relief, in the first instance, has been given in the form of weekly allowances until the men have received their pensions and the "back pay" due to them, or have become fit for some light occupation; whilst a large number of men on discharge from hospital have been supplied with clothes and been paid for in Convalescent Homes, or have received extra medical attendance and surgical appliances. Many have entered the Corps of Commissionaires; some have been given outfits for domestic service, or tools and instruments to resume or learn trades; others have been started in shops or in small farms; a number have been set up with barrows, or ponies and carts, and stock, as hawkers; and for many situations have been found by the various Soldiers' and Sailors' Employment Agencies.

Towards the permanent provision of those utterly incapacitated, the Trustees have made a grant to the Cottage Homes in memory of Prince Christian Victor, and have received a bequest of £1,050 under the Will of the late Lieut. H. S. McCorquodale of Thorneycroft's Mounted Infantry, to provide annuities for two such men.

For the benefit of officers whose means have not enabled them to meet the expenses of serious operations and nursing homes, with the necessary change of air during convalescence, the Trustees have made grants towards the Funds started by Georgina, Countess of Dudley, and the Duke of Abercorn, and have in some cases given assistance direct.

STATEMENT OF RECEIPTS AND PAYMENTS.
October, 1899, to 31st December, 1901.

RECEIPTS.	£ s. d.	£ s. d.	PAYMENTS.	£ s. d.	£ s. d.
To Cash per the Lord Mayor	£109,959 3 10		By Grants to—		
,, ,, ,, McCorquodale Bequest	1,050 0 0		Officers direct	£347 8 6	
		111,009 3 10	Lady Dudley	7,224 12 10	
,, ,, ,, Discretionary Fund		1,331 0 6	Duke of Abercorn	500 0 0	
,, Contributions direct		11,118 18 0			8,072 1 4
,, Interest on Deposit		3,599 2 11	Disabled men		26,037 16 1
			Colonies		9,900 0 0
			India Office Doolie Bearers	500 0 0	
			,, ,, Lumsden's Horse	500 0 0	
					1,000 0 0
			Soldiers' and Sailors' Help Society		1,150 0 0
			Prince Christian Memorial Homes		1,000 0 0
			Miss Ker Dunlop's Convalescent Home		200 0 0
			McCorquodale Trust		1,050 0 0
			Expenses of Management		2,333 3 9
			Balance		76,315 4 1
		127,058 5 3			127,058 5 3

Brook House, Walbrook, E.C.

GEORGINA, COUNTESS OF DUDLEY'S FUND.

This Fund was initiated in December, 1899, and has been carried on with a twofold object—

1st, to assist Sick and Wounded Officers returning from South Africa; and

2nd, to provide a Home of rest for Nurses, many of whom being Colonials had no friends in England.

The aid to Officers, which included a large number of Colonials, has been chiefly connected with wounds, dangerous operations, after effects of fever, dysentery, and nervous exhaustion.

These have been placed in Nursing Homes in London, and at health resorts both at home and abroad free of all expenses, including Nursing and Medical attendance.

Voluntary help has been generously given in a large number of cases by many distinguished members of the Surgical and Medical profession, Many Hotel Proprietors both in England and abroad have rendered invaluable assistance in the matter of hospitality and by the reduction of tariffs.

In the case of married Officers, their wives—and in the case of unmarried Officers a mother or sister, have accompanied them to health resorts when they have been too ill to travel alone.

Altogether 1,057 cases, or 1,684 officers, their wives and children have been thus helped.

About 50 per cent. of the nurses assisted have been connected with the Army and the Army Nursing Reserve, the remainder were Colonial and Volunteer Nurses in charge of sick and wounded on each home-coming Transport. Many of these women were themselves invalids greatly in want of rest, and in the case of these latter their pay ceased on the date of disembarkation.

282 Nurses have been provided for, and 28 relatives or friends of those who needed care while at health resorts.

STATEMENT OF RECEIPTS AND PAYMENTS.

December, 1899, to 31st March, 1902.

RECEIPTS.	£	s.	d.	PAYMENTS.	£	s.	d.
To Contributions	32,245	0	8	By Expenses of Officers	54,691	9	7
,, Lord Mayor's Discretionary Fund	24,500	0	0	,, Expenses of Nurses	4,514	19	5
,, The Central British Red Cross Society	5,000	0	0	,, Advertising, &c.	2,383	0	8
				,, Balance	155	11	0
	61,745	0	8		61,745	0	8

N.B.—The Grant from Lloyd's Patriotic Fund is kept as a separate account and not included in the above statement.

THE LAYARD HOME FOR OFFICERS.

The Layard Home for invalided Officers started in March, 1900, was in the first instance opened at Madeira, and subsequently at Matjesfontein, Cape Colony, where some useful work was done, especially in supplying comforts and medical attention to the trains full of sick and wounded on their way to Cape Town.

From the Lord Mayor's Discretionary Fund a grant of £500 was received; from the National Bazaar £250; and from the Central British Red Cross Committee £100.

MEDICAL AND SURGICAL AID FOR SICK AND WOUNDED OFFICERS.

THE DUKE OF ABERCORN'S FUND.

The above Fund, having for its object "to aid sick and wounded officers whose means were inadequate to secure that efficient medical and surgical treatment which was needed on their return home to restore to them that health they had sacrificed in the service of their country," was, with the sanction of the Secretary of State for War, inaugurated at a meeting held at Hampden House on the 22nd January, 1900.

At this Meeting a Committee was formed, with the Duke of Abercorn as President and the Hon. Arthur Brodrick as Honorary Secretary and Treasurer; Hampden House having, by the invitation of the President, been made the Headquarters of the Fund, whilst the necessary office accommodation, services of clerks, &c., were supplied by the British South Africa Company.

The general principles laid down were that the Committee should limit itself to contributing to the *exceptional* expenses incurred during treatment or convalescence exceeding those which an officer would be able to defray under the ordinary circumstances of his position.

Upwards of eighty consulting Physicians and Surgeons in England, Scotland, and Ireland, who joined the Committee, undertook to give their invaluable services to any patients properly recommended to them, and with this object a Sub-Committee, of which Sir Thomas Smith, Bart., acted as Chairman, was appointed, and drew up Regulations towards attaining this end. The very onerous responsibility of making preliminary examinations into the condition of every applicant was undertaken by Dr. Donald Hood and Mr. J. H. Morgan. These gentlemen reported weekly to the Committee upon each case on the books, acting as intermediaries between the Committee and consultants, and further bestowing constant personal attention upon a large number of invalids.

It is not too much to say that the services rendered to officers by the hard-worked leaders of the medical profession have been priceless. Those services have been freely, unremittingly, and ungrudgingly bestowed; yet they could seldom have been of any avail unless met by a liberal provision for the care and nursing of the patients whilst under treatment.

Of about 400 officers who have been treated, one half have been surgical cases.

Many officers have also received treatment without needing to apply to the Committee, through the inexhaustible kindness of individual members of the medical profession, and the generosity of private persons who have received them into their houses as into a Nursing Home.

STATEMENT OF RECEIPTS AND PAYMENTS.

January, 1900, to 31st December, 1901.

RECEIPTS.	£ s. d.	PAYMENTS.	£ s. d.
To Contributions	5,081 19 1	By Expenses of Invalid Officers	6,797 2 11
,, Grants from Lord Mayor's Discretionary Fund	1,500 0 0	,, Administration Expenses	376 8 11
,, ,, Lloyd's Patriotic Fund	500 0 0	,, Balance, 31 December, 1901	449 10 1
,, ,, *Daily Mail* (Kipling Poem)	500 0 0		
,, Interest	41 2 10		
	7,623 1 11		7,623 1 11

Deloitte, Dever, Griffiths & Co., *Hon. Auditors.*

THE INCORPORATED SOLDIERS' AND SAILORS' HELP SOCIETY.

(Communicated.)

The Objects of the Society are—

(1) To help soldiers and sailors by providing them with the name and address of a "Friend" in each Parish or Ward throughout the Kingdom, to whom they may be commended on discharge from the Army or Navy for aid in obtaining employment or other forms of help suited to their needs.

Every soldier or sailor from the War, who, on quitting the Army or Navy for return to civil life, or on sick furlough, has been visited and helped as needed by an office-holder of the Society. In 1900, employment was found for 450 men, and 580 were helped by clothing and money. During 1901, exclusive of London and County General Agencies, employment was found for 550 men by the Central London Employment Branch of the Society, and 603 were equipped in articles of clothing to fit them for special employments, or aided by monetary grants for emergent necessities.

(2) In time of war to arrange for accommodation of sick and wounded convalescent soldiers and sailors in temporary convalescent homes and private houses.

Since the outbreak of War in South Africa, 3,001 sick and wounded convalescents have been admitted into temporary convalescent homes of the Society, without any expense to the men, in addition to the convalescents who were visited and helped in their own homes throughout the country.

(3) To establish and maintain convalescent homes and homes of rest for discharged soldiers and sailors who are disabled and necessitous, and to contribute to the support of such cases in their own homes, if considered necessary.

For the permanently disabled, the Society's permanent Home at 57, High Street, Portsmouth, for about 12 disabled soldiers and sailors, was kept filled during 1901, and another large permanent Home on the Grand Parade at Portsmouth for 20 men has been acquired, and was publicly opened by H.R.H. the President of the Society on 21st April, 1902. The Society has also built extensive permanent (inland) Homes at Bisley, Surrey. In addition to the fixed Homes, 52 Princess Christian's Cottage Homes have been established at this date in various counties in England, Wales, Scotland, and Ireland, for married disabled soldiers with their wives; rent and up-keep of the Cottage Homes being borne by the Society.

STATEMENT OF RECEIPTS AND PAYMENTS.

October, 1899, to 31st December, 1901.

RECEIPTS.		£ s. d.	PAYMENTS.	£ s. d.
To Homes a/c in general, "permanent" for permanently disabled soldiers and sailors, "temporary" for sick and wounded convalescents, and for relief of War cases in their own homes (including donation of £9,000 from Naval and Military Bazaar, less £600 for endowment of a bed), and "Children's Home" Fund,* £11,840		28,474 0 0	By Homes "permanent" at Portsmouth; Bisley; cottages in counties; and "temporary" convalescent homes ..	19,749 0 0
" Endowment of beds in permanent Homes		5,574 0 0	" Endowments invested ..	5,574 0 0
" Subscriptions and donations for general purposes (including Portland Hospital donation of £4,634) ..		9,585 0 0	" Grant's in personal relief of South African War cases only ..	5,359 0 0
" Special War Funds:—			" Grants to other than South African War cases; rents; salaries; advertising, &c. ..	3,982 0 0
Mansion House Transvaal War Fund, for Bisley Homes ..	£3,000		" Balance, unexpended ..	15,704 0 0
Mansion House Transvaal War Fund, for Portsmouth Home ..	400		" " " "Children's Home" Fund * ..	11,840 0 0
Mansion House Transvaal War Fund, for relief of War cases only ..	4,500	7,900 0 0		
Mansion House Transvaal War Fund, for Irish branch of the Society † ..	—	—		
" Lloyd's Patriotic (out of Mansion House Transvaal War Fund) ..	£1,000			
" Lloyd's Patriotic (out of Mansion House Transvaal War Fund for Portsmouth Home)..	100	1,100 0 0		
" Central British Red Cross Society (instalment of £5,000) ..		3,000 0 0		
" National Bazaar ..		5,000 0 0		
" Imperial Yeomanry and Duke of Cambridge's Own Yeomanry ..		1,050 0 0		
" Soldiers of the Queen Canadian Fund ..		525 0 0		
		£62,208 0 0		£62,208 0 0

110, Victoria Street, S.W.

* Fund not closed on 31 December, 1901, since closed and handed over to the Society.
† £2,000 remitted direct to Dublin by the Lord Mayor of London.

REGIMENTAL COTTAGE HOMES FOR DISABLED SOLDIERS.

The scheme of Regimental provision for disabled men after they have left the service, commenced in 1901 as a memorial of H.H. Prince Christian Victor of Schleswig-Holstein, and after sufficient funds had been subscribed for the establishment of eighteen regimental cottages, an endowed bed in the Princess Christian Home at Portsmouth, and a Cottage Homes Fund for Middlesex, the appeal was closed.

The General Committee which had been formed, with Lord Roberts as president and Mrs. Papillon, honorary secretary, remained after the closing of the Memorial with the object of raising Funds to assist regiments to establish rent-free Cottages where deserving soldiers may live in comfort with their families. These Cottages, which are free from all restraint or disciplinary supervision, are attached to the Regiments for which they are respectively endowed, each Regiment selecting the inmates of its own particular Cottages, the Soldiers' and Sailors' Help Society being prepared, if desired, to hold the Regimental Homes in trust for the respective Regiments, and undertaking as far as possible the maintenance of the inmates. No expense whatever attaches to the Cottages after their establishment—yearly repairs, insurance, rates and taxes, being met in perpetuity by an Endowment Fund provided by each Regiment.

Cottages have also been presented by individuals with the desire either of making them private Memorials of relatives or friends; or helping Regiments or Corps in which they are specially interested. In some cases also Cottages are being built—in others purchased—all being as far as possible situated in or within easy reach of some town or village.

STATEMENT OF RECEIPTS AND PAYMENTS.

12TH MARCH, 1901, TO 30 APRIL, 1902.

RECEIPTS.	£ s. d.	PAYMENTS.	£ s. d.
To Contributions, H.H. Prince Christian Victor's Memorial	7,798 11 5	By Printing, typewriting, etc.	151 9 3
,, Lloyd's Patriotic Fund	1,000 0 0	,, Clerical assistance	35 9 0
,, Lord Mayor's Discretionary Fund	500 0 0	,, Messengers, travelling expenses, etc.	10 4 2
,, Contributions additional	7,195 5 11	,, Advertising, postage, &c...	71 0 4
(includes £65 3s. 11d. interest on deposit at Bank)		,, Balance	16,225 14 7
	16,493 17 4		16,493 17 4

Horse Guards, Whitehall, S.W.

THEIR MAJESTIES' CONVALESCENT HOME AT BABINGLEY.

IN January 1900 the King and Queen personally inspected a Farm House at Babingley, on the Sandringham Estate for the reception of wounded and invalided officers from South Africa.

Part of the Farm House had in former years been reserved as a hospital for the Estate. By their Majesties' instructions, a Cottage was built for the accommodation of the tenant and caretaker then living there, while structural improvements were at once put in hand on the Farm House, which was also entirely redecorated and newly furnished throughout. The Hospital or Home when reconstructed consisted of a dining-room, a panelled oak smoking and sitting room, and four bed-rooms for officers, in addition to rooms and usual offices for Matron and servants. Attached to the Home was a large tent in a pleasant garden with a good croquet lawn. By desire of their Majesties, the War Office Authorities were requested to give preference to Colonial officers. The Home was opened on the 29th June, 1900, and during that summer twenty-one officers were received. In the summer and autumn of 1901, thirty-one officers were admitted, and a masseur from London engaged, so that any such treatment ordered by the Medical Staff could be carried out. Carriages were provided for the officers' use from the Sandringham stables, enabling those who were well enough to take drives on the Estate and to different country seats, from the owners of which they received much kindness and hospitality.

Visits to the Sandringham Gardens, Studs, Farm and the Hall, were much appreciated, especially when on several occasions they were honoured by Her Majesty personally conducting them over the Hall.

The knowledge also that the Queen had with her own hands hung many of the pictures, and had personally supervised the arrangements of their rooms in the Home was highly treasured. In an Autograph Book of the King and Queen every officer left a short written account of his career, and also a photograph of himself, with expressions of gratitude for the benefits they had derived and for their life-long remembrance of the special honour of having been their Majesties' guests.

THE PRINCESS LOUISE (DUCHESS OF ARGYLL'S) TRANSFER HOSPITAL FOR SOLDIERS.

Roseneath, Dumbartonshire.

This Hospital was opened early in 1900, and has been carried on ever since. The building, which is self-contained, is close to the old "Ferry" Inn at Roseneath, and was built by Her Royal Highness for her own use. It is situated on the Garelock, in beautiful scenery, and the position being above the sea level and in pure air, lends itself to the quick recovery of patients.

Soon after the commencement of the War it was entirely refurnished and equipped throughout as a Hospital for sixteen patients. It was originally offered as a Convalescent Home for the sick and wounded of the various Scottish Regiments returning from South Africa; but in September 1900 it was nominated by the Secretary of State for War as a "Transfer" Hospital, and receives patients from the Military Hospitals under the direction of the Principal Medical Officer of the Scottish District.

The Funds have been provided by Her Royal Highness the Princess Louise, supplemented by a grant from the Lord Mayor's Discretionary Fund and various contributions, including the proceeds of a concert given by the Glasgow Highlanders (Volunteers) and by one given at Helensburgh. Since the Hospital opened 120 patients have been received and treated, of whom about forty were wounded, some very severely, the rest being invalided from enteric and other diseases. Many of these have returned to duty and some to South Africa, only one death, that of Private E. Morrison, of the Gordon Highlanders, having occurred. The Staff consists of Sisters Liddell and Taylor (who have been in charge since the Hospital was opened), a cook and a wardwoman. Professor MacEwen, Dr. I. MacEwen, and Dr. James Allen, of Glasgow, have given their constant attendance whenever needed, Dr. Alexander, of Kilcreggan, being the daily Medical Attendant. Great kindness in various ways has been shown to the patients by all classes in the neighbourhood. The patients have frequently expressed themselves as thoroughly happy and comfortable, and many interesting letters have been received from men since they left the Hospital, especially from those who have returned to South Africa.

KING EDWARD'S HOSPITAL,

17, Grosvenor Crescent, S.W.

In personal devotion to work in connection with the War probably none have exceeded, if any have equalled, Miss Keyser and "Sister Agnes," her sister.

Their offer to convert their large house into a Hospital, to undertake the entire management, and to defray all expenses, was approved by the King (then Prince of Wales), and gladly accepted by the Authorities.

Four Wards containing seven beds—rooms for nurses, a bath room (with a lift from the basement) were established on one floor. The drawing-room floor was rearranged with a billiard-room, two sitting-rooms, and a dining-room, all communicating, and comfortably and suitably furnished.

The Staff consisted of Nurse Louise Flangan, a second day nurse and one night nurse, with extra and special nurses as required. The household servants (seventeen in number) have all worked in the most willing and praiseworthy manner.

Ever since the Hospital was opened Sir Thomas Smith and Dr. Charles Morris, as surgeon and house surgeon respectively, have given their gratuitous services, while over forty of the leading physicians and surgeons in London have, in the same way, been constant visitors to and attendants on the patients. It would be impossible to speak too highly of the kindness and devotion shown by these gentlemen. Two masseurs have been continually employed, in addition to Mr. Lindahl, who gave the Swedish Medical Manual treatment gratuitously. Over 225 officers (amongst them many Colonials) have passed through the Hospital, several having been inmates for long periods, and in two cases for more than a year.

At periods when the Wards were full, "out" patients have been lodged through the kindness of friends at 47, Belgrave Square, and treated in the Hospital. Those who had homes or friends in London have also attended to be seen by the doctors and receive massage and electric treatment.

By permission of the King, the Hospital was named after His Majesty early in 1901, and the frequent visits of His Majesty were highly valued and appreciated by the patients.

Her Majesty Queen Alexandra, the Duke and Duchess of Connaught, and the Duke of Cambridge, have also been visitors. In the autumn of 1901 the inmates of the Hospital were temporarily moved for three months to Windsor, where Mr. and Mrs. Kennard placed their house at their disposal. M. Ritz also placed suites of rooms at the disposal of the patients in his hotel at Salsomaggiore, the invitation including the cure, baths and medical attendance.

The domestic management of the Hospital was undertaken by Miss Keyser, whilst Sister Agnes devoted herself to the nursing and work in the Wards, neither ladies having been absent from the Hospital since it was opened in January 1900.

THE EARL OF SANDWICH'S HOME,

Hinchingbrooke, Huntingdon.

In January, 1900, Lord Sandwich offered to receive Convalescent Officers from South Africa, and from February of that year to May, 1902, almost continuously entertained these at Hinchingbrooke.

About fifty officers availed themselves of his hospitality, many being Colonials, who made Hinchingbrooke their home while in England, and the great majority having been patients in the Misses Keyser's (King Edward's) Hospital in London. In almost every instance the improvement has been remarkable, although in some cases it was slow, necessitating a stay of over several months.

Lord Sandwich looked after the patients himself, assisted only by an excellent masseur. Entertainments have been from time to time provided to enliven the weary hours of the patients, and on more than one occasion Madame Melba and other artistes have given their services for their recreation.

The officers were treated as personal guests, no trouble being too great in seeing after their wants and comforts.

WOUNDED OFFICERS' FUND,

Cannes.

Early in 1901 a Committee was formed at Cannes, with Sir Sydney H. Waterlow as Chairman and Treasurer, and Mademoiselle de Labrosse as Honorary Secretary, for the purpose of providing suitable accommodation for the reception, as guests of the English community, of wounded officers who might be desirous, or who had been recommended to recruit their health and strength by a sojourn for a short time on the Riviera, instead of having to face the rigour of the early spring weather in England.

During that year sixteen officers were received, and in 1902 six more, some each year having remained the whole winter, and all having materially benefited by their residence and treatment, and on leaving individually expressed themselves deeply thankful for the kindness extended to them during their stay.

Much hospitality and good feeling was shown to the officers by the French residents, especially by the Military Authorities and officers of the French Army.

PRIVATE MILITARY HOSPITAL,

The Gables, Surbiton.

Authorised by Government under private management.

SIR ALFRED (then Mr.) COOPER equipped, and at his own expense maintained, the above, by converting the private theatre attached to his residence as an adjunct to the Princess of Wales's Hospital Ship, for the reception of sick and wounded soldiers brought home from the front by that vessel.

The Hospital, or converted theatre, contained two wards of 11 beds each, the division being made at the proscenium line separating the stage from the auditorium. On the same floor was a perfectly-appointed surgery and operating room, washhouse, and a room for the matron—private quarters for the nursing staff being provided in the lodge adjoining and communicating with the Hospital. In the basement were two auxiliary wards, a commodious mess-room, a well-equipped kitchen, lavatories, and bath-room. The grounds of the mansion were always open to the patients, with the use of an asphalted tennis court and a miniature shooting range; while indoors, games, books, illustrated papers, materials for writing (a popular occupation) were fully provided. Smoking concerts and other amusements were continually organised, and a never-failing source of pleasure was a musical box, the thoughtful and gracious gift of Queen Alexandra, then Princess of Wales.

Mr. F. C. Abbott, the eminent surgeon of St. Thomas's Hospital, in addition to giving his advice in fitting up the Hospital, very generously offered his services as consulting and operating surgeon, and through his instrumentality many eminent specialists at St. Thomas's, when required, also gave their services.

Dr. Ackerley (Sir Alfred Cooper's private medical adviser), his partner, Dr. Groome, and many other local practitioners, all worked gratuitously on the staff of the Hospital.

Lady Cooper, with the true instinct of her sex, with her own hands arranged the fresh-cut flowers each morning throughout the wards, and was ever constant in her sympathetic devotion to the welfare of her guests, from whom she received her best reward in their invariable good conduct and behaviour during the period of their visit. Only one death, out of 141 patients admitted, occurred, although many critical operations were performed.

The Hospital was honoured on two occasions by visits from Queen Alexandra and the Princess Victoria, the King accompanying the Queen on the first visit. The Queen on both occasions presented each man with a souvenir of her visit, each present having the man's name and the battle in which he was wounded engraved upon it.

To perpetuate the memory of the Hospital, a medal, bearing on the obverse side a bust of Queen Alexandra, and on the reverse a facsimile of the exterior of the Hospital, with an appropriate inscription on each side, was presented to every patient who passed through the Hospital, as also to the medical and nursing staff.

The Hospital was closed on the Princess of Wales's Hospital Ship being put out of commission.

GLENEARN CONVALESCENT HOME,
Crieff, Perthshire.

IN January, 1900, Miss Ker Dunlop offered her house to the Government free of all expense, and the same having been accepted, the House was opened in March of that year with a staff of trained nurses, Miss Ker Dunlop having undertaken the sole management, to which she has since devoted herself. Over one hundred soldiers, chiefly men from Highland Regiments, have been successfully treated, no death having occurred. Her late Majesty Queen Victoria took a personal interest in the Home, and accompanied a signed photograph of herself with a message of grateful thanks for the kind care of her dear, brave soldiers.

The expenses of the Home have been almost entirely borne by Miss Ker Dunlop and her friends.

THE GROSVENOR HOME,
18, East Cliff, Dover.

THIS Home, which has been utilised now for over two years, was taken and furnished by Miss L. Hardy and her friends, and has been supported by private subscriptions.

There has been no Committee of Management and no fixed Rules and Regulations, all men entering the Home being placed on their honour as to their behaviour and good conduct, which has been much appreciated, and proved in every way successful. Miss L. Hardy has during the whole period acted as matron; but a great deal of the success of the Home has been due to a young caretaker, Corporal Jefferson, late of the Coldstream Guards, one of the early inmates in consequence of a wound received at Belmont, an earnest Scotchman and respected by all the men. The Home has been under the care of Dr. Ian Howden, who has given his services gratuitously, and has been cordially supported by the Chief of the Staff at Dover. 192 men have passed through the Home, 52 of whom have been Colonials from Australia, New Zealand, Tasmania, South Africa, and from India, Canada, and Ceylon.

GOLDER'S HILL, HAMPSTEAD.

THE above, lent by the London County Council, containing 36 beds, and established in April, 1900, first as a Convalescent Home, and subsequently used as a Section of the Station Hospital, London, under the Principal Medical Officer of the Home District, was limited to men of the Brigade of Guards.

Subscriptions amounting to about £10,000 were received, £2,000 being from the inhabitants of Hampstead, and £8,000 from the officers and friends of the Brigade. 250 men have passed through the Home.

SYRACUSA CONVALESCENT HOME,

Torquay.

This Home, to accommodate thirty patients, was instituted by Mr. and Mrs. Mallock, of Cockington Court, in December, 1899; Mrs. Mallock's brother-in-law, Mr. Lee, having placed the house at their disposal. A Committee was formed, with Colonel Stovell as Honorary Secretary, and in answer to an appeal through the local press, £3,002 13s. 8d. was subscribed, which with interest amounted to £3,042 8s., besides presents of furniture, &c.

The necessary alterations and fittings being completed, the Home was opened the following month, and from that date until its close in December 1901, 256 men were admitted. In June, 1900, Princess Henry of Battenberg honoured the Home with a visit, at which time there were twenty-eight patients, eighteen of whom were Canadians.

The Home was closed in consequence of the Authorities being no longer pushed for room, and having more accommodation offered for Convalescent Homes than could be utilised.

There was a balance in hand after all expenses had been met of £550.

WESTERN COUNTIES' CONVALESCENT HOME,

Combe Down, Bath.

Early in 1900 a Committee, of which General Sir John McQueen was Chairman and Mrs. Hawthorn, Honorary Secretary, was formed, and subscriptions invited for the establishment of the above Home of ten beds, which was opened on the 19th of the following month, and has continued its operations since that date. The staff consisted of a trained nurse as matron and two servants, with a paid Medical Officer who attended twice a week or oftener as required.

The Home has been almost constantly full, and at times three or four men have had to be boarded out in the village.

The majority of cases have been those suffering from rheumatism, who have received special benefits from the mineral water baths, generously given by the Corporation of Bath free of charge.

STATEMENT OF RECEIPTS AND PAYMENTS.

January, 1900, to 24th May, 1902.

RECEIPTS.	£	s.	d.	PAYMENTS.	£	s.	d.
To Contributions	2,134	5	7	By Expenses of Home	*2,409	1	5
,, Grant from Lord Mayor's Discretionary Fund	300	0	0	,, Balance	175	4	2
,, ,, Soldiers' and Sailors' Help Society	150	0	0				
	2,584	5	7		2,584	5	7

* Includes £300, the expenses of furniture, sanitary, and other work.

CONVALESCENT HOMES, PRIVATE HOUSES, AND HOSPITALS

Offered for the use of Wounded and Invalided Officers and Men.

ENGLAND.

NOTE.—The suggestion as to the above provision originated with Mr. C. Hampden Wigram, Chairman of Lloyd's Patriotic Fund, who early in December, 1899, appealed for tickets of admission to the established Convalescent Homes throughout the kingdom, which, as the work of that Fund was confined to "Disabled Soldiers and Sailors" and as they were in constant communication with the authorities at the Naval and Military Hospitals, he considered his Fund the best medium through which such benefits could be utilised.

Name and Address and by whom offered.	Number of Beds.	Total Number admitted.	Remarks.	Name and Address and by whom offered.	Number of Beds.	Total Number admitted.	Remarks.
BEDFORDSHIRE	...	...	None.	HEREFORDSHIRE	...	...	None.
BERKSHIRE.				HERTFORDSHIRE.			
Reading, Aldermaston Court. By C. E. Keyser, Esq., Aldermaston Court.	6	45	Doctor, nurse, and all found.	Buntingford Isolation Hospital. By the Committee.	8	...	Not utilised.
Reading, Colesberg House. By Miss Radcliffe Balmore, Caversham.	8	50		Harpenden Convalescent Home. By Maple and Co.	40	7	
Windsor (Old) Convalescent Home. By Hon. Lady Murray, Windsor.	16	2		New Barnet, Gloucester House. By Mrs. Twentyman, Green Hill Park.	6		No information.
Windsor, St. Andrew's Convalescent Hospital. By Miss Hull, Hayward's Heath.	1		No information.	HUNTINGDONSHIRE.			
BUCKINGHAMSHIRE.				Hinchingbrooke House. By Earl of Sandwich.	No limit.	50	See Page 107 of this Part.
High Wycombe, Daws Hill Lodge. By Lord and Lady Carrington.	9	26	Doctors attended free of charge.	KENT.			
CAMBRIDGESHIRE	...	...	None.	Dover, The Grosvenor House. By Miss Hardy, 3, Victoria Park, Dover.	15	*192	*51 of whom have been Colonials. See Page 109 of this Part.
CHESHIRE.				Dover Friendly Societies' Convalescent Home. By the Committee.	10		Not utilised.
Knutsford Convalescent Home. By Lord Egerton of Tatton.	12	35		Dover (St. Margaret's Bay), Morley Convalescent Home. By the Committee.	11	15	
Northwich, Victoria Infirmary. By the Committee.	5	18		Folkestone, St. Andrew's Convalescent Home. By Colonel A. Grubb.	Several.	61	
Springfield, Hazel Grove, Stockport. By Robert Farmer, Esq.	1	...	No information.	Herne Bay, Passmore Edwards' Convalescent Home. By the Trustees.	20		Not utilised.
Winsford, Albert Infirmary. By F. B. Cooke, Esq., Middlewich.	1	9		Hythe Convalescent Home. By Colonel Allatt.	2		No information.
CORNWALL.				Sandgate, The Alfred Bevan Convalescent Home. By the Committee.		4	Also lent to Government as a hospital for 15 months.
Falmouth, Royal Cornwall Sailors' Home. By the Committee.	10	1		Swanley, Parkwood Convalescent Home. By the Committee.	24	15	
Newquay, Glendorgal. By Sir Richard Tangye	5		Not utilised.	Swanley Convalescent Hospital. By the Committee.	5		No information.
Perranport Convalescent Home. By the Committee.	10	2		Wingham, Elmstone Court. By Major G. W. L. Gwatkin.	2	2	
St. Austell Convalescent Home. By Lady Graves Sawle.	4		Not utilised.	LANCASHIRE.			
Trelawne, Dulce. By Lady Trelawney	4		Not utilised.	Blackburn, Balderstone. By R. C. Radcliffe, Esq., Inglewood.	6	35	
CUMBERLAND.				Bolton, Blair Convalescent Home. By Miss E. F. Wood.	3	20	
Silloth, near Carlisle. By Mrs. Ullock, Quarry House, Windermere.	2	2		Manchester, Fairfield Convalescent Home. By the Committee.	24	145	
DERBYSHIRE.				Ormskirk Cottage Hospital. By the Committee.	6	...	Not utilised.
Matlock Bank Convalescent Home. By the Committee.	10	9		Pendlebury, Westwood House. By Lees Knowles, Esq., M.P.	12	6	5 from Lancashire Fus.
DEVONSHIRE.				Southport Convalescent Hospital. By the Committee.	20	51	
Bovey Tracey, St. Mary's. By Lady Halifax.	4		Not utilised.	LEICESTERSHIRE.			
Exeter, Devon and Exeter Hospital. By the Committee.	20		Not utilised.	Leicester, Ilston Grange. By the late Mrs Baillie.	2	6	
Exeter, South Devon and East Cornwall. By the Committee.	22		Not utilised.	Loughborough, Mountsorrel Cottage Hospital. By the Committee.	3	13	
Exeter, Royal Albert Hospital. By the Committee.	26		Not utilised. A ward, fully equipped, was held in readiness for 3 months.	LINCOLNSHIRE.			
Ilfracombe, Convalescent Home, Morthoe. By Lord Ebrington.	12	5		Louth, Mabelthorpe Convalescent Home. By Rev. J. W. Hancock.	Several.	*2	*Through private subscribers.
Lapford. By Mr. and Mrs. Radford, Nymett Rowland.	2		No information.	Louth Cottage Hospital. By T. F. Allison, Esq.	2	2	
Torbay, Redcliff Towers. By Mr. Singer	20	...	Not utilised.	Scawby, Scawby Hall. By Hon. Mrs. Sutton Nelthorpe.	2		Not utilised.
Torquay, Syracusa House. By Subscribers	30	256	See Page 110 of this Part.	Scawby, The Grove. By Mrs. Cliff	2		Not utilised.
DORSETSHIRE.				Skegness, Seathorne. By the Committee	7	4	
Sherborne School House. By Rev. F. B. Westcott.	10		Not utilized.	Woodhall Spa, Alexandra Hospital. By Rev. J. O. Stephens.	25	18	
DURHAM	...	...	None.	LONDON.			
ESSEX.				King Edward's Hospital, 17, Grosvenor Crescent (the Misses Keyser).	7	225	See Page 106 of this Part.
Brentwood Cottage Hospital. By Mr. Ravenhill, Park House.	10	3		London Hospital, Whitechapel Road. By the Governors.	No limit.	140	
Clacton-on-Sea Convalescent Home. By Mrs. Stephenson.	20	16		St. John and St. Elizabeth Hospital, 40, Grove End Road. By the Committee.	No limit.	5	
Theydon Bois. By Gerald Buxton, Esq., Birch Hall.	2		No information.	St. John's Wood. By Mrs. Witham, 2, Hall Road, Hamilton Terrace.	2	2	For Roman Catholics.
Walton-on-Naze. By H. Padfield, Esq., Portobello Hotel.	12		Not utilised.	Medical and Electrical Gymnastics. By J. Richert, 33, Cambridge Street, W.	No limit.		Not utilised.
GLOUCESTERSHIRE.				Society of Trained Masseuses. By Miss Grant 12, Buckingham Street, Strand.	No limit.	...	No record kept.
Bristol, Durdham Down. By Society of Merchant Vintners.	Several.	20		Jaw Specialist. Dr. F. M. Farmer, 53, Wimpole Street, W.	No limit.	37	
Bristol Royal Infirmary. By the Committee.	24	10		MIDDLESEX.			
Cheltenham General Hospital. By the Committee.	9	...	Not utilised.	Golder's Hill, Hampstead. By London County Council.	50	250	See Page 109 of this Part.
Tedbury Cottage Hospital. By Rev. E. W. Estcourt, Newnton Rectory.	3	5		MONMOUTH	...	...	None.

CONVALESCENT HOMES, PRIVATE HOUSES, AND HOSPITALS, &c. ENGLAND—cont.

Name and Address and by whom offered.	Number of Beds.	Total Number admitted.	Remarks.
NORFOLK.			
Cromer, Fletcher Convalescent Home. By the Committee.	4	16	Not utilised.
Hunstanton Convalescent Home. By Rev. H. Earle Bulwer.	40	...	
Sandringham, Their Majesties' Convalescent Home at Babingley.	4	52	See Page 104 of this Part.
NORTHAMPTONSHIRE.			
Brackley Cottage Hospital. By Hon. Mrs. G. Campbell.	2		Not utilised.
Earls Barton, The Grange. By Mrs. M. Hornby	2		Not utilised.
East Haddon Nursing Home. By Mrs. Guthrie, East Haddon Hall.	4		Not utilised.
Harlestone. By Duchess of Grafton, Harlestone House.	2	5	
NORTHUMBERLAND.			
Chester, Humshaughs. By Mrs. Clayton	6		No information.
Newcastle, Gibside Hall. By Lord Strathmore.	25	...	No information.
Whitley, Prudhoe Memorial Home. By Sir G. H. Phipson, M.D.	20	38	
Whitley, Priory House. By Miss Philipson, 77, Lancaster Gate, W.	4		Not utilised.
NOTTINGHAMSHIRE.			
Newark Hospital and Dispensary. By the Duke of Portland.	6	6	
OXFORDSHIRE.			
Chadlington, Layston House. By Mrs. Scholfield.	1		Not utilised.
Charlbury, The Vicarage (private house). By Rev. A. Smith.	1		No information.
Charlbury, Ramsden. By Mrs. Baker	1	...	No information.
Charlbury, Wilcote. By Mrs. G. H. Dawkins, Wilcote.	No limit.	4	
Chipping Norton, Bruern Abbey (private house). By Mrs. Samuda.	3	6	
Chipping Norton, Old Bank House (private house). By Mrs. Burbidge.	No limit.	10	
Chipping Norton, The Castle Farm (private house). By Mrs. Ingle.	1		Not utilised.
Chipping Norton (private house). By Mrs. Fowler.	1	...	No information.
Chipping Norton, Heythorp (private house). By Hon. Mrs. Brassey.	1	6	
Chipping Norton, Kingham. By Mrs. Evans	1		Not utilised.
Chipping Norton, Kingham Rectory. By Rev. D. Lockwood.	1		No information.
Chipping Norton, Fifield Rectory (private house). By Rev. S. Yorke.	1		Not utilised.
Chipping Norton, Fifield (private house). By Mrs. Matthews.	1	...	Not utilised.
Chipping Norton, Leafield. By Mrs. Spicer...	1	2	
Chipping Norton, Leafield. By P. S. Yapp, Esq., and Rev. T. W. Lee.	6		Not utilised. Two men privately.
Chipping Norton, Over Norton (private house). By Mrs. Denis Daly.	2	1	
Chipping Norton, Over Norton. By Mrs. Walford.	1		No information.
Enstone, The Vicarage. By Rev. T. Phillips...	2		Not utilised.
Enstone, Tew Park. By M. E. Bolton, Esq.	3		No information.
Great Rollright, The Vicarage. By Rev. W. Guest Williams.	No limit.		Not utilised.
Henley, Checkendon. By Mrs. Fife, Goring-on-Thames.	3	1	
Henley, Harpsden Court. By Mrs. Noble, Park Place.	6	4	
Milton-under-Wychwood (private house). By Mrs. Damant.	4	17	
Swerford, The Rectory. By Miss Shebbeare.	1		Not utilised.
Thame, Victoria Nursing Home. By the Committee.	2	2	
Watlington Cottage Hospital. By Lady Macclesfield, Shirburn Castle.	2	5	
Watlington, Victoria Nursing Home. By Colonel Ballard.	2		No information.
RUTLAND.			
Oakham, Hambleton Hall. By C. A. Cooper, Esq.	4		No information.
Oakham, Somerby, by Hon. Mrs. Candy	4		Not utilised.
SHROPSHIRE.			
Shrewsbury, Petton Park. By Mrs. Cunliffe...	2	1	
SOMERSETSHIRE.			
Bath, Coombe Down Convalescent Home. By Mrs. Hawthorn.	13	100	See Page 110 of this Part.
Bath, Royal Mineral Water Hospital. By Col. Vaughton-Dymock.	20	90	
Bath, Royal West of England Sanatorium. By the Committee.	6	*30	Not utilised by Govt. 30 admitted privately.
Bath, Lansdowne Grove Hospital and Home. By the Committee.	6		Not utilised.
Crewkerne, Merriott. By A. E. V. Nicholls Barnes, Esq.	1		Not utilised.
Shepton Mallet District Hospital. By F. G. Bradbury, Esq.	1		Not utilised.
Taunton, Taunton and Somerset Hospital. By the Committee.	10		Not utilised.

Name and Address and by whom offered.	Number of Beds.	Total Number admitted.	Remarks
SOMERSETSHIRE—cont.			
Wells, Mendip Hill Grove. By Samuel Owen, Esq.	30	...	Not utilised.
Wells District Cottage Hospital. By the Committee.	1	1	
Yeovil, The Hospital. By the Committee ...	2		Not utilised.
SOUTHAMPTON (Hants).			
Basingstoke Cottage Hospital. By the Committee.	6	10	
Bournemouth, Needwood Hinton Road. By Miss Wykeham Fiennes.	10	35	
Bournemouth, St. Joseph's House. By the Committee.	2	25	
Emsworth, St. Faith's Home. By Mrs. Ernald Smith.	12	29	
Farnborough, Minley Manor. By Miss Currie	2		No information.
Longparish, The Cottage. By Owner... ...	2		No information.
Lymington, Lisle Court. By Mr. Whittaker...	18		Not utilised.
Lyndhurst. By Mrs. Eyre, Matcham	2	3	
Milford-on-Sea Cottage Hospital. By Miss Magnay.	2	4	
Romsey Home and Cottage Hospital. By Major Spencer Chichester.	2	...	Not utilised.
Portsmouth, 57, High Street. Soldiers' and Sailors' Help Society.	12	26	
Portsmouth, Grand Parade. Soldiers' and Sailors' Help Society.	20		Opened 21 April, 1902.
SOUTHAMPTON (Isle of Wight).			
Bonchurch, The Grange. By Mr. C. H. Combe	6		No information.
Cowes Memorial Home. By A. James, Esq., Coton House, Rugby.	18	150	
Ryde, Southlands. By Dr. R. Barrow... ...	18	...	No information.
Ryde Home and Infirmary. By Mrs. E. Croft Murray, Perrivale.	4	6	
Shanklin, Leslie, Hope Road. By Sister Julie	10		No information.
Ventnor National Consumption Hospital. By the Committee.	1		No information.
STAFFORDSHIRE.			
Hanchurch, Newcastle. By the Subscribers.	10		Not utilised.
Milford, Sister Dora Convalescent Hospital. By Captain W. S. Levett.	10	2	Admitted privately.
SUFFOLK.			
Aldeburgh Convalescent Home. By Mrs. Garrett.	4		No information.
Easton, Glenn House. By Duchess of Hamilton	6		Not utilised.
Felixstowe Convalescent Home. By Lady Gwendolen Herbert.	No limit.	28	
Felixstowe, Rougham Cottage Home. By Mrs. M. Johnstone.	4		Not utilised.
Lowestoft Convalescent Home. By the Committee.	13	2	
SURREY.			
East Grinstead. By C. Bagally, Esq., K.C., The Grange.	2	1	
Haslemere. By Mrs. Cox, Oakhurst, Grayshott	2		Not utilised.
Limpsfield, Charing Cross Hospital Home. By the Committee.	50		No information.
Reigate, Quex House. By A. H. Wrey, Esq....	1		No information.
Surbiton, the Gables. By Sir Alfred Cooper, Private Military Hospital.	6	141	See Page 108 of this Part.
Tooting Common, Furzedown Park. By Sir Charles Seeley.	40	...	Not utilised.
Walton-on-Thames, Metropolitan Convalescent Institution. By the Committee.	20	*6	*On recommendation of subscribers. None officially.
SUSSEX.			
Arundel Castle. By the Duke of Norfolk ...	6	29	
Billinghurst, Rowner Mills. By Mrs. Locke King.	3		No information.
Bognor, Merchant Taylors' Home. By the Governors.	7		No record kept.
Brighton, Miss Marsh's Home. By the Superintendent.	2	...	Not utilised.
Brighton, Police Seaside Home. By Miss Gurney.	20	3	
Chichester, Goodwood. By the Duke of Richmond.	60	134	
Chichester, Sennicotts. By Mrs. Farrell ...	2		Not utilised.
Eastbourne, Home, Royal Parade. By Colonel Cardwell.	10	93	
Hassocks, Danny. By Mrs. Brown	4	...	No information.
Hastings, Beau Site Convalescent Home. By the Committee.	11	28	No information.
Hastings, 28, St. Andrew Square. By Mrs. Morrell, Headington, Oxford.	6		
Little Hampton, Belle Vue. By Mrs. Fletcher, Dale Park.	6		Not utilised.
Little Hampton, Rustington Convalescent Home. By Sir H. Harbern.	10	39	
Pulborough, West Burton. By Colonel Ansell	2		No information.
Seaforth, Surrey, Convalescent Home. By the Committee.	10		No information.
Uckfield, Heron's Ghyll. By Mrs. Hope ...	3		No information.

CONVALESCENT HOMES, PRIVATE HOUSES, AND HOSPITALS. ENGLAND, WALES, &c.

Name and Address and by whom offered.	Number of Beds.	Total Number admitted.	Remarks.	Name and Address and by whom offered.	Number of Beds.	Total Number admitted.	Remarks.
ENGLAND—cont.				**SCOTLAND**—cont.			
WARWICKSHIRE.				EDINBURGH.			
Kenilworth Convalescent Home. By F. Stranger-Leathes, Esq.	4	12		Leith, Starbank Park. By Leith Council	12		Not utilised.
Leamington, Baths and Waters. By the Committee.	No limit.		Not utilised.	Ravenscroft, Convalescent Home. By the Committee.	6	21	
Stratford-on-Avon, The Hospital. By the Committee.	No limit.	1		ELGINSHIRE.			
WILTSHIRE.				Grantown, Ian Charles Cottage Hospital. By Dowager Countess of Seafield.	2	5	
Savernake, Cottage Hospital. By Marchioness of Aylesbury.	4		No information	FIFESHIRE.			
Tetbury, Cottage Hospital. By Rev. E. W. Estcourt.	3		No information.	Inverkeithing, Ladywell Cottage. By D. Gillespie, Esq.	2	6	
WORCESTERSHIRE.				St. Andrews, Memorial Cottage Hospital. By the Committee.	2		No information.
Bromsgrove, Hanbury Convalescent Home. By Sir H. Vernon, Bart.	12	191		Springfield, Crawford Priory. By Lady Cochrane.	1	1	Nurse, doctor, and all found. Only 1 man sent.
Malvern, Convalescent Home. By Colonel de Berniere.	12		No information.	Wemyss, West Wemyss Hospital. By Lady Eva Wemyss.	6		No information.
Malvern, Hornyold Road. By Mrs. Williams	12		Not utilised.	FORFARSHIRE.			
Worcester, Basford Court. By Mrs. Agg	1		Not utilised.	Arbroath, Infirmary and Convalescent Home. By the Committee.	12		Not utilised.
YORKSHIRE.				Dundee, Broughton Ferry. By A. B. Gilroy, Esq.	10		Not utilised.
Bridlington Quay, St. Anne's Convalescent Home. By Lord Halifax.	50	*)	Mostly by subscribers' tickets, 4 of which were from Colonel Vickers, C.B. (Maxim & Vickers).	HADDINGTONSHIRE.			
Harrogate, Police Convalescent Home. By Miss Gurney.	10		Not utilised.	Prestonkirk, Biel. By Mr. and Mrs Hamilton Ogilvy.	4		Not utilised.
Hull, Withernsea Convalescent Home. By Captain Gurney.	25	8		INVERNESSHIRE.			
Ilkley, Hospital and Convalescent Home. By the Committee.	30	45		Orich, Callart Cottage. By Mrs. Cameron Lucy.	4	9	
Leeds, Cookridge Convalescent Hospital. By the Committee.	4		No information.	KIRKCUDBRIGHTSHIRE.			
Pontefract, Wentbridge Convalescent Home. By Mrs. J. E. Neilson.	7		Not utilised.	Anworth, Cottage Hospital. By Mrs. Maxwell	2		Not utilised.
Rawdon, Convalescent Home. By Committee at Bradford.	50	6	Local cases only.	LANARKSHIRE.			
Scarborough, Northern Sea Bathing Infirmary. By Captain Bower.	13		No information.	Carnwath, Cottage Hospital. By Sir Simon Lockhart, Bart.	4		Not utilised.
Sheffield, Hathersage, Brookfield Manor. By Mrs. Cammell.	2	3		PERTHSHIRE.			
Skelton-in-Cleveland, Cottage Convalescent Home. By Lieut.-Col. Wharton.	9	44		Crieff, Glenearn. By Miss A. Ker Dunlop	6	101	See Page 109 of this Part.
				Errol, Murie Cottage. By J. Brown-Morison, Esq.	2	2	
				Grantully, Comly Bank. By Lady Stewart	5		
WALES.				ROSSHIRE.			
BRECKNOCKSHIRE.				Avoch, Kincurdy, Rosehaugh. By I. Douglas Fletcher, Esq.	20		Not utilised. A matron and assistant kept at house for some months.
Brecon, Builth Cottage Hospital. By the Committee.	5	1					
CARDIGANSHIRE.							
Borth, Brynellew. By Major Barry Taunton.	2		Not utilised.				
CARMARTHENSHIRE.							
Carmarthen, Infirmary. By the Committee.	8		Not utilised.				
CARNARVONSHIRE.				**IRELAND.**			
Llanfairfechan, Heath Memorial Home. By the Committee.	50	2		DOWN.			
GLAMORGANSHIRE.				Bangor, Home of Rest. By the Committee	50	31	
Cardiff, Infirmary. By the Committee	50		Not utilised.	Donald Lodge. By Earl of Annesley	60		No information.
				Dromore, Cowan Heron Hospital. By the Committee.	10		No information.
				Mount Stewart, Donard Lodge. By Marquess of Londonderry.	6		No information.
SCOTLAND.				DUBLIN.			
ABERDEENSHIRE.				Blackrock, Linden Convalescent Home. By the Mother Superior.	10	31	
Cults, Blair-Devenick. By Dr. Arthur	4	2	Nurse, doctor, and all found. Kept open for many months—only 2 men sent.	Merrion, St. John's Home of Rest. By Mrs. Clements, Cellridge.	1	...	
Fyvie, Cottage Hospital. By Mrs. Forbes-Leith.	5	3		Stillorgan, Convalescent Home. By the Committee.	7	14	
ARGYLLSHIRE.				MEATH.			
Lochawe, Blythswood. By Miss Campbell	4	2	(a) Colonel with his family. (a) Lieut. with his mother	Slane, Beau Parc. By Hon. H. Bourke	12		No information.
AYRSHIRE.				MONAGHAN.			
Kilmarnock, Dundonald Convalescent Home, Auchaus. By the late Hon. Mrs Greville Vernon.	14	25	Three nurses.	Monaghan, the Infirmary. By Mrs. Guthrie, Glasslough.	15		No information.
BANFFSHIRE.							
Keith, Terrace Memorial Hospital. By the Provost.	2	1		**ISLE OF MAN.**			
DUMBARTONSHIRE.				Douglas, Belmont Convalescent Home. By Hon. M. Henniker.	24		No information.
Roseneath. By H.R.H. Princess Louise, Duchess of Argyll.	16	120	See Page 105 of this Part.				

SUMMARY

OF

APPROXIMATE AMOUNT SUBSCRIBED.

PART III.

	£	s.	d.	£	s.	d.
Lloyd's Patriotic Fund—						
Received from the Mansion House ...	112,340	4	4			
,, ,, other sources ...	14,718	0	11			
	127,058	5	3			
Less accounted for in other Funds...	13,050	0	0			
				114,008	5	3
Georgina, Countess of Dudley's Fund ...				61,745	0	8
The Layard Home for Officers ...				850	0	0
Medical and Surgical Aid for Sick and Wounded Officers (The Duke of Abercorn's Fund) ...				7,623	1	11
The Incorporated Soldiers' and Sailors' Help Society				62,208	0	0
Regimental Cottage Homes ...				16,493	17	4
Their Majesties' Convalescent Home at Babingley ...				—		
The Princess Louise's (Duchess of Argyll) Transfer Hospital, Roseneath ...				—		
King Edward's Hospital (The Misses Keyser) ...				—		
The Earl of Sandwich's Home, Hinchingbrooke				—		
Wounded Officer's Fund (Cannes) ...				—		
Sir Alfred Cooper's Private Military Hospital, Surbiton				—		
Glenearn Convalescent Home (Miss Ker Dunlop)				—		
The Grosvenor Home, Dover (Miss L. Hardy) ...				—		
Golder's Hill, Hampstead (Brigade of Guards)				10,000	0	0
Syracusa Convalescent Home (Torquay) ...				3,042	8	0
Western Counties' Convalescent Home, Combe Down, Bath ...				2,584	5	7
Convalescent Homes, Private Houses, &c. (Tabular Statement)				—		
				278,544	18	9

PART IV.

EXTRA COMFORTS, &c.

CONTENTS.

	PAGE
Queen Victoria's Chocolate Box ...	117
Queen Alexandra's Pipe	119
The "Absent-minded Beggar" Fund ...	120
Women and Children from South Africa (Southampton) ...	121
Field Force Fund	122
Literature for the Troops	123
Lady White's Ladysmith Fund ...	124
Kimberley and Mafeking (In Memoriam Soldiers') Fund ...	125
Summary of Approximate Amount Subscribed	126

EXACT SIZE.

QUEEN VICTORIA'S CHOCOLATE BOX.

WITH the recollections of the Crimean War in Her Majesty's mind, when warm clothing and comforters, knit by her own hand, were despatched to her soldiers and sailors at the seat of war, it was not to be wondered at that her late Majesty Queen Victoria should have been the first to think of her brave troops in South Africa at Christmas-time. The example thus set by the Sovereign was quickly followed by her subjects, and a bountiful supply of extra comforts were henceforth readily forthcoming. Such supplies were in some cases for the Field Force generally, in others for particular Regiments or Corps; but probably the far greater proportion came from the relatives and friends of those at the front, to the extent of which, owing to the same not having passed through any organised channel, it is impossible to give even an approximate estimate.

The original number of Chocolate Boxes sent out was 120,000, which were procured to the number of 40,000 each from Messrs. J. S. Fry and Sons, of London and Bristol, Messrs. Rowntree and Co., of York, and Messrs. Cadbury Bros. of Birmingham. A supplementary issue of 3,000 from Messrs. Fry and Sons was made later on, it being found that the garrisons of Kimberley and Mafeking had been omitted in the first distribution, and among the former were included sailors from H.M.S. *Powerful*. The Queen's gift was originally only intended for the non-commissioned officers and men; but later on in the distribution, officers were included.

Letter from the Queen's Private Secretary to the Secretary of State for War, and from the Marquis of Lansdowne to Sir Fleetwood Edwards:—

Windsor Castle,
November 19th, 1899.

Dear Lord Lansdowne,—The Queen commands me to inform you of Her Majesty's anxiety to make some little personal present as soon as possible to each of the soldiers serving in South Africa.

Her Majesty has decided upon sending Chocolate, which she is given to understand will be appropriate and acceptable. It will be packed for each man in a tin that has been specially designed for the occasion. The Queen hopes that you may be able to arrange for its conveyance and distribution. Believe me

Yours truly,

FLEETWOOD I. EDWARDS.

The Marquis of Lansdowne, K.G.

War Office,
November 20th, 1900.

My Dear Edwards,—Her Majesty's thoughtfulness for her troops serving in South Africa will, I am sure, be cordially appreciated by them, and we shall, I need not say, be ready to make arrangements for the delivery of the Chocolate as expeditiously as possible to the whole of the Field Force.

I have already conferred with the Quartermaster-General, who has undertaken to provide for the conveyance of the packages, and we shall ask the General in Command to see to the distribution.

I have asked the Quartermaster-General to communicate with you later on as to the port from which the Chocolate should be shipped. If it is not ready *here* for six or seven weeks, there may not be many opportunities of sending it out on board transports, as most of them will have left by that time. Pray assure Her Majesty that no pains will be spared to give effect to her gracious intentions.

I am, my dear Edwards,
Yours sincerely,

LANSDOWNE.

Sir Fleetwood I. Edwards, G.C.V.O.

The Quartermaster-General having undertaken their despatch from this country, and Sir Francis Evans, Chairman of the Union Steamship Company, having offered on behalf of the Company to convey the Chocolate free of charge to the Cape, the following letter, conveying the Queen's thanks, was addressed to the latter:—

Osborne,
January 3rd, 1900.

Dear Sir,—The Queen has learnt that, on behalf of the Union Steamship Company, of which you are the Chairman, you recently communicated to the Secretary of State for War an offer on behalf of the Company to convey free of cost the whole of the Chocolate that Her Majesty is presenting to the Force in South Africa.

The Queen desires me to say that she is glad to think that this very generous offer was accepted, which Her Majesty much appreciated, as well as the kind interest that your Company has been good enough to take in the matter.

Yours faithfully,

FLEETWOOD I. EDWARDS.

Sir Francis Evans, K.C.M.G.

NOTE.—It may be stated that the design on the Queen's Chocolate Box has been registered, so that its value shall not be deteriorated by its being copied or adapted for any other purpose.

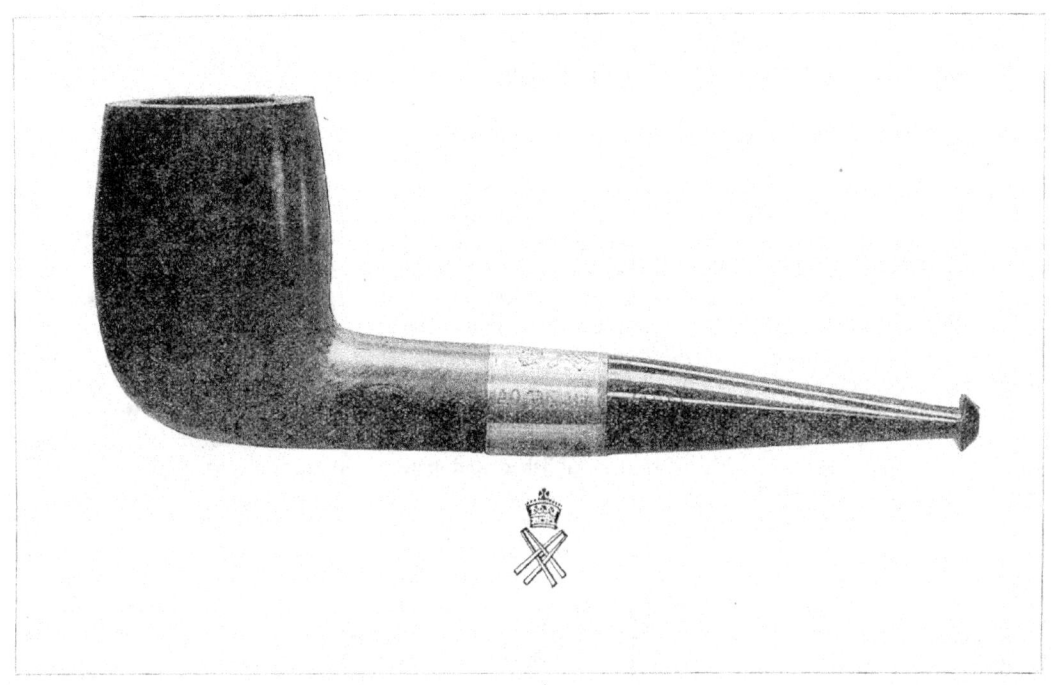

EXACT SIZE.

QUEEN ALEXANDRA'S PIPE.

Her Majesty Queen Alexandra having completed her work of the previous two years in connection with The Princess of Wales' Hospital Ship, and with the thought ever uppermost in her mind of doing some kind act, more frequently unknown than known, determined in the winter of 1901 to send what, to the sailor or soldier is always his best and most valued friend—his pipe. 5,500 of these with the Queen's monogram engraved, packed in five cases and addressed, "A present from Queen Alexandra to Lord Kitchener, Commanding the Troops in South Africa," were despatched with a request that Lord Kitchener would distribute the same at his discretion. The pipes were given to the Warrant Officers, Staff-Sergeants, and Sergeants, or to specially distinguished soldiers in the following proportions:—

Regular Cavalry (15 per Regiment)	285	Army Ordnance Corps	54
Royal Artillery	305	Army Pay Corps ...	70
Royal Engineers	146	Post Office Corps ...	42
Regular Infantry (22 per Battalion)	1,848	Remount Department ...	24
Militia Infantry (18 per Battalion)	540	Headquarter Staff Clerks ...	24
Imperial Yeomanry	399	Army Veterinary Department ...	17
Colonials (Oversea and South African)	633	Military Police	6
Army Service Corps	278	Signalling Staff	4
Royal Army Medical Corps ...	144	Headquarters Office	1

The balance was, at the time that the above return was rendered, being distributed.

Numerous letters of humble and grateful thanks have been received from the Officers in Command of the various Corps, stating how much Her Majesty's thought had been appreciated, and how highly the gift was valued.

One of the recipients, a private in the Grenadier Guards, a West Newton boy, and a grandson of the old kennelman at Sandringham, especially wrote asking that his thanks might be conveyed to the Queen.

A separate case was also addressed to Lord Kitchener from Princess Charles of Denmark for sick and wounded soldiers in South Africa.

THE KIPLING POEM FUND.

THE "ABSENT-MINDED BEGGAR" RELIEF CORPS and THE ALTON HOSPITAL FUND.

(Communicated.)

In November, 1899, just after the beginning of the War, Mr. Rudyard Kipling sent to the *Daily Mail* the now famous poem, "The Absent-Minded Beggar," with a request that the *Daily Mail* should "give what it was worth to some charity in aid of the soldiers and reservists." The *Daily Mail* exploited the poem, and received about £135,000 from the public the world over. It is computed that the poem earned in addition, for other funds in various places and in all the Colonies, over £165,000, making, with some £40,000 (£5,000 for the working expenses of the Relief Corps and £35,000 to the "A.M.B." Hospital Fund) contributed to the Fund by the proprietors of the *Daily Mail*, a total of over £340,000 earned by this poem of four verses.

Of the £175,000 which came into the hands of the *Daily Mail*, about £40,000 was donated to other funds, £65,000 spent on the "Absent-Minded Beggar" Fund, and £70,000 on the Alton "A.M.B." Hospital.

Originally it was intended to raise money only for the purpose of helping funds and Committees already established, but the arrival at Southampton on December 16th, 1899, of a large number of soldiers' wives and children in a deplorable condition as to food and clothing, led to the foundation of the "Absent-Minded Beggar" Relief Corps, whose only rule was to "help deserving cases," no matter what were the conditions. All the other funds were restricted in various ways in the granting of relief. In the execution of this work, depôts of the "A.M.B." were established and maintained until the early months of 1901 at London, Queenstown, Southampton, St. Vincent, Cape Town, East London, and Durban. In South Africa the Red Cross Society took the work in the field, and the "A.M.B." Relief Corps took the work on the transports. The work of the "A.M.B." embraced anything and everything, from clothing wounded men to caring for their parrots; from supplying Government Hospitals with medical stores to saving a man for the Service by furnishing a set of false teeth; from wiring and writing relations to inducing fifteen soldiers in special cases to marry and paying for the licences. Then the Patriotic Fund in every Colony that sent a contingent to South Africa was started by the Kipling Fund with a substantial contribution. Relief was afforded to Kimberley, Mafeking, and Ladysmith, to the expedition to Tientsin and Pekin, and that to Ashantee in 1900.

Summarised, the work is partly shown in these figures:—

GENERAL WORK.

Transports visited	445
Sick and wounded and discharged men attended to	90,595
Free telegrams sent	23,262
Letters, post-cards, and parcels forwarded	35,906
Free meals supplied	123,675

NECESSARY COMFORTS SUPPLIED.

Handkerchiefs	46,183
Pairs of socks	45,455
Shirts	40,612
Tam o'Shanters and Balaclavas	36,376
Vests	24,581
Mufflers	17,607
Caps	9,265
Cardigans	6,664
Pairs of pyjamas	3,327
Hospital suits (regulation)	1,000
Articles of old and new clothes distributed for donors	25,000
Army overcoats (regulation)	2,236
Pairs of gloves and mittens	6,836
Cushions and down pillows	6,222
Towels	2,832
Blankets	848
Walking-sticks	2,306
Pairs of crutches	623
Air cushions	146
Arm slings	282
Deck chairs	318
Cigarettes	684,270

NECESSARY COMFORTS SUPPLIED—*cont.*

Pipes	51,094
Tobacco (lbs.)	11,944
Articles of new clothing distributed to 667 soldiers' wives and 1,102 soldiers' children	14,581

EXTRA COMFORTS.

Chocolate (lbs.)	2,761
Tins of cocoa	2,268
Bottles of wine and turtle jellies	3,232
Tins of preserved game	1,355
Tins of condensed milk	1,984
Jars of beef tea	1,650
Bottles of beef extract	1,128
Mixed biscuits (lbs.)	2,569
Bottles of lime-juice	1,835
Tins of soup	1,356
Cases of soap	12
Bottles of brandy	428
Cases of arrowroot	10
Cases of fruit	34
Bandages and packages of medicated gauze, medicated wool, hospital lint, and other hospital supplies	4,000

Many other things were given in sixteen hospitals dealing with war sufferers, additionally, at request of the Commanding Officer in Natal and the distribution of an immense number of soldiers' parcels was undertaken.

The activity of the Fund was brought to a close in the presentation to the Government of 66 acres of freehold land at Alton, Hants, upon which the *Daily Mail* had erected a model hospital with 300 beds and all necessary quarters, offices, and outbuildings. The cost of this hospital was £70,000—£35,000 having been contributed by the public to the "A.M.B." Hospital Fund, the other £35,000 being a contribution from the *Daily Mail*.

WOMEN AND CHILDREN FROM SOUTH AFRICA.

A COMMITTEE was formed by Colonel Stacpole, C.V.O., in December, 1899, for the purpose of helping the soldiers, their wives and families, returning from South Africa and India, on their arrival at Southampton, by providing them with extra warm clothing for their further journey, and in helping them in any way that suggested itself.

A stall of clothing was arranged in the shed to meet each transport, and all who needed warm clothing were amply provided. In this way upwards of 25,000 garments have been distributed; a large number being received from Miss Evelyn Moreton, Honorary Secretary of the Hampshire Clothing Branch of the Soldiers' and Sailors' Families Association.

When a ship arrived conveying women and children who could not be despatched to their destinations the same day, they were not kept on board ship, which would be the ordinary course, but were taken off and placed in comfortable lodgings by the Ladies of the Committee, where they had good food, hot baths, and every comfort till they were despatched to their destinations the next day.

Hospitality has been given to women and children too ill to proceed on their journey; for instance: A young widow arrived in an almost dying condition; it was impossible for her to proceed on her journey unless special arrangements had been made for her comfort. An invalid carriage was provided, and after a week's rest she was able to make the journey in comfort.

Another case was that of a soldier's wife suffering from an ulcer on the eye and needing special advice. Board and lodging was provided for her until arrangements could be made for her admittance into Moorfields Hospital; further help was given on her discharge from hospital.

Grants of money have been given to the women requiring immediate help, or to the relatives of orphans; for instance: A Colonial soldier's wife was allowed to return home in the same ship with her husband; they had six young children with them. The husband was badly wounded, and sent on to Netley; the wife was left stranded with only £1. The children's wardrobes were replenished and a cheque given to the wife, which enabled her to provide for herself and her children until she could communicate with her friends.

But the work commenced at the docks did not end there. By special request of the men they were visited weekly at Netley Hospital. Comforts were distributed, such as tobacco, cigarettes, books, games, and various kinds of work. Christmas presents were also given to the sick and wounded in Netley in 1900 and 1901. The sick and wounded have been helped in various ways—warm clothing given, when necessary, on their arrival; and, if the men were too ill to write themselves to their relatives, this has been done for them or a telegram sent. In reference to this, the following case may be mentioned: A young dying soldier, wearying for the sight of his mother's face, said, "I should like to see mother, but she is too poor to come and see me; father only earns eleven shillings a week." The mother was communicated with, her expenses paid, and she was in time to be with her boy for a few days before he died.

The Committee have always felt it especially incumbent on them to do what they could for the sick and wounded Colonials It was a means of showing appreciation of the valuable service they have rendered, and also that they had friends in the Mother Country ready to render them a service if called upon. Many have required further surgical and medical attendance after leaving hospital, and they had the opportunity given them of consulting a specialist, and the means provided for carrying out his advice.

The special thanks of the Committee are due to the indefatigable zeal and work of Miss Nowell and Miss Lucretia Nowell their Honorary Secretaries.

Since December, 1899, £410 17s. 6d. has been received, of which £209 15s. 7d. has been expended, leaving a balance in the Capital and Counties Bank of £201 1s. 11d.

Embarkation Office, Southampton.

THE FIELD FORCE FUND.

This Fund, having for its object the supply of comforts to the troops at the Front, was initiated by the Countess of Airlie, Lady Charles Bentinck, and Lady Edward Cecil, in March, 1900, all of whom were then at the Cape, the hearty approval of Lord Roberts having been first obtained.

The Drill Hall, which was placed at their disposal, was used as a store, where these ladies, as each consignment arrived from England, themselves unpacked and repacked the goods into smaller parcels of two kinds—one containing $\frac{1}{4}$ or $\frac{1}{2}$ lb. of chocolate, $\frac{1}{4}$ lb. of tobacco, two boxes of cigarettes, two boxes of matches, one handkerchief, one piece of soap, stationery, and bootlaces, the other and larger containing, in addition to the above, a shirt or suit of warm underwear, warm cap, muffler, pair of gloves, cholera belt, pair of socks, and a towel—ready to forward immediately on receipt of a wire from the Officers commanding Regiments, Corps, or Columns.

On the return in November, 1890, of these ladies to England, the work at Cape Town was entrusted to Mrs. Sclater, while their attention at home was directed to raising further funds, and sending out larger supply of goods, the receiving of the latter on this side being undertaken by Mrs. Currey, of The Pit House, Ewell.

A second appeal for "Christmas Gifts," supported by a Committee of ladies which had been formed, was made in September, 1901, who collected £9,000, and with the co-operation of the proprietors of the *Morning Post*, through whom nearly £20,000 was raised, one plum pudding (1 lb.), a packet of tobacco (1 lb.), and one pipe was sent to every soldier at the Front, making altogether 224,144 pounds of plum puddings, 220,000 pounds of tobacco, and 182,528 pipes. Several cases of tobacco and clothing were in addition supplied by the Mayor of Cape Town, 1,450 complete Christmas Parcels by the Mayor and ladies of Woodstock, and nine similar cases by the Mayor and ladies of Wynberg, Her Majesty Queen Alexandra's patronage having been of the greatest assistance in the success of the Appeal.

Approximately, the number of goods sent out was as follows, viz., 229,656 articles of clothing, in addition to a vast quantity of literature—books, magazines, illustrated papers—tobacco, toffy, and bootlaces, all packed and sent through Mrs. Currey.

STATEMENT OF RECEIPTS AND PAYMENTS.

RECEIPTS.		£	s.	d.	PAYMENTS.	£	s.	d.
To Contributions, first Appeal		7,670	2	9	By Goods purchased, etc.	33,545	1	4
,, ,, Second Appeal	£10,986 19 7				,, Balance	4,990	2	6
,, ,, Morning Post	19,506 17 7							
		30,493	17	2				
,, Received from Mrs. Sclater		371	3	11				
		38,535	3	10		38,535	3	10

LITERATURE FOR THE TROOPS.

N.B.—ALTHOUGH, as stated in the Preface, much has been done by individuals which cannot be recorded in the supply of Extra Comforts, with which were included in a number of instances Literature of every description, the work of Ex-Sergeant H. J. Johnson, of the 5th West Middlesex Rifle Volunteers, is given with a two-fold object (see Footnote) and may prove of interest.

This work may be classified under two heads:—

1st. The receiving, packing, and forwarding, in boxes (163 of which were despatched), Books, Magazines, Games, and Extra Comforts.

2nd. The directing and issuing gratis, assorted addressed Postal Wrappers, to those who desired personally to forward newspapers weekly, the wrappers being addressed from a book in which was recorded the town or locality where fixed Camps and Hospitals had been established.

Subsequently Centres were established, chiefly undertaken by the Military Chaplains, for their distribution to the several Blockhouses. One hundred thousand of these wrappers have been issued, and the hundreds of letters of grateful thanks which were received, not only from the Chaplains, but from Officers and Men themselves (of which three extracts are given), show how well this system has been utilised by those at home.

The Officers and Patients of Deelfontein Hospital desire through their Commandant and Chaplain to convey to Mr. Johnson their warmest appreciation and gratitude for the literature he has forwarded. His kind work and generosity has been a great help to them, and enabled them to pleasantly pass many an otherwise weary hour. (Signed by 6 Officers and 19 Men.)

We have just come in from a 2½ months' trek, and the troops are simply devouring the papers you have sent us. How the Irishman gloats over the *Irish Times*, the Scotchman over the *Scotsman*, and the Welshman over the *Cardiff Mail*, is a sight to be remembered. You are indeed conferring a great pleasure and happiness on us all.

I make a special point of supplying the Blockhouses. There 8 or 12 men, sometimes more, are from week's end to week's end, often many miles from the main point or railway station. You can imagine how heavily time hangs on their hands, and how grateful they are for the supply of literature which you sent out.

STATEMENT OF RECEIPTS AND PAYMENTS.
1900-1-2.

RECEIPTS.	£	s.	d.	PAYMENTS.	£	s.	d.
To Contributions	139	8	2	By Printing, Postage, Purchases, &c.	233	0	6
,, Lord Mayor's Discretionary Fund	50	0	0	,, Balance, 6 May	26	14	6
,, H. J. Johnson (out of pocket)	70	6	10				
	259	15	0		259	15	0

NOTE.—I have given the particulars of this work first and chiefly that full credit should be rendered to Ex-Sergeant Johnson, who has unostentatiously devoted his whole time to an object of as much benefit to the active as well as the sick and wounded man; and, secondly, in the hope that under similar circumstances arising in the future, a Central Store or Office may be established where, with greater publicity, all desiring to help in this direction should be able to contribute, and as Sergeant Johnson says, be able to carry out such work in a complete and thorough way, which no individual, however great his exertions, can possibly do.

J. G.

LADY WHITE'S "LADYSMITH FUND."

The following Appeal appeared in the Press on 18th November 1899:—

England's generosity to the sick and wounded is unbounded, nor are the wives and families of our gallant soldiers fighting in South Africa forgotten. All classes have combined with enthusiasm to do their utmost for these, but will some one now come forward to help me in sending to those men who have not been wounded, and who have gone through the past trying weeks at Ladysmith, some articles of clothing, tobacco, pipes, and cigars, to reach them about Christmas time?

I have ascertained from a reliable source that the gifts most acceptable to the soldier would be woven vests or woollen jerseys, Tam O'Shanter caps, Cardigan jackets, comforters, and socks. All necessities are liberally supplied by Government.

My readers may ask, "Why send these warm garments to a hot climate?" but in Natal the variations of temperature are very trying. The day is hot, the night and morning often very cold. The Jersey vest or Cardigan jacket never comes amiss, and we all know how soon socks wear out.

Will some of our large Firms, who are always so ready to help, send me contributions of any of these garments, and will the public help me with money?

If my appeal meets with a ready response, I should like to send our gifts to Natal at once.

The troops now at Ladysmith number about 10,000, and it is on their behalf chiefly that I wish to enlist your generosity.

The Canteen and Mess Co-operative Society, Ltd., have kindly consented to receive at their Warehouse, at 23, Regency Street, Westminster, any contributions of the articles enumerated above (and which, of course, should be restricted to clothing not previously worn).

Subscriptions may be sent to Lady White, 4, Draycott Place, Cadogan Gardens, or to Lloyd's Bank, Ltd., Law Courts Branch, to be placed to the account of "Lady White's Fund for the Ladysmith Garrison."

All contributions, whether in kind or in money, should be accompanied by a letter of advice and marked "Lady White Fund," stating nature of contribution and name of sender, and will be acknowledged as received, and also periodically through the Press.

I hope those who wish to help will try to enable me to send all out by December 1st next.

The following were sent to Natal under the gratuitous supervision of the Staff and Secretary (Mr. Heygate) of the Canteen and Mess Co-operative Society, no charge being made by Messrs. W. Davis & Sons, who carted the goods to the packers; by Messrs. Perrott & Perrott, who delivered them at the Docks; by Messrs. Staley, Radford & Co., who checked and prepared the necessary documents, or by Messrs. Renine & Sons, and by Messrs. Bullard, King & Co., who conveyed the goods to Durban. The above charges would, under ordinary circumstances, have amounted to £410.

Socks	44,832	
Scarves	29,610	
Cardigans and Jerseys	22,455	
Caps	18,265	In 806 Packages weighing 150 tons, and Insured for £5,000.
Vests and Drawers	2,098	
Shirts	1,200	
	118,460	
Pipes	31,418	
Pouches	140	
Tobacco, Cigars, and Cigarettes	11,000 lbs.	
	161,018	

N.B.—Included in the above (not purchased) were the following gifts: Clothing, 48,784; Pipes, 2,340; Pouches, 140.

STATEMENT OF RECEIPTS AND PAYMENTS.

RECEIPTS.	£	s.	d.	PAYMENTS.	£	s.	d.
To Donations	4,355	12	8	By Goods, purchases	3,516	9	11
				„ Packing, Insurance, &c.	62	15	7
				„ Passage and expenses of officer in charge of goods	351	5	0
				„ Balance	425	2	2
	£4,355	12	8		£4,355	12	8
To Balance	425	2	2	By Soldiers' and Sailors' Families Association	200	0	0
				„ Soldiers' and Sailors' Help Society (Convalescent Homes)	125	0	0
				„ Georgina, Countess of Dudley	50	0	0
				„ Memorial Church, Ladysmith	50	2	2
	£425	2	2		£425	2	2

KIMBERLEY AND MAFEKING FUND,

SUBSEQUENTLY

The "In Memoriam" Soldiers' Fund.

FOLLOWING the example of Lady White's Ladysmith Fund, a similar appeal for the troops in Kimberley and Mafeking was made by Mrs. Scott Turner, Mrs. Henry Scott Turner, and Mrs. Conrad Howell, and a large assortment of suitable clothing, pipes, tobacco, etc., was forwarded, the first supply reaching the beleaguered towns very soon after they were relieved.

The response to the appeal having been so great, the supply far exceeding the necessities for which the appeal was first made, it was decided to continue the work for the troops in South Africa generally, and further large consignments were continued to be sent to Bloemfontein, Pretoria, the General Hospital at Wynberg, and in some instances to the various Divisions direct.

Among the many thousand garments and sundries received and despatched, besides those purchased, were 3,300 small editions of the Gospels, the gift of the British and Foreign Bible Society, and 250 pairs of socks and 100 shawls, knitted by the Irish Industry, the gift of the Duke of Abercorn.

The following, among many other acknowledgments, was received from Lady Roberts, through Lady Settrington:—

"Pretoria, 9th August, 1900.

"Lady Roberts has asked me to write and thank you for the splendid cases of clothing and other comforts that have been sent out by the 'In Memoriam' Fund. The last lot of cases you sent contained almost the first comforts that arrived here. We gave a great number to the Hospitals; but all the shirts and socks are gone to the Eleventh Division, which marched through Pretoria about three weeks ago. Hardly any of the men had a shirt, and none a pair of socks that was not quite worn out. You can imagine, therefore, what a Godsend your clothes were for these men, and how heartily grateful they were.

"HILDA SETTRINGTON."

STATEMENT OF RECEIPTS AND PAYMENTS.

DECEMBER, 1899, TO 31ST DECEMBER, 1901.

RECEIPTS.	£ s. d.	PAYMENTS.	£ s. d.
To Contributions, Kimberley and Mafeking	297 16 10	By Clothing	514 12 7
" " "In Memoriam" Fund	526 6 0	" Extra Comforts, etc.	217 11 2
		" Expenses, Carriage	74 17 0
		" Balance	17 2 1
	824 2 10		824 2 10

45, *Queensborough Terrace, W.*

SUMMARY

OF

APPROXIMATE AMOUNT SUBSCRIBED.

PART IV.

	£	s.	d.
Queen Victoria's Chocolate Box ...	—		
Queen Alexandra's Pipe	—		
The "Absent Minded Beggar" Fund ...	175,000	0	0
Women and Children from South Africa	410	17	6
Field Force Fund ...	38,535	3	10
Literature for the Troops	259	15	0
Lady White's Ladysmith Fund	4,355	12	8
Kimberley and Mafeking (The In Memoriam Soldiers') Fund ...	824	2	10
	£219,385	11	10

PART V.

VARIOUS FUNDS.
EQUIPMENT.

CONTENTS.

VARIOUS.

	PAGE
THE COUNTESS CARRINGTON'S FUND (COLONIALS) ...	129
MAFEKING RELIEF FUND	130
THE BARALONG RELIEF FUND	131
THE AUSTRALIAN BUSHMEN CONTINGENT FUND	131

EQUIPMENT.

YEOMANRY AND VOLUNTEER EQUIPMENT	132
LORD LOCH'S HORSE	132
THE CITY OF LONDON IMPERIAL VOLUNTEERS (THE C.I.V.)	132
THE MOUNTED SHARPSHOOTERS' CORPS	133
SUMMARY OF APPROXIMATE AMOUNT SUBSCRIBED ...	134

NOTE { For Lord Strathcona's Horse, *see* Part VI. under the "Canadian Patriotic Fund Association"
No information obtainable of Lovat's Scouts, Paget's Horse, and Rimington's Guides.
No special Fund raised for "Roughriders."

THE COUNTESS CARRINGTON'S FUND FOR INVALIDED COLONIAL SOLDIERS IN ENGLAND.

LADY CARRINGTON, on being informed in October, 1900, by some Australian soldiers who were staying at her convalescent home at High Wycombe, that, of 170 wounded and invalided Colonial soldiers then in England, many were in serious temporary financial difficulties on account of their being unable to obtain payment of their arrears of pay, in some cases amounting to £115 per man, appealed to the Lord Mayor, who made an advance out of the Mansion House Discretionary Fund to insure a loan of £1 a week to each individual soldier whilst in England.

The Colonel Commanding the Corps of Commissionaires kindly granted the use of a room at the barracks of that Corps as an office, where weekly payments, commencing the 11th October, 1900, were made, amounting together to £524, as per the following summary, viz.:—

			£	s.	d.
Canadians	48 men to the amount of		173	10	0
South Africans	33 ,, ,,		199	0	0
New South Wales	13 ,, ,,		110	0	0
Queensland	4 ,, ,,		6	0	0
New Zealand	3 ,, ,,		8	0	0
West Australia	2 ,, ,,		8	0	0
Sundry	3 ,, ,,		20	0	0
Total	106		£524	10	0

Arrangements were made with the Orient Steamship Company and the Union Castle Line to provide second-class saloon dietary, deck and comforts to all convalescents sent home as steerage passengers by the Government, the total cost in respect of 55 men being £507 4s. The Dominion Line made *special* provision for the necessary comfort of all Canadian Volunteers sent home in the steerage of their steamers.

These extra comforts on board ship proved a great boon, for, although the steerage fare is excellent for those in good health, it is hardly such as was required by convalescing enteric and dysentery patients.

An order having been issued at Shorncliffe Camp that any Colonials who had claims for back pay could receive advances in respect thereof, the necessity for the continuation of this Fund, which had proved such a timely benefit, ceased.

The sums refunded by men to 31st December, 1901, amounted to £20.

STATEMENT OF RECEIPTS AND PAYMENTS.

OCTOBER, 1900 TO 31 DECEMBER, 1901.

RECEIPTS.	£	s.	d.	PAYMENTS.	£	s.	d.
To Received from Mansion House Discretionary Fund	1,000	0	0	By Loans to Colonials	524	10	0
,, Loans repaid	20	0	0	,, Extra Comforts on Board Ship	507	4	0
,, Balance due to Lady Carrington	26	6	8	,, Expenses, etc.	14	12	8
	1,046	6	8		1,046	6	8

MAFEKING RELIEF FUND.

Letter to the Press from Major=General BADEN=POWELL, C.B.

SIR,—I have frequently found that letters sent by me home have—through the attention of our enemies—failed to reach their destinations during the past year. It seems, therefore, only too probable that many of those generous friends thoughout our Empire who came forward to assist the poor folk of Mafeking in the hour of their need, have never received even the bare acknowledgment of their donations.

May I, therefore, on this the Anniversary of our relief, by them as well as by Colonels Mahon and Plumer, ask your kind offices to make known to them the following points, which may be of interest.

In view of the large amount contributed, I formed a representative Committee for the control of its expenditure. This Committee included Lieut.-Colonel C. B. Vyvyan, the Commandant of Mafeking; Mr. C. G. Bell, the resident Magistrate, and Mr. A. H. Frend, the Mayor. These gentlemen worked hard and zealously to distribute the Funds with discrimination among the really deserving cases, and with such promptitude as to prevent any real distress, as well as to keep regular account and control of the money placed in their hands. I may add that their efforts appear to have been successful, for I have not so far had a single complaint as to the disbursements, &c.

The total amount made available for distribution was £29,267 6s. 1d., as per particulars attached. The collection of so vast a sum has necessarily also been a labour—albeit to many a labour of love—and the gratitude of Mafeking is largely due to Lady Sarah Wilson, who suggested the idea of the Fund; to Lady Georgina Curzon, who thereupon, with characteristic and whole-hearted energy raised the sum of £24,000; to my school comrades of Charterhouse, who sent, in addition to very large supplies of clothing and comforts, £1,150 in cash; to Lady Snagge and the *Birmingham Argus*, who collected £643 and £353 respectively towards sending the nerve-strained nurses, women and children to the seaside; to the Conservative Club, Liverpool; to the Melbourne Club; to Luton; to Mr. Butler, of Wellington, New Zealand; to Tunbridge Wells Imperial Association; to the Right Hon. C. J. Rhodes; to Swansea, Wales; to Salisbury, Mashonaland; to Mr. J. Garlick, Cape Town; to the Mayor of Brighton; to the Raleigh Club, London; to Ilfracombe; to Mr. William Nicol, all of whom sent over £100 a piece; to the Lord Mayor of London, who, in addition to sending £200 from the Mansion House Fund as an immediate advance, offered any further sum that might be required; to Mr. Leonard Rayne, the theatrical impresario of South Africa, who inaugurated the "Rainy! Day Fund," with a view to ultimate calls for relief by members of the Garrison in years to come. To all of these, and to the many more who so promptly contributed, according to their means, is due the heartfelt gratitude of Mafeking for their generous anticipation of her most pressing needs, and perhaps more than the gift of money did we in Mafeking appreciate the warm and loving sympathy which, first beaming on us through the gracious message of Her Majesty, then thrilled to us from every corner of the Empire.

It went as far in restoring head to the overstrained people of Mafeking, as have their liberal Funds since gone in repairing their more material damages, and a deep and lasting sense of gratitude now binds them with their friends across the world.

Trusting that through your kindness our benefactors may know how fully their generosity is appreciated,

I am, Sir, your obedient servant,

R. S. S. BADEN-POWELL, Major-General.

Zumfontein, Transvaal, May 17, 1901.

STATEMENT OF RECEIPTS AND PAYMENTS.

RECEIPTS.	£	s.	d.	PAYMENTS.		£	s.	d.
To Contributions	29,267	6	1	By Grants to Widows and Orphans..		6,538	15	0
				,, ,, Refugees		4,630	19	8
				,, ,, Town relief		3,741	2	10
				,, ,, Seaside Fund		2,912	6	6
				,, ,, Convent .. £1,500 0 0				
				,, ,, St. John's Church 300 0 0				
				,, ,, Wesleyan Church 300 0 0				
				,, ,, Public Schools .. 300 0 0				
				,, ,, Victoria Hospital 200 0 0				
				,, ,, Public Library .. 150 0 0				
				,, ,, Cemetery 150 0 0				
						2,900	0	0
				,, ,, Wounded Men ..		2,245	0	0
				,, ,, Small Tradesmen		1,765	0	0
				,, ,, Hospital Staff, Nuns, etc.		1,115	0	0
				,, ,, Col. Plumer's Rhodesian Column		1,000	0	0
				,, ,, Farmers (repayable)		750	0	0
				,, ,, Railway Fares and Passages		710	19	6
				,, Expenses		306	16	7
				,, Balance		651	6	0
	29,267	6	1			29,267	6	1
To Balance	651	6	0	By Reserve Contingent Allowance for Refugees returning to their homes		250	0	0
				,, ditto for Town Relief Fund		150	0	0
				,, Reserve for "Rainy Day"		251	6	0
	651	6	0			651	6	0

THE BARALONG RELIEF FUND.

The object and distribution of this Fund is contained in the following letter, addressed to Major H. Goold-Adams, C.B., C.M.G., Bloemfontein, Orange River Colony, by the undersigned:—

Mafeking, October 3rd, 1901.

Sir,—In response to the appeal on behalf of the Baralong addressed by you to the Press on May 5th, 1900, subscriptions amounting to £225 18s. 4d. were received by the Agent-General for this colony in London, and were placed to the credit of the Baralong Relief Fund, which, in accordance with the suggestion made in your letter, we were asked to administer.

Of this amount £18 8s. 6d. was expended last year in providing food for some destitute Baralong.

It was proposed that the balance should be used for the relief of members of the Baralong tribe, partially or totally disabled through wounds received during the siege.

The existence of the fund was made generally known, and the committee held two meetings, at which 21 applications for relief were dealt with.

Of these, 17 were found to be worthy of consideration, and, after taking statements as to the nature of the injuries sustained, personally interviewing applicants, where practicable, and getting information as to their circumstances, we decided to award £30 each to three men, one of whom was struck by a shell and lost half one leg and the foot off the other; another was wounded during the fight in the native stad on May 12th, and had a leg amputated; the third was injured in the thigh by a shell, and is now unable to work.

To a man who lost his left foot £15 was awarded, and the same was done for a man who was wounded through both thighs.

A grant of £10 was made to a widow who is quite helpless owing to wounds received in endeavouring to pass through the Boer lines.

It was decided that these amounts should be lodged in the Post Office Savings Bank, and should be expended at the discretion of the Civil Commissioner in the purchase of food or in providing other necessaries for the several persons mentioned.

In the cases of three women who were injured by shells, £30 was set aside for the purchase of heifers to be handed over to them. These will be bought as soon as a favourable opportunity of acquiring them presents itself.

The remaining eight applicants were granted sums of from £2 to £5 each, amounting in the aggregate to £24.

The total amount thus allotted is, therefore, £184, leaving a balance of £23 9s. 10d. available to meet any fresh cases that may be brought to our notice.

In conclusion, we have the honour, at the request of the chiefs and headmen, to thank you, on behalf of the Baralong tribe, for your kind interest in their welfare, and the subscribers to the fund for their generous response to your appeal.

We have the honour to be, Sir, your obedient servants,

J. B. MOFFAT, Civil Commissioner.
FRED J. BRISCOE, Supt. Wesleyan Mission.
EDGAR ROWLAND.

STATEMENT OF RECEIPTS AND PAYMENTS.

RECEIPTS.	£ s. d.	PAYMENTS.	£ s. d.
To Contributions	225 18 4	By Grants	184 0 0
		„ Food	18 8 6
		„ Balance	23 9 10
	225 18 4		225 18 4

THE AUSTRALASIAN BUSHMEN CONTINGENT FUND.

At a meeting of Australasians held at the Bank of New South Wales, Old Broad Street, on 15th January, 1900, it was resolved to raise a Fund in England to which all Australasians were invited to contribute, and thus support their Governments in their efforts to raise this Corps. The following was the result of the Appeal and the allocation of the Fund:—

STATEMENT OF RECEIPTS AND PAYMENTS.

RECEIPTS.	£ s. d.	PAYMENTS.	£ s. d.
To Contributions	13,299 14 8	By Remitted to Governor of New South Wales to distribute amongst various Colonies in proportion to men forwarded from each	12,740 9 3
		„ ditto to Victoria (earmarked for that Colony)	242 0 0
		„ „ New Zealand ditto	205 5 0
		„ Expenses	112 0 5
	13,299 14 8		13,299 14 8

E. C. Hitching, Esq., Hon. Sec., 17, Tokenhouse Yard, E.C.

YEOMANRY AND VOLUNTEER EQUIPMENT.

Funds for this object were generally contributed in answer to Appeals from Lords Lieutenants of Counties, although in some few instances Equipment Funds were raised independently for Companies of local Volunteers. The approximate amount subscribed throughout the kingdom, exclusive of the following special Funds for the same purpose, was £205,376.

LORD LOCH'S HORSE.

The late Lord Loch raised the above Corps consisting, with the Colt Gun detachment, of 12 officers and 207 men in January, 1900.

The cost of equipping and despatching the Corps amounted to £11,365 14s. 1d., of which the Government contributed £8,360, the remaining sum of £3,291 0s. 11d. being found by Lord Loch and his friends. From this latter amount £285 was given to the men for the support of their families for five weeks in order to give them time to remit money home; and subsequently Lady Loch raised a further sum of £550 for the Insurance of the men's lives. Forty-four wives and five dependent relatives were thus supported for five weeks; but in consequence of the delay in the men remitting their pay a large number of these were for a considerable time supported by the Soldiers' and Sailors' Families Association.

In its twelve months of "active" service, the Corps lost eleven men through wounds and disease, and in each case the widow or next-of-kin was paid the sum of £50, the amount for which the life of each officer and man was insured.

STATEMENT OF RECEIPTS AND PAYMENTS.
January, 1900 to April, 1901.

RECEIPTS.	£	s.	d.	PAYMENTS.	£	s.	d.
To Contributions (Lord Loch)	3,291	0	11	By Equipment, Passages, etc.	11,365	14	1
„ Grant from Government	8,360	0	0	„ Grants to Wives, etc.	285	6	10
„ Contributions (Lady Loch)	550	0	0	„ Insurance	550	0	0
	12,201	0	11		12,201	0	11

Sidney H. Farrer, Esq., *54, Old Broad Street, E.C.*

THE CITY OF LONDON IMPERIAL VOLUNTEERS.
(More commonly known as the C.I.V.)

At a meeting convened by the Lord Mayor (Sir Alfred Newton, Bart.) at the Mansion House on the 19th of December, 1899, when Masters of City Companies, Merchants, and Bankers attended; and at a meeting of the Common Council held the following day, when £25,000 was voted for the purpose, it was decided (the Commander-in-Chief having previously given his approval) to offer to the Government on behalf of the City of London, to fully equip and transport to the seat of War a Regiment of Volunteer Marksmen, a thousand strong. Public subscriptions were at the same time invited.

The Corps ultimately consisted of—(a) a Four Gun Battery of Field Artillery; (b) two Companies of Mounted Infantry; and (c) a Battalion of Infantry with Four Maxim Guns, and consisted of 1,671 officers and men, afterwards reinforced by a draft of 140 men. The men were clothed and equipped at the expense of the Fund with horses, saddlery, guns, and fixed ammunition, rifles only being supplied by Government, who also guaranteed that each Volunteer should, from the date of his enlistment, receive the same pay-rations, allowances, etc., of his rank as a regular soldier of the arm to which he belonged. Each officer and man received the Freedom of the City of London before embarkation. By the liberality of Messrs. Wilsons, the Castle and Union Lines, and Mr. Ellerman, a large part of the expenses of the transport of the Corps to South Africa was saved.

A Committee of the Field Officers' wives, under the Presidency of the Lady Mayoress, with Miss Muriel Newton as Hon. Secretary, undertook the care of the families of the men during their absence, and a payment of £100 was made to the families of men dying during the campaign, the total number being 71.

RECEIPTS AND PAYMENTS.
15th December, 1899 to 31st May, 1901.

RECEIPTS.	£	s.	d.	PAYMENTS.	£	s.	d.
To Subscriptions, including Interest and Dividends	118,282	2	10	By Equipment, Armament, Horses, Transport, Extra Rations, etc.	93,724	16	5
				„ Grants to Relatives of deceased men, &c.	8,842	19	1
				„ Reception Expenses, Mural Tablets, and other expenses as detailed	8,796	7	3
				„ Balance in hand 31st May, 1901	*6,918	0	1
	118,282	2	10		118,282	2	10

W. H. Pannell & Co., *Chartered Accountants, 20th June, 1901.*

The Corps was enrolled on 20th December, 1899 and disbanded on 30th October, 1900.

* A final statement, issued May 1902, shows a balance of £5,203 17s. 10d. in hand, which has been placed in trust "for the benefit of deserving poor, sick or disabled freemen of the City of London Imperial Volunteers."

THE MOUNTED SHARPSHOOTERS' CORPS.

The special feature of this Corps initiated in January, 1900, by H. Seton-Karr, Esq., M.P., who acted as Vice-Chairman to a Committee then formed, and as Honorary Secretary from May, 1900, was to provide men of a standard of rifle shooting, higher than the ordinary marksmen's test.

Three and a half battalions of this Corps were raised; the 1st battalion in 1900; the 2nd and 3rd battalions and a draft of about 300 men in 1901; some 1700 men in all.

In addition to the usual Government grants, a Fund amounting to £9,758 was received from the public in response to the above appeal, and from the Sharpshooters' Committee and their friends.

All the Recruits of the 1st battalion (483 men) were guaranteed a special bounty of £10 (apart from all Government bounties) payable on discharge. The lives of those with dependents were also insured for £250 each for one year, this insurance being subsequently renewed for £100 for a second year by the Committee, the insured or next-of-kin in many instances themselves paying the balance of the premium for the renewal of the full amount.

This special bounty and insurance was offered, in the first instance, by the Sharpshooters' Committee in order to attract good rifle-shots, and thus to ensure a higher standard of marksmanship than that required by the Imperial Yeomanry generally. At this time the Imperial Yeomanry pay was at the ordinary Cavalry rates of 1s. 3d. per day and upwards according to rank.

In 1901, when the 2nd and 3rd battalions and draft (1,205 men) were recruited, the Imperial Yeomanry pay had been raised to the special rate of 5s. per day and upwards according to rank, and the special inducements offered by the Sharpshooters' Committee were then fixed at £1 cash Bounty on enlistment in lieu of any Bounty on discharge; and a Life Policy for £100 for one year to recruits with dependents, subsequently renewed by the Committee for £50 for a second year.

Binoculars and telescopes were also supplied to all Officers and a majority of the men of the 1st battalion, as well as a large supply of tobacco, pipes, cigarettes, and food, extra comforts, etc., to all three battalions and draft.

APPROXIMATE STATEMENT OF RECEIPTS AND PAYMENTS.

RECEIPTS.	£	s.	d.	PAYMENTS.	£	s.	d.
To Contributions	9,758	0	0	By Bounties	5,715	0	0
				,, Insurance	2,013	0	0
				,, Binoculars and Telescopes, Gifts, Comforts, etc.	1,587	0	0
				,, Administration (exclusive of Government allowance)	443	0	0
	9,758	0	0		9,758	0	0

SUMMARY

OF

APPROXIMATE AMOUNT SUBSCRIBED.

PART V.

VARIOUS.

	£	s.	d.
The Countess Carrington's Fund (Colonials)	1,000	0	0
Mafeking Relief Fund	29,267	6	1
The Baralong Relief Fund	225	18	4
The Australian Bushmen Contingent Fund ...	13,299	14	8

EQUIPMENT.

	£	s.	d.
Yeomanry and Volunteer Equipment	205,376	0	0
Lord Loch's Horse (omitting Government Grant) ...	3,841	0	11
The City of London Imperial Volunteers (The C.I.V.) ...	118,282	2	10
The Mounted Sharpshooters' Corps ...	9,758	0	0
	381,050	2	10

PART VI.

INDIA.

BRITISH DOMINIONS BEYOND THE SEAS.

CONTENTS.

INDIA.

	PAGE
THE NORTH-WESTERN PROVINCES AND OUDH TRANSVAAL WAR FUND	137
THE INDIAN FOLLOWERS' RELIEF FUND	138
THE INDIAN STRETCHER-BEARERS' FUND ...	139

BRITISH DOMINIONS BEYOND THE SEAS.

THE CANADIAN PATRIOTIC FUND ASSOCIATION	140
LORD STRATHCONA'S HORSE ...	140
THE SOUTH AFRICAN WIDOWS' AND ORPHANS' FUND	141
GOOD HOPE SOCIETY FOR AID TO SICK AND WOUNDED ...	142
NATAL VOLUNTEER WAR FUND ...	143
SOUTH AUSTRALIA TRANSVAAL PATRIOTIC FUND ...	144
TASMANIA TRANSVAAL PATRIOTIC FUND	145
SUMMARY OF APPROXIMATE AMOUNT SUBSCRIBED ...	146

NOTE.—No information received from New South Wales, Victoria, Queensland, Western Australia, or New Zealand.

THE NORTH-WESTERN PROVINCES AND OUDH TRANSVAAL WAR FUND.

This Fund was raised in the winter and spring of 1899-1900, in response to an appeal from members of the Civil Service and others, the administration of the Fund being entrusted to the Bengal Branch of the Soldiers' and Sailors' Families Association.

In the early part of 1900 large subscriptions were received from Native Princes, influential Native gentlemen and others—the contributions received by December, 1900, amounting to over a lac of Rupees.

Of this sum Rs. 8,000 was expended in India on the relief of cases arising from the despatch of the Indian contingent to South Africa. A sum of Rs. 60,000 was transmitted to the Mansion House, ear-marked for the Soldiers' and Sailors' Families Association; and a sum of Rs. 35,000 handed to the Indian Followers Relief Fund, at the request of the Simla Committee of that Fund.

No fixed principle was followed in the distribution of relief, each case being treated, after full enquiry, on its merits.

STATEMENT OF RECEIPTS AND PAYMENTS.

October, 1899, to 31st December, 1901.

RECEIPTS.	Rs.	a.	p.	PAYMENTS.	Rs.	a.	p.
To Contributions	119,590	0	0	By Grants	8,000	0	0
				,, Remitted to Mansion House earmarked for S. & S.F.A.	60,000	0	0
				,, Indian Followers Relief Fund, Simla	35,000	0	0
				,, Expenses	90	0	0
				,, Balance	16,500	0	0
	119,590	0	0		119,590	0	0

INDIAN FOLLOWERS' RELIEF FUND.

In December, 1899, Lady Lockhart (the late Sir William Lockhart being then Commander-in-Chief), in conjunction with Lady Palmer, Lady Blood, Lady Luck and others, instituted a Fund in connection with the Soldiers' and Sailors' Families Association, for the benefit of the families of those native followers who had proceeded with the troops from India to Natal. These followers (syces, bheesties, stretcher-bearers, etc.) receive little pay, are quite unable to put by anything, and had, as a rule, left India without making any provision for their families; moreover, as the majority were shut up in Ladysmith, they were unable to remit any of their pay to India. Lady Lockhart and the other ladies mentioned, assisted by several officers, commenced collecting subscriptions for their benefit.

About the same time Messrs. King, King & Co., Bombay, who were collecting subscriptions for the Mansion House Fund, asked and obtained the permission of the Lord Mayor to allot some of the money subscribed for that Fund for the benefit of these people.

Subsequently, at the suggestion of the Commander-in-Chief, a Central Fund for all India was created at Simla, under the above designation, and under the management of a Committee, and all collections made by private individuals (amounting to Rs. 9,555 11a. 5p.) were transferred to this Fund for distribution. Owing to the fact, however, that people in India had already subscribed to the Mansion House Fund, and that the Lord Mayor was willing to allot moneys from the Fund for the benefit of the Indian Followers, special subscriptions were not asked for.

The distribution of relief was entrusted to the Officers commanding regiments, batteries, departments, etc., who administered the same locally, grants being made from the date on which the "follower" left India to the date of his return. In case of death or incapacity through the effects of active service, a bonus equal to six months' allowance was made to the family.

The monthly average of cases relieved has been between five and six hundred.

STATEMENT OF RECEIPTS AND PAYMENTS.
OCTOBER, 1899, TO 31ST DECEMBER, 1901.

RECEIPTS.	Rs.	a.	p.	PAYMENTS.	Rs.	a.	p.
To Contributions in India	9,555	11	5	By Relief of Cases	52,816	10	7
,, Further Contributions	30,048	2	10	,, Expenses	1,607	5	0
,, Received from S. & S.F.A.	35,000	0	0	,, Balance	58,324	11	2
,, ,, ,, Durban (Stretcher-bearers Fund)	20,165	14	6				
,, The Mansion House	15,000	0	0				
,, The Globe (Stretcher-bearers Fund)	638	11	0				
,, Contributions from Home	240	0	0				
,, Interest on Deposit	2,100	3	0				
	1,12,748	10	9		1,12,748	10	9

THE INDIAN STRETCHER BEARERS' FUND.

This Fund, with the exception of £133 19s. 6d., subscribed in Natal, was raised by the Proprietor of the *Globe* Newspaper in London.

Its objects were to aid:—

First, those Indian followers who had been through the siege of Ladysmith, and the War generally from its beginning.

Secondly, those who had participated in the relief of Ladysmith; and

Thirdly, those who came from India at a later date.

The total amount of articles of clothing distributed was as follows, viz.:—

Pairs of Woollen Socks	1,830
Warm Woollen Scarves capable of conversion into Caps	1,790
Pairs of Warm Pants	1,296
Warm Flannel Shirts	491
Woollen Vests	588
Cardigan Jackets	210
Pyjamas Suits	18
Pairs of Boots	4

The amount of Food Stuffs distributed were 4,956 lbs. of ghee, 218¼ lbs. of curry powder, 142 lbs. of cardamoms, 47 lbs. of betel nuts, and 80 lbs. of turmeric.

STATEMENT OF RECEIPTS AND PAYMENTS.

RECEIPTS.	£	s.	d.	PAYMENTS.	£	s.	d.
To Contributions	2,447	4	5	By Remitted to Durban	2,600	0	0
,, Grant from Lord Mayor's Discretionary Fund	250	0	0	,, Examiner Military Accounts, Simla	42	14	11
				,, Telegrams, &c.	54	9	6
	2,697	4	5		2,697	4	5

NATAL ACCOUNT.

RECEIPTS.	£	s.	d.	PAYMENTS.	£	s.	d.
To Remittance from the *Globe*	2,600	0	0	By Clothing	591	10	3
,, Contributions in South Africa	133	19	6	,, Food	276	2	3
				,, Gifts in Natal	367	4	0
				,, ,, ,, Capetown	100	0	0
				,, Examiner Military Accounts, Simla	1,386	16	10
				,, Expenses	12	6	2
	2,733	19	6		2,733	19	6

THE CANADIAN PATRIOTIC FUND ASSOCIATION.

This Association was organised on 1st January, 1900, with the object of raising a Fund for the benefit of Canadian soldiers and their dependents.

First. For the benefit of the Widows, Orphans, and other dependents of Officers and Men of the Military Forces of Canada who may lose their lives in, or in connection with, the War in South Africa.

Second. For the benefit of the Soldiers themselves or others (whether combatant or non-combatant) on duty in South Africa, with the authority of the Government of Canada, and their families or dependents, who may have been disabled by wounds, sickness, etc.

Third. For the benefit of the Wives and Children and dependents separated at home from those serving in South Africa.

Relief under the latter head was chiefly made monthly, the Committee being greatly assisted by officers and members of the Soldiers' Wives League in the different districts of the Dominion.

In addition to the amount contributed to this Association, local Funds were also raised at Halifax, N.S., St. John, N.B., and Hamilton, Ont., and in other cities amounting approximately to £30,000 in aid of the members of the Contingents sent from such cities.

Independently also of this work, assistance was rendered by the Red Cross Society in Canada, and large consignments of articles of comfort sent out.

STATEMENT OF RECEIPTS AND PAYMENTS.

1st January, 1900, to 31st October, 1901.

RECEIPTS.	£	s.	d.	PAYMENTS.	£	s.	d.
To Contributions	69,544	0	0	To 10 Widows, 1 Orphan, and 48 Dependents	9,505	0	0
				,, 471 Invalided or disabled Soldiers	20,558	0	0
				,, 340 Wives and Dependents	6,501	0	0
				,, Balance	32,980	0	0
	69,544	0	0		69,544	0	0

NOTE.—£30,000 also in Cities named above.

LORD STRATHCONA'S HORSE.

No mention of work carried out in Canada would be complete without referring to the patriotism of Lord Strathcona, in the raising and equipping of 600 men known as Strathcona's Horse. Not only was the Corps fully equipped in respect of uniform for officers and men, accoutrements, carbines and two Maxim guns; but all expenses of transport to South Africa, and the pay of officers and men up to the date of their embarkation, and until they landed, defrayed; after which time they were paid by Government. While serving in South Africa Lord Strathcona, in addition, paid to officers and men the difference between Imperial pay and the pay given to the North West Mounted Police in Canada.

No particulars of this outlay is obtainable, but it is estimated to be not less than £300,000.

THE SOUTH AFRICAN WIDOWS' AND ORPHANS' FUND.

CAPE OF GOOD HOPE.

This Fund was started by Sir Alfred (now Lord) Milner and Lieut.-General Sir F. W. E. Forestier-Walker, in July, 1900, for the purpose of supplementing the Royal Patriotic Fund, the grants from which were not considered sufficient to meet the high cost of living in South Africa; and also to give immediate relief to Widows and Orphans suddenly deprived of their means of subsistence by the death of the breadwinner.

The Fund is for the assistance of Widows or Orphans, resident in South Africa, of all soldiers, Colonial and Imperial, who have lost their lives during the war.

In the administration of the Fund the investigation and payment in every case has been made by and through the clergy or Resident Magistrate.

The relief has generally taken the form of a monthly allowance for the payment of rent. This has, in some cases, been supplemented by the gift of a sewing machine, and once, in the case of a music teacher, of the gift of a piano, the object being to enable the beneficiaries, if possible, to earn their own living.

Number of cases relieved, 85.

STATEMENT OF RECEIPTS AND PAYMENTS.

July, 1900, to 31st December, 1901.

RECEIPTS.	£ s. d.	PAYMENTS.	£ s. d.
To Contributions	2,486 0 0	To Grants	1,706 15 1
		,, Expenses	7 17 7
		,, Balance	771 7 4
	2,486 0 0		2,486 0 0

NOTE.—No General Fund except the above appears to have been raised in Cape Colony. Committees were formed for the distribution for the objects for which they were subscribed of grants made from Lloyd's Patriotic Fund, *The Daily Telegraph* Shilling Fund, the National Bazaar Fund, and the British Empire League, and no less than thirty Committees for the Lord Mayor's Transvaal Refugees' Fund.

THE GOOD HOPE SOCIETY FOR AIDING THE SICK AND WOUNDED.

This Society owes its initiation chiefly to Mrs. Hanbury Williams (wife of Colonel Hanbury Williams, Military Secretary to the Governor), and was formed at a public meeting held on the 3rd November, 1899. The movement was warmly supported by the Governor, Sir Alfred (now Lord) Milner, General Sir W. Forestier-Walker, the Bishop of Cape Town, and many influential ladies and gentlemen. On the arrival of the Commissioner of the Central British Red Cross Committee in South Africa it was agreed that the two bodies should join and work hand in hand for the one cause. In order to avoid any overlapping it was further agreed that at first the Good Hope Society should confine its sphere of action to the Base and other Hospitals in the Cape Peninsula and the Hospital Trains. This arrangement was subsequently modified by the extension of the work throughout South Africa, always keeping in touch with the Agents of the Central British Red Cross Committee. Working in this way, and sharing the burden between them, the best interests of the cause were served. Throughout the whole period that the Commissioners of the Central British Red Cross Committee were in South Africa, up to the time of their leaving at the close of 1900, the two bodies worked together without a hitch, when the Good Hope Society took over the entire control of Red Cross Work, henceforth acting as agents for the Central British Red Cross Committee, by whom they were supplied with funds and materials. In order to enable the Society to cope with the heavy demands for edible comforts, sub-committees were formed of ladies and gentlemen at Wynberg, Rondebosh, Maitland, Woodstock and Sea Point for the supply of such wants to the Hospitals and Convalescent Camps in their respective centres. Affiliated committees were also formed at East London, Naauwpoort, De Aar, Kimberley, Beaufort West, Touws River, and Wellington, to provide for the wants of the sick and wounded on their journeys from the Field Hospitals to the Base. The necessity for supplying clothing to men in Hospital, etc., led to the organization of working parties of ladies in Cape Town and elsewhere who manufactured garments from materials supplied by the Society. Among the comforts supplied, probably what was most valued and appreciated was the issue, on the arrival of the wounded at the dressing stations and to those in the Ambulance Trains, of "kit bags," the happy idea of Lady Charles Bentinck. These kits consisted of a flannel shirt, suit of pyjamas, pair of socks and pair of slippers, towel, sponge and bag, hair brush, tooth brush, and cake of soap, contained in a stout canvas haversack, bearing the inscription, "Gift from the British Red Cross and Good Hope Societies." It is computed that 20,000 of these kits, which became the exclusive property of the recipient, were distributed.

Mr. Fairbairn has been the Hon. Secretary of the Society almost from its initiation.

STATEMENT OF RECEIPTS AND PAYMENTS.

6TH NOVEMBER, 1899, TO 13TH JANUARY, 1902.

RECEIPTS.	£ s. d.	PAYMENTS.	£ s. d.
To Contributions	*14,170 17 11	By Clothing, Materials for Kit Bags, Chairs, Tobacco, &c., Books, &c. Paper and Stamps	13,180 10 0
		,, Expenses	782 12 8
		,, Balance	207 15 3
	14,170 17 11		14,170 17 11

* An account of the moneys advanced (approximately between £5,000 and £6,000) and goods supplied to the Good Hope Society by the Central British Red Cross Committee, will be found set out on pages 8 and 20 of the Report of the Central British Red Cross Committee published by Harrison & Co., St. Martin's Lane.

NATAL VOLUNTEER WAR FUND.

This Fund was raised in response to the following extract of an appeal through the Press of 27th November, 1899, by Sir Walter Peace, K.C.M.G., Agent-General for Natal in London:—

"Notwithstanding the generous subscriptions which have been made to the Transvaal Refugees' Fund and the Transvaal War Fund, I feel sure I shall not ask in vain for subscriptions for the relief of those who in Natal are dependent on the Natal Volunteers and Local Forces, who, at great sacrifice, are nobly doing their duty to their Queen and country in the present war.

"The fact that I make this appeal with the sanction of the Natal Government shows that there is an urgent need for funds for the object stated, in anticipation of which several handsome subscriptions have been already forwarded to me for transmission.

"A list of all subscriptions will be duly published in the Press, and the funds will be transmitted to the Natal Government for distribution by responsible local committees."

No expenses were charged against the Fund in this country, excepting the cost of advertising subscriptions in the Press. The funds were remitted to Natal by the Standard Bank of South Africa free of charge.

Included in the amounts transmitted to the Colony were the following contributions:—From the Mansion House Refugees' Fund and *The Daily Mail* Kipling Poem Fund, £5,000 each; from Lloyd's Patriotic Fund, £3,000; from Mr. Walter Morrison, M.P., £2,500; from *The Daily Telegraph* and Mauritius Relief Fund, £2,000 each; and from the Soldiers' and Sailors' Families Association and Officers' Wives and Families Fund, £1,000 each.

EXTRACT FROM STATEMENT OF RECEIPTS AND PAYMENTS.
Received from the Natal Committee.

November, 1899, to 31st January, 1902.

RECEIPTS.	Sir W. Peace. £ s. d.	Other Sources. £ s. d.	PAYMENTS.	£ s. d.	Balance. £ s. d.
To *Daily Mail* Armour Train Relief Fund	1,000 0 0	—	By Grants	900 0 0	100 0 0
,, Volunteer Relief Fund (*Daily Mail* £1,000)	2,000 0 0	445 2 11	,, ditto	2,445 2 11	—
,, Volunteer Relief and Sufferers' Fund (*Daily Telegraph* £1,000, *Daily Mail* £1,000)	16,540 17 11	669 6 6	,, ditto	17,209 4 5	1 0 0
,, Mauritius Relief Fund	2,000 0 0	141 0 3	,, ditto	2,141 0 3	—
,, *Telegraph* Widows' and Orphans' Fund	1,000 0 0	711 5 0	,, ditto	1,711 5 0	—
,, *Daily Mail* (Kipling Poem) Fund	2,000 0 0	—	,, ditto	2,000 0 0	—
,, Special Relief Fund (Mansion House £5,000)	6,000 0 0	152 18 10	,, ditto	6,152 18 10	—
,, Mauritius Volunteer Relief Fund	.. ..	739 14 0	,, ditto	414 16 6	324 17 6
,, Transvaal War Fund (Patriotic Commissioners)	.. ..	350 0 0	,, ditto	350 0 0	—
,, Officers' Wives and Families (Lansdowne) Fund	1,000 0 0	—	,, ditto	1,000 0 0	—
,, Sir John W. Akerman's Fund	.. ..	100 0 0	,, ditto	100 0 0	—
,, Lloyd's Natal Patriotic Fund	3,000 0 0	22 0 0	,, ditto	1,064 2 11	1,957 17 1
,, General Widows' and Orphans' Fund	1,211 5 0	3,978 17 10	,, ditto	2,062 10 0	3,127 12 10
,, South African Colonists' Fund	.. ..	569 17 2	,, ditto	168 10 0	401 7 2
	35,752 2 11 7,880 2 6	7,880 2 6		37,719 10 10 5,912 14 7	5,912 14 7
	43,632 5 5			43,632 5 5	

26, Victoria Street, Westminster, S.W.

SOUTH AUSTRALIA.

TRANSVAAL PATRIOTIC FUND.

Two Funds were raised in this Colony.

(*a*) For wives, widows, dependents, and men.

(*b*) For the equipment and partial maintenance of 100 men of the South Australian Bushmen Contingent.

In both cases the Funds received substantial help from the Proprietors of *The Register* Newspaper, who initiated a Shilling Fund, collecting for object (*a*) £10,000, and for (*b*) £4,100.

For Fund (*a*) £11,000 was forwarded to the Mansion House, earmarked for widows and orphans, and £881 given in relief to 58 wives, widows, and men.

From Fund (*b*) the Contingent was partly maintained in South Africa for 12 months.

STATEMENT OF RECEIPTS AND PAYMENTS (*a*).

RECEIPTS.	£ s. d.	PAYMENTS.	£ s. d.
To Contributions	6,376 0 0	By Remitted to Mansion House	11,000 0 0
,, *Register* Shilling Fund	10,000 0 0	,, Grants, etc.	881 0 0
,, Interest	190 0 0	,, Balance	4,685 0 0
	16,566 0 0		16,566 0 0

STATEMENT OF RECEIPTS AND PAYMENTS (*b*).

RECEIPTS.	£ s. d.	PAYMENTS.	£ s. d.
To Contributions	13,942 0 0	By Maintenance of Contingent	18,042 0 0
,, *Register* Shilling Fund	4,100 0 0		
	18,042 0 0		18,042 0 0

Total amount subscribed   £34,608 0 0

TASMANIA.

TRANSVAAL PATRIOTIC FUND.

Seven Funds for different objects were raised in this Colony, amounting together to £12,068 12s.; but few detailed particulars of the allocation of the Funds are given, making it difficult to give any clear statement.

It is stated that insurance was effected for the

1st Contingent:—On Officers, for £200 each; on Non-commissioned Officers and men, for £100 each.

2nd Contingent:—That the lives of the members were not insured, the Government having accepted the liability and paid £100 in each case to the relations of three men of the Contingent who died on service; and that the

3rd Contingent was treated as the First.

STATEMENT OF RECEIPTS AND PAYMENTS.

RECEIPTS.	£ s. d.	£ s. d.	PAYMENTS.	£ s. d.	£ s. d.
Mansion House War Fund:—			By Remitted to Mansion House that the same might be applied to any one or more Divisions of the Fund ..		10,278 2 0
To Contributions:					
No. 1. Widows and Orphans					
No. 2. Sick and Wounded		10,278 2 0			
No. 3. Disabled Soldiers					
No. 4. Wives and Families					
To Tasmania Contingent Fund (For assistance of Soldiers)		980 0 0	By Grants „ Balance	947 0 0 33 0 0	980 0 0
To *Daily Mail* Kipling Fund (For relief of Dependents)	500 0 0		By Grants „ Insurance .. „ Balance ..	60 0 0 114 10 0 636 0 0	810 10 0
To Lloyd's Patriotic Fund (For Disabled Soldiers) ..	200 0 0				
To Australian Benefit Matinée (For Widows and Families)	20 0 0		Note.—These four last Funds have all been transferred to the *Daily Mail* Kipling Fund.		
To National Bazaar War Fund (For use of Soldiers Sufferers)	30 10 0				
To British Empire League (For men unable to resume their occupation) ..	60 0 0	810 10 0			
		12,068 12 0			12,068 12 0

SUMMARY

OF

APPROXIMATE AMOUNT SUBSCRIBED.

PART VI.

INDIA.

		£	s.	d.
The North-Western Provinces and Oudh Transvaal War Fund ... (say)		7,947	0	0
The Indian Followers' Relief Fund—				
Received from Mansion House ... ... (say) 2,000 0 0				
„ „ other sources 5,516 0 0				
		7,516	0	0
The Indian Stretcher Bearers' Fund—				
Received from Mansion House 250 0 0				
„ „ other sources 2,581 3 11				
		2,831	3	11

BRITISH DOMINIONS BEYOND THE SEAS.

	£	s.	d.
The Canadian Patriotic Fund Association 69,544 0 0			
Halifax (N.S.), St. John (N.B.), Hamilton (Ont.) 30,000 0 0			
	99,544	0	0
The South African Widows' and Orphans' Fund ...	2,486	0	0
Good Hope Society for Aid to Sick and Wounded	14,170	17	11
Natal Volunteer War Fund	43,632	5	5
South Australia Transvaal Patriotic Fund ... ... { (a) = 16,566 0 0 / (b) = 18,042 0 0 }			
	34,608	0	0
Tasmania Transvaal Patriotic Fund	12,068	12	0
	£224,803	19	3

PART VII.
REFUGEES, ETC.

CONTENTS.

	PAGE
THE MANSION HOUSE TRANSVAAL REFUGEES FUND	149
BRITISH REFUGEES FUND } VICTORIA LEAGUE	151
THE DUTCH WOMEN AND CHILDREN'S FUND }	
SOUTH AFRICAN WOMEN AND CHILDREN'S DISTRESS FUND	152
THE BOER WOMEN AND CHILDREN'S CLOTHING FUND	152
THE JOHANNESBURG REFUGEES FUND	153
SUMMARY OF APPROXIMATE AMOUNT SUBSCRIBED ...	154

THE
MANSION HOUSE TRANSVAAL REFUGEES FUND

RAISED DURING THE MAYORALTIES OF

Sir John Voce Moore	1899.
Sir Alfred James Newton, Bart.	1899-1900.
Sir Frank Green, Bart.	1900-1901.

Private Secretary—WM. JAMESON SOULSBY, Esq., C.B., C.I.E.

APPEAL OF SIR JOHN VOCE MOORE.
Letter to the Press.

Sir,—I have to-day received the subjoined letter from the Secretary of State for the Colonies with the enclosure from Sir Alfred Milner, and I have lost no time in opening a fund at the Mansion House for the immediate relief and succour of the thousands of unhappy refugees from the Transvaal and the Orange Free State, whose pitiable and unfortunate condition must appeal to the sympathy of us all.

Help, to be effectual, must be rendered without delay, and I shall take care that the remittances which the benevolent public may send to me shall be placed by telegraph at the Relief Committee's disposal from time to time as the money comes in.

I would especially commend this appeal to the attention of my brother Mayors and the clergy and ministers of religion, whose aid and assistance I earnestly invite.

I am, Sir, your obedient servant,
JOHN VOCE MOORE, Lord Mayor.

The Mansion House, London, Oct. 11, 1899.

Letter from the Secretary of State for the Colonies to the Lord Mayor, and enclosure from Sir Alfred, now Lord Milner.

Downing Street, Oct. 11, 1899.

My Lord Mayor,—I have the honour to transmit to you a copy of a telegram which I have to-day received from the High Commissioner for South Africa.

In communicating to you his message, which is addressed to Lord Mayors and Lord Provosts of the United Kingdom, I desire to associate myself most cordially with him and with the Governor of Natal in the appeal which they make to the sympathy and generosity of the British public on behalf of those who have been compelled by the unfortunate course of events to leave the South African Republic and the Orange Free State, a very large number of whom, through no fault of their own, are in great straits and in urgent need of prompt assistance.

As Sir Alfred Milner points out, both in the Cape Colony and Natal there has been no lack of a helpful response to the claims of these sufferers, but the exodus from Johannesburg and from other parts has assumed such enormous proportions that it has become imperative to seek aid from beyond the limits of British South Africa, and I trust you will be able to initiate a fund for the relief of these refugees.

They are in the vast majority of cases of British birth, and I feel sure that their fellow-countrymen will recognize the claim upon their liberality involved in this fact, and will provide such funds as may be necessary, which I have no doubt will be carefully and wisely administered.

I have the honour to be, my Lord Mayor, your lordship's most obedient servant,
J. CHAMBERLAIN.

The Right Hon. the Lord Mayor of London.

Telegram. High Commissioner Sir Alfred Milner to Mr. Chamberlain.
(Received, Colonial Office, 1.56 a.m., 11th October, 1899.)

10th October.

In consequence of the enormous exodus of British subjects from Johannesburg, as well as from other parts of the South African Republic and the Orange Free State, the British colonies in South Africa, and especially the seaport towns, are now flooded with refugees, many of them already in needy circumstances, and many more whose savings will shortly be exhausted. Hitherto local charity, working in connection with the relief committee at Johannesburg, which has displayed great generosity, has been able to cope with the influx, at least to extent of providing for women and children. But the numbers now pouring into British territories are more than our local resources can possibly deal with for long; the arrivals at Cape Town alone exceed 1,000 per diem, and it must be borne in mind that the vast majority of the refugees are not of colonial but of British origin, the white population of the gold fields amounting to at least 100,000. It is estimated that nearly half of these have left, and as almost all work is stopped many more will follow. In this time of great trial the refugees are as a body showing a courage and independence worthy of all praise; those who can are helping themselves. But there are thousands who need, or will need, some assistance either to return home or to maintain themselves in this country, which, in the long run, can ill spare their skill and energy till the normal course of industry is restored.

In order to assist local effort to achieve these objects, I appeal, in the name of British South Africa, to the generosity of the British public, trusting that your lordships will see fit to take up our cause and to ask your fellow-citizens to come to the aid of this vast body of British working people in their undeserved suffering. Relief is being organised by local committees in a practical way. Wherever possible employment is found and readily accepted. Where the refugees are anxious to go home and it seems wiser that they should do so, help is, if necessary, given in that direction. But it is impossible to find work at once for more than a few, nor can those returned home be sent off all at once.

In the meantime food and shelter has to be found for ever-increasing numbers; a strong central committee is being formed containing representatives from all the principal places to which refugees resort [in] large numbers to superintend the distribution of the fund according to their needs among the several local relief committees; the Standard Bank of South Africa has kindly undertaken to transmit to us without charge any funds subscribed in Great Britain, and the Bank of Africa will assist in the same direction. The Governor of Natal, to which colony a considerable number of refugees are resorting, desires to associate himself with me in making this appeal; hitherto Natal has coped with the difficulty out of its own resources, but on Natal also the burden will soon be too great.

THE MANSION HOUSE TRANSVAAL REFUGEES FUND.

1899 TO 1901.

RECEIPTS.	£ s. d.	PAYMENTS.		£ s. d.
To Contributions	178,950 19 10	By Cash transmitted to—		
		The Cape	£164,243 4 4	
		Natal	5,000 0 0	
				169,243 4 4
		„ Cash to the Jewish Board of Guardians for the relief of Jewish Refugees	624 5 0	
		„ Families relieved in England ..	6,210 2 4	
				6,834 7 4
		„ Charges of Crown Agents for the Colonies for transmission of Gifts of Clothing		271 0 10
		„ Expenses of Advertising, Printing, Stationery, Postage, and Clerical Staff		2,602 7 4
	178,950 19 10			178,950 19 10

9 May, 1901.

Examined and found correct,
(Signed) TURQUAND, YOUNGS, BISHOP & CLARKE.
Honorary Auditors.

APPROXIMATE STATE OF THE FUND IN SOUTH AFRICA
ON 31 DECEMBER, 1901.
(From particulars supplied to the Mansion House.)

RECEIPTS.	£ s. d.	PAYMENTS.	£ s. d.
To Contributions in South Africa, including amounts sent direct to Lord Milner from England	108,664 13 11	By Amount expended in Relief	264,606 13 10
„ Amounts received from the Mansion House	169,243 4 4	„ Balance	13,301 4 5
	277,907 18 3		277,907 18 3

Approximate number of Persons relieved in South Africa ... ... 50,679 } 51,379.
Ditto ditto England ... ... 700 }

The Mansion House Fund was closed 9th May, 1901, but the work of distribution in South Africa is still proceeding. The Victoria League subsequently took up the work of collection in London.

BRITISH REFUGEES' FUND.

VICTORIA LEAGUE.

A Sub-Committee of the Victoria League (under the Chairmanship of Lord Windsor) was formed in July, 1901, to continue the work previously carried on from the commencement of the war by The Mansion House Transvaal Refugees' Fund, viz., the relief of British Refugees, chiefly women and children, scattered throughout South Africa.

The chief function of the Sub-Committee was to collect funds and remit the same to South Africa to be disbursed by the local committees already formed, although in some instances assistance was also given to families who had returned to England as refugees.

STATEMENT OF RECEIPTS AND PAYMENTS.

July, 1901, to 31st March, 1902.

RECEIPTS.	£ s. d.	PAYMENTS.	£ s. d.
To Contributions	6,083 0 0	By Grants in England and to South Africa	5,200 0 0
		,, Advertising and Expenses	162 0 0
		,, Balance	721 0 0
	6,083 0 0		6,083 0 0

THE DUTCH WOMEN AND CHILDREN'S FUND.

Another Sub-Committee of the Victoria League (with Lady Gwendolen Cecil as Chairman) was formed the same month with the object of providing clothing, medicine, and comforts for the Boer women in the Concentration Camps.

The Sub-Committee were guided in the administration of the Fund by the Lady Commissioners sent to South Africa by the Government. On the report of these ladies after arriving in South Africa, that the Government were providing everything that was necessary in the Camps, and that there was no longer any call upon the Funds, it was decided to await their return to England before taking further action. Subsequently, after hearing the views of two of the lady Commissioners, who deprecated any further distribution of clothing, the Sub-Committee decided to remit £800 for educational purposes (for which they thought the Government could not reasonably be asked to supply funds) to Mr. Sargant, the Commissioner for Education in the Transvaal and Orange River Colony, who undertook to apply the same to the best advantage.

The balance of the Fund the Sub-Committee decided to retain in their hands until the breaking up of the Camps believing that great distress might then prevail.

STATEMENT OF RECEIPTS AND PAYMENTS.

July, 1901, to 31st March, 1902.

RECEIPTS.	£ s. d.	PAYMENTS.	£ s. d.
To Contributions	1,942 9 2	By Purchase of Clothing, Medicine, etc.	160 0 0
		,, Advertising and Expenses	117 7 11
		,, Education remittance to Mr. Sargant	800 0 0
		,, Balance	865 1 3
	1,942 9 2		1,942 9 2

Dacre House, Victoria Street, S.W.

SOUTH AFRICAN WOMEN AND CHILDREN'S DISTRESS FUND.

THIS Fund was opened early in December, 1900 (with Sir Thomas Dyke Acland as Chairman), for the assistance of women and children who had been rendered homeless during the military operations in South Africa, and who were chiefly located in what are known as the Concentration Camps.

A Provisional Committee was formed in England with Sir Thomas C. D. Acland, Bart., as Chairman, as also a Committee at Cape Town over which Lady de Villiers, wife of the Chief Justice of Cape Colony, presided.

Later in the month, Miss Hobhouse proceeded to South Africa to ascertain the extent and nature of the distress, and to learn what relief was desirable or possible while the war continued. After an extended tour through Cape Colony and the Orange River Colony, in which, among others, the Women's Camps at Bloemfontein, Kimberley, Edenburg, Kronstadt, Norval's Pont, and Springfontein were visited, Miss Hobhouse returned to England. On the reports received from her while in South Africa, and on her subsequent reports after her return home, the Committee were able to supply Funds to the Committee at Cape Town and such necessaries as were considered would be most useful.

The Honorary Secretaries were, in the first instance, Mr. E. W. Lawrence, and, subsequently, Mr. C. E. Maurice.

A Clothing Branch was also established in London by a different Committee.

STATEMENT OF RECEIPTS AND PAYMENTS.
4TH DECEMBER, 1900, TO 28TH OCTOBER, 1901.

RECEIPTS.	£ s. d.	PAYMENTS.	£ s. d.	£ s. d.
To Contributions	6,390 13 2	By Relief, through Miss Hobhouse—		
,, Sale of Reports	115 19 6	Food, Soap, Clothing, etc.	307 0 11	
,, Sale of Tickets	12 6 0	Building Materials	265 0 0	
		Rents, School Fees, etc.	147 5 6	
		Sundries (not yet accounted for)	108 10 8	
		Telegrams, etc.	13 6 5	841 3 6
		,, Two other Representatives in South Africa		540 0 0
		,, Passages of ditto		142 17 6
		,, Sums to Local Committees		379 10 0
		,, Mr. Rendell Harris for Food and Clothing		500 0 0
		,, London Committee—		
		Foodstuffs and Freight		53 1 3
		Photographs of Boer Children		8 14 3
		Printing Miss Hobhouse's Report (55,000 copies)		520 1 4
		Office expenses, Advertising, etc.		273 11 1
		,, Balance		3,259 19 9
	6,518 18 8			6,518 18 8

31, Golden Square, W.

THE BOER WOMEN AND CHILDREN'S CLOTHING FUND.

UNDER the auspices of the Women Workers of the South Africa Conciliation Committee a scheme (with Lady Osborne Morgan as Chairman and Miss E. D. Bradby as Honorary Secretary) was set on foot in November, 1900, for helping to provide clothing for the distressed Boer women and children.

Since the Fund was opened, 100 Bales and Cases have been dispatched to a Committee of ladies in Cape Town, for distribution, containing clothes to the number of—

New	{ 7,306	Women's and girls' garments
	{ 10,379	Children's and babies' garments
Old	{ 3,579	Women's and girls' garments
	{ 2,804	Children's and babies' garments
Total ...	24,068	in addition to 200 workbags fitted with haberdashery, sent in each bale.

Pieces of dress material, flannel, flannelettes, lining, stuffs, cottons, combs, sponges, maternity bags, and household linen have also been sent out. The goods on arrival, after clearing the Customs, were warehoused, and unpacked and repacked into bundles of complete outfit, according to size, by the Ladies' Committee at Cape Town, and forwarded, as opportunity occurred, to the Camps most in need. The Camps chiefly supplied were those at Mafeking, Warrenton, Kimberley, Springfontein, Bloemfontein, Bethulie, Norval's Pont, and Aliwal North.

STATEMENT OF RECEIPTS AND PAYMENTS.
NOVEMBER, 1900, TO 31ST DECEMBER, 1901.

RECEIPTS.	£ s. d.	PAYMENTS.	£ s. d.
To Contributions	1,298 0 6	By Purchase of Woollen Stuffs, etc.	923 0 9
		,, Expenses, Carriage, etc.	183 9 9
		,, Balance	191 10 0
	1,298 0 6		1,298 0 6

19, Linden Gardens, Bayswater, W.

THE JOHANNESBURG REFUGEES' FUND.

APPEAL OF SIR JOSEPH C. DIMSDALE, M.P.

Letter to the Press.

Sir,—I have the honour to invite you to give publicity to the accompanying letter addressed to me by the Secretary of State for the Colonies, and to allow me heartily to commend the appeal which he and Lord Milner make after serious consideration in behalf of the loyalist refugees at Johannesburg, who, like so many others in various parts of South Africa, have suffered terribly from the prolonged operations of the war. I feel certain that the benevolent public at home will desire to give these much-tried people a helping hand in their praiseworthy efforts to start afresh after their severe privations.

I shall be glad to receive at the Mansion House donations in money to be expended in the manner indicated by Mr. Chamberlain, or they may be sent to the bankers of the fund, Messrs. Prescott, Dimsdale, and Co., 50, Cornhill, and their branches. Gifts of furniture or other goods of the descriptions mentioned in the Secretary of State's letter should be forwarded to Messrs. Hayter and Hayter. Public acknowledgment will be made of the receipt of all contributions, whether in money or in kind.

I am, Sir, your obedient servant,

JOSEPH C. DIMSDALE, Lord Mayor.

The Mansion House, London, E.C., April 7, 1902.

Colonial Office, Downing Street, April 5, 1902.

My Lord Mayor,—I have the honour to inform you that I have received a telegram from Lord Milner stating that the Refugee Aid Committees in Johannesburg continue to report the serious condition of the houses of the artisan class who have not yet returned. The smaller houses are said to be practically looted of all necessaries.

2. Lord Milner suggests that an appeal from you to the large wholesale firms, both in the City and outside, for gifts of the articles most urgently required would have a good result and be the means of alleviating much suffering. These articles are stated in Lord Milner's telegram to be—first, house and table linen and woollen blankets; secondly, mattress cases and bales of coir for filling them; thirdly, single and double iron bedsteads; fourthly, cutlery, comprising knives, forks, and spoons; fifthly, tinned or enamelled kitchen utensils; sixthly, coal stoves (sizes 5, 6, and 7); seventhly, clothing for adults and children; eighthly, simple furniture, including bentwood chairs and kitchen tables; and ninthly, medical comforts, including infants' and invalids' foods. It is expected that provision will have to be made for not less than 1,000 families, and the cost will be about £50,000 in money or in its equivalent in goods.

3. Any such goods which may be contributed will, if forwarded to Messrs. Hayter and Hayter, of 36, Upper Thames Street, E.C., the packing firm employed by the Crown Agents for the Colonies, be packed and despatched by them to Johannesburg.

4. I have no doubt that there are many persons, not being manufacturers of the goods specified, who will sympathise with the object of this appeal, and will be willing to make donations in furtherance of it. In this case the Crown Agents for the Colonies will be instructed to devote such contributions to the purchase of the articles specified above.

5. I venture to bring this matter to your notice in the hope that you will use your great influence to promote so worthy a cause, and I am sure that, if you feel able to comply with this request, your action will be deeply appreciated by our fellow-countrymen in South Africa.

I have the honour to be, my Lord Mayor, your lordship's most obedient servant,

J. CHAMBERLAIN.

The Right Hon. the Lord Mayor, London.

STATEMENT OF RECEIPTS AND PAYMENTS.

7TH APRIL TO 30TH MAY, 1902.

RECEIPTS.	£	s.	d.	PAYMENTS.	£	s.	d.
To Contributions	5,830	0	0	By Cash transmitted to Johannesburg ..	5,500	0	0
				„ Balance	330	0	0
	5,830	0	0		5,830	0	0

Large contributions of Furniture and other goods have also been despatched.

SUMMARY

OF

APPROXIMATE AMOUNT SUBSCRIBED.

PART VII.

	£	s.	d.
The Mansion House Transvaal Refugees' Fund ...	287,615	13	9
British Refugees' Fund (Victoria League)	6,083	0	0
The Dutch Women and Children's Fund (Victoria League)	1,942	9	2
South African Women and Children's Distress Fund	6,518	18	8
The Boer Women and Children's Clothing Fund ...	1,298	0	6
The Johannesburg Refugees' Fund	5,830	0	0
	309,288	2	1

PART VIII.

MISCELLANEOUS.

CONTENTS.

	PAGE
Soldiers' Christian Association,—Work in South Africa ...	157
South Africa General Mission	158
The Church Army Work in South Africa ...	159
Army Scripture Readers' and Soldiers' Friend Society	160
Royal Army Temperance Association ...	161
Transvaal Clergy Relief Fund	163
The Girls' Friendly Society (Two Orphans) ...	163
Soldiers' Graves (Victoria League)	164
Cape Town Cathedral Memorial Fund ...	165
Summary of Approximate Amount Subscribed	166

SOLDIERS' CHRISTIAN ASSOCIATION,—WORK IN SOUTH AFRICA.

Since the commencement of hostilities the Council have sent fifteen workers from home: twelve more were engaged by the Representative of the Association at Cape Town, and five others worked for some time in an auxiliary capacity, making altogether thirty-two Christian Association workers sent into the Field.

These Christian men have laboured among our troops during the Campaign from Cape Town to Pretoria, and from Kimberley to Durban, many of them sharing in the arduous marches and trying privations of the soldiers, ever seeking to help them by brotherly sympathy, but never forgetting that their supreme object was to win them for Christ. The many letters that have been and still are being received prove how greatly their services were appreciated, not only by the rank and file, but by very many of the officers, and by the Commander-in-Chief himself, who on leaving South Africa for England directed the following letter to be addressed to the Representative of the Association:—

"I am desired by Field-Marshal Lord Roberts to assure you of his Lordship's high appreciation of the good work done by your Association. Lord Roberts has watched your work with much interest, and feels sure that the success which has attended your efforts in the past will continue in the future. His Lordship wishes me to ask you to tender to the members of your staff and co-workers his best thanks for their excellent services, and in leaving South Africa to-day he wishes you all good-bye and God speed."

As an equipment for the workers, eight large and ten smaller tents, completely fitted and furnished, were sent out; as also four iron buildings, one of which is erected at Pretoria, one at Bloemfontein, one at Newcastle, and one at Woodstock Hospital Camp. Forty-four cases, weighing eleven tons, containing stationery, literature, tracts, and 2,500 Testaments, were also sent out and distributed among the troops.

STATEMENT OF RECEIPTS AND PAYMENTS.

October, 1899, to 31st December, 1901.

RECEIPTS.	£ s. d.	PAYMENTS.	£ s. d.
To Contributions	7,721 9 9	By Cost of Tents, Furniture, etc.	1,255 9 11
		,, Salaries, Passages, Medical, etc. …	4,119 10 3
		,, Grants	472 10 0
		,, General Expenses ..	580 9 6
		,, Balance	1,293 10 1
	7,721 9 9		7,721 9 9

Exeter Hall, Strand, W.C.

SOUTH AFRICA GENERAL MISSION.

ORIGINATED in the founding by Mrs. Osborne of a Soldiers' Home at Cape Town twenty years ago, and since extended to similar Homes at Wynberg and Pietermaritzburg, etc.

Being on the spot when the war broke out, it was natural that the men in charge of these Homes should be the first to volunteer to go to the front, and with the permission of the authorities they were allowed to follow the army, in the first instance to the relief of Kimberley. It is believed that the first Soldiers' Home established on a battlefield was that by this Mission in an old school house at Modder River within a day or two after the battle at that place. During the war the workers of the Mission have accompanied the troops to Paardeburg, Bloemfontein, Johannesburg, Pretoria, and other places, and have on all occasions not only afforded valuable aid in bringing in the wounded, but have in a hundred other ways been a friend to the soldier in camp and in hospital, in addition to the spiritual work in which they were engaged.

Copies of Letters received from

Field-Marshal VISCOUNT WOLSELEY, K.P.:—

"All who take an interest in the welfare of the army must cordially approve of the good work being done amongst our soldiers in South Africa by your Mission. From my heart I wish the South Africa Mission every success in its efforts to help men whom I know to be so deserving of it."

Field-Marshal EARL ROBERTS, K.G., V.C.:—

"I fully appreciate the good and noble work which has been carried on with such untiring zeal and devotion amongst our soldiers by the members of the South Africa General Mission."

And from General SIR GEORGE WHITE, V.C.:—

"I thoroughly appreciate and am glad to testify to the splendid work done by Mr. James Taylor and the late Mr. Tom Smith, whose sad death was a great loss to the garrison at Ladysmith. The zeal and devotion of the members of the South Africa General Mission cannot fail to have any but the best results on our soldiers in the field, and I have the highest admiration of their work."

STATEMENT OF RECEIPTS AND PAYMENTS.

NOVEMBER, 1899, TO 31ST DECEMBER, 1901.

RECEIPTS.	£ s. d.	PAYMENTS.	£ s. d.
To Contributions	5,587 10 9	By Relief ..	547 5 7
		,, Expenses	3,769 5 2
		,, Balance towards Soldiers' Homes	1,271 0 0
	5,587 10 9		5,587 10 9

17, Homefield Road, Wimbledon, S.W.

THE CHURCH ARMY WORK IN SOUTH AFRICA.

(Communicated.)

IMMEDIATELY after the commencement of the war a number of our evangelists volunteered for the front. In conjunction with the Chaplain-General to the Forces and the Archbishop of Capetown, and with the warm approval of the Archbishop of Canterbury, nine of the more experienced officers of the Society were selected and sent out to assist and supplement the work of the Army Chaplains at the front. Upon arrival at Capetown they were drafted by the senior Chaplain to their various posts. Some were attached to regiments, while others worked amongst the men who guarded the lines of communication. Another took charge of the Mission Church and Soldiers' Home at Brandfort.

Long marches and self-denial were cheerfully undertaken in the effort put forth to win the men for Christ.

Extracts from Letters of Army Chaplains:—

Pretoria, June 15th, 1900.

"I have been for a long time intending to send you a line of thanks for having sent out to our help Mr. A———, your Church Army Evangelist, and to tell you how extremely useful he has been to me. He is a good earnest fellow, and very ready to do anything he can. Very simple, and his simplicity and goodness and earnestness very soon secured the attention and affection of the men, who liked him very much. At Bloemfontein, where our work was very scattered, and beyond our powers, Mr. A——— was invaluable, and I was able confidently to leave the sick visiting in my Field Hospital to him. He did not spare himself, and conducted his meetings when and wherever he had the chance, and lost no opportunity of getting in amongst the men and quietly and tactfully helping and encouraging them in their duties and intervals of rest."

Bloemfontein, October 28th, 1900.

"For many weeks I have wished to write to you, but have not been able to find time. Of O———, as before, I cannot speak too highly. The longer I know him the more I like and admire and respect him. He 'takes' with both officers and men, and he is a most valuable worker.

"D——— does excellently. Everyone likes and respects him. His singularly happy manner wins favour and openings for him everywhere. He was most successful working here on the line, where he had to rough it very much. Now he is in charge of our Branch Soldiers' Home at Brandfort, and doing extremely well there. His intense piety and thoroughness are bound to impress everyone he spends any time with."

Cape Town, July 10, 1901.

"I must write and tell you that I have very warmly appreciated S———'s steady, thorough, and earnest work. I can most conscientiously say that he is one of the best men you have sent out. No one could have worked better."

Bloemfontein, October 26, 1901.

"The Church Army Evangelist has done a splendid work in South Africa. The greater part of his time has been spent in taking sole charge of the garrison of Brandfort and troops in its neighbourhood. All ranks of three successive regiments stationed at Brandfort—the 3rd East Lancs, 3rd Royal Lancaster, 2nd Dorset—have spoken most highly of his character, worth, and work. He is a very great loss to the army in South Africa, the more so as there is no one to take his place, which has to be filled to the loss of other garrisons."

"The four Church Army men are a very great help. One is posted at Vet River to work there and at Smaldeel; another at Brandfort, to work there and at Karree; another travels constantly to smaller outposts on the line, and is most successful. Often all the men who are off duty will attend the week-day service. Another stays here with me, and spends the week riding round outposts a few miles off, and works on Sunday here."

STATEMENT OF RECEIPTS AND PAYMENTS.

JANUARY, 1900, TO DECEMBER, 1901.

RECEIPTS.	£ s. d.	PAYMENTS.	£ s. d.
To Subscriptions	1,423 1 6	By General Expenses, including Outfits	1,565 12 5
„ Balance Deficit	142 10 11		
	1,565 12 5		1,565 12 5

130, Edgware Road, W.

ARMY SCRIPTURE READERS' AND SOLDIERS' FRIEND SOCIETY.

(Communicated.)

IMMEDIATELY upon the outbreak of the war in South Africa the Committee of the Army Scripture Readers' and Soldiers' Friend Society, recognising the importance of Readers accompanying the troops, issued a special appeal to the public for funds to cover the additional cost. The response was speedy and large; so that it was at once decided to send out six Readers. The War Office not only provided free passages (the Society being called upon to pay merely for their messing), but arranged also for the extra field-pay being issued by the Army Paymasters (chargeable to the Society), and that the Readers should be taken on the strength and provided with free rations. Very shortly afterwards, six more Readers were sent out to meet urgent demands: and later on, as some were invalided home, more were sent out, Field-Marshal Lord Roberts having cabled his willingness to receive them.

The Reports from our Readers at the Front, and of their work from others, have been most encouraging. Eternity alone will reveal the blessing and comfort they have been to our gallant soldiers, and the result of this campaign, as far as human knowledge goes, is that hundreds are already growing into thousands of those who have passed into the Kingdom of our Lord and Saviour Jesus Christ. As one worker writes:—"If the blessing continues at this 'rate,' truly it will be one of the greatest revivals ever known in the annals of the British Army."

A General Officer commanding a Brigade writes from Heidelberg, South Africa:—"The Scripture Reader to the 4th Brigade being about to leave for England, I cannot allow him to do so before expressing my high appreciation of his good services during this campaign. He has been Scripture Reader during the whole time of the war, and came out with the Brigade from Aldershot; he has worked hard and well in the cause of God, and has been a great help to the sick and wounded, as also to all ranks. He leaves with my best wishes and thanks of the Brigade and myself for the good work he has done among us."

STATEMENT OF RECEIPTS AND PAYMENTS.

OCTOBER, 1899, TO 31ST DECEMBER, 1901.

RECEIPTS.	£ s. d.	PAYMENTS.	£ s. d.
Contributions, etc.	2,024 8 9	By Scripture Readers' Salaries	899 7 0
		,, Outfits, etc.	421 12 7
		,, Books, etc.	190 11 8
		,, Insurance	4 14 6
		,, Office Expenses	75 6 4
		,, Balance	*432 16 8
	2,024 8 9		2,024 8 9

112, *St. Martin's Lane, Trafalgar Square, W.C.*

* A large sum is due to the War Office on account of Field Pay advanced to the Readers.

ROYAL ARMY TEMPERANCE ASSOCIATION.

A LARGE number of branches of the Association, including some thousands of members, having been sent to the War, the Council, with the approval of Lord Roberts, despatched their Secretary, Mr. Clare White, with full powers to take whatever steps might be practicable and necessary to promote the interests of the Association amongst the troops forming the Field Force.

An indulgence passage was kindly granted by the Secretary of State for War, and the Secretary left England on the 30th October, 1900.

On arrival in South Africa facilities were granted for his proceeding to visit the troops in all the principal garrisons and camps in Cape Colony, Orange River Colony, Transvaal, and Natal, the following message from Lord Roberts on his departure for England of " Tell them I hope they will feel they are not forgotten " being highly appreciated by the men during the Secretary's tour.

A very ready and generous response on the part of the residents of Cape Town, Port Elizabeth, Durban and Pietermaritzburg, and other places, was made to the appeal for financial support of the work of the Association, with the result that not only were the expenses of the tour defrayed, but a considerable balance was left for future operations. The Railway authorities contributed largely to this by placing a railway carriage at his disposal. The Secretary arrived in England on the 5th of April, 1901.

THE following are copies of letters addressed by Lord Wolseley and Lord Roberts to the Press on the evils of "treating":—

"THE time draws near when we may hope to welcome home many of the gallant soldiers who have so nobly fought our battles for us in South Africa.

"Their reception will, I know, be cordial, and it is this assured cordiality that impels me to ask those wishing to do them honour to refrain, while extending to them a hearty welcome, from offering them intoxicating liquor.

"Our soldiers are recruited from all classes of Her Majesty's subjects, and only differ from their brothers in civil life by the habits of discipline they have acquired in the Army. Like all of us, they are open to temptation.

"Many of them must soon resume the occupations and positions their employers have patriotically kept open for them; others will have to seek for new situations, and will require a helping hand in doing so.

"It is, therefore, most important that all should endeavour to preserve a good name for steadiness and sobriety before entering upon their civil work.

"I trust that our greetings to the brave soldiers returning from this War may be something better than simply an incitement to excessive drinking, and that all will remember that whoever encourages them in this, far from being their friend, is really their worst enemy.

"WOLSELEY, F.M.

"*War Office, October 3rd*, 1900."

"WILL you kindly allow me, through the medium of your paper, to make an appeal to my countrymen and women upon a subject I have very much at heart, and which has been occupying my thoughts for some time past?

"All classes in the United Kingdom have shown such a keen interest in the Army serving in South Africa, and have been so munificent in their efforts to supply every need of that Army, that I feel sure they must be eagerly looking forward to its return, and to giving our brave soldiers and sailors the hearty welcome they so well deserve when they get back to their native land.

"It is about the character of this welcome, and the effects it may have on the reputation of the troops whom I have been so proud to command, that I am anxious, and that I venture to express an opinion. My sincere hope is that the welcome may not take the form of 'treating' the men to stimulants in public-houses or in the streets, and thus lead them into excesses which must tend to degrade those whom the nation delights to honour, and to lower the "Soldier of the Queen" in the eyes of the world—that world which has watched with undisguised admiration the grand work they have performed for their Sovereign and their country.

"From the very kindness of their hearts, their innate politeness, and their gratitude for the welcome accorded them, it will be difficult for the men to refuse what is offered to them by their too generous friends.

"I therefore beg earnestly that the British public will refrain from tempting my gallant comrades, but will rather aid them to uphold the splendid reputation they have won for the Imperial Army.

"I am very proud that I am able to record, with the most absolute truth, that the conduct of this army from first to last has been exemplary. Not one single case of serious crime has been brought to my notice—indeed, nothing that deserves the name of crime. There has been no necessity for appeals or orders to the men to behave properly. I have trusted implicitly to their own soldierly feeling and good sense, and I have not trusted in vain. They bore themselves like heroes on the battlefield and like gentlemen on all other occasions.

"Most malicious falsehoods were spread abroad by the authorities in the Orange Free State and the Transvaal as to the brutality of Great Britain's soldiers, and as to the manner in which the women and children might be treated. We found on first entering towns and villages doors closed and shops shut up, while only English-born people were to be seen in the streets. But very shortly all this was changed. Doors were left open, shutters were taken down, and people of all nationalities moved freely about in the full assurance that they had nothing to fear from "the man in khaki," no matter how battered and war-stained his appearance. This testimony will, I feel sure, be very gratifying to the people of Great Britain, and of that Greater Britain whose sons have shared to the fullest extent in the suffering as well as the glory of the war, and who have helped so materially to bring it to a successful close.

"I know how keen my fellow subjects will be to show their appreciation of the upright and honourable bearing as well as the gallantry of our soldiers and sailors, and would entreat them, in return for all these grand men have done for them, to abstain from any action that might bring the smallest discredit upon those who have so worthily upheld the credit of their country.

"I am induced to make this appeal from having read, with great regret, that when our troops were leaving England, and passing through the streets of London, their injudicious friends pressed liquor upon them, and shoved bottles of spirits into their hands and pockets—a mode of "speeding the parting" friend which resulted in some very distressing and discreditable scenes. I fervently hope there may be no such scenes to mar the brightness of the welcome home.

"ROBERTS, F.M.

"Headquarters of the Army in South Africa.

"*Pretoria, September 30th, 1900.*"

STATEMENT OF RECEIPTS AND PAYMENTS.

October, 1899, to December, 1901.

RECEIPTS.	£ s. d.	PAYMENTS.	£ s. d.
To Collections in South Africa	971 19 1	By Secretary's Expenses to South Africa	147 12 7
,, Appeal for "anti-treating" Posters	154 2 9	,, Expenses of issue of Posters	322 17 1
		,, Balance	*655 12 2
	1,126 1 10		1,126 1 10

47, Victoria Street, S.W.

* £400 of this sum has been allocated to South Africa.

TRANSVAAL CLERGY RELIEF FUND.

Letter from the Bishop of Pretoria to the Lord Mayor of London.

Town Hall, Durban, Natal, *November 11th.*

My Lord Mayor.—An exile myself from Church and Diocese and home in Pretoria, through the needless and cruel action of the Government of the South African Republic, I venture to appeal to your Lordship on behalf of one class of my fellow sufferers, whose case has peculiar features of hardship—the Clergy serving under me—and to plead for them with your Lordship and the other managers of your Lordship's Mansion House Fund for some special consideration and relief. The Clergy of the English Church have been specially obnoxious to the Transvaal Government, not only as English, but as, in the opinion of that body, "members and ministers of the Queen's Church," and therefore sure to be peculiarly faithful to Her Majesty, and on that account peculiarly obnoxious to that Government. From the diminution of their congregations through the now long-continued flight of families and members of their congregations, the sources of their incomes have been drying up for some time past—*e.g.* in Pretoria the offertories, on which we mainly depend, have fallen from an average of £10 and £12 a week to £2 and £5. Most of them have been compelled to leave the South African Republic, and are here and at the Cape without income, employment, or means. Some of them have been allowed to remain—to what straits reduced I can only fear and conjecture from the occasional scraps of news which reach me. With small incomes at best, in a land where the Church is the Church of a few, and therefore having no such reserves to fall back upon in a day of trouble as their lay friends and associates; while a Church which has had to pass through two revolutions and three wars in the twenty-five years of its existence has no funds to support them in such an emergency as at present. Unless I can obtain for them special aid some of them must be reduced to the condition of paupers. With perhaps three exceptions none of them have given cause of offence by unwise political speeches or actions. I therefore venture to ask your Lordship and those associated with you for a grant of £1,000 for the peculiar and really hard cases, at least twenty-five of whom I know to be in very great distress. I offer myself as almoner, as knowing fully the cases of all and the leader to whom they turn in their distress, and I will keep and give you full account of any money entrusted to me and that in any form prescribed. I may add, for the information and gratification of your Lordship, your committee and subscribers, that the efforts and arrangements made by the relief committees both here and at Delagoa Bay are most gratifying and satisfactory. In my own enforced exile, I am visiting my fellow sufferers, and cannot speak too highly of the arrangements I have witnessed and the grateful appreciation of them by the recipients.

I have the honour to remain, my Lord Mayor, your Lordship's faithful servant,

H. B. PRETOR.

The Right Hon. the Lord Mayor.

STATEMENT OF RECEIPTS AND PAYMENTS.

October, 1899, to 31st December, 1901.

RECEIPTS.	£ s. d.	PAYMENTS.	£ s. d.
To Contributions	1,535 15 11	By Cash remitted to the Bishop for distribution at his discretion	1,535 15 11
	1,535 15 11		1,535 15 11

99, Gresham Street, E.C.

THE GIRLS' FRIENDLY SOCIETY.

TWO ORPHANS.

NOTE.—There have been instances innumerable of offers, by private families and Institutions, to adopt the orphans of both officers and men; but the following is given as a typical case:—

In February, 1900 the Diocesan Council of the Girls' Friendly Society, in the Diocese of Winchester, decided to raise a Fund to support the daughter of a soldier or sailor whose life had been lost in the War in South Africa, and invited the various Branches of the Society in the Diocese to co-operate in the matter.

An enthusiastic response was made, notably in the Winchester and Dorking Branches, although the members and associates of the Society had, in almost every Branch, already subscribed to the various War Funds.

It was proposed to keep and educate a girl of seven until she was able to work for her living; but it was found that this age limit was almost prohibitive in consequence of the children of Reservists especially, being generally younger. In the following February, however, the following case was brought to the notice of the Committee: Private Gatcum, of the Queen's (Royal West Surrey Regiment), the father, had died of enteric shortly after being invalided home. The mother, herself a member of the Girls' Friendly Society, who was very ill when he landed, lived only a few days after his return. There were two children, a girl of five and a boy of three the former of which the Committee decided to adopt and place with some motherly woman in a Cottage Home while inquiries were being made. A lady Associate of the Girls' Friendly Society, who had lost a brother in the War, hearing of the children, and of the provision being made for the girl, offered to adopt the boy in memory of her brother, and arranged that both children should be placed in a comfortable home in her own locality, under her supervision. Several Branches of the Society have also undertaken from time to time to provide suitable clothing.

The Fund subscribed amounted to £122 11s. of which £100 has been placed in the Post Office Savings Bank.

SOUTH AFRICAN GRAVES.

VICTORIA LEAGUE.

A Sub-Committee of the Victoria League was formed in May, 1901, under the Presidency of Lady Edward Cecil, with Miss Tillard as Honorary Secretary, having for its object the raising of Funds for the purpose of identifying and caring for the Graves of all who had served in the Field Force in South Africa.

The actual work was first undertaken by the Loyal Women's Guild of South Africa from a deep sense of gratitude towards the men who had fallen in the war, and it is in conjunction with, and as representatives in this country of the Guild, that the South African Graves Fund is working. A general record of the names, regimentally and alphabetically, has been begun of those who have lost their lives during the war.

The mementos, so frequently left by comrades after an engagement, have been of material assistance in identifying the graves. The work is one of considerable difficulty, owing to the vast extent and unsettled state of the country over which the graves are scattered; but through the members of the Guild being spread over so many parts of South Africa, and the cordial assistance rendered both by the Military Authorities, Chaplains, and others, greater progress has been made than could have been anticipated. Lord Roberts and Lord Milner have both expressed their cordial and hearty support and sympathy in the work which the Guild of Loyal Women have undertaken.

It is impossible at present, and until the country is more settled, to state the number of graves located and cared for.

In Cape Colony, Natal, Orange River Colony, Transvaal, and Rhodesia over 6,000 graves, at least, in the cemeteries have been named and cared for, as well as, wherever possible, numberless isolated graves on battlefields and on the veldts. The care of the graves, after the conclusion of the war, when the land in which they are situated is purchased by the Government, will, owing to the climate, require constant attention to preserve any memorials.

STATEMENT OF RECEIPTS AND PAYMENTS.

May, 1901, to 31st March, 1902.

RECEIPTS.	£	s.	d.	PAYMENTS.	£	s.	d.
To Contributions	2,701	5	0	By Guild of Loyal Women, Cape Town	2,300	0	0
				,, Expenses	199	0	5
				,, Balance	202	4	7
	2,701	5	0		2,701	5	0

13, Victoria Street, Westminster, S.W.

M. HARRIS SMITH, *Public Accountant.*

CAPE TOWN CATHEDRAL MEMORIAL FUND.

Letter to the Press.

Sir,—

We ask to be allowed to appeal to the British public through your columns on behalf of the proposal to erect in Capetown a building which shall serve both as a Memorial to those who have fallen in the South African War, and as a Thank-offering for those whose lives have been spared. In pursuance of the precedent of the erection of the English Church at Constantinople after the Crimean War, it has been decided that the present Memorial shall take the form of the Eastern portion of the new Cathedral about to be erected in Capetown. There is a widespread desire that there should be built on South African soil a dignified and stately monument, hallowed by religious sanctions and dedicated to the service of Almighty God, in memory of the soldiers and sailors of all ranks and of all parts of the Empire, who have given their lives for their Sovereign and their country. For this Memorial portion of the Cathedral, a sum of at least £30,000 is required. Opportunity will be given to preserve on the walls of the building the names, so far as may be possible, of all those who have fallen. It is only right to say that towards the adjacent portion of the new Cathedral a sum of about £20,000 has been subscribed, mainly from Colonial sources.

The Memorial has received the cordial approval of His Majesty the King, who has most graciously consented to become the Patron of the fund; and we are authorised to say that Her late Majesty Queen Victoria "took a great interest in the success of the proposed Memorial."

The names of an influential Committee were announced through the press on Monday, May 20th. A Committee of Ladies is also now being formed, of which H.R.H. Princess Christian has graciously accepted the office of President. Her honoured and beloved son was, it is known, very deeply interested in this proposal, and took an active part in its promotion when he was attacked by his fatal illness in Pretoria.

The new Cathedral will be regarded, we trust, as a pledge of the responsibilities both of the Church and of the Empire towards the future well-being of South Africa as well as a glorious temple for the service of God, and a noble Memorial to the courage and heroism of the fallen. In this spirit we most earnestly commend this our appeal, and trust that it may be most generously responded to by rich and poor alike in every part of the Empire.

Contributions will be most thankfully received by the Secretary, Capetown Cathedral Memorial Fund, Church House, Westminster, S.W.

(Signed) F. CANTUAR.
ROBERTS.
MILNER.
HARRY H. RAWSON.
W. W. CAPETOWN.

6th June, 1901.

The Committee, which has been formed in England for the purpose of raising the necessary funds for the Memorial portion of the Cathedral (about £35,000), while fully realising that the bulk of the money must be provided by the Mother Country, earnestly hope that the various Colonies and Dependencies may contribute, so as to make the Building a true Memorial of the whole Empire.

For this purpose plans are being arranged between the Committees in Capetown and England by which definite portions of the Cathedral can be allocated to the various parts of the Empire, in each of which suitable inscriptions and memorials can be placed to Sons of the Colony or Dependency which has contributed to its erection. Arrangements will in any event be made for preserving within the walls of the Cathedral the names of all who have given their lives in the war, no matter to what Denomination they may have belonged.

If this scheme can be carried out, the whole of the Memorial portion of the Cathedral must then, from the bond of a common sorrow and common mercies, form one more link in the Unity of the Empire, and will go down to future generations as a priceless inheritance.

On the 22nd August, 1901, His Royal Highness the Prince of Wales, on his memorable voyage to the Colonies, laid the Foundation Stone of the new Cathedral, and Her Majesty Queen Alexandra and the Prince and Princess of Wales have since become Patrons of the Fund.

STATEMENT OF RECEIPTS AND PAYMENTS

For Half-year ending 31st December, 1901 (*English Committee*).

RECEIPTS.	£	s.	d.	PAYMENTS.	£	s.	d.	£	s.	d.
To Contributions	5,442	11	1	By Rent of Office	8	6	8			
,, Interest	22	4	2	,, Electric Light	3	5	6			
				,, Office Furniture	10	11	1			
				,, Secretary's Salary	100	0	0	122	3	3
				,, Printing and Stationery	144	9	9			
				,, Postage and Telegrams	12	16	4	157	6	1
				,, Advertisements	23	6	0			
				,, Expenses of Meetings	7	19	7			
				,, Sundries	4	18	7	36	4	2
				,, Balance				5,149	1	9
	5,464	15	3					5,464	15	3

AVEBURY,
EVELYN HUBBARD, } Hon. Treasurers.

Church House, Westminster, London, S.W.
29th January, 1902.

Audited and found correct,
CHATTERIS, NICHOLS, & Co., *Chartered Accountants.*

NOTE.—The total amount received and promised up to April, 1902, was £10,805 17s. 6d., as well as £335 for Special Memorials such as Windows and Tablets.

SUMMARY

OF

APPROXIMATE AMOUNT SUBSCRIBED.

PART VIII.

	£	s.	d.
Soldiers' Christian Association Work in South Africa	7,721	9	9
South Africa General Mission	5,587	10	9
The Church Army Work in South Africa	1,423	1	6
Army Scripture Readers' and Soldiers' Friend Society	2,024	8	9
Royal Army Temperance Association	1,126	1	10
Transvaal Clergy Relief Fund	1,535	15	11
The Girls' Friendly Society (Two Orphans) ...	122	11	0
Soldiers' Graves (Victoria League)	2,701	5	0
Cape Town Cathedral Memorial Fund ...	11,140	17	6
	£33,383	2	0

SUMMARY

OF

APPROXIMATE AMOUNTS SUBSCRIBED.

	£	s.	d.
PART I.—Widows and Orphans—Wives and Families	2,930,538	19	8
PART II.—Sick and Wounded—Hospitals, &c.	750,000	0	0
PART III.—Disabled Officers and Men—Convalescent Homes, &c.	278,544	18	9
PART IV.—Extra Comforts, &c....	219,385	11	10
PART V.—Various Funds;—Equipment	381,050	2	10
PART VI.—India—British Dominions beyond the Seas	224,803	19	3
PART VII.—Refugees, &c.	309,288	2	1
PART VIII.—Miscellaneous	33,383	2	0
GRAND TOTAL	*5,126,994	16	5

---

* Exclusive of amounts expended on objects shown in the different Parts, of which no particulars can be given, but which with Lord Strathcona's Horse cannot b less than another £1,000,000.

THE LARGEST FUNDS.

AMOUNTS RECEIVED OVER £20,000.

		£	s.	d.
1.	The Soldiers' and Sailor's Families' Association	1,320,231	4	3
2.	The Patriotic Fund	466,353	2	1
3.	The Transvaal Refugees' Fund { The Mansion House £178,950 19 10; South Africa £108,664 13 11 }	287,615	13	9
4.	*The Daily Telegraph* (including £45,699 18s. from *The Scotsman*)	254,800	0	6
5.	The National Aid Society	178,950	0	0
6.	*The Daily Mail*, Kipling Poem Fund, &c.	175,000	0	0
7.	Lloyd's Patriotic Fund	127,058	5	3
8.	Glasgow—The Lord Provost's Fund	98,002	0	0
9.	The Officers' Families' Fund (Lady Lansdowne's)	82,636	16	5
10.	Manchester—The Lord Mayor's Fund	76,552	6	1
11.	The Canadian Patriotic Fund Association	69,554	0	0
12.	The Incorporated Soldiers' and Sailors' Help Society	62,208	0	0
13.	Georgina, Countess of Dudley's Fund	61,745	0	8
14.	*The Scotsman* (£45,699 18s. to *The Daily Telegraph*)	54,683	18	6
15.	*Birmingham Daily Mail* Fund	54,592	1	6
16.	Liverpool—The Lord Mayor's Fund	53,988	10	3
17.	Edinburgh—The Lord Provost's Fund	53,775	7	4
18.	Northumberland and Tyneside Reservists' Fund	52,840	4	5
19.	The Scottish National Red Cross Hospital (St. Andrew's Ambulance Association)	45,833	15	6
20.	Natal Volunteer War Fund	43,632	5	5
21.	American Hospital Ship *Maine*	41,597	13	2
22.	The Field Force Fund	38,535	3	10
23.	*The Liverpool Courier Express*	36,680	0	0
24.	Sheffield—The Lord Mayor's Fund	23,670	0	0
25.	Bristol—The Lord Mayor's Fund	23,081	0	0
26.	The Edinburgh and East of Scotland Hospital	21,325	5	4

The largest Lord Lieutenant's Fund was that in Northumberland (Earl Grey) £42,977 16s. 1d.

APPENDIX.

CONTENTS.

	PAGE
LETTER FROM LORD LANSDOWNE AND LORD WOLSELEY ...	171
LETTER FROM LORD ROBERTS ...	172
SUBSIDIARY FUNDS { THE ARTISTS' WAR FUND ...	173
THE NATIONAL BAZAAR	174
THE NAVAL AND MILITARY EXHIBITION, CRYSTAL PALACE	174
THE GREAT COUNTY SALE, EARL'S COURT	175
THE CHILDREN'S PENNY FUND	176
BRIGADE OF COLLECTING DOGS ...	177
THE CRICKETERS' NATIONAL WAR FUND ...	178
HIS MAJESTY THE KING'S (AS PRINCE OF WALES) COMMITTEE ...	179
THE WAR RELIEF FUNDS COMMITTEE	180
WAR RELIEF FUNDS ORGANISATION ...	188
JOINT SELECT COMMITTEE OF THE HOUSE OF LORDS AND COMMONS ...	189
THE FORCES IN SOUTH AFRICA	193
TABLE OF CASUALTIES ...	194
DIARY OF THE WAR ...	195
HOMES FOR OFFICERS' WIDOWS AND DAUGHTERS ...	198

LETTER FROM THE MARQUESS OF LANSDOWNE AND VISCOUNT WOLSELEY.

The following important letter was issued by the Marquess of Lansdowne, K.G., Secretary of State for War, and Field-Marshal Viscount Wolseley, K.P., Commander-in-Chief, to the Press:—

Sir,—The War Office has received many requests for advice from persons desirous of giving a practical shape to the interest which they take in the wives and families of soldiers serving in South Africa.

Such assistance should, in our opinion, be organised so far as possible on local lines. Local agencies can alone distribute the funds which may be available with a thorough knowledge of the merits of each case, and now that a territorial connection has been established between each Line Regiment, with its reservists and Militia battalions, and a particular portion of the United Kingdom, we may hope that on an occasion like the present every county will readily avail itself of the opportunity of recognising that connection and helping that portion of the Army which is peculiarly its own.

No doubt a certain number of men join a regiment though previously unconnected with its district; and, again, a certain number after serving with the colours of a regiment leave its district to marry and settle elsewhere. But the only organisation which will prevent cases of hardship from being either overlooked or dealt with twice over is that which we recommend.

Under such a system Committees would be formed representing the counties which include the regimental districts where Regulars have been mobilised or Militia embodied.

The Lord Mayor of London has appealed to the public for subscriptions to funds, one of which is for the benefit of "the wives and children separated at home here from their husbands and fathers by the exigencies of the war," and has intimated that contributions to this fund will be handed to that excellent Institution, The Soldiers' and Sailors' Families Association, of which her Majesty the Queen is Patron and the Princess of Wales President. We cordially support the Lord Mayor's action, and we trust that it will be imitated by local organisations in many parts of the Kingdom.

The Soldiers' and Sailors' Families Association has branches in every county, and indeed in every town of importance. It is prepared to place its machinery and all the valuable information which it possesses at the disposal of any Local Committees which may be formed. We trust that its co-operation may be generally resorted to. The central funds collected by the Lord Mayor and others could then be handed over to the Soldiers' and Sailors' Families Association for distribution to each district in proportion to the burden which each is called on to bear. And, lastly, the branches of the Soldiers' and Sailors' Families Association, in collaboration with the district and regimental staffs, would be in a position to deal effectively with every case of hardship incidental either to the mobilisation of the Regulars or the embodiment of the Militia in any one district. A proportion of the central funds would, of course, have to be set aside for Cavalry and Artillery and other corps which have no territorial connection.

We venture to express our hope that those who have the interests of the Army at heart will respond liberally to the Lord Mayor's appeal, either by direct subscription to his Fund or through the medium of local Committees, and we are in a position to state that it would be in accordance with his Lordship's views that, in all counties whose territorial regiments have been mobilised, local efforts should be specially directed to providing relief for the wives and children of soldiers belonging to the territorial regiment.

We take this opportunity of explaining that the Association is prepared to assist the wives and families of soldiers, whether they are or are not on the married establishment of the regiment.

Yours, &c.,

LANSDOWNE.

WOLSELEY, Field-Marshal.

War Office, Oct. 31, 1899.

LETTER FROM EARL ROBERTS.

Letter of Field-Marshal Earl Roberts, K.G., Commander-in-Chief, to the Press, on his return from South Africa :—

I feel confident that I can count on the courtesy of the Press, as the only medium available to me, to enable me to express to the people of London my heartfelt and sincere thanks for the generous reception accorded to me on my arrival in the Metropolis, which touched me more than I can describe.

I regard the welcome I received yesterday not only as one tendered to me personally, but also as a testimony from the people of this great city of their appreciation of the valour and endurance of my brave comrades who have fought and are still fighting the battles of the Empire in South Africa. I know that the echoes of yesterday's cheers will reach our soldiers far away, and be as gratifying to them as they were to me, for it will show them that they are not forgotten, and that an equally warm welcome awaits them on their return to England.

It is impossible for me to describe what I owe to them for their services. The only way I can ever hope to repay the debt is, as I have already said, by devoting myself to furthering their interests. It is with this object in view that I venture most strongly to support the recent appeal made by Her Royal Highness the Princess of Wales on behalf of the Soldiers' and Sailors' Families Association.

I can assure the public that nothing has cheered the hearts of our soldiers more through the long period they have been serving in South Africa than the knowledge that those who are nearest and dearest to them are being cared for in their absence by their fellow countrymen and women. The prolongation of the campaign in South Africa has taxed the resources of the fund so heavily that I am informed ere long it may be necessary to consider whether a debt should be incurred by the Committee in order to continue the help given to the families of our soldiers, or to cease altogether assisting them. The latter contingency is one so painful, indeed I may say so impossible, to contemplate, that I feel it my duty to make a personal appeal to the generosity of all classes of the community, and ask them to assist once more the fund, the needs of which have been placed before them so clearly by Her Royal Highness the Princess of Wales.

I feel confident that it is only necessary for the general public to be informed of the facts of the case for them to do what is necessary to bring relief to the homes of those whose breadwinners are daily risking their lives in the service of our Queen and for the honour of the Empire.

ROBERTS, F.M.

War Office, Jan. 4, 1901.

FOR KING AND COUNTRY.

THE ARTISTS' WAR FUND.

Guildhall Exhibition, 22nd January to 10th February, 1900.
Exhibition at Christie's, 17th to 24th February, 1900.
Sale at Christie's, 24th and 26th February, 1900.

NOTE.—This Fund affords a unique, and probably the only instance of all the "subsidiary" War Funds, where the "gross" were also the "nett" profits for allocation, *no deductions whatever* having been made for working expenses.

Patron:
HER LATE MAJESTY QUEEN VICTORIA.

President:
SIR EDWARD J. POYNTER, P.R.A.

A committee consisting of Sir L. Alma-Tadema (Chairman), Frank Dicksee, Esq., R.A. (Vice-Chairman), Val C. Prinsep, Esq., R.A. (Hon. Treasurer), and M. H. Spielmann, Esq. (Hon. Secretary), and other well-known artists representing all the great art societies of England except one, being formed, issued invitations to over 300 artists to contribute. A total number of 328 artists (including Her late Majesty Queen Victoria, H.I.M. the Empress Frederick, and H.R.H. the Princess Louise, Duchess of Argyll) contributed 346 works, several works being also presented by artists who had not been specially invited. About 60 artists and architects unable to contribute works, together with some unsolicited sympathisers, presented the Fund with £1,085. This amount includes the corporate donations of the following affiliated clubs and societies, viz., the Arts Club (London), the Berwick Club (Newcastle-on-Tyne), the Chelsea Arts Club (London), the Derby Sketching Club, the Dudley Gallery Art Society (London), the St. John's Wood Art Club (London), and the Winchester Art Society. The Committee of the Glasgow Artists' War Fund, though not affiliated, collected and handed over £2,800 to the Scottish Funds. The Lord Mayor and Corporation of London gave the use of the Guildhall Art Gallery free, as well as the labour connected therewith, the exhibition being opened by the Princess Louise, accompanied by the Duke of Argyll, and subsequently visited by His Majesty the King, who bid for works on the walls as also at the sale. Messrs. Christie, Manson, and Woods lent their galleries for the week's exhibition and two days' sale, and conducted the whole without any charge whatever. Messrs. Clowes and Son presented all catalogues to be sold for the benefit of the Fund at the Guildhall Gallery and at Messrs. Christie's. Messrs. Arthur Dicksee and Co. acted as agents free of charge, an arrangement voluntarily concurred in by their workmen, and Mr. Val C. Prinsep and Mr. Spielmann defrayed all the expenses of insurance and other outgoings.

STATEMENT.

	£ s. d.
Amount of Fund with interest available for allocation...	10,593 11 9
Less Berwick Club ... £405 14 4 ⎫*	
Arts Club (London) ... 34 0 0 ⎭	
Winchester Art Club ... 19 0 0 †	
Lady Butler's contribution ... 110 5 0 ‡	
	568 19 4
	10,024 12 5

Two-fifths of £10,024 12s. 5d. to No. 1, and one-fifth to Nos. 2, 3, and 4 of the following Funds:—

(1) The Patriotic Fund ... £4,009 17 0			=	4,009 17 0
(2) Lloyd's Patriotic Fund ... 2,004 18 6 +	£146 11 5 +	£19 0 0	=	2,170 9 11
(3) The Soldiers' and Sailors' Families Association... 2,004 18 6 +	146 11 5 +	110 5 0	=	2,261 14 11
(4) Lord Mayor's Discretionary Fund ... 2,004 18 6 +	146 11 5		=	2,151 9 11
				10,593 11 9

* One-third of this sum of £439 14s. 4d. (*i.e.*, £146 11s. 5d.) specially appropriated to Funds (2), (3), (4).
† Specially appropriated by donors to Lloyd's Patriotic Fund.
‡ Specially appropriated by donor to Devonport and Plymouth Branch (Soldiers' and Sailors' Families Association).

THE NATIONAL BAZAAR.

May 24th, 25th, 26th, 1900.

STATEMENT OF RECEIPTS AND PAYMENTS.

RECEIPTS.	£	s.	d.	PAYMENTS.	£	s.	d.	£	s.	d.
To Admissions	4,601	4	8	By Grants to—						
„ Stalls, Subscriptions, etc.	22,848	8	9	Soldiers' and Sailors' Help Society (London)				5,154	1	7
„ Interest	94	14	4	Soldiers' and Sailors' Families Association				5,000	0	0
				Soldiers' and Sailors' Help Society (Dublin)				2,600	0	0
				Officers' Families Fund (Lady Lansdowne)				2,500	0	0
				Daily Telegraph War Fund				1,000	0	0
				Daily Mail War Fund				1,000	0	0
				Lloyd's Patriotic Fund				1,000	0	0
				Dr. Barnardo's Homes				1,000	0	0
				Belfast War Fund				500	0	0
				The Layard Home, Matjesfontein				250	0	0
				Colonial War Funds *—						
				Cape Colony	2,400	0	0			
				Natal	700	0	0			
				Canada	300	0	0			
				New South Wales	264	0	0			
				New Zealand	177	16	0			
				Victoria	142	4	0			
				Queensland	112	18	0			
				South Australia	57	8	0			
				West Australia	47	12	0			
				Tasmania	30	10	0			
				Ceylon	12	10	0			
								4,244	18	0
				By Expenses				3,295	8	2
	£27,544	7	9					£27,544	7	9

* Allocated *pro rata* according to the number of Troops provided by each Colony.

NAVAL AND MILITARY EXHIBITION, Crystal Palace, 1901,
AND
GRAND NAVAL AND MILITARY CONCERT, 6th July, 1901.

ALLOCATION OF PROFITS FROM SALE OF EXHIBITION AND CONCERT TICKETS.

	Sale of Exhibition Tickets.			Expenses.			Nett.			Sale of Concert Tickets. Nett.			Total.		
	£	s.	d.	£	s.	d.	£	s.	d.	£	s.	d.	£	s.	d.
The Soldiers' and Sailors' Families Association	2,775	6	9	70	6	1	2,705	0	8	380	0	0	3,085	0	8
Officers' Families Fund (Lady Lansdowne)	468	10	0	—			468	10	0	100	0	0	568	10	0
Convalescent Officers' Fund (Lady Dudley)	287	17	0	—			287	17	0	180	0	0	467	17	0
Royal School for Officers' Daughters (Army)	134	18	6	—			134	18	6	50	0	0	184	18	6
Soldiers' and Sailors' Help Society	40	19	0	—			40	19	0	100	0	0	140	19	0
The Gordon Boys' Home	11	11	0	—			11	11	0	50	0	0	61	11	0
The Central British Red Cross Society	7	7	0	—			7	7	0	—			7	7	0
The Soldiers' Daughters' Home (Hampstead)	5	5	0	—			5	5	0	—			5	5	0
Royal School for Naval and Marine Officers' Daughters	4	4	0	—			4	4	0	20	0	0	24	4	0
The Royal Naval Fund	3	3	0	—			3	3	0	—			3	3	0
	3,739	1	3	70	6	1	3,668	15	2	*880	0	0	4,548	15	2

£4,548 15s. 2d.

* Concert organised by Colonel Barrington Foote, Commandant School of Music, Kneller Hall.

THE GREAT COUNTY SALE (Earl's Court).

JUNE 27TH, 28TH, 29TH, 1901.

The following were the nett takings at each County Stall of The Soldiers' and Sailors' Families Association, including the sum of £61 1s. 2d. remitted to each County from the Nett Profits of the General Fund.

	£	s.	d.		£	s.	d.
Berkshire (H.R.H. The Princess Christian)	831	1	2	Brought Forward	£8,477	4	10
Cornwall (The Countess of St. Germans and Lady Trelawney)	734	6	4	Sussex (Lady Fletcher)	301	0	6
Surrey (The Viscountess Knutsford)	620	4	8	Southampton, Hants (Mrs. Charles Orman) ..	289	1	2
Essex (Lady Rayleigh and Lady Alice Archer Houblon) ..	561	13	11	Flintshire (Lady Mostyn)	281	16	1
Oxfordshire (The Duchess of Marlborough)	556	18	6	Wiltshire (Lady Methuen)	259	19	8
Warwickshire (The Marchioness of Hertford)	551	13	7	Worcestershire (The Countess of Coventry) ..	251	5	8
Leicestershire (The Countess of Lanesborough)	540	0	8	Rutland (Mrs. Henry Fludyer)	242	15	2
Kent (The Viscountess Falmouth)	508	8	2	Derbyshire (The Duchess of Devonshire) ..	241	11	2
London (H.R.H. Princess Louise, Duchess of Argyll):—				Nottinghamshire (The Viscountess Galway) ..	241	1	2
North District 192 4 0				Merionethshire (Mrs. Wynne of Peniarth) ..	236	5	7
South ,, ... 103 5 0				Monmouthshire (Lady Raglan)	234	12	9
West ,, ... 90 6 0				Carnarvonshire (Mrs. Duff Assheton Smith) ..	219	5	2
East ,, ... 87 16 2				Devonshire (Lady Clinton)	218	1	2
	473	11	2	Cambridgeshire (Mrs. Adeane)	188	0	11
Gloucestershire (The Duchess of Beaufort)	449	7	2	Cumberland (The Countess of Lonsdale) ..	186	2	5
Glamorganshire (Lady Aberdare and Miss Talbot)	367	18	9	Midlothian (Lady Gibson Craig)	168	7	8
Dorsetshire (Lady Digby)	354	6	2	Huntingdonshire (Lady Caroline Duncombe)	166	10	6
Lincolnshire (Victoria Countess of Yarborough)	342	2	0	Haddingtonshire (Mrs. Fletcher of Saltoun)	161	1	2
Norfolk (The Countess of Albemarle)	340	8	9	Yorkshire, E. Riding (The Countess of Londesborough)	147	11	2
Buckinghamshire (Lady Rothschild)	314	16	6	Middlesex (Lady Hillingdon)	135	8	8
Denbighshire (Mrs. Cornwallis West)	313	17	8	Irish Lace Stall (Lady Arthur Hill), to Ulster Branch	134	8	10
Suffolk (Lady Florence Barnardiston)	308	16	6	Dumbartonshire (Lady Colquhoun and Mrs. Morant)	91	1	9
Yorkshire, N. Riding (The Marchioness of Zetland)	307	13	2	Westmoreland (The Countess of Bective)	87	8	8
Carried Forward	£8,477	4	10	Total ..	£12,960	1	10

Aberdeenshire (The Countess of Aberdeen), in hand, £227 1s. 5d.
Australia (Lady Wittenoom) £586 14s. 2d. yet to be divided—Georgina Countess of Dudley's stall, £489 5s. 11d.

The following Stalls were also held, the takings being paid into the General Fund towards the expenses of the Sale, viz :—

Furniture (Mrs. Harold Hartley), £314 17s. 8d.; Hampshire (The Duchess of Wellington), £305 4s. 4d.; *The Gentlewoman* (Mrs. J. S. Wood and Mrs. Warden), £245 1s.; Lady Faudel Phillips, £220 1s. 6d.; Pets, Ladies' Kennel Association (H.R.H. Princess Victoria of Schleswig-Holstein), £180 17s. 7d.; Dogs (Lady Norbury and Mrs. Edgar Farman), £173 8s.; City of London (The Lady Mayoress), £139 10s. 6d.; South Africa (H.S.H. Princess Lowenstein Werthiem), £96 13s. 8d.; Linen (Lady Furley and Mrs. Pratt), £61 17s. 10d.; Sweets (Maynard and Co.), £59 5s.; Children's Salon (Mrs. Jack Johnson), £50 18s. 9d.; Hat and Bonnet (Mrs. Aubrey Wallis and Mrs. Rawley Turpin), £45; Cigars (Mrs. Perryman), £40 18s. 9d.; India (Lady Blood and Mrs. James Heath), £40 7s. 6d.; Leather (Miss Hammond), £31 6s. 4d.; San Jose Fruit Stall, £2 4s. 7d.; Newball and Mason, 10s. 8d. Total, £2,008 3s. 8d.

STATEMENT OF RECEIPTS AND PAYMENTS.
(GENERAL FUND.)

RECEIPTS.	£	s.	d.	PAYMENTS.	£	s.	d.
To Gate Money and Miscellaneous	3,499	4	10	By Expenses	2,636	18	10
,, Taking at Stalls other than County Stalls ..	2,008	3	8	,, Endowment of Cot for Children of Soldiers and Sailors, Cheyne Walk, Hospital	295	19	9
				,, Balance paid to Counties, at rate of £61 1s. 2d. each County	2,574	9	11
	£5,507	8	6		£5,507	8	6

225, Gresham House, Old Broad Street, E.C.

BLANDFORD AND LAURENCE, *Incorporated Accountants.*

THE CHILDREN'S PENNY FUND.

Schomberg-house, Pall-mall, S.W., May 5, 1902.

In handing over the Children's Penny Fund, which has been raised in my name from British children, I have thought it advisable to do so in such a manner as to ensure that the sixteen beds shall be endowed in perpetuity, and have, therefore, had the attached agreement prepared for the acceptance of the Executive Committee of the Society.

I also attach a statement of the receipts and expenditure of the Fund, which will be audited and handed to the Committee, together with the donation book, cash book, and ledger, when the transfer of the securities is completed.

A tabulated list of donations by Counties is attached.

By the wish of the Lord Provost of Glasgow, the deposit interest, amounting to £24 8s. 11d., on the Glasgow donation, should be added to the amount shown to their credit, thereby making the total Glasgow donation £1,474 8s. 11d.

The Jubilee Children's Silver Donation balance-sheet is also presented herewith, and, as will be seen, the sum of £46 17s. 4d. has been reserved by their Committee, with my consent, to be expended by them on the purchase of books for the Children's Home.

I have also now the pleasure of handing over to the Finance Committee a cheque for £2,982 8s. 1d. for the purpose of building and furnishing the Home. Of this sum, £113—collected by Her Royal Highness the Princess Henry of Battenberg from the children of the Isle of Wight—is to be devoted to furnishing, and a sum of £50—from the children of Colchester—to furnishing "a ward," and I have promised that a notification of this fact is to be placed in the room.

The securities—for the purchase of which I have now the pleasure of handing you the broker's contract note—are £3,000 London, Brighton, and South Coast Railway second preference stock, and £5,000 West Australian 3½ per cent. stock, which I have bought at a price that will yield annually £325—being rather over the sum of £20 a bed.

In fulfilment of my promise that collectors of £600 should be entitled to name beds, the following is a list in accordance with the wishes of the donors:—Beds—No. 1. Children of Sunderland, Queen Victoria Jubilee bed. 2. Children of Newcastle and Northumberland, Queen Victoria Jubilee bed. 3. Children of Leeds, Yorkshire, and Lancashire, Queen Victoria Jubilee bed. 4. Queen Victoria Jubilee children's bed. 5. From the children of Glasgow in memory of his Highness Prince Christian Victor of Schleswig-Holstein. 6. From the children of Glasgow, in memory of many brave sons of St. Mungo who fell in the South African War. The remaining ten beds to be named as follows:—all counties which have contributed £100 and upwards will thus have their names always associated with a bed. All counties having given less than £100 are included under the name of the British children's bed:—7. Children of Scotland bed. 8. Children of Middlesex bed. 9. Children of Surrey bed. 10. Children of Berks, Bucks, and Oxon bed. 11. Children of the Isle of Wight, Hants, and Sussex bed. 12. Children of Somerset, Devon, and Wales bed. 13. Children of Lancashire, Yorkshire, Cheshire, and Durham bed. 14. Children of Norfolk, Essex, and Kent bed. 15. Children of Warwickshire, Gloucestershire, Staffordshire, and Nottinghamshire bed. 16. The British children's bed.

HELENA, Princess Christian of Schleswig-Holstein,
President Incorporated Soldiers' and Sailors' Help Society.

CHILDREN'S PENNY FUND.
Receipts and Expenditure from January 16, 1900, to the Close of the Fund in May, 1902.

RECEIPTS.

	£ s. d.	£ s. d.
To Donations, general	8,598 18 9½	
„ Donations from the Lord Provost of Glasgow	1,450 0 0	
„ Donations from Jubilee Children's Silver Donation Fund, per Mrs. Priestly	2,400 0 0	
		12,448 18 9½
„ Deposit interest on the Lord Provost of Glasgow's collection	24 8 11	
„ Deposit interest on general and Jubilee Children's collection	364 3 7	
		388 12 6
		12,837 11 3½

PAYMENTS.

	£ s. d.	£ s. d.
By General expenses—		
Office furniture and appliances	27 11 1	
Less amount on resale	15 17 6	
		11 13 7
„ Printing, Stationery, etc.	140 5 4	
Less surplus resold	0 17 0	
		139 8 4
„ Postages		92 11 3
„ Typewriting and clerical assistance		61 1 6½
„ Bank charges on Scotch and Irish cheques		2 1 6
„ Payment to the Soldiers' and Sailors' Help Society for the building and furnishing of the home at Bisley		2,982 8 1
„ Sum invested for the endowment in perpetuity of the 16 beds, viz.:—£5,000 Western Australian Three-and-a-Half per cent. Inscribed Stock at cost of	5,059 8 6	
„ £3,000 London, Brighton, and South Coast R. 2nd Consolidated Preferred Five per Cent. stock at cost of	4,488 18 6	
		9,548 7 0
		12,837 11 3½

JUBILEE CHILDREN'S SILVER DONATIONS.
Receipts and Expenditure from September 24, 1900, to April 16, 1902.

RECEIPTS.

	£ s. d.	£ s. d.
Donations, entertainments, etc.		2,681 12 1
Bank interest		4 0 9

SUMMARY.

	£ s. d.
England and Wales	2,288 17 5
Scotland	273 17 6
Small Sums not tabulated	113 13 11
Bankers' interest	4 0 9
	2,685 12 10

PAYMENTS.

	£ s. d.
May 25, 1901—	
To H.R.H. Princess Christian's (General) Children's Penny Fund	1,200 0 0
„ H.R.H. Princess Christian's (Sunderland) Children's Penny Fund	600 0 0
April 16, 1902—	
„ Ditto (Northumberland and Newcastle)	600 0 0
„ Printing, Stationery, &c.	86 18 5
„ Stamps, Parcels, Post, Advertising, and Travelling Expenses	72 12 1
„ Clerical assistance	50 0 0
„ Expenses of Entertainments	29 5 0
„ Amount to be retained to be handed over for purchases and buying books for the use of Sailors and Soldiers in the Bisley Homes	46 17 4
	2,685 12 10

BRIGADE OF COLLECTING DOGS.

The Committee of the Ladies' Kennel Association, of which Her Majesty Queen Alexandra is Patron, being anxious that as many Dogs as possible should aid the Funds in connection with the War, issued the following Appeal:—

A PROCLAMATION
BY THE
LADIES OF ENGLAND TO ALL PATRIOTIC BRITISH DOGS.

WHEREAS it is considered right and proper, at this present juncture of national strain and stress, that Dogs—the Friends of Man and the Favourites of the Soldier—should be given the opportunity of showing, by some signal example of special service, their long-proven loyalty, we, the Ladies of England, call upon all patriotic British Dogs to come forward at once and volunteer for the Brigade that is now collecting money for the relief of the Widows and the Orphans of British Soldiers killed in the War in South Africa. In accepting Recruits, our Staff will make no difference whatsoever between Dogs with Stud-book pedigrees and those without; Dogs belonging to Men or to Women, whether Members of the L.K.A. or not; great Dogs or little ones; British subjects or friendly Foreigners; Dogs who live at home in the British Isles, or those who serve British-born masters in our Empires beyond the seas which England calls her Colonies. Come forward, then, all loyal Dogs, and enrol.

VIVAT REGINA-IMPERATRIX!

Pursuant to the above, and in order to simplify and regulate the services of our Bow-wow Volunteers, we have resolved to raise one Troop of Cavalry, one Battery of Artillery, and one Battalion of eight Companies of Infantry, with due proportions of Commissioned and Non-commissioned Officers to each, and a suitable Headquarters Staff for the Brigade.

Constitution of the Ladies' Brigade of Collecting Dogs.

Cavalry—One Troop of fifty men and two Non-commissioned Officers. One Colonel, one Major, one Captain, one Lieutenant, one Second Lieutenant.
  The Cavalry will be recruited from English Greyhounds, Scottish Deerhounds, Irish Wolfhounds, and Borzois (Russian auxiliaries).

Artillery—(Heavy guns) One Battery. Fifty men, with one Colonel, one Major, two Captains, one Subaltern, and two Non-commissioned Officers.
  The Artillery will be recruited from the Mastiffs, Bloodhounds, Mount St. Bernards, Great Danes, and Newfoundlands.

Infantry—One Battalion of Eight Companies. Each Company of (not more than) 100 men and five Non-commissioned Officers. Battalion Officers: one Colonel, one Lieut.-Colonel, eight Majors, Eight Captains, sixteen Lieutenants, sixteen Second Lieutenants, one Quarter-master, one Paymaster, one Warrant Officer.
  The Infantry will be recruited from all Dogs other than of the breeds selected for the Cavalry and Artillery, and as the enlistment returns come in the composition of the different Companies will be duly gazetted.

No. 1 Company. "The British Bulldogs," or "English Company."
  Recruited from Bulldogs, Bull Terriers, Toy Bulldogs, White English Terriers.

Infantry—*cont.*

No. 2 Company. "The Die Hards," or "Scotch Company."
  Recruited from Scotch Terriers, Aberdeens, Dandie Dinmonts, and Skyes.

No. 3 Company. "The Dare Devils," or "Irish Company."
  Recruited from Irish Terriers, Welsh Terriers, Airedales, and Bedlingtons.

No. 4 Company. "The Loyal Dutchmen."
  Recruited from Pugs, Schipperkes, Toy Griffons.

No. 5 Company. "The Ladies' Own."
  Recruited from all varieties of Toy Spaniels, Pomeranians, and Toy Terriers.

No. 6 Company. "The Sportsmen's Own."
  Recruited from Retrievers, Sporting Spaniels, Setters and Pointers, and Hounds of all varieties not enlisted in the Cavalry and Artillery, and Fox Terriers.

No. 7 Company. "The British Watch Dogs."
  Recruited from Old English Sheepdogs, Scotch Collies, and Houseguard Dogs of any breed or of none.

No. 8 Company. "The Friendly Foreigners."
  Recruited from "Foreign Dogs," Chows, Dalmatians, and Mongrelians of all sorts and sizes.

ALLOCATION OF COLLECTIONS.

	£	s.	d.	
The Daily Telegraph	2,400	0	0	
The Daily Mail	106	4	0	
Princess of Wales' Hospital Ship	250	0	0	= £3,047 19 1
Princess Christian's Homes	100	0	0	
The Great County Sale, "Pets" Stall	180	17	7	
Miscellaneous Funds	10	17	6	

13, Wyndham Place, Bryanston Square.

Mrs. A. Stennard-Robinson, *Hon. Secretary.*

THE CRICKETERS' NATIONAL WAR FUND
IN AID OF
THE SOLDIERS' AND SAILORS' FAMILIES ASSOCIATION. (Queen Alexandra's Appeal.)

Lord Howe, the president of the M.C.C., and Mr. F. E. Lacey, the secretary, have issued the following circular to cricketers in aid of Queen Alexandra's appeal for the Soldiers' and Sailors' Families Association:—

"The committee of the M.C.C. invite the co-operation of all cricket clubs and persons interested in cricket in the furtherance of the following scheme:—

"(1.) In view of the prolongation of the war in South Africa and the great suffering caused thereby to the wives and families of our soldiers and sailors, the committee think that cricket clubs and cricketers would like to join in contributing to their relief.

"(2.) The committee of the M.C.C. propose that a fund be instituted entitled 'The Cricketers' National War Fund.'

"(3.) The committee of the M.C.C. propose to inaugurate this fund by contributing the sum of 1,000 guineas.

"(4.) The Cricketers' National War Fund, in support of Queen Alexandra's appeal, shall be paid to 'The Soldiers' and Sailors' Families Association,' which shall be the sole administrators of the fund after it has passed into their possession.

"(5.) It is proposed that cards, such as are usually issued for 'benefit' matches, be printed by the M.C.C. and issued to all cricket clubs which apply for them, to be placed in their pavilions and other conspicuous places. Such applications to be addressed to the Secretary of M.C.C. and enclosed in envelopes marked 'Cricketers' National War Fund.'

"(6.) In addition to the placing of the above-mentioned cards, it is suggested that clubs might devote the whole or part of the profits of one match played during the coming season to the above-mentioned fund.

"(7.) Three trustees shall be appointed by the committee of the M.C.C., in whose names 'The Cricketers' National War Fund' shall be banked. When cheques are drawn on the said fund the signatures of one trustee and the secretary of M.C.C. shall appear on the cheques.

"(8.) The trustees shall be Earl Howe, Lord Alverstone, and the Right Hon. Sir Spencer Ponsonby-Fane.

"(9.) The Secretary of the M.C.C. is authorised to receive and give receipts for the contributions sent by the various cricket clubs and cricketers, and also to open an account at the London and South-Western Bank, N.W., in the names of the said trustees, to be called 'The Cricketers' National War Fund' account.

"(10.) The said accounts shall be audited by a firm of chartered accountants appointed by the committee of the M.C.C., and their statement shall be furnished to the Press as soon as possible after the accounts are closed.

"(11.) The committee of the M.C.C. venture to express a confident hope that this appeal in aid of such an object will be greeted with enthusiasm by all lovers of cricket."

The result of this Fund cannot be stated, as "the innings" had only just begun when going to Press; but from the following letter it will be seen that the score has already reached the handsome figure of One Thousand with the loss of no wickets.

THE QUEEN'S THANKS.

The following letter has been received by Mr. F. E. Lacey, the Secretary of the Marylebone Club:—

"23, Queen Anne's Gate, Westminster, S.W., April 19th.

"Dear Mr. Lacey,—I am commanded by the Queen, who has seen the announcement of the opening by the committee of the M.C.C. of 'The Cricketers' National War Fund' in aid of Her Majesty's appeal for the Soldiers' and Sailors' Families Association, to ask you to convey to Lord Howe and your committee the Queen's grateful appreciation not only of their handsome contribution of 1,000 guineas, but also of the inauguration of such a fund to support the work which Her Majesty has so much at heart.

"The Queen will watch with much interest the progress of the fund, which, initiated by such an influential body, Her Majesty feels sure will be supported with enthusiasm by all lovers of cricket throughout the kingdom, and probably by cricketers in the King's Dominions beyond the Seas.

"Yours very truly,

"JAMES GILDEA,

"Chairman, Soldiers' and Sailors' Families Association."

THE PRINCE OF WALES'S COMMITTEE.

His Majesty the King, as Prince of Wales, was the first to take the initiative towards drawing together into closer co-operation the Managers of the several Funds, by summoning a Meeting of Lords Lieutenants, Representatives of War Funds and others at Marlborough House on the 1st of March, 1900, when a Sub-Committee with His Royal Highness, the Duke of York, as Chairman, was appointed to consider the various points and suggestions brought forward, and to draw up a scheme for consideration at a further Meeting of the Committee.

The following is the Report of the Sub-Committee.

The Sub-Committee appointed by the Committee which met at Marlborough House on the 1st instant, His Royal Highness the Prince of Wales presiding, met on the 3rd, 6th, and 9th instants, at York House, to consider the matters referred to us, viz. :—

> "To consider the various points and suggestions brought forward, and to draw up a scheme for consideration at a further meeting of the Committee."

On the occasion of our first Meeting, attention was drawn to the appointment of a Committee by the Government to which is referred :—

> "To consider, with the assistance of the managers of the various charitable Funds available for the relief of persons who have served or are serving in the field, or of the families of such persons, how these funds may be distributed with the least waste and to the best advantage of those for whom they were intended."

We thought it advisable to ascertain whether the objects of the Committee, summoned by His Royal Highness, would be likely to lead to conflict in any way with the objects of the Committee appointed by the Government, and pending some assurance on this matter we decided to adjourn.

At our Meeting on the 6th instant, a letter was read addressed to our Chairman, His Royal Highness the Duke of York by the First Lord of the Treasury, Mr. Arthur Balfour, in which it is stated that no such difficulty need be apprehended, and this point having been settled we proceeded to consider the matters referred to us.

For the purpose of effecting the objects which were fully explained by His Royal Highness the Prince of Wales at the Conference, various suggestions have been made at our meetings, and after full consideration we have come to the conclusion that it is desirable to establish a central authority, sitting in London, through the medium of which funds subscribed throughout the country for much the same objects might be brought into touch with each other. We suggest that this Central Committee be composed

> (a) Of representatives chosen by the Committees of the larger general funds, one representative from each.
> (b) Of gentlemen nominated at a further meeting of the Conference.

The function of the Central Committee thus to be constituted should be wholly consultative and advisory. The Committee would not exercise control over any funds, neither would it interfere, except by way of suggestion and advice, with the administration of any of the funds.

The Committee would be in a position to invite those responsible for the various relief funds throughout Great Britain and Ireland to place themselves in communication with it, in order that all might work harmoniously together, and by interchange of information bring about closer co-operation and more uniform principles of action on the part of the different War Funds throughout the country—an object which is urgently desirable.

We are further of opinion that for the purpose of securing good management, the existence of a central consultative Council or Committee such as that now contemplated, is a permanent necessity, but the precise form the committee should ultimately assume as a permanent institution, and the duties with which it might be charged, are matters the consideration of which had better be deferred until the Committee recently appointed by the Government has made its report.

We would add in conclusion that in our opinion the most desirable objects which His Royal Highness the Prince of Wales has in view would be greatly advanced if His Royal Highness, who has taken the initiative as well as so great an interest in the movement, could graciously consent to be Chairman of the newly constituted Central Committee.

(Signed) GEORGE,
Chairman.

9th October, 1900.

At a second Meeting held at Marlborough House on the 23rd of March, 1900, at which His Royal Highness the Prince of Wales presided, it was decided that no further steps should be taken pending the issue of the Report of the War Relief Funds Committee.

At a third and final Meeting held at Marlborough House on the 28th of May, 1900, His Royal Highness the Prince of Wales again presiding, an extract from the Report of the War Relief Funds Committee, bearing on the action which the Government proposed to ask His Royal Highness' Committee to take, was read and discussed and a small Sub-Committee appointed to meet at the Mansion House to report as to the best means of carrying out the recommendations of the Report.

THE WAR RELIEF FUNDS COMMITTEE.

The Lord Justice R. Henn Collins (*Chairman*).
The Earl of Northbrook, G.C.S.I.
The Right Hon. William Lidderdale, P.C.
The Lord Mayor (Sir Alfred Newton, Bart.).

Mr. Robson, Q.C., M.P.
Mr. Whitmore, M.P.
The Rev. Cosmo Gordon Lang.
Colonel Twynam, C.B.

REPORT.*

Report of the Committee appointed to consider, with the assistance of the managers of the various charitable Funds available for the relief of persons who have served or are serving in the field, or of the families of such persons, how these Funds may be distributed with the least waste and to the best advantage of those for whom they were intended.

To the Right Honourable A. J. BALFOUR, M.P., First Lord of the Treasury.

Sir,

We have the honour to inform you that in pursuance of the Treasury Minute dated 17 February 1900, instructing us " to " consider, with the assistance of the managers of the various charitable Funds available for the relief of persons who have " served or are serving in the field or of the families of such persons, how these Funds may be distributed with the least " waste and to the best advantage of those for whom they were intended," we heard evidence from the managers of the principal Funds above-mentioned, and elicited opinions from them upon the matters referred to us, and we now have to report as follows:—

The Central Funds having their headquarters in London may be divided broadly into three classes:—

1. Those which deal with the wives and dependents of living soldiers and sailors;
2. Those which deal with the widows and dependents of soldiers and sailors dying in the service;
3. Those which deal with sick and wounded soldiers and sailors at the front or invalided home, or discharged disabled.

Of the first class, by far the most important is the Fund administered by the Soldiers and Sailors' Families Association, which was founded by Colonel Gildea in 1885. It deals with wives whether "on" or "off the strength," *i.e.* whether married with or without leave, and the children and dependents of the absent soldier. If the wife becomes a widow, its aid is withdrawn as soon as she comes under the care of those societies which deal with widows.

Of the second class, the most important is the Fund in the hands of the Royal Commissioners of the Patriotic Fund, known as the Transvaal War Fund. The system of the Commissioners is to make a payment of £5 to every widow, whether "on" or "off the strength," immediately on learning the fact of her husband's death, and, subject to some qualification which will be mentioned hereafter, to grant a pension on a fixed scale according to rank during widowhood, together with certain allowances for children. When we began our inquiry there were two other Funds, viz., the *Daily Telegraph* Fund and the Imperial War Fund, from which relief was given to widows and orphans; but relief to such persons is no longer granted from the latter Fund.

The third class embraces Lloyds' Patriotic Fund, the Society for the Aid of the Sick and Wounded in War, to which is affiliated the Central British Red Cross Committee, and so far as these deal with disabled soldiers and sailors, the Soldiers and Sailors' Help Society and the *Daily Mail* Fund.

There are in addition numerous local Funds which deal with one or more of these objects, but a portion of the Funds raised in local centres has been sent to the Lord Mayor of London, and forms part of the Mansion House Fund. This latter Fund

---

* Can be purchased (Price 2s. 4d.) either directly or through any Bookseller from Eyre and Spottiswoode, East Harding Street, Fleet Street, E.C.; John Menzies and Co., 12, Hanover Street, Edinburgh, and 90, West Nile Street, Glasgow; or Hodges, Figgis and Co., 104, Grafton Street, Dublin.

has been raised by public subscription in response to an appeal by the Lord Mayor of London on the outbreak of the present war, and amounted on Thursday, May 24th, to £913,159 of which £897,876 has been allocated as follows:—

 £394,304 to the Royal Commissioners of the Patriotic Fund,
  89,524 „ Red Cross Society,
  96,646 „ Lloyds' Patriotic Fund,
 172,861 „ Soldiers and Sailors' Families Association,
 144,541 „ Lord Mayor's Discretionary Fund, of which £15,974 has been disbursed, and the balance will be allocated where most needed.

The nature and objects of all the principal Funds above named, except those raised by newspapers, are fully set out in the Report of the Select Committee of the House of Commons of 1896, and it is therefore unnecessary to refer to them in greater detail here.

Leaving out of consideration the various local Funds not administered through one or other of the bodies above named, it will be seen that the area of possible overlapping among these central Funds is principally in the domain of those which deal with widows, *i.e.*, the Patriotic Fund, the *Daily Telegraph* Fund, and till recently the Imperial War Fund. Some slight room for overlapping exists between the Patriotic Fund and the Soldiers and Sailors' Families Association, as it may happen that the latter continue to assist a widow in ignorance of the fact that she is already receiving aid from the former.

There is also to a very slight extent a possibility of overlapping between the Soldiers and Sailors' Families Association and the Soldiers and Sailors' Help Society, where the latter are aiding the husband while the former are helping the wife. The two societies are, however, already acting as much as possible in concert, and this overlapping need not be considered.

Neither would it appear that overlapping to any considerable extent takes place between the societies which aid the sick and wounded and the disabled.

The *Daily Mail* Fund is designed not to clash with any other, and deals with special emergencies unprovided for elsewhere. It seems to fulfil a most useful purpose, and as far as possible acts through and utilises the information of existing agencies. It will be seen, therefore, that so far as the central Funds are concerned their overlapping with each other is practically limited to the Patriotic Fund, the *Daily Telegraph* Fund, and till lately the Imperial War Fund. In order to make this clear it will be necessary to explain shortly the mode in which these Funds are administered.

The administration of the Patriotic Fund and all the other Funds which are placed under the control of the Royal Commissioners was fully inquired into and reported upon by a Committee of that body, presided over by the late Lord Herschell, in 1895, and by the Select Committee in 1896, and certain recommendations were made in very similar terms by both Committees, of which the following are for present purposes the most important.

Lord Herschell's Committee reported as follows:—

"We suggest the creation of a Consultative Committee on which the several bodies administering Funds for similar "purposes should be represented. This Committee should meet at stated intervals; they should arrange for the communication "to the authorities administering the different Funds of all applications for relief and of the manner in which it was proposed "to deal with them, and an arrangement might perhaps be made that where a pension appeared the most suitable form "of relief, it should be given by one of these bodies, whilst relief in the form of gratuity should be afforded by another.

"We give these merely as illustrations of the advantages which would arise from the constitution of such a committee in "securing harmonious action and thus ensuring that all the Funds would be administered in the most efficient manner.

"The Royal Commission by which the Patriotic Fund was constituted contemplated the formation of local Committees "with the view of assisting the work of the Commissioners.

"If the operations of the Commission be extended in the manner suggested, obvious advantages would accrue from "inviting such co-operation."

The Select Committee of the House of Commons reported as follows:—

"Your Committee are of the opinion that steps might advantageously be taken by the Patriotic Commissioners to bring "themselves into closer touch with those who are responsible for the administration of the Greenwich, War Office and "outside Funds, and with this in view they suggest that each administration should be asked to nominate one of this body "to form part of a separate and independent Consultative Council, between which and the Patriotic Commission there "should be a cordial alliance, by which means valuable interchange of ideas and information might be secured. Your "Committee hope that by such a course not only would overlapping be avoided but a very beneficial extension of relief "be assured.

"That local committees should, as far as can be found practicable and convenient, be established in military centres, "garrison towns and naval ports, whose reports and recommendations shall be submitted to the Consultative Council.

"That these local committees shall be requested to advise particularly as to the best manner in which relief may be

"advantageously given, whether in the form of gratuity or continuing allowance, and to report instances in which, from
"sickness or other need, it is desirable to administer special relief in any other form, regard being had to the obligation,
"while making assistance adequate and its distribution sympathetic, to encourage industry and self-dependence on the part
"of the recipients. The Consultative Council may, with the information thus furnished, be then able to say from what
"particular Fund the aid can most properly be afforded."

We have not deemed it to be any part of our duty to enter afresh upon a similar inquiry except so far as was necessary in order to see generally what Funds in the hands of the Commissioners were available for the sufferers by the present war, and to what extent the mode of administration invited or lent itself to overlapping or waste. It would appear from the evidence tendered on behalf of the Commissioners of the Patriotic Fund, that with one or two possible exceptions all the Funds under their control at the outbreak of the present war have been specially allocated to other purposes, and that practically the only Fund in their hands which is available for the relief of the widows and orphans of soldiers and sailors who have lost their lives in the war in South Africa, is the sum above named which has been handed to them by the Lord Mayor. It was strongly pressed upon us by Mr. Kearley, M.P., that after exhausting special objects there would be an available surplus to a large amount in their hands. This is a matter of actuarial calculation, and the Commissioners are advised by an expert of the highest standing. But however this may be, we can see no reason why some portion, at all events, of the capital of the Soldiers' Effects Fund should not be available for the relief of the widows and orphans of soldiers who have lost their lives in the present war.

The Select Committee above referred to recorded their opinion that in fixing the rates of relief to widows and orphans the Commissioners should not necessarily restrict their grants to the sum which the deceased relative might have been able to contribute to those dependent on him, but should consider what sum would secure to applicants a moderate maintenance according to their class in life. A Committee of the Commissioners, presided over by Lord Davey, has recently drawn up the following statement of the principles by which they seek to guide their action :—

" The Royal Commissioners have set before them as a guide in the administration of the various Funds committed to
" their trust two great principles—
" 1st. That the Funds should be looked upon, not as of right belonging to all, but as a Charity to be carefully
" administered among all who are truly deserving assistance. This has necessitated a limit of income beyond which the
" widow of an officer or soldier has no claim on the Fund. And it has further required careful inquiries into the position
" of the applicant.
" 2nd. That the corpus as well as the interest of the Funds should be dealt with for the benefit of those for whom
" they were originally subscribed. Our object has been to secure to the widow during her widowhood a moderate
" maintenance, according to her class of life. In acting upon this rule, we have found it better policy not materially to
" improve the position which the widow was in before the loss of her husband, but rather to reserve the surplus for any
" benefits in placing out the children, and in providing increased allowances in time of sickness and old age."

The present practice of the Commissioners is to send at the earliest possible moment a sum of £5 to every widow, the death of whose husband has been reported to them by the War Office. A sum of £1 for each child is also sent as soon as its existence becomes known. These sums are sent direct to the widow through the Post Office, with a form of receipt attached which she is required to fill up with details, and return authenticated by the signature of responsible persons. A copy of this form is printed in the Appendix. There is no preliminary inquiry before the £5 is sent. A pension is afterwards granted practically as a matter of course, upon a scale graduated according to rank (a copy of which is also printed in the Appendix), beginning in the case of private soldiers and sailors at 5s. a week, with an allowance of 1s. 6d. a week for each child under 14. The pension is given during widowhood. If the widows marry again they are put on half the scale during re-marriage. If they again become widows the case is again considered, and they are replaced on the full scale if their position requires it. If it comes to the knowledge of the Commissioners that the widow is receiving a pension from another source they reduce the allowance to 2s. 6d. a week. No inquiries except those contained on the form are made, nor are the answers otherwise tested; nor, as far as we can learn, has any attempt been made by the Commissioners to carry out the recommendations of the two Committees as to joint action above set out, or as to securing the co-operation of local committees generally throughout the country.

It was explained to us that it would complicate the machinery of distribution too much if any individual inquiries on the spot were attempted, and that there were advantages in treating the allowances made by the Commissioners as though they were pensions payable with the regularity and certainty of a Government Department. The scale on which these allowances are made, though the Commissioners hope to be able to raise it, is perhaps as high as is reasonably consistent with the amount at the disposal of the Commissioners, and with the standard which they are applying in the case of the other specially allocated Funds which they administer, but it is obvious that in most cases it falls not only below the standard which the public would desire for the objects of their bounty, but also below that which the Commissioners have themselves laid down in the passage above cited, and therefore renders overlapping not only probable but desirable.

This is the view of the managers of the *Daily Telegraph* Fund and of the Imperial War Fund. It has been the object of both to supplement the grants which they assumed would be made by the Commissioners. The practice of the *Daily Telegraph* has been to make a present grant of £20 to the widow of every man killed or dying on service, and in addition to buy an annuity for her at the rate of 5s. 9d. a week for life. These annuities will not in many cases become payable before July of this year. Mr. Richardson, who is the manager of the *Daily Telegraph* Fund and gave evidence before us, has invented an elaborate and ingenious system of tabulating information as to all widows, relieved by this Fund. He avails himself, as far as is compatible with his system, of local assistance, but he explained that in the case of a Fund raised and administered by a newspaper, it was impossible to keep a staff adequate to conduct special inquiries from time to time into each case, and that a system had therefore been chosen which worked automatically when set in motion. Each recipient has to answer questions on a printed form, and the answers have to be attested by some responsible person. The money is not sent until this paper has been returned. If the return is satisfactory, £3 is sent to the widow, and she is required to open an account at the Post Office Savings Bank. This involves a fresh inquiry by the Post Office for the purpose of identification if she has not already got an account. A sum of £17 is then paid into her account by the *Daily Telegraph*, who remove her name from their books if the account is not kept alive. It is thought that this acts to some extent as a check on squandering. Occasionally the money is paid into the joint account of the widow and a trustee, usually some member of a Soldiers and Sailors' Families Association Committee, but as a general rule it is paid direct into the banking account in the widow's own name. It is claimed that the Fund is by this means administered at very slight cost.

The Imperial War Fund consisted of a sum of about £9,200 contributed from various sources, and embracing a sum of £2,600 from the Mansion House, £500 from the Lord Mayor of Liverpool, £1,250 from the *Daily Telegraph*, and £400 from the *Daily Mail*. Its founder and manager was Lieut.-Colonel Tully. His practice was to send a sum of £10 to the widow of every soldier or sailor killed or dying on service. He worked as far as possible in conjunction with the Soldiers' and Sailors' Families Association, and sought information from them, and from the *Daily Telegraph*, as well as from officers commanding at depôts. He has devised a simple method of exchanging information as to applicants and recipients by means of cards. Both he and Mr. Richardson are strongly of opinion that the aggregate of the sums paid by the Commissioners and themselves is not too much. The initial payments are designed to cover immediate expenses, as well as to supply a means of subsistence, before the recipient becomes entitled to permanent relief.

It will be seen from the above summary that, in the case of the central Funds, overlapping is, or was, in the main deliberate, and intended to give effect to the supposed desire of the public to deal generously with the widows and orphans of those who have lost their lives in the service of the country. Mr. Richardson, of the *Daily Telegraph*, was of opinion that the chief danger of unintentional overlapping was in the case of local Funds raised and administered on the spot. We obtained Returns from which it appears that such Funds have been raised in almost every county, and in a great many of the towns in the United Kingdom, and that in many cases the amount so raised is very considerable. A summary of these Returns has been prepared and is printed in the Appendix.

We have heard evidence from Liverpool, Manchester, Portsmouth, Edinburgh, Glasgow, and Birmingham, in all of which substantial Funds have been raised.

In Liverpool a portion of the local Fund has been allocated to the central Funds above mentioned; but by far the larger portion, about £37,000, is being held over pending further information and guidance as to the best mode of distributing it.

Manchester and Salford have raised a large Fund—about £60,000—which is being locally administered to cases in the district. It is confined to wives, widows, children, and dependents of those who have gone to the front. No distinction is made between wives and widows. Relief is given in accordance with a scale whereby the weekly income of the family of a soldier, reservist, embodied militiaman, or volunteer, from all sources, excepting the proceeds of the wife's own labour, and any grant from a club to which the husband may have contributed, is made up to 15s. a week where there are no children, rising to 25s. a week where there are five children. It deals alike with those married with leave and without leave, making up to the latter out of the Fund the separation allowance which is granted by the War Office to the former. The sum of 15s. a week is based on a rough estimate of the average sum likely to have been contributed by the breadwinner when present to the maintenance of the family.

There is a centre in each of the principal divisions of Manchester and Salford, and the work of distribution is carried out through the agency of the District Provident Society, which is described as a very old established organisation in Manchester. It will be seen, therefore, that this Fund covers the same field as the Patriotic Fund and the Soldiers and Sailors' Families Association together, and we were told by the Lord Mayor of Manchester that there had been a practical difficulty, through local circumstances, in co-operating with the Soldiers and Sailors' Families Association, but his belief was that the vigilance of the officers of the District Provident Society was such as to neutralise the danger of overlapping.

In Edinburgh, Glasgow, Birmingham, and Portsmouth, temporary relief to wives, dependants, and widows is successfully administered through local committees generally acting in concert with the Soldiers and Sailors' Families Association, and in each place much the same standard is adopted, viz.: to make up the income to that which the family might be expected to receive from the bread-winner if he were present. Edinburgh has made a considerable contribution to the

Patriotic Fund on conditions which will be found set out in Lord Nelson's evidence. Glasgow has, so far, made no arrangements for permanent relief, and has not yet decided how it will dispose of the expected surplus of its Fund after the war.

The evidence as to the practice in all these places is important as showing the standard adopted by thoroughly practical men as that to which relief ought to be adjusted.

We are of opinion that the evidence justifies the conclusion that, with the exception of the lump payments above mentioned, temporary relief is, on the whole, being now administered without much injurious overlapping or waste.

It is now necessary to state somewhat more specifically the objects aimed at and the system adopted by the Soldiers and Sailors' Families Association. It should be premised, however, that underlying all schemes and standards of relief by voluntary subscriptions is the fact that certain separation allowances, allotments, grants, and pensions, or gratuities, are made by Government to the wives and widows of soldiers and sailors. These are made according to scale, either fixed or easily ascertainable, and can therefore be readily allowed for, as is shown in the scale adopted by Manchester, in administering further assistance. The evidence as to these Government allowances and pensions and as to the allotments from their pay by men at the front will be found in the Minutes of Evidence, and it is not necessary to deal with it further here. The separation allowance is paid monthly. There are also certain Funds for the benefit of soldiers and sailors, such as certain regimental Funds and the Royal Cambridge Fund, which supplements the pensions of necessitous soldiers in their declining years, and the Wolseley Fund, which is formed out of a portion of the profits of the Royal Military Tournament, and is applied at the discretion of the Commander-in-Chief to the relief of soldiers and soldiers' widows in destitute circumstances, which though not war Funds, cannot be ignored by those who administer relief. There are also various county Funds out of which equipments are provided for the Yeomanry and Volunteers going to the front, and in some cases their lives insured. These Funds are also in some cases applicable to other purposes connected with the war.

The Soldiers and Sailors' Families Association is the only voluntary organisation which claims to have a complete system of local committees extending throughout the Kingdom. In addition to the sum received from the Lord Mayor it raises money by local subscriptions throughout the country. It has raised a large sum specially allocated to the relief of officers' widows, and has also provided a nursing branch for the visitation of the wives and families of soldiers and sailors in their own homes and quarters at large stations at home and abroad. But, as already stated, its principal field of effort is among the wives and families of living soldiers and sailors during separation. The principles on which relief should be administered in cases arising out of the present war were laid down in a circular addressed by Colonel Gildea from the central office, and distributed among all the various local committees shortly after the war broke out. This will be found set out in the Appendix. The cardinal principle of the society has always been to encourage self help. Its aim is that its allowances made during the war should be on such a scale "that the total amount received by the wife from all sources "should not exceed the pay or wages of the bread-winner previous to separation," and such that the wife might be relieved from the sense of "struggle." It attaches the greatest importance to personal supervision by competent persons on the spot through whom the relief is administered weekly.

The evidence before us and the Returns from local centres show in many instances a want of confidence in the management of the Patriotic Fund which has led to a withholding of contributions. This may give rise to anomalies. For instance, of two adjoining centres one may remit the Fund raised locally in whole or in part to the Patriotic Commissioners, and the other may retain it wholly for administration by itself; with the result that the latter can supplement out of its own Funds kept in hand the pension paid to its widows by the Patriotic Commissioners, to whom it has contributed nothing, while the former has denuded itself of the means of supplementing the sum coming to its widows from the same source. Unless this inequality is redressed through concerted action between the Commissioners and the local Funds, it is probable that there will be increasing reluctance on the part of local bodies to contribute to the Commissioners' Fund. On the other hand, if it were publicly known that relief would in all cases be administered through the committee administering local Funds, there is good reason to think that such reluctance would be diminished or removed. The evidence shows that such local committees as have in a few centres been already appointed by the Patriotic Fund Commissioners, do not meet the difficulty.

GENERAL CONCLUSIONS.

From the above sketch some general observations arise. For instance:—

That in the case of many, if not of most of the recipients, the gift of lump sums such as those of the Patriotic Fund, the *Daily Telegraph*, and the Imperial War Fund, may not only be wasteful, but actually mischievous if paid to the recipient direct.

That the danger of waste would be reduced if the Government allowances could be paid weekly instead of monthly. At present the aggregate of four weeks' separation allowance is in the hands of many of the recipients a temptation to waste. The same remark applies to the pensions granted by the Patriotic Commissioners, which are paid monthly. This mischief, as well as that of the lump sums paid by them as above-mentioned, would be avoided if they could be induced to administer their relief through the local committees hereafter mentioned.

That in the absence of some general agreement as to the standard of relief to be aimed at, there must be a want of uniformity.

That such general standard is desirable, subject to particular modifications in special local conditions.

That unless the sums contributed exceed in the aggregate the desired standard, overlapping is not illegitimate but desirable.

That when relief cannot be administered once for all from one central Fund, complete information as to what has been done by others ought to be at the disposal of each separate giver.

That where no such single central Fund exists adequate to the complete relief of each case or of each of a particular class of cases, still the mischief of overlapping may be avoided if it is certain that relief on a fixed scale will be given from one Fund to a small ascertained amount in every case of a particular class. The contributions from such Fund being universal, and certain, like a Government pension, all others might be modified accordingly. This (except as to the initial lump payments) would be to some extent a practical justification of the method pursued by the Patriotic Fund Commissioners in making their allowances uniform and certain and independent of all others. At all events, as long as their rate of pension is fixed on their present scale, the danger of its being too large in a particular instance is not formidable. If, however, they should be able to raise their rate, consultation and co-operation with other possible donors would be just as important for them as for others.

That the total aggregate of subscriptions is likely to be much larger where they are raised locally for separate Funds and special objects than if collected only by one central body.

That pooling of such Funds, and therefore the formation of one central Fund, would be impracticable.

That all relief should be administered as far as possible by persons on the spot.

That while inquiry into the circumstances of individual cases is necessary and desirable, it ought not to be of an inquisitorial character, and that the Funds administered are not to be regarded as primarily or exclusively eleemosynary.

That it is desirable that any organisation framed for the purpose of administering the present war Funds should be adaptable for the administration of permanent relief after the war is over.

While, as above pointed out, the existing system of the Patriotic Fund Commissioners does not, except in the points named, involve to any considerable extent waste or injurious overlapping, we desire to record our opinion that unless they radically change their present method of administration so as to make it at once more businesslike and more elastic, and also take steps to ensure complete and cordial co-operation with the persons distributing local Funds, the public confidence, which has been rudely shaken, will never be restored, and thus the only central Fund in the country for the permanent relief of the widows and orphans of soldiers and sailors will cease to exist. This would be a great public misfortune. It is of the utmost importance that the flow of subscriptions should not be interrupted at the present crisis, and if the Patriotic Fund Commissioners adopt the suggestions here made we venture to hope that Funds will be entrusted to them adequate to the needs of the present war.

Causes of Overlapping and Waste, and Possibility of Removing them.

The chief danger of overlapping and waste would seem to arise from—

Want of knowledge on the part of the givers of what others have done or are able and willing to do in each case.

Want of agreement as to the standard to be aimed at.

Want of efficient local organisation and supervision.

Valuable evidence was given to us on these points by Major-General Sir F. Maurice, K.C.B., Commanding the Woolwich District, and Mr. Loch of the Charity Organisation Society. There would not, we think, be any practical difficulty in devising simple means for the tabulation and distribution of information. Practical methods were suggested to us by more than one witness.

Neither does it seem that there is much divergence of view as to what the standard of relief should be. Expressed in varying language and reached by different methods it would seem to be an equivalent for what the husband, when present, contributed to the support of the family, provided that it should not fall short of a moderate maintenance, according to the class in life of the recipient.

As has been already explained, a system of local committees throughout the Kingdom has been, to a great extent, organised by the Soldiers and Sailors' Families Association, with which the Soldiers and Sailors' Help Society already to a great extent co-operates; but being the nominees of one Society only these committees are not universally accepted, and though the scheme may be admirable the efficiency of each committee must depend on the skill and experience of its individual members. These consist at present exclusively of voluntary workers, and there is no security for skilled supervision of their work. The evidence shows also that in London especially the relations between the central authority and the local committees require revision and clearer definition. To make local committees at once thoroughly efficient and to secure to them the confidence of all donors, it would be desirable to give all the principal voluntary Funds a voice in their nomination, and also to provide for their being started, and occasionally supervised by trained organisers. This would probably involve some expense, though it is possible that even for this skilled work competent volunteers might be forthcoming.

Importance of Co-operation, and Proposals for Securing it.

As will be seen from the extracts above cited, Lord Herschell's Committee and that of the House of Commons both advised the formation of a central consultative Council, composed of representatives of the different Funds administering relief. A similar resolution has recently been passed by a committee brought together by His Royal Highness the Prince of Wales, but no practical steps have as yet been taken to call such a council into existence. Co-operation on the part of the persons managing the various local and central Funds is indispensable to the success of such a proposal, and, short of legislation, this can, we think, be attained only by such powerful influence as can be brought to bear by the committee called together by His Royal Highness the Prince of Wales.

A great step towards simplifying the problem would have been taken, if even all the central Funds could be induced to act in concert through the same local committees, and it is precisely such concert that we hope may be brought about at once by the action of the Prince of Wales' Committee as already constituted. Such co-operation would secure what is most desirable, namely, a permanent nucleus in each local committee which would remain to administer permanent relief after the present War is over. The evidence shows a very efficient local organisation already existing in many parts of the country, and there seems to be no disinclination whatever on the part of the country and municipal authorities to co-operate with the central Funds, if the latter would lend themselves to such co-operation. The action suggested by the Prince of Wales' Committee might do much to secure this.

In order, however, to create an authoritative, permanent, central, consultative council, such as their resolution contemplates, it will, we think, be necessary to make it thoroughly representative, and for this purpose to bring together a body composed of nominees from the principal local and central Funds and other Organisations concerned in the distribution of relief. This body would then appoint the required committee or council. An invitation to the principal county and municipal authorities and to the managers of the principal central Funds and Organisations, emanating from the Committee already constituted under the auspices of His Royal Highness, to come together for the purpose of agreeing upon a common course of action, and arranging for the constitution of a consultative Committee, could not, we think, fail of success.

Such a Committee, thus constituted, might, we think, readily arrange for the complete tabulation and interchange of all necessary information as to applicants for relief and cases relieved. They might come to some general understanding as to a common standard, and as to what share each Fund should take in maintaining it, and they might provide for the organisation of local committees in the various counties, boroughs, petty sessional divisions, and other smaller centres, through whose agency all relief might be locally administered, and lay down general principles for their guidance. A body so composed might indeed in future become the repository of all Funds raised for the relief of soldiers and sailors, their wives, families and dependents.

If each Local Centre confined its relief to cases arising in its own area, while all were in touch with a central County Committee, and through it with the consultative body in London, injurious overlapping and waste would become simply a question of the efficiency of the workers in each district. The investigation made in the case of a wife, and the standard of relief adopted, would be applicable if she became a widow, the relief being administered by the same persons, though possibly drawn from different Funds in each case, while any change of circumstances requiring modification would come under their observation. The key to the position, in our opinion, is co-operation coupled with local administration, and this we think can be most probably secured in the manner indicated. Though, as above pointed out, the Commissioners of the Patriotic Fund have not, so far, availed themselves of the assistance of local committees to any appreciable extent, Colonel Young told us that they were willing to do so, and he and Colonel Gildea have both propounded schemes for co-operative working, which will be found in the Appendix.

The Returns from Leicestershire and other counties and the evidence of Captain Holland afford illustrations of successful county organisation.

Suggestion as to Government Pensions.

Although it does not come within the scope of the reference to this Committee that we should inquire how far the Funds now available are sufficient to secure adequate pensions to the widows of soldiers and sailors serving in South Africa, the question is of such great importance that we think it right to offer some observations upon it.

It is obvious that in most cases the scale of allowance granted by the Patriotic Fund Commissioners to widows must fall far below the sum received by the family during the lifetime of the husband. The supplementary grants from other sources, such as the *Daily Telegraph*, cannot be relied upon as likely to continue, and it is impossible before the conclusion of the War to be certain whether the Fund in the hands of the Patriotic Commissioners will suffice to provide pensions even on the present scale, and certainly it will not be sufficient to provide those additions which are necessary in order to secure a moderate maintenance for the widows.

If Parliament should consider it right to give a small pension to widows at a fixed rate, the whole of the subscriptions of the public could be applied to making such additions to that pension as may be found necessary after inquiry by local committees into each particular case, and so the intentions of the subscribers would be fulfilled.

If no such action is taken, there must not only be very many cases of distress, but also great inequality in the relief given to widows. In some places where considerable subscriptions are held in hand for local administration, widows may receive substantial additions to the Patriotic Fund pension of 5s. a week. In other places, where the subscriptions have been remitted to the Patriotic Fund, the widows will receive nothing beyond 5s. a week.

We have not considered it our function to take evidence with regard to the amount of the charge which would have to be provided by Parliament for the pensions. We confine ourselves to stating the case as it presents itself to us, and we are of opinion that it deserves the careful consideration of Her Majesty's Government.

Recommendations.

We therefore recommend :—

That relief should in all cases be administered locally through committees on the spot.

That such committees should include nominees of the central as well as the local Funds.

That representatives of the principal local and central Funds be called together in London for the purpose of forming a consultative council, who should provide for the formation of local committees and carry into effect the conclusions at which we have arrived, and which are embodied in this Report.

We desire to express our high sense of the ability and discretion with which the Hon. Malcolm M. Macnaghten has discharged his duties as Secretary on this Inquiry.

28th May, 1900.

WAR RELIEF FUNDS ORGANISATION.

The Report of the Sub-Committee (appointed by His Majesty the King, as Prince of Wales, on the 28th of May, 1900) which met at the Mansion House on the 8th, 15th, and 27th of June, recommending the summoning of a Conference of Representatives of the principal War Relief Funds and the principal county and municipal authorities, was approved at a meeting of the Prince of Wales's Committee held at the Mansion House on the 11th of July, 1900, as also a draft letter of invitation which had been submitted to and approved by His Royal Highness.

On the 31st of July, 1900, at a Conference of Representatives referred to in previous paragraph, held at the Mansion House, to consider the Report of the War Relief Funds Committee, and to adopt means whereby the recommendations of that Committee could be best carried out, it was resolved that a Central Consultative Council be formed of not less than fifty members, being Lords Lieutenants of Counties, Lord Mayors and Mayors, Lords Provosts and Provosts of towns, and representatives of the principal Central and Provincial Funds; and that invitations be issued to all concerned to elect their own representatives.

At the first meeting of the Central Consultative Council held at the Mansion House on the 19th of October, 1900, in addition to the Earl of Derby appointed Chairman, an honorary secretary, a secretary, and an Executive Committee consisting of the whole Council were appointed, as also a small Sub-Committee formed "to draw up 'questions' to be addressed to the various central and local Funds, as well as a scheme on the basis of these returns for the future work of the Committee."

On the 21st of November, 1900, a meeting of the Executive Committee was held at the Mansion House to consider an interim Report of the Sub-Committee, when the questions recommended were, with certain alterations, approved and directed to be issued.

The final Report of the Sub-Committee was submitted, discussed, and, as altered by the Executive Committee, reported to, and with further alterations approved by the Central Council at a meeting held at the Mansion House on the 2nd of April, 1901.

At this meeting it was resolved "that a letter through its Chairman should be addressed to the Lords Lieutenants of Counties, Lord Mayors of Cities, and Mayors of County Boroughs, requesting them to take the initiative in the formation of local Committees in their respective Counties, Cities, and County Boroughs," as recommended by the Central Council. It was also announced that a sum of one thousand pounds had been voted by the Lord Mayor out of his Discretionary Fund to provide for the salary of the secretary and the necessary office expenses. The actual sum paid was £1,280 18s. 5d. (See Mansion House statement, page 5.)

No further meetings have been held, nor the response to the above letter promulgated up to this date (June, 1902).

THE JOINT SELECT COMMITTEE

OF

THE HOUSE OF LORDS AND HOUSE OF COMMONS

ON

CHARITABLE AGENCIES FOR RELIEF OF WIDOWS AND ORPHANS OF SOLDIERS AND SAILORS.

MEMBERS.

The Right Hon. Lord James of Hereford (*Chairman*).

The Marquess of Bath.	Mr. G. C. T. Bartley.
The Earl of Dartmouth.	Mr. W. Hayes Fisher.
The Earl of Malmesbury.	Mr. J. H. C. Hozier.
The Earl of Westmeath.	Mr. Hudson E. Kearley.
Viscount Hampden.	Mr. G. Lambert.
Lord Newton.	Colonel Nolan.
Mr. E. M. Archdale.	

REPORT.*

THE SELECT COMMITTEE appointed to join with a Committee of the House of Lords "to consider the various
" Charitable Agencies now in operation, and the funds available for relieving Widows and Orphans of Soldiers
" and Sailors with a view to insuring that the funds subscribed by local and private benevolence are applied to
" the best advantage in supplementing a scheme of Government Pensions for Widows and Orphans of Soldiers
" and Sailors who have lost their lives in War "

Have met and have examined many Witnesses, and have agreed to the following REPORT, viz. :—

At the commencement of the present war the State made no provision for the payment of pensions to the widows and orphans of soldiers in the ranks killed in action, or dying of wounds or disease contracted on active service; whereas in the case of sailors and marines killed or drowned on service the State has long ago recognised its obligations to pension their widows and orphans, and a sum, averaging yearly about £5,000, has for some 20 years been paid out of the funds of Greenwich Hospital. To such general funds of the Hospital a yearly sum of £21,000 is contributed by the State.

In 1854, at the outbreak of the Crimean War, "The Royal Patriotic Fund Commission" was called into existence for the purpose of administering any sums that might be subscribed to assist the widows and orphans of soldiers and sailors killed in action or dying on active service. The original powers conferred on the Commissioners referred only to the widows and orphans and other dependents of soldiers and sailors killed or dying of wounds or disease during the Crimean War.

Since the constitution of the Patriotic Commission, Parliament, by the passing of various Statutes, has shown its approval of the principle of voluntary assistance.

In 1866 a Statute was passed giving power to the Crown to authorise the Commissioners to apply the Patriotic Fund and its income as they might think fit for the relief—first, of the widows and children of soldiers, sailors, and marines killed in battle, or dying from wounds, or by other casualties in the war with Russia; and secondly, "In the education, training, and advancement of children of soldiers, seamen, and marines of Her Majesty's Army and Navy who have lost or hereafter lose their lives in battle, or from wounds, or by other casualties in any other war."

By this Statute power was also given to the Commissioners to contribute to any Royal or other institution established for similar purposes.

---

* Can be purchased (Price 1s. 8d.) either directly or through any Bookseller from Eyre and Spottiswoode, East Harding Street, Fleet Street, E.C.; John Menzies and Co., 12, Hanover Street, Edinburgh, and 90, West Nile Street, Glasgow; or Hodges, Figgis and Co., 104, Grafton Street, Dublin.

In 1867 a Statute further extended the powers of the Commissioners by enabling them to expend any balance of funds that may have been applicable to the purposes mentioned in the Act of 1866 to the maintenance, education, training, and advancement of children of soldiers, sailors, and marines who had lost or might thereafter lose their lives in the service of the Crown.

Again, in 1881, power was given to the Crown to confer by commission power on the Patriotic Fund Commissioners to apply the Patriotic Fund and all other funds then in their possession and of which they might hereafter become possessed and the income and accumulations thereof (so far as not appropriated for the Royal Victoria Patriotic Asylum for Girls, and for the purposes mentioned in the schedule to the Patriotic Fund Act, 1867, and so far as not required to meet liabilities and claims existing prior to the date of such commission) for the benefit of the widows and children of officers and men of Her Majesty's Military and Naval Forces.

By a Statute passed in 1886 the Commissioners were empowered to apply to the public and to collect funds for the purpose of applying them for the benefit of the widows and children of the officers and men of Her Majesty's Military and Naval Forces.

And this power was in 1899 extended so as to allow "other dependents" to receive the advantage of the funds previously applicable to widows and orphans.

To carry into effect these statutory powers commissions were at different times issued by the Crown.

As a result of voluntary efforts at the time of the commencement of the South African War the Trustees of the Royal Patriotic Fund held large sums in their hands. A statement of these funds is to be found in the document handed in by Colonel Young, which is set out as an Appendix to this Report. The Committee, although they received very valuable evidence from Mr. Higham, the President of the Institute of Actuaries, as to the present value of the different funds in the hands of the Royal Patriotic Fund Commissioners, were unable to pursue the subject to the extent of determining the exact amount of the surplus which, after meeting all liabilities attaching to such funds, will come into existence.

In addition to the funds above referred to, the Royal Patriotic Fund Commissioners hold a very valuable property, consisting of a large building and 40 acres of land at Clapham. This building is devoted to the purposes of an orphanage, capable of receiving 300 girls, daughters of soldiers and sailors killed in action, and the land is let for agricultural purposes. This land and other eleven acres were purchased in the year 1854, under the advice of the late Prince Consort, for £3,000. But in consequence of the growth of London and of the proximity of the land to the now existing Clapham Junction Railway Station, the value of the estate has undoubtedly very largely increased, and therefore consideration may well be given to the desirability of realising the full value of this land and obtaining at a less cost suitable accommodation for the orphanage in a different locality.

It is presumed that the existing trusts, denominational or otherwise, affecting the various funds will be respected. But if the amount necessary to fulfil these trusts be ascertained and held in hand there seems no reason why the surplus should not be applied, if it be thought fit, to providing pensions for the widows and orphans of soldiers and sailors who have lost their lives in war.

Such being the funds vested in and administered by the Royal Patriotic Fund Commissioners, the Committee have considered whether it is advisable in the public interests that the funds should continue to be so held and administered.

The Committee desire to express their recognition of the care and ability with which the Royal Patriotic Commissioners have discharged the onerous duties entrusted to them. It is also desirable to bear in mind the unselfish views expressed by His Royal Highness the Duke of Cambridge in the following letter, dated "8th February, 1900. Dear Mr. Balfour,— The duration of the war and the increasing list of casualties in South Africa make it evident that a vigorous effort must be made to provide for those who suffered in the service of the nation. I understand that His Majesty's Government will submit to Parliament on its reassembling a scheme of State pensions for the widows and children of soldiers and sailors who have lost their lives on active service, and that it will be a feature of the proposal that the pensions so granted will be supplemented by the united efforts of private benevolence. This is a new departure, and Parliament will doubtless require to be assured that the administration of the public and private funds, which have been raised or will be raised for the relief of disabled soldiers and sailors or for pensions to widows and children, is organised on principles which will prevent overlapping and secure efficiency. I need not say to you how heartily the Patriotic Fund Commissioners will concur in proposals directed to this end, but I am afraid that the movement for bringing existing funds into correspondence and co-ordination has not progressed sufficiently to enable you to give a decisive answer to the questions which will be put. The Patriotic Fund Commissioners venture to hope that His Majesty's Government may themselves take up the question, and in that event I desire to say how anxious we are to co-operate with and assist you, and I can assure you that no question of our charter will stand in the way of measures which the Government may think desirable.—Yours sincerely, (signed) GEORGE."

With the opinion expressed by Mr. Balfour in his reply to the above letter dated 10th February, 1900, that "the Country owes a great debt of gratitude to those who have administered the Patriotic Fund," the Committee fully agree.

At the same time the Committee feel that the publication of the Report of the Commission presided over by Lord Justice Henn Collins must have weakened the position and authority of the Patriotic Fund Commissioners as an Administrative Body.

After full consideration the Committee have arrived at the conclusion that the discharge of the duties of the Royal Patriotic Fund Commissioners and the funds vested in them should be transferred to the Pension Boards hereinafter suggested. The maintenance of the Commission, as at present constituted, and its continued exercise of the duties discharged by it would be inconsistent with the creation of the system now recommended by the Committee.

It now becomes necessary to review the state of affairs that has to be dealt with in the immediate future.

The Government have announced the intention of granting pensions on the following scale:—

—	Rank.		Widow's Pension.	Scale for each Child.
	Army.	Navy.	s. d.	s. d.
Class I.	Quartermaster-Sergeant.	—	10 0	2 0
Class II.	Colour-Sergeant	Chief Petty Officer, Colour and Staff Sergeant of Marines and Marine Artillery.	9 0	2 0
Class III.	Sergeant	First Class Petty Officer, Sergeant of Marines and Marine Artillery.	7 6	2 0
Class IV.	Corporal	Second Class Petty Officer, Corporal of Marines and Marine Artillery.	6 0	1 6
Class V.	Private	Able Seaman, Private of Marines and Marine Artillery	5 0	1 6

From the evidence before them the Committee have arrived at the conclusion that the sums allotted under it will not sufficiently meet many of the cases that have to be dealt with, and there certainly will be numerous cases in respect of which supplemental assistance will have to be obtained from private sources.

Apart from the Patriotic Fund Commission there was, at the commencement of the war in South Africa, no general body which afforded relief to the widows and orphans of soldiers killed in action or dying when engaged on active service.

But as soon as the war broke out, the public took steps to make provision for those widows and orphans, and also for the families of our soldiers engaged on active service.

The Lord Mayor of London initiated a subscription of a national character.

In the large cities, and throughout the counties of the United Kingdom, committees were formed for collecting subscriptions to carry out these objects. Large sums of money were collected: some of this money was remitted to the Lord Mayor, some retained by the local committees for distribution. Different newspapers opened subscription lists in their columns, and thus collected very large sums of money.

The Patriotic Fund Commissioners made an appeal through the Lord Mayor, in response to which £437,800 was received and handed over to the Commissioners.

At the time of taking the evidence large sums had been applied by the Commissioners in the relief of 2,960 widows, 3,900 children, and 1,900 "other dependents"; all these cases arising out of the South African War.

The rate of relief given was:—

	s. d.	
To widows of privates	5 0	per week.
To children "	1 6	"
To widows of corporals	5 6	"
To children "	1 6	"
To widows of sergeants	6 0	"
To children "	2 0	"
To widows of colour-sergeants and ranks above	6 6	"
To children " " "	2 0	"

The *Daily Telegraph* and *Scotsman* Fund amounted to upwards of £250,000, of which £182,125 has been expended on the purchase of permanent annuities payable to 659 widows, the rates varying from 8s. to 4s. per week. The balance of the fund has mainly been applied to granting temporary relief to widows, and rendering assistance to children. These pensions are mainly paid by Government annuities, and are irrevocable.

It is apparent that in respect to the future the proposed grant of Government pensions will raise questions deserving full consideration.

Under the Government scheme the grant to the widow is not a matter of discretion. She will be entitled to demand it substantially as a right. So a widow totally destitute and one who is in receipt of a pension from a private source or has private means of support will receive the same amount of pension from the Government.

It is not for the Committee to suggest any alteration in the Government proposals, and it will be difficult where from other sources permanent pensions have already been granted to recommend that they should be withdrawn in consequence of the Government pensions being granted. But doubtless in the future those who make provision for these widows and orphans will fully recognise the existence of the Government pension and content themselves merely with supplementary grants.

The Committee desire to express a strong opinion that notwithstanding the granting by the Government of pensions on the above scale, the necessity of rendering assistance by voluntary effort will still continue. By such agency much has to be accomplished: (1) Government pensions will have to be substantially supplemented in amount. (2) Immediate relief before the pension comes into operation has to be afforded. (3) Widows married off the strength and children born of such marriages will have to be provided for. (4) Widows and children of Colonial soldiers, in the cases of those Colonies which do not grant pensions, will have to be assisted, and (5) in addition, although this subject is not within the reference to this Committee, "other dependents" will have to be dealt with.

In administering the funds applicable to pensions to the widows and orphans in question the Committee are of opinion that each pension and any addition to it should be paid in one sum at the same time and by the same hand.

To effect this result the Committee recommend that two Boards, to be termed respectively the Naval and Military Pension Board, shall be established.

The duties of such Boards shall be (1) to administer the Government pensions; (2) to supplement such Government pensions by administering the funds now vested in the Royal Patriotic Fund Commissioners, which should, subject to the necessary conditions, be transferred to the Boards; and (3) to administer any other moneys which may be placed at their disposal for the purpose of being expended in pensions to widows and orphans.

The Committee also recommend that all the funds and property now vested in the Royal Patriotic Fund Commissioners should be vested in the Boards and administered by them according to the trusts attaching to such funds. The funds to be thus vested may be apportioned to either Board according to the nature of the trusts now affecting such funds.

The Boards should also hold themselves out as being willing to receive from any source any contributions for the purpose of granting pensions or assistance to the widows and orphans of soldiers and sailors, and should undertake to distribute all such sums when received. It should also be the duty of the Board to make all necessary inquiries in respect of the granting of supplementary or other pensions.

The Committee recommend that each Board should consist of seven Members. As the primary object of the existence of the Boards will be the payment of pensions derived from funds voted by Parliament, the Committee think that two members of each Board should be officers of the Department whose duty it would be to administer the Government Funds. The other members of the Boards should be appointed by the Crown, as distinguished from the heads of other Departments, and should be unpaid. The Crown should also have power on occasion to add to the permanent members of the Board special members, such as the Lord Mayor of London or any other person whose services for the time being might be deemed to be of importance.

The distribution of the Government pensions being the principal duty of the Boards, the expense of the secretarial and necessary staff for carrying out the work might well be borne by the State.

It is also desirable that the Boards should be subject to the control of Parliament. Reports of their proceedings should be made to both Houses of Parliament, and as the payment of the officers of the Board would have to be voted by the House of Commons, an opportunity for discussing such proceedings would be found.

The Boards should also be ready at all times to afford any advice that may be sought by any collecting body or by any local body or agency distributing the funds at its disposal.

26th July, 1901.

THE FORCES IN SOUTH AFRICA.

Strength of Garrison on 1st of August, 1899, Reinforcements and Casualties, &c., since, and strength on 1st of January, 1902:—

	Officers Exclusive of Staff.	Non-commissioned Officers and Men.					Total Officers and Men.
		Cavalry.	Artillery.	Infantry and Mounted Infantry.	Others.	Total.	
I. Garrison on 1st August, 1899	318	1,127	1,035	6,428	1,032	9,622	9,940
II. Reinforcements, 1st August, 1899, to 11th October, 1899 (outbreak of war)—							
(1.) From Home	280	—	743	5,620	—	6,363	6,643
(2.) From India (some of these did not reach South Africa until after the outbreak of hostilities)	259	1,564	653	3,427	—	5,644	5,903
	539	1,564	1,396	9,047	—	12,007	12,546
III. Further reinforcements from 11th October, 1899, to end of July, 1900—							
Regulars—							
(1.) From Home and Colonies	5,748	11,003	14,145	110,292	14,347	149,787	155,535
(2.) From India	132	713	376	670	—	1,759	1,891
	5,880	11,716	14,521	110,962	14,347	151,546	157,426
Colonials—							
(1.) From Colonies other than South Africa	550	287	692	9,788	267	11,034	11,584
(2.) Raised in South Africa	1,387	—	—	—	—	28,932	30,319
	1,937	—	—	—	—	39,966	41,903
Militia	831	—	617	19,753	256	20,626	21,457
Imperial Yeomanry	536	—	—	—	—	10,195	10,731
Volunteers from United Kingdom	342	—	358	9,995	434	10,787	11,129
Total all arms sent to, and raised in South Africa, up to 1st August, 1900, including garrison on 1st August, 1899	10,383	—	—	—	—	254,749	265,132
IV. Further reinforcements from 1st August, 1900, to 30th April, 1901—							
Regulars—							
From Home and Colonies	1,157	5,427	1,129	12,588	2,686	21,830	22,987
Colonials—							
(1.) From Colonies other than South Africa	265	—	—	—	—	5,525	5,790
(2.) Raised in South Africa	937	—	—	—	—	21,158	22,095
Militia from Home and Colonies	116	—	—	3,823	—	3,823	3,939
Imperial Yeomanry	429	—	—	—	—	16,304	16,733
Volunteers from United Kingdom	164	—	—	—	—	5,641	5,805
South African Constabulary from United Kingdom	2	—	—	—	—	5,178	5,180
	13,453	—	—	—	—	334,208	347,661
V. Further reinforcements from 1st May, 1901, to 31st December, 1901—							
Regulars—							
(1.) From Home and Colonies	1,244	3,871	1,115	14,286	2,230	21,502	22,746
(2.) From India	108	1,206	—	2,540	3	3,749	3,857
Colonials—							
(1.) From Colonies other than South Africa	54	—	—	—	—	1,140	1,194
(2.) Raised in South Africa		Numbers uncertain.					
Militia	301	—	289	7,869	103	8,261	8,562
Imperial Yeomanry	44	—	—	—	—	877	921
Volunteers	14	—	—	—	—	393	407
Scottish Horse	7	—	—	—	—	447	454
South African Constabulary, from Home	13	—	—	—	—	1,696	1,709
,, ,, ,, ,, Canada	29	—	—	—	—	1,209	1,238
Total sent to and raised in South Africa from 1st August, 1899, to 31st December, 1901, including garrison on 1st August, 1899	15,267	—	—	—	—	373,482	388,749
VI. Numbers—							
(1.) Killed to 31st December, 1901	469	—	—	—	—	4,762	5,231
(2.) Wounded to 31st December, 1901	1,685	—	—	—	—	19,242	20,937
(3.) Died of wounds or disease, or accidentally killed in South Africa to 31st December, 1901	462	—	—	—	—	13,271	13,733
(4.) Disbanded and discharged in South Africa	377	—	—	—	—	6,308	6,685
(5.) In Hospital in South Africa on 27th December, 1901 (latest returns)	328	—	—	—	—	11,392	11,720
VII. Numbers left South Africa—							
(1.) For England, not invalids	3,027	—	—	—	—	46,159	49,186
(2.) For England, sick, wounded, and died on passage	2,664	—	—	—	—	61,666	64,330
(3.) For India direct from South Africa, including 6 Batteries Royal Field Artillery	88	—	—	—	—	843	931
(4.) For Colonies direct from South Africa							
(a.) Regulars, including 2 Battalions to Ceylon, and 3 Companies Royal Garrison Artillery, and 1 Battalion to Bermuda	145	—	—	—	—	3,087	3,232
(b.) Colonials	363	—	—	—	—	8,016	8,379
VIII. Strength of Forces in South Africa on 1st January, 1902—							
(1.) Regulars	4,700	16,000	10,000	97,000	14,000	137,000	141,700
(2.) Militia	750	—	—	—	—	19,000	19,750
(3.) Imperial Yeomanry	650	—	—	—	—	13,000	13,650
(4.) Volunteers	200	—	—	—	—	5,200	5,400
(5.) Colonials (including Town Guards, &c.)	*2,300	—	—	—	—	*55,000	*57,300
Total	8,600	—	—	—	—	229,200	237,800

February 11th, 1902.   T. K.-KENNY, A.G.

* These numbers are uncertain.

THE WAR.
OFFICIAL TABLE OF CASUALTIES.

The War Office issued the following Table of Casualties in the Field Force, South Africa, reported during the Month of April, 1902, and the Total Casualties reported since the beginning of the War, up to and including the Month:—

Casualties in Action.	Killed. Officers.	Killed. N.C.O.'s and men.	Wounded (not including wounded prisoners). Officers.	Wounded. N.C.O.'s and men.	Died of Wounds in South Africa (included in wounded). Officers.	Died of Wounds. N.C.O.'s and men.	Missing and prisoners.* Officers.	Missing and prisoners. N.C.O.'s and men.	Total killed, wounded, missing, and prisoners. Officers.	Total. N.C.O.'s and men.
Reported during the month:—										
Boschbult, Mar. 31	3	22	17	129	—	5	—	—	20	151
Leeuwkop, Apr. 1	2	14	5	61	—	8	—	—	7	75
Rooival, Apr. 11	1	6	11	60	2	4	—	2	12	68
Other casualties	8	57	22	197	3	24	1	15	31	269
	14	99	55	447	5	41	1	17	70	563
Total casualties reported up to and including the month:—										
Belmont, Nov. 23, 1899	3	50	25	220	1	21	—	—	28	270
Blood River Poort, Sep. 17, 1901	2	19	4	31	2	2	7	240	13	290
Boschbult, Mar. 31, 1902	3	22	17	129	—	5	—	—	20	151
Brakenlaagte, Oct. 30, 1901	7	59	16	149	5	11	—	1	23	209
Colenso, Dec. 15, 1899	7	140	43	719	2	22	21	176	71	1,035
Driefontein, Mar. 10, 1900	5	58	19	342	1	18	—	2	24	402
Dundee, Oct. 20, 1899	8	46	11	84	3	—	25	296	44	426
Elandslaagte, Oct. 21, 1899	5	50	30	169	—	6	—	4	35	223
Enslin (Graspan), Nov. 25, 1899	3	14	6	162	1	4	—	9	9	185
Farquhar's Farm and Nicholson's Nek, Oct. 30, 1899	6	57	9	245	—	12	43	925	58	1,227
Johannesburg and Pretoria, capture of.	3	20	34	132	1	8	5	38	42	190
Karee, near Brandfort, Mar. 29, 1900	1	20	9	152	1	11	—	—	10	172
Klerksdorp, Feb. 25, 1902	5	48	7	125	—	13	2	106	14	279
Klip Drift, near Lichtenburg, Mar. 7, 1902	4	56	9	144	—	6	3	42	16	242
Ladysmith, relief of, Feb. 19 to 27, 1900	22	245	91	1,530	3	86	1	3	114	1,778
Magersfontein, Dec. 11, 1899	23	182	45	645	3	36	—	76	63	903
Monte Christo, Colenso, &c., Feb. 15 to 18, 1900.	1	13	8	180	—	3	—	4	9	197
Modder River, Nov. 28, 1899	4	66	20	393	—	32	—	2	24	461
Nooitgedacht, Dec. 13, 1900	9	65	7	179	1	13	15	327	31	571
Paardeburg, Feb. 16 to 27, 1900	18	253	74	1,136	6	71	6	53	98	1,442
Potgeiter's Drif, Feb. 5 to 7, 1900	3	23	17	326	—	8	—	5	20	354
Pretoria, east of, June 11 and 12, 1900	8	6	16	128	1	4	1	3	25	137
Reddersburg, Apr. 3 and 4, 1900	2	10	2	33	1	1	8	397	12	440
Rietfontein, Oct. 24, 1899	1	11	6	98	—	4	—	2	7	111
Sanna's Post, Mar. 31, 1900	3	18	16	122	2	7	18	403	37	543
Senekal, May 29, 1900	—	38	7	127	1	5	—	12	7	177
Spion Kop, &c., Jan. 17 to 24, 1900	30	294	53	1,060	6	53	4	299	87	1,653
Stormberg, Dec. 10, 1899	—	28	7	51	—	1	13	620	20	699
Tweefontein, Dec. 25, 1901	6	52	9	75	3	6	6	244	21	371
Uitval's Nek, July 11, 1900	3	16	3	53	—	3	4	186	10	255
Willow Grange, Nov. 23, 1899	—	11	1	66	—	2	1	8	2	85
At Ladysmith during Investment—Battle of, Jan. 6, 1900	14	164	33	287	4	25	—	2	47	453
Other Casualties	6	60	36	280	3	29	—	12	42	352
At Kimberley during Investment	2	36	15	124	—	4	1	3	18	163
At Mafeking during Investment	5	64	10	152	—	9	1	41	16	257
Other casualties	294	2,897	1,124	11,028	130	1,274	199	4,638	1,617	18,563
Total casualties in action reported up to April 30.	516	5,211	1,839	20,876	181	1,815	384†	9,179†	2,739	35,266

Other Casualties.	Officers.	N.C.O.'s and men.
Reported during the month—		
Died of Disease in South Africa	15	261
Accidental deaths in South Africa	1	90
Invalids sent home	93	2,631
Total up to and including the month—		
Died of Disease in South Africa	328	12,664
Accidental deaths in South Africa	25	733
Invalids sent home—		
Wounded	}	8,121
Sick	} 3,030	61,519
Not specified which	}	1,302
Total reduction of the Field Force, South Africa, due to casualties.		
Reported during the month—		
Killed in action	14	99
Died of wounds in South Africa	5	41
Died of disease in South Africa	15	261
Accidental deaths in South Africa	1	90
Missing and prisoners	1	17
Sent home as invalids	93	2,631
Total	129	3,139
Totals reported up to and including the month—		
Killed in action	516	5,211
Died of wounds	181	1,815
Prisoners who have died in captivity.	5	97
Died of disease	328	12,664
Accidental deaths	25	733
Total deaths in South Africa	1,055	20,520
Missing and prisoners (excluding those who have been recovered or have died in captivity).	1	131
Sent home as invalids	3,030	70,942‡
Total, South African Field Force	4,086	91,593
	95,679§	
Total reduction of the Military Forces through war in South Africa.		
Deaths in South Africa	1,055	20,520
Missing and prisoners	1	131
Invalids sent home who have died	7	487
Invalids sent home who have left the service as unfit	—	5,531
	1,063	26,669
	27,732§	

* Officers and men reported missing, but afterwards found not to have been taken prisoners, are deducted from the figures in these columns.
† Of these, 378 officers and 8,951 men have been released or have escaped, and five officers and 97 men have died in captivity.
‡ Of these, 487 have died, 5,531 have been discharged from the service as unfit, and 907 are in hospital.
§ The difference between these two numbers is due to the fact that the great majority of the men invalided home have recovered and rejoined for duty. (See note ‡.)

DIARY OF THE WAR.

1899.
Oct. 11. Time fixed by the Boers for compliance with their "ultimatum" expired at 5 p.m.
Oct. 14. Boers march on Kimberley and Mafeking.
Oct. 15. KIMBERLEY ISOLATED.
Oct. 20. Boer position on TALANA HILL captured by the British under Symons.
Oct. 21. White moves out force under French to eject Boers from ELANDSLAAGTE. Boers routed.
Oct. 22. Yule retires from Dundee on Ladysmith via Beith.
Oct. 23. Death of General Symons at Dundee.
Oct. 30. General sortie from Ladysmith. Naval guns silence Boer siege artillery.
Surrender of part of two battalions and a Mountain Battery at Nicholson's Nek.
Oct. 31. General Sir Redvers Buller lands at Cape Town.
Nov. 1. Boers invade Cape Colony.
Nov. 2. LADYSMITH ISOLATED.
Nov. 9. General attack on Ladysmith repulsed with heavy loss to Boers.
Nov. 15. Armoured train wrecked by Boers near Chieveley. Over 100 British troops captured.
Nov. 19. Lord Methuen's column for the relief of Kimberley concentrated at Orange River.
Nov. 23. Methuen attacks Boers at BELMONT with Guards Brigade and 9th Brigade. Boers driven from their position.
Nov. 25. Methuen attacks Boers in position at Enslin and dislodges them.
General Sir Redvers Buller arrives in Natal.
Nov. 28. Methuen engages 11,000 Boers at MODDER RIVER. Battle lasting all day. Boers evacuate position.
Nov. 30. Sixth Division for South Africa notified.
Dec. 1. Australian and Canadian contingents leave Cape Town for the front.
Dec. 10. Gatacre attempts night attack on STORMBERG, but is surprised and driven back with heavy loss.
Dec. 11. Methuen attacks Boer position at MAGERSFONTEIN and is repulsed with heavy loss. General Wauchope killed.
Dec. 15. Buller advances from Chieveley against Boer positions near COLENSO. British force repulsed on Tugela with 1,100 casualties and loss of 12 guns.
Mobilization of Seventh Division ordered.
Dec. 18. Lord Roberts appointed Commander-in-Chief in South Africa, with Lord Kitchener as Chief of Staff.
Dec. 19. Regulations issued for employment of Yeomanry and Volunteers in South Africa.
Dec. 20. Formation of City of London Volunteer Corps for South Africa announced.

1900.
Jan. 6. Suffolk Regiment loses heavily near Rensburg, over 100 prisoners taken.
BOER ATTACK ON LADYSMITH REPULSED.
Jan. 10. LORD ROBERTS AND LORD KITCHENER ARRIVE AT CAPE TOWN.
Forward movement for relief of Ladysmith resumed.
Jan. 11. Dundonald seizes pont on Tugela at Potgeiter's Drift.
Jan. 18. Buller makes SECOND ATTEMPT to relieve Ladysmith. Dundonald having crossed Tugela engages Boers near Acton Homes.
Crossing of Tugela by Warren and Lyttelton concluded.
Jan. 21. Warren attacks Boers' right flank.
Jan. 23-24. SPION KOP captured and held during 24th, but evacuated on the night of Jan. 24-25. General Woodgate fatally wounded.
Jan. 26-27. Buller's force recrosses the Tugela.
Feb. 3. MacDonald with Highland Brigade marches out from Modder River.
Feb. 5. Buller's THIRD ATTEMPT to relieve Ladysmith commenced. Lyttelton crosses Tugela, and delivers attack on VAAL KRANTZ, which he captures and occupies.
Feb. 7. Vaal Krantz evacuated and British force withdrawn across the Tugela.
Feb. 9. Lord Roberts arrives at Modder River.
Feb. 11. French, having been summoned from Southern Frontier, leaves Modder River with Cavalry Division and Horse Artillery.
Feb. 13. Lord Roberts at Dekiel's Drift.
Feb. 15. Lords Roberts at Jacobsdal.
RELIEF OF KIMBERLEY.
Feb. 17. Rearguard action between Kelly-Kenny and Cronje en route to Bloemfontein.
FOURTH ATTEMPT to relieve Ladysmith.
Buller presses advance on Monte Cristo Hill.
Feb. 19. Buller takes Hlangwane Hill.
Feb. 20. Boers under Cronje, having laagered near Paardeberg, are bombarded by Lord Roberts.
Feb. 21. Fifth Division crosses Tugela.
Feb. 23. Buller unsuccessfully attacks Railway Hill.
Feb. 26. Buller makes fresh passage of Tugela.
Feb. 27. CRONJE SURRENDERS AT PAARDEBERG.
PIETER'S HILL, the main Boer position between Ladysmith and the Tugela, carried by Hildyard.
Feb. 28. RELIEF OF LADYSMITH.
Clements occupies Colesberg.
Mar. 5. Gatacre occupies Stormberg.
Brabant again defeats and pursues Boers.
Overtures of peace made by Boer Presidents.
Mar. 6. Field Force arrives at Carnarvon to quell rising in North-West.
Mar. 7. Lord Roberts routs a large force of Boers at Poplar Grove.
Mar. 10. Lord Roberts defeats Boers at Driefontein.
Mar. 11. Overtures of peace rejected by Lord Salisbury.
Mar. 13. Lord Roberts, without further fighting, takes possession of BLOEMFONTEIN. Boers retire on Kroonstad.
Mar. 27. DEATH OF GENERAL JOUBERT.
Mar. 31. Broadwood attacked at Waterworks. During retirement R.H.A. and convoy entrapped at Koorn Spruit. Six guns lost, 350 casualties.
April 3. Detachment of Royal Irish Rifles and Mounted Infantry surrounded near Reddersburg.
April 7. Colonel Dalgety isolated near Wepener.
April 15. Chermside leaves Reddersburg to relieve Wepener.
April 25. Dalgety relieved. Boers retreat northwards, under Botha.
May 10. Zand River crossed, Boers rapidly retreating before Lord Roberts's advance.
May 12. Lord Roberts enters KROONSTAD without opposition, President Steyn having retired to Heilbron, which he proclaims his new capital.
Attack on Mafeking repulsed, 108 Boer prisoners, including Commandant Eloff, taken.
May 13. Mahon with Mafeking Relief Column repulses attack at Koodoosrand.
May 15. Buller occupies Dundee and Glencoe, having driven the Boers from the Biggarsberg.
Plumer, reinforced by Canadians and Queenslanders from Carrington's Division, joins hands with Mahon.
May 17-18. RELIEF OF MAFEKING.
May 24. Advance portion of Lord Roberts's force crosses the Vaal near Parys.
May 28. ANNEXATION OF ORANGE FREE STATE under name of Orange River Colony formally proclaimed at Bloemfontein.
May 30. FLIGHT OF PRESIDENT KRUGER FROM PRETORIA.
May 31. BRITISH FLAG HOISTED AT JOHANNESBURG.
Surrender of 500 Yeomanry at Lindley.
June 2-4. Futile negotiations between Buller and Christian Botha for armistice.
June 5. OCCUPATION OF PRETORIA.
June 8. Hildyard takes Botha's Pass.
Surrender of 4th Derbyshires at Roodeval.
June 11. Stubborn fight at Allemans Nek. Heavy Boer losses.
June 12. Boers evacuate Laings Nek.
Roberts defeats Botha at DIAMOND HILL, east of Pretoria.
June 14. Boer attack on Sand River repulsed.
July 4. Roberts and Buller join hands at Vlakfontein.
Railway to Natal clear.
July 11. Surrender of Scots Greys and Lincolns at Uitval Nek.
July 21. Advance eastwards towards Komati Poort begins.
July 30. SURRENDER OF PRINSLOO and 3,000 Boers to Hunter in Brandwater basin.
Aug. 16. Eland's River garrison relieved.
Aug. 25. Execution of Cordua for conspiracy to kidnap Lord Roberts.
Aug. 26-27. Fighting at DALMANUTHA.

Aug.	30.	British occupy Nooitgedacht and release 2,000 prisoners.
Sept.	6.	Buller occupies Lydenburg.
Sept.	11.	KRUGER, FLYING FROM THE TRANSVAAL, takes refuge at Lorenzo Marques.
Sept.	13.	Proclamation issued by Roberts calling on burghers to surrender. French occupies Barberton.
Sept.	25.	British force occupies Komati Poort. Many Boers cross Portuguese frontier and surrender to Portuguese.
Oct.	9.	De Wet driven across the Vaal out of Orange River Colony.
Oct.	19.	Kruger sails from Lorenzo Marques for Marseilles on Dutch man-of-war.
Oct.	24.	Buller sails from Cape Town for England.
Oct.	25.	FORMAL ANNEXATION OF SOUTH AFRICAN REPUBLIC, to be styled Transvaal Colony.
Nov.	6.	De Wet defeated at Bothaville.
Nov.	22.	Kruger lands at Marseilles.
Nov.	23.	Garrison at Dewetsdorp captured by De Wet.
Nov.	29	LORD KITCHENER TAKES OVER SUPREME COMMAND.
Dec.	5.	De Wet's first attempt to enter Cape Colony frustrated by Knox.
Dec.	11.	Roberts sails from Cape Town for England.
Dec.	13.	Clements defeated with heavy loss by Delarey at NOOITGEDACHT. Mishap to Brabant's Horse at Zastron.
Dec.	14.	De Wet and Steyn escape through Sprinkhaans Pass.
Dec.16-20.		BOER RAID INTO CAPE COLONY.
Dec.	20.	Martial law proclaimed over northern districts of Cape Colony.
Dec.	22.	War Office announce despatch of reinforcements to South Africa.
Dec.	28.	De Wet fails in attempt to break back into Cape Colony. Cape raiders driven northwards.
Dec.	29.	Surrender of Liverpools at Helvetia.

1901.

Jan.	1.	Colonial Defence Force called out in Cape Colony.
Jan.	3.	Defeat of bodyguard near Lindley by Botha.
Jan.	7.	Determined Boer attack on Belfast and other stations on railway to Lorenzo Marques.
Jan.	18.	Delarey's force defeated near Ventersburg.
Jan.	28.	French enters Ermelo. Smith-Dorrien repels determined attack on Botha. Sweeping movement continues in South-Eastern Transvaal, finally resulting in capture of eight guns, 734 prisoners, and large quantities of ammunition, transport, cattle, &c.
Feb.	7.	War Office announce despatch of additional 30,000 mounted troops.
Feb.	10.	De Wet slips through into Cape Colony.
Feb.	13.	Botha writes to Kitchener proposing an interview.
Feb.	28.	After desperate chase DE WET RECROSSES ORANGE RIVER, having lost all guns, ammunition, transport, and many prisoners. KITCHENER MEETS BOTHA in response to the Boer Commandant's desire to confer with him with a view to peace negotiations.
March	3.	Unsuccessful attack by Delarey on Lichtenburg.
March	16.	BOTHA BREAKS OFF NEGOTIATION.
Mar.22-23.		Babington routs Delarey at VENTERSDORP and captures three guns and six Maxims.
April	8.	Plumer occupies Pietersburg.
April	10.	Civil jurisdiction resumed in Transvaal.
April	14.	Rawlinson captures laager and two guns at KLERKSDORP.
April	20.	Winter operations in the Bush veld begin. During following two weeks many small captures are almost daily reported.
May	8.	Milner leaves Cape Town for England. Municipal government started in Johannesburg.
May	24.	MILNER RECEIVED BY THE KING and raised to peerage.
May	29.	Delarey defeated by Dixon at VLAKFONTEIN.
June	2.	Kruitzinger captures James Town, Cape Colony.
June	6.	Elliot engages De Wet near Reitz and captures his convoy.
June	12.	Disaster to Victorians near Wilmansrust.
June	26.	Boer attack on blockhouses along Delagoa railway.
July	4.	Train wrecked by Boers near Naboomspruit.
July	5.	In reply to Botha's inquiries about ending war Kruger telegraphs to Botha to CONTINUE FIGHTING.
July	13.	Broadwood surprises Reitz and captures Steyn's correspondence. Narrow escape of Steyn.
July	14.	French drives Scheepers's commando with heavy loss out of Camdeboo Mountains.
July	20.	Death of Mrs. Kruger.
July	30.	General W. Kitchener captures one gun, 32 prisoners, from B. Viljoen near Middleburg.

Aug.	1.	Kitchener reports shooting of native prisoners by Boers.
Aug.	6.	PROCLAMATION BY LORD KITCHENER of permanent banishment from South Africa of all Boer leaders taken in arms after September 15.
Aug.	8.	Commandant de Villiers and two field cornets surrender at Warmbaths.
Aug.	13.	Kitchener reports the largest return of Boer losses yet made in a week. More than 800 prisoners, 700 waggons, and 33,000 cattle.
Aug.	13.	Kruitzinger's commandos routed near Steynsburg by Colonel Gorringe.
Aug.	17.	Boer laager near Middelsburg captured by S. A. Constabulary with heavy loss.
Aug.	19.	Duke of Cornwall lands at Cape Town.
Aug.	21.	Kitchener's despatch published commenting on inefficiency of certain reinforcements.
Aug.	25.	Kitchener announces receipt of letters from Steyn, De Wet, and Botha, declaring their intention to continue fighting.
Aug.	27.	LORD MILNER RETURNS TO SOUTH AFRICA.
Aug.	31.	Train wrecked by Boers near Waterval.
Sept.	5.	LOTTER'S COMMANDO CAPTURED by Colonel Scobell. Commandants Lotter and Breedt prisoners.
Sept.	10.	Colonel Crabbe routs Scheeper's commando at Lainsburg; Van de Merwe killed.
Sept.	17.	British force under Major Gough surprised near UTRECHT. Smuts's commando surprises 17th Lancers at Elands River Poort.
Sept.	20.	Kruitzinger fails to force a crossing of the Orange River, after inflicting heavy loss on Lovat's Scouts.
Sept.	26.	Botha's attack upon FORTS ITALA and PROSPECT, on the Zulu border, repulsed with severe loss.
Sept.	29.	Proclamation issued at Pretoria, providing for sale of the properties of Boers still in the field, in accordance with previous proclamation.
Sept.	30.	Delarey's attack upon Kekewich's camp at Moedwill beaten off with heavy loss on both sides.
Oct.	6.	Botha breaks back to the north and crosses Pivaan River.
Oct.	8.	Martial Law extended throughout Cape Colony.
Oct.	11.	Commandant Lotter executed. Commandant Scheepers captured.
Oct.	16.	Angelo Mine allowed to drop 50 stamps. Rhenoster River blockhouse line attacked.
Oct.	20.	Rebels enter Oudtshoorn District, Cape Colony. Colonel Dawkins captures three laagers in the Nylstroom district.
Oct.	21.	Lord Kitchener reports Botha driven back from Natal border.
Oct.	22.	Sir Redvers Buller relieved of his command of the 1st Army Corps. Sir J. French appointed to succeed him. Col. Benson surprises a laager near Clippoortje.
Oct.	23.	Lord Kitchener reports recovery of the two guns captured at Scheepers Nek.
Oct.	24.	Viljoen attacks blockhouse line near Badfontein. Kemp attacks Von Donop's convoy near Marico River.
Oct.	25.	Lord Milner visits Natal. Mr. Chamberlain's Edinburgh speech. Major Damant disperses a Boer force near Villiersdorp. Colonel Byng captures Spanneberg's laager.
Oct.	27.	Miss Hobhouse refused permission to land.
Oct.	29.	Maritz captures a convoy from Lambert's Bay to Clanwilliam.
Oct.	30.	7th Hussars and 2nd Dragoons ordered to South Africa. Colonel Benson's column attacked at Brakenlaagte.
Nov.	1.	Colonel Kekewich captures Van Albert's laager.
Nov.	7.	General Sir Ian Hamilton appointed Chief of the Staff in South Africa. Maritz attacks Picquetberg.
Nov.	11.	De Wet collects a following in North-East Orange River Colony. Major Pack Beresford, S.A.C., captures Dutoit's laager at Doornhoek.
Nov.	14.	De Wet attacks Colonel Byng near Heilbron.
Nov.	15.	Despatch from Lord Kitchener describing progress of campaign and capture of Lotter.
Nov.	20.	Commandant Buys defeated near Villiersdorp. Conspiracy reported from Johannesburg.
Nov.	25.	New Canadian Contingent accepted. Cape Colony assumes control of Colonial forces in certain of its districts.
Nov.	26.	General Charles Knox's columns capture Commandant Joubert (Freestater).
Nov.	27.	Committee appointed to inquire into the working of the Gold Law.
Dec.	3.	Louis Botha reported to have collected a following of 1,300 at Lake Chrissie. Despatch from Lord Kitchener covering Blood River, Moedwill, and Itala engagements.

Dec. 4. General Bruce Hamilton captures a laager south-west of Ermelo, and Colonel Dawkins a portion of Beyer's laager near Nylstroom.
Dec. 7. The National Scouts Corps inaugurated.
Dec. 8. De Wet with 2,000 men reported in vicinity of Heilbron.
Dec. 10. General Bruce Hamilton captures practically whole of Bethel commando.
Dec. 11. Lord Kitchener reports considerable extensions to block-house lines.
Dec. 12. Lord Kitchener sends despatch tabulating murders by Boers. Lord Kitchener permits 100 stamps to be dropped weekly in Johannesburg mines. General Bruce Hamilton captures Piet Viljoen's laager.
Dec. 14. Kritzinger's impudent proclamation published in London. New Zealand offers 1,000 more men.
Dec. 15. Colonel Colenbrander captures Commandant Badenhorst.
Dec. 16. Lord Rosebery speaks at Chesterfield. Commandant Kritzinger captured near Hanover Road.
Dec. 17. Johannesburg Stock Exchange reopened.
Dec. 18. Lord Kitchener inspects National Scouts at Brugspruit. Colonel Dartnell heavily engaged with De Wet in North-East Orange River Colony.
Dec. 19. Colonel Allenby captures residue of Staats Artillerie under Major Pretorius.
Dec. 20. Additional drafts for Imperial Yeomanry called for. Majors Damant's and Bridgeford's columns severely handled by Boers.
Dec. 22. Federal Government of Australia determine to offer another contingent of 1,000 men.
Dec. 23. Blockhouse line completed from Kroonstad to Lindley.
Dec. 24. De Wet captures Colonel Firman's camp at Tweefontein.
Dec. 28. Horse and Field Artillery in South Africa organised into a Mounted Infantry Corps.
Dec. 29. General Bruce Hamilton captures General Erasmus east of Ermelo.

1902.
Jan. 10. War Office determines to raise fresh Volunteer companies for service in South Africa.
Count von Bülow's hostile speech in the Reichstag.
General Bruce Hamilton captures Major Wolmaran's laager. General L. Botha narrowly escapes capture at Knapdaar.
Jan. 12. General Elliott's columns still in pursuit of De Wet on Liebenberg Vlei River.
Jan. 16. Lord Kitchener's September correspondence with General Schalk Burger published.
Jan. 17. Trial of Dr. Krause commenced. Commandant Scheepers executed at Graaf Reinet.
Jan. 22. Commandant Beyers forces his way into the concentration camp at Pietersburg.
Jan. 25. General Ben. Viljoen captured near Lydenburg.
Jan. 28. Colonel Du Moulin killed at Abraham's Kraal.
Jan. 30. Statements with regard to Dr. Kuyper's mission.
Colonel Price takes Wessel's laager in Cape Colony.
Feb. 4. Anglo-Dutch papers issued as a Blue-book. De Wet's last gun captured by Colonel Hon. Byng. Major Leader captures Commandant Saeel Alberts of Delarey's commando.
Feb. 5. Lord Kitchener commences the Wolvehoek drive against De Wet.
Feb. 6. De Wet breaks through the Lindley-Kroonstad blockhouse line.
Feb. 8. British convoy captured near Fraserburg.
Feb. 10. Twenty-three Boers surrendered on their own initiative at Middelburg.
Feb. 12. Mishap to 28th Co. Mounted Infantry at Klip River.
Feb. 13. Debate on Remount Question in the House of Lords. Mr. Chamberlain's speech in the City.
Feb. 16. Certain Boers removed from concentration camps in Transvaal to Natal as an experiment.
Feb. 17. Lord Kitchener reports Midland District Cape Colony clear of armed Boers. Judge Kock captured in the Cape Colony.
Feb. 18. Mishap to Scots Greys at Klipdam.
Feb. 20. Colonel Park, A D.C., captures a commando in the Bothasberg.
Feb. 22. Colonel Mackenzie captures Hans Grobelaar's commando near Lake Chrissie.
Feb. 24. Delarey captures Von Donop's convoy near Wolmaranstad. Boers attempt to rush Bothasberg (O.R.C.) outpost line. New Zealanders repel attack with great gallantry.
Feb. 27. Six hundred Boers captured in combined operations on Vanreenen-Harrismith blockhouse line.
March 4. Colonel Rimington unearths a Boer magazine near Reitz.
March 5. South of the blockhouse line from Williston-Calvina reported clear of armed Boers.
March 7. Major Paris's column overwhelmed near Tweebosch by Delarey. Lord Methuen wounded and captured.
March 15. General Bruce-Hamilton surprises Emmett's commando. Captures General Cherry Emmett.
March 19. Sir J. Maxwell relinquishes the military governorship of Pretoria.
March 23. The Boer Government arrives in Pretoria under a flag of truce and then proceeds to Kroonstad to consult with the Orange Free State leaders.
March 24. In combined operations against Delarey General W. Kitchener captures five guns and 179 prisoners.
March 26. DEATH OF MR. RHODES.
March 28. Boer Government still at Kroonstad.
March 30. Mr. Schalk Burger finds difficulty in getting into communication with De Wet. A serious railway accident near Barberton.
March 31. General W. Kitchener's columns again repulse Delarey. Canadians meet the attack at Hart's River with great gallantry.
April 1. 2nd Dragoons surprise a laager at Boschman's Kop.
April 3. First general meeting of the Chamber of Mines at Johannesburg since the war.
April 5. Mr. Schalk Burger gets into communication with Mr. Steyn.
April 6. General Kritzinger acquitted of the charges of murder.
April 8. Colonel Colenbrander attacks Beyers near Pietersburg. Two hundred Boers captured.
April 9. Boer peace delegates move to Klerksdorp from Kroonstad. MR. STEYN, GENERAL DELAREY and DE WET join the Transvaal delegates at Klerksdorp.
April 11. Kemp's men make a spirited attack on Kekewich's column at Rooiwal. Repulsed with heavy losses.
April 12. BOER DELEGATES MOVE TO PRETORIA.
April 16. Official trial of the Bloemfontein-Sanna's Post railway extension.
April 18. Boer peace delegates disperse to consult their commandos.
April 22. Mr. Reitz proceeds to Pietersburg to consult with Commandant Beyers.
April 24. Special meetings convened by burghers in the field to discuss the question of peace.
April 30. The extension to Natal territory was announced to be Vryheid and Utrecht districts.
May 1. Colonel Barker captures Manie Botha. Rebels invest Ookiep in Cape Colony.
May 7. Colonel Cooper relieves Ookiep. Serious accident to armoured train near Pretoria.
May 8. Lord Kitchener reports 221 prisoners.
May 12. Principal Boer leaders begin to arrive for the conference to be held at Vereeniging on May 15.
May 16. Conference at Vereeniging. Jack Hindon, train wrecker, surrenders at Balmoral. Mr. Seddon arrives at Durban.
May 17. Lord Milner arrives in Pretoria.
May 18. Aberdeen (Cape Colony) attacked by 120 Boers. Six chief delegates, with Generals Delarey and De Wet, leave Vereeniging for Pretoria to confer with Lord Milner and Lord Kitchener.
May 20. Visaye surrenders at Balmoral with 50 men.
May 21. Lord Lovat captures Fouché's camp at Stapleford. Mr. Seddon at Pretoria.
May 25. J. Hindon's corps surrenders at Balmoral.
May 27. Commandant Malan, mortally wounded, captured at Ripon Road, Cape Colony.
May 29. The Boer delegates, after receipt of the British Government's definite answer, return to Vereeniging for the final ballot.
May 31. Conditions of Surrender signed.

HOMES FOR OFFICERS' WIDOWS AND DAUGHTERS
(Naval and Military)

AMALGAMATED WITH

THE OFFICERS' BRANCH OF THE SOLDIERS' AND SAILORS' FAMILIES ASSOCIATION.

The scheme for the establishment of these Homes was initiated by a member of the Council in the summer of 1899—before the outbreak of the war, and for which privately £1,500 was raised, including annual subscriptions to the amount of £140. It is intended to supply the same want to a much larger class, as apartments at Hampton Court and Kensington are granted by His Majesty the King to exceptional cases. In September, 1900, the scheme having been adopted by the Association, a beginning was made by renting a portion of a flat in Elm Park Mansions, Chelsea, containing 12 suites of rooms (one sitting, two bedrooms, and offices each), and the same month twelve ladies were elected by the votes of the subscribers.

The following are shortly the qualifications:—

Candidates, being the widows or unmarried daughters of officers of the Army or Navy, must not be under 50, not more than 80 years of age, and must have an assured income of not less than £40 and not more than £100 per annum.

It is hoped when the present War is over, and the claims for different objects become less, that this provision for officers' widows and daughters may be largely extended (there being already 20 candidates for the first vacancy), nay, more, that, considering the generosity of owners of mansions and houses in placing these (furnished and unfurnished) temporarily at the disposal of sick and wounded officers and men, a similar offer or offers may in the near future be made for the establishment of a permanent home for officers' widows and daughters, many of whom, with very limited means, and through no fault of their own, are bravely battling against altered circumstances, and who, from the natural delicacy of their position, seldom make their wants known. The balances of unused funds would also be gladly accepted.

23, Queen Anne's Gate, Westminster, S.W.

www.ingramcontent.com/pod-product-compliance
Lightning Source LLC
Chambersburg PA
CBHW080635230426
43663CB00016B/2874